P9-DXN-283

Recreation Program Planning Today

Richard G. Kraus
Temple University

SCOTT, FORESMAN AND COMPANY
Glenview, Illinois   London

Library of Congress Cataloging in Publication Data.

Kraus, Richard G.
  Recreation program planning today.

  Includes index.
  1. Recreation—United States—Planning.
2. Recreation leadership.   I. Title.
GV181.43.K7   1985   790′.0973   85-2394
ISBN: 0-673-18141-3

1 2 3 4 5 6—KPF—90 89 88 87 86 85

PREFACE

Traditionally, a course in recreation programming has prepared students for positions as leaders in publicly sponsored playgrounds and community centers. Programs emphasized serving children and youth, and the activities presented consisted chiefly of sports and games, arts and crafts, and similar pastimes.

Recreation Program Planning Today views recreation programming in a sharply different light—as a reflection of significant changes that have taken place in the leisure-service field. These changes include:

1. *The diversification of the field itself.* Today, recreation agencies include at least eight distinctly different types of organizations, such as public, voluntary nonprofit, private, commercial, armed forces, campus, corporate/employee, and therapeutic recreation services. Ideally, students should become familiar with recreation program planning approaches in several of these different settings.

2. *The variety of populations served.* Contemporary leisure-service programs must serve all age groups, with increased emphasis on adult and aging populations. In addition, new kinds of family constellations, including single adults, the physically or mentally disabled and other special populations, require innovative recreation programming approaches.

3. *Expanded range of program activities.* Today, broadened public tastes and leisure interests necessitate a fuller range of program offerings. Beyond this, many recreation agencies or administrative units today offer varied human-service or health-related functions; typically, recreation staff members may coordinate services related to education, counseling, transportation, vocational development, and discount purchasing.

4. *Alternative philosophical orientations.* In addition to the familiar "quality-of-life" approach, a number of other philosophical orientations to recreation programming have emerged recently. These include the "marketing" and "human-services" models of recreation service, as well as several other approaches which are discussed in Chapter 4.

If recreation is to justify adequate support in today's tight economic climate, it *must* be goal-oriented and purposeful. It must have clearly stated objectives, and it must demonstrate accountability through a systematic evaluation process and full documentation of outcomes. At the same time, recreation must respond to the needs and interests of participants and must provide real pleasure and enjoyment—surely the most compelling motivation for taking part in recreation.

In preparing this book, I divided my original text, *Recreation Today: Program Planning and Leadership*, into two separate books covering the two key aspects of the subject. Chapter 3 of this book presents a model of recreation program planning and implementation based both on several other models appearing in the literature and on the actual programs of dozens of leisure-service agencies. Each of the following chapters deals with successive steps of the eight-stage programming process.

The book steers a middle course between a highly practical and "how-to-do-it" approach and a more conceptual or theoretical approach. Much of its content reflects current writing about social change and the structure of organizations in contemporary life, including information on networking and participative management approaches. At the same time, the book provides numerous practical guidelines and examples of programming in various types of leisure-service agencies. Emphasis is placed on the process of developing programs rather than on the activities themselves. The reader will find a wide selection of program activities in the book's companion volume, *Recreation Leadership Today*.

The questions and suggested student projects that appear at the end of chapters are designed to help readers develop applied skills in analyzing problem situations or evolving program plans that are innovative and fit today's changing needs and societal circumstances. It is not expected that all students undertake all of these projects. Instead, they may be assigned to individuals or small groups well in advance of the date when a chapter would be covered in class. At that time, presentations could be made to help illustrate or enrich the text material in the chapter itself.

I hope that both instructors and students will find this text useful and enjoyable—both for specific course purposes and as a valuable addition to their professional libraries.

Acknowledgments

Appreciation is extended to the following organizations and individuals who assisted in preparing this book by sending brochures, program reports, manuals, and photographs, or by providing other useful information.

The largest amount of material received came from local, public recreation and park agencies in the United States, including the following: Des Moines, Iowa, Park and Recreation Department (William Foley); Essex County,

New Jersey, Department of Parks, Recreation and Cultural Affairs (Lisa Popusz-niak); Howard County, Maryland, Department of Parks and Recreation (Shirley Miner); Kansas City, Missouri, Department of Parks and Recreation; Leawood, Kansas, Recreation Department; City of Miami, Florida, Recreation Department (Albert Howard); Milwaukee, Wisconsin, Division of Municipal Recreation, Public Schools (Mike Magulski); Oakland County, Michigan, Department of Parks and Recreation (Janet Pung); Omaha, Nebraska, Parks and Recreation Department; Portland, Oregon, Parks Bureau, and Project S.O.A.R. (Mary Douglas); Portsmouth, Virginia, Park and Recreation Department; Tampa, Florida, Recreation Department (Donald Saltzman); and Willamalane, Oregon, Park and Recreation District. A number of Federal agencies in the United States also provided useful materials, including the U.S. Forest Service, Army Corps of Engineers, and Tennessee Valley Authority.

In Canada, a number of provincial agencies and municipalities sent valuable program reports and brochures. These included: Province of Alberta Recreation and Parks Department and Blue Mountain Centre; Manitoba Department of Cultural Affairs and Historical Resources (Jill Lhotka); Nepean, Ontario, Parks and Recreation Department (Betty Usher); Province of Saskatchewan Department of Culture and Recreation (Ven Begamudre); and Vancouver, British Columbia, Parks and Recreation Board (Terri Clark).

Numerous therapeutic recreation agencies provided program outlines and manuals. In the United States, these included: Camp Confidence in Brainerd, Minnesota (Bill Lewis); Camp Courage, in Monticello, Iowa; Robert Wood Johnson, Jr. Rehabilitation Institute, Edison, New Jersey; Maryland School for the Blind; Moss Rehabilitation Hospital, in Philadelphia; Napa State Hospital, in Imola, California (Steve Weeks); and the Pennsylvania Special Olympics (Rick Brown). In Canada, therapeutic recreation contributors included: Ontario Crippled Children's Centre in Toronto; Ontario March of Dimes in Toronto (Gillian Kearney and Kirsty Griffiths); Penetanguishene, Ontario, Mental Health Centre; and Souris Valley Regional Care Centre, Weyburn, Saskatchewan.

A number of voluntary, non-profit organizations provided materials, including the Girl Scouts of the U.S.A.; the National Board of the Young Women's Christian Association; the Police Athletic League of Philadelphia; and the Boys' Clubs of America. Among commercial organizations in the leisure-service field that assisted were : Busch Entertainment Corporation, including The Old Country and Adventure Island (Laurie Halladay); GameTime (Frances Wallach); Sesame Place, Langhorne, Pennsylvania; and Wave Tek Corporation (Betsy Cogan). Major corporations that sent materials either regarding their own employee recreation programs or national sports and fitness programs they sponsored included: Hershey Corporation, including the National Track and Field Youth Program; Honeywell, Inc., in Minneapolis; and the Wells Fargo National Fitness Campaign.

Several armed forces bases sent excellent program materials, including the Naval Air Station in Leemore, California (Ron Stamphill); the Charleston, South Carolina Air Force Base; and the Eighth Army Command in Korea (EUSA ROK).

Among the individuals who contributed particularly valuable assistance were: Prof. Delores Andy of Temple University, who offered materials from the National Youth Sports Program; Pamela Crespi of the Operations Division of the Naval Material Command in Washington, D.C., who contributed a wealth of outstanding documentation on armed forces recreation; Karen Fernsten and Dr. Jane Kaufman of the Children's Seashore House, Atlantic City, New Jersey; Kenneth Joswiak of the Center for Individuals with Disabilities in San Bernardino, California; Anne Mattes, formerly of the Cigna Corporation and Temple University, who contributed many useful materials on corporate/employee recreation; Prof. Larry Neal of the University of Oregon; Janet Pomeroy, founder and executive director of the Recreation Center for the Handicapped in San Francisco, California; and Arnold Sperling of the Clinical Center of the National Institutes of Health, U.S. Public Health Service, Bethesda, Maryland.

Finally, I would like to thank my reviewers, Glenn W. Cheatham, Arizona State University; Charles B. Corbin, Arizona State University; and M. Jean Keller, University of Georgia, whose comments and suggestions on the manuscript were extremely helpful.

Without the assistance of all these organizations and individuals, this book could not have been written.

Richard Kraus

CONTENTS _____

CHAPTER **8**
Alternative Approaches to Program Design: Formats and Facilities   185

CHAPTER **9**
Developing the Program Plan   213

Recreation _____

Program _____

Planning _____

Today _____

PART 1

Introduction
to Recreation
Program
Planning

Sports and fitness are among the most popular of all recreation program activities. Here, boys and girls compete in the Hershey Track and Field Youth Program, while crewmen compete at basketball in crowded quarters on the USS *Mount Hood*. Participants take part in ice-skating at the South Mountain Arena, while others "work out" in a fitness court and lawn bowl, all in Essex County, New Jersey.

Recreation Program_____
Planning in_____
a Changing Society_____

_____

_____

"Well, Jim, we're very excited that the Mayfield Village Board has agreed to hire you as our first recreation director," said Mary Carter, head of the community's Recreation Committee.

"I'm excited about it too," replied Jim Schmidt. "You're taking a bit of a chance, hiring me right out of college. But I've had good experience in other programs like this, and feel that I'm well-qualified."

Mary Carter smiled. "We think you're the person for the job. But let me warn you, people are going to expect a lot from this program, although our budget will be small to start with. Now, the Village Board will be meeting in three weeks. We'll want a beginning statement from you—not a final plan, of course, but some of your ideas about what Mayfield's recreation program should include, and how we ought to develop it. You'll be able to give us some ideas at that time, won't you?"

"Of course I will," said Jim. "I've already started on it. It's going to be a real challenge."

Over the past three decades, recreation has emerged as a major aspect of modern life in all industrialized societies. Thanks to the growth of leisure time, economic capability, and favorable attitudes that encourage varied forms of play, the provision of organized recreation service today represents a highly significant form of community service and career opportunity.

While many of the pursuits that people engage in during their leisure time are casual and unstructured, many other activities are sponsored by various community agencies. At the heart of such organizations is the task of planning, organizing, and conducting diversified program activities and services. Russell has written:

The program is what recreation services are all about. All else—personnel, supplies, areas and facilities, budgets, public relations—exists primarily to see that the program occurs and that people enjoy participating. Planning is the tool that makes programs happen.[1]

The purpose of this book is to provide the reader with a full understanding of the nature of recreation program planning, both in terms of its underlying concepts and the wide range of programs typically emphasized by different kinds of leisure-service agencies today. In addition to such understandings, the book's purpose is also to present the reader with an analysis of different types of program activities and formats, and to examine the skills involved in designing and implementing programs.

DEFINITION OF TERMS

Before describing the social factors that have created a dramatically new climate for recreation programming, it is necessary to define the two terms that are used throughout this text: *recreation* and *leisure*.

Recreation is generally viewed as the act of participating in voluntarily chosen, pleasurable activities in one's free time. It has also been increasingly defined as the emotional experience involved in participation rather than simply the act of taking part. Recreation must also be seen as a social institution in the sense that it represents a major economic force in society, an important area of governmental responsibility, and a source of employment for millions of men and women.

Leisure may be narrowly defined as unobligated time—that is, time free from the responsibilities of work, self-maintenance responsibilities, or other mandated tasks. In a broader sense, leisure represents freedom and the opportunity for self-enrichment through participation in a wide range of pursuits and hobbies, including many of a cultural or community-service nature. Leisure may also be seen as a state of mind and as a source of creative and spiritual values.

Many educators and social scientists prefer to use the word *leisure* when discussing this field, and to be concerned with its philosophical and psychological implications. In contrast, most members of the public are accustomed to using the term *recreation* and most agencies that provide such services refer to the services as *recreation*. In actual practice, the term *leisure-service agency* is usually regarded as synonymous with *recreation provider*, and is used in that way throughout this text.

UNDERSTANDING THE NATURE
OF RECREATION PROGRAMMING

Having clarified these basic terms, we may then ask, "Exactly what is recreation programming?"

At its simplest level, it consists of the process of providing opportunities for recreational participation to the public at large, or to selected clienteles or target audiences. It includes varied types of activities—such as sports, games, hobbies, arts and crafts, music, drama and dance, or social events—which meet the needs of participants for enjoyable leisure activity.

It is essential to realize that programs are not an end in themselves. As Edginton, Hanson, and Compton point out, *people* are the real reasons for the existence of leisure-service agencies, and should be considered the focal point of their services:

> Programs are the tools of the recreation and leisure professional—the vehicle for service delivery. Through the use of programs, values are formed, skills developed, and processes learned.[2]

Beyond this, the reader should recognize that recreation programming involves more than simply planning and carrying out group recreation activities. As later chapters will show, it encompasses a number of other important functions, such as the provision of facilities for self-directed use, the assistance and coordination of other community leisure-service programs, leisure education and counseling, and even the provision of related nonrecreational programs and services.

Past Development of Community Recreation

During the early years of its development as a form of organized community service in the late nineteenth and early twentieth century, recreation programming tended to be heavily child- and youth-oriented and to be carried on primarily in playgrounds and community centers. It was provided chiefly by municipal or other local, tax-supported recreation and park agencies, with limited opportunities offered by voluntary, industrial, or other specialized types of organizations.

At that time, community recreation was generally regarded as a significant form of social service, designed chiefly to meet the needs of the urban poor and newcomers to America's changing cities. During the period of the 1920s through the 1960s—as it merged with the growing urban and county parks movement—it came to be conceptualized chiefly as an *amenity,* a fun-oriented activity that contributed to the quality of life, but did not have other important social purposes or outcomes.

During this period, a philosophy of municipal or community recreation service developed, which stressed the need to provide equal leisure opportunities to all, regardless of age, sex, race, or religious background. Despite this philosophy, it was evident that most publicly sponsored recreation programs tended to serve middle-class, white populations, and that facilities and program activities in many lower-income or minority-group neighborhoods tended to be inadequate. Similarly, within the traditional pattern of recreation sponsorship, boys and men were much more fully served than girls and women, who generally were regarded as having a lower level of priority, particularly in such leisure pursuits as sports or other active program areas.

SOCIAL FACTORS AFFECTING RECREATION PROGRAMMING

During the second half of the twentieth century, a number of important social trends and changes in the fabric of society have dramatically affected the nature of recreation programming. These changes have important implications for all leisure-service planning and operations, and should be clearly understood by students and practitioners in the field of professional recreation service.

Growth of Leisure

Obviously, the steady increase in discretionary time in recent years has been a key force in the growth of public recreation involvement and the expansion of organized forms of leisure-service agencies.

Traditionally, this trend has been attributed chiefly to the shortened workweek, which provides employees in varied fields of employment with many free hours each week, in contrast to the conditions experienced by past generations. However, increased leisure also stems from such other factors as (1) added numbers of holidays and expanded vacations for employees; (2) the use of flextime or the four-day week to provide added blocks of useful time; (3) earlier and longer periods of retirement for elderly employees, linked to the lengthened life span, caused chiefly by medical advances; and (4) the use of varied forms of labor-saving devices or equipment, such as power mowers, vacuum cleaners, washers, driers, and frozen foods.

The U.S. Department of Commerce stresses the link between growing leisure and consumer spending power:

> The growth of the recreation services industry can be traced to expanding consumer expenditures, increasing mobility, higher family income, and more leisure time. During the past two decades, Americans have seen almost steady improvements in the amount of their time and money available for leisure pursuits. While the basic 40-hour work week has remained unchanged since World War II, the advent of the 4-day work week and the introduction of flexitime has helped considerably in creating more leisure time. The average worker also gets longer vacation time and more holidays now.[3]

Changing Values and New Lifestyles

Beginning with the human potential movement and the emergence of the "Me Generation" in the 1960s, there has been a dramatic change in the social values held by Americans and Canadians of all ages.

The traditional Protestant work ethic—which saw work as a major form of human commitment, a source of self-worth and important life satisfactions—declined markedly during this period. Young people in particular tended to reject so-called middle-class or establishment values, and to see work chiefly as a means of finding monetary support—that is, "selling" one's time for money, but without a sense of loyalty or deep affiliation with one's work or employer.

Other values related to family life and the normal expectation of marrying and raising a family have also shifted during this period. The single life has become widespread and is recognized as a respectable choice for many adults. As indicated earlier, the number of single-parent families or households has expanded rapidly, and alternative lifestyles such as homosexuality have become far more open.

The formerly strict social and religious values that condemned and sought to control such marginal forms of leisure activity as nonmarital sexual involvement, gambling, drinking, and drug-taking, have declined sharply in influence. Often laws are not enforced, and even when they are—as in the case of the use of marijuana or cocaine—huge segments of middle-class, presumably responsible Americans and Canadians are still able to use such drugs as part of a hedonistic approach to leisure.

Influence on Recreation Programming.   Such trends affect recreation programming in the sense that marginal forms of leisure activity tend to overshadow or crowd out other more wholesome kinds of recreational activity. Public and voluntary agencies are increasingly pressured to make use of such *leisure* activities as gambling or drinking in their programs in order to "meet the competition." Without making a moral judgment at this point, it should be stressed that recreation programs—particularly for youth and young adults—must consider such issues on the basis of a sound philosophical position before determining their appropriate policies and strategies in meeting public leisure needs.

At the same time, there appears to be a countertrend among various segments of society. The decline in church membership of the past three decades appears to have been halted and religious programs are becoming popular on many campuses. There are increased efforts to control pornography, and growing resistance to legalized gambling in many areas. Casual sexual activity is reported to be declining, and the marriage rate has begun to rise. Old-line youth groups, which had suffered severe membership drops in the 1960s and 1970s, appear to be growing again—all as part of what has been described as a return to traditional social values.[4]

New Kinds of Recreation Sponsors

Whereas the recreation movement was first thought of in terms of publicly sponsored municipal recreation and park agencies, today it is recognized that a number of other major types of organizations sponsor extensive leisure programs and services.

These include the following eight types of leisure-service organizations: (1) public or governmental agencies, operating on federal, state, and local levels of service, (2) voluntary, nonprofit organizations, both nonsectarian and sectarian, (3) private membership associations, (4) commercial, profit-oriented recreation businesses, (5) armed forces which, while a branch of government, constitute a distinctly separate form of recreation programming, (6) campus recreation, serving college and university students and staff members, (7) corporate recreation programs serving company employees, and (8) therapeutic recreation service for special populations.

Each of these types of sponsors has a uniquely different set of goals and objectives, accompanied by sharply contrasting types of staff and facilities. For a realistic and accurate understanding of the contemporary leisure-service system, it is necessary to understand these differences.

Variety of Populations Served

Just as the sponsoring agencies themselves have become more diversified, so the populations being served today are far more heterogeneous. In the recent past, the typical view of the American household saw it as consisting of Mom, Dad, and two or three children, neatly scrubbed and dressed, living in an attractive one-family home on a tree-lined suburban or small-town street. Today, there is the inescapable fact that we live in a far more complex society. Instead of being in a so-called melting pot in which people of every background have blended together homogeneously, our society continues to become more of a mosaic or patchwork quilt of cultural differences all existing at the same time.

Leisure-service agencies today must consider the need to serve people of every age, ranging from unborn babies whose mothers are attending courses in the natural childbirth method to the very elderly in senior centers or nursing homes. Overall, we are rapidly becoming a more long-lived and elderly society. A 1984 report by the Metropolitan Life Insurance Company indicated that children born today can expect to live 74.6 years, and that before long the average American will live into his or her eighties.

We are changing as a society in other important respects. We are no longer a predominantly white, middle-class society of northern European or Anglo-Saxon heritage. Instead, many of our largest cities now have a majority of "minority-group" blacks and Hispanics; increasingly people of Asian or other foreign extraction are entering American and Canadian communities.

Numerous other changes have also occurred. In 1983, the U.S. Census Bureau reported:

> Americans are marrying later in life and divorcing more often, trends that have increased the number of children living with single parents by two-thirds in the last dozen years.[5]

As a result, there are not only growing numbers of single-parent families (with many more men heading households) but also more extended families with intricate relationships because of divorce and remarriage. The strong push toward equal economic, social, and political rights for women has resulted in a much greater emphasis on programming for this segment of the overall population. Similarly, disabled people of every type—the physically and mentally disabled, the emotionally ill, the dependent aging, and those with social disabilities—have become important priorities for recreation programmers both in institutions and in the modern community setting.

In summary, the growing diversity of community residents means that recreation programmers must seek to understand and satisfy the leisure needs and interests of the elderly as well as the young, of different ethnic and racial groups, of the rich and poor, of the physically and mentally disabled, of people of both sexes, and of people with widely varying life-styles and leisure inclinations.

At the same time, different types of agencies serve markedly different populations and therefore have sharply contrasting goals for meeting public leisure needs.

For example, professionals in armed forces recreation programs are normally concerned only with programming for the members of military units and their dependents. Therapeutic recreation specialists are involved only in providing services for special populations in institutional or community settings, although they may also relate to nondisabled citizens in terms of advocacy, referral, clients, or integrated leisure programs. Like those in armed forces recreation, employee recreation specialists have an obligation to serve only their own companies' employees and the employees' families. Commercial recreation planners, while they may choose to meet the extremely varied needs of all groups in society, normally restrict their offerings on the basis of the patron's ability to pay.

In reality, then, it is chiefly the public and voluntary agency recreation professional who is faced with the obligation of serving many of the other special populations identified in this chapter.

Trends in Recreational Interests

With the steady growth in free time, spending capability, and awareness of the values of leisure involvement, many new recreational interests have emerged in recent years. Often these have important implications for those who sponsor organized recreation services.

TABLE 1–1 How Americans Stay Fit: Number Who Participate in Activities[6]

Swimming	102.3 million
Bicycling	72.2
Fishing	63.7
Camping	61.6
Boating	42.0
Bowling	40.3
Body building (with equipment)	34.9
Jogging	34.3
Roller skating	30.2
Softball	28.0
Tennis	25.5

Health and Fitness Programming. One of the most remarkable waves of enthusiasm in recent years has been the dramatic increase of concern about health and fitness in American and Canadian society. Education, government, business and medical and other social agencies have all joined in the effort to promote total, functional health—best described by the holistic term of *wellness*.

Smoking and drinking habits, nutrition, freedom from excessive stress, and sustained and enjoyable regular exercise all play a part in promoting fitness. Without question, the greatly increased participation in varied forms of physical activity, including exercise and training programs, jogging, and running is linked to the need to improve cardiovascular fitness and bodily endurance and strength. However, physical recreation also contributes to the release of tension and stress, and to a balanced outlook and emotional well-being—which in turn support the individual's sense of total wellness.

As later chapters will show, this important trend represents a major focus of many recreation programs today, and will continue to do so in the years ahead. It is important to recognize that, for most people, the urge to be fit is closely linked with an interest in sports and other forms of active leisure participation. In 1984, for example, *U.S. News & World Report* summarized the most popular forms of fitness activity in the American public at large (Table 1–1).

Impact of Modern Technology. Another major influence on today's recreational participation comes from modern technology. Scientists and engineers have helped to create many new forms of play, including outdoor recreation activity in the sky (skydiving, hang gliding, sport flying, and ballooning); on land (off-road vehicles, including dune buggies, snowmobiles and trail biking, and numerous winter sports with newly created environments like artificial snow or ice surfaces), and in aquatic environments (waterskiing and kite-skiing, scuba diving and other forms of boating play).

Electronic Entertainment. A related form of currently popular play consists of electronic entertainment; *Time* magazine reports that Americans spend more than half their leisure time in front of the television set, an average of almost three hours per person each day. Indeed, *Time* refers to television as the new fireplace; it has become

> the new American hearth—a center for family activities, conversation and companionship. . . . Consumers are putting the sets to more varied uses and demanding more from their TVs. . . . First they began playing video games, whose fancy graphics show up best with a sharp display. Now people are showing movies on their TV with laser-disc machines and video-cassette recorders, and they want picture and sound quality at home that approaches what they can get in a movie theater.[7]

Beyond this, growing numbers of young people are involved with computers as a fascinating combination of hobby, social outlet, and career interest. Today, so-called hackers constitute an intensive subculture of students that has cropped up at the nation's top universities:

> The term hacker derives from "hack," meaning a subtle, sometimes elegant fix for a flaw in a computer program. Hackers spend hours typing commands on terminal keyboards to learn as much as possible about the strengths and weaknesses of a particular program or network. They tinker for the sheer fun of it, delving deeper and deeper into the mysteries of software.[8]

Clearly, this has become an immensely popular form of leisure pursuit in an area of personal development that was totally unknown twenty years ago.

Other Recreation Trends

Numerous other examples of widely expanded recreational interest might be cited. One of the most popular broad areas of activity is outdoor or nature-oriented recreation. The growth in popular participation is illustrated in a summary of statistics of involvement in selected outdoor pursuits drawn from the 1982–1983 Nationwide Recreation Survey (Table 1–2).

Similarly, there has been an impressive growth of involvement in such recreational activities as arts and crafts, the performing arts, travel and tourism, and numerous other hobbies and forms of popular amusement. Thanks to such growth, recreation has emerged as a major economic force and source of employment in modern society.

TABLE 1–2   Percentage of Respondents Taking Part in Outdoor Recreation[9]

Activity	Summer 1960	Summer 1982
Bicycling	9%	28%
Horseback riding	6%	7%
Fishing	29%	30%
Canoeing or kayaking	2%	8%
Sailing	2%	4%
Swimming	45%	51%
Camping	8%	19%

Recreation as an Economic Force

The tremendous expansion of recreational participation in the United States is illustrated by citing a figure estimating the total amount of annual leisure spending. For example, *U.S. News & World Report* estimated in the early 1980s that over $260 billion a year was spent on leisure in the United States. Two years later, it reported that total outlays for sports, recreation, and entertainment amounted to $310 billion annually, with the bulk of it spent on commercial products and services.[10]

Indeed, based on reports that tourism and travel alone involve an expenditure of over $200 billion a year and that other forms of leisure spending amount to $152 billion (not including money spent on alcohol and similar activities, or on government or voluntary agency programs), it seems clear that actual recreation spending is well over $350 billion annually. Seen broadly, leisure represents a vast interlocking economic system in which varied agencies provide services at a cost, and different segments of the public consume them, based on their own tastes and financial capability.[11]

Need for Accountability.   Particularly when economic forces compel a reduction in funding support—as in many cities or other governmental units in recent years—it has become increasingly necessary for leisure-service agencies to justify their existence or to gain support in other ways.

This effort has taken two forms: (1) an acceptance of a marketing model of program service, and (2) a shift to a human-service orientation in program planning.

The *marketing model* requires that recreation agencies take a new, harder look at their programs in economic terms with a growing expectation that they must pay their own way. Stress is placed on businesslike management approaches and the use of systems-based planning and assessment methods—along with a stronger emphasis on expanded revenue sources, including the use of fees and charges, concessions, contracting methods, solicitation of gifts and grants, and similar techniques.

The *human-service model* involves a distinct shift away from the view of recreation as an activity carried on for its own sake, *without* extrinsic value or purpose. Instead, a number of important factors have compelled the redefinition of recreation as purposeful activity, designed to achieve significant social goals.

One such factor was the role assumed by recreation during the 1960s and 1970s, when municipal and voluntary-agency recreation programs were funded by the federal government to meet important social needs in low-income urban areas, as part of the so-called war on poverty. Similarly, the expansion of therapeutic recreation service has sharpened the serious, purposeful image of recreation as a goal-oriented community service.

Today, many leisure-service agencies sponsor such programs as health-related classes or clinics; vocationally oriented activities; personnel services related to stress or burnout, or other areas of employee concern; educational functions; and referral, counseling, advocacy, or specific forms of therapeutic treatment or rehabilitation.

Beyond these changes in program emphasis, which are discussed more fully in Chapter 4, program planners must be aware that it is no longer acceptable to speak in vague generalities or clichés about the value of leisure in our lives or the contribution made by recreation in community life. Defining the specific goals and objectives of organized recreation service has become increasingly necessary to measure the outcomes of programs carefully, and to document these convincingly.

This trend has not been the result of fiscal pressures alone. Instead, it stems from a much more sophisticated and analytical approach to all forms of social service which are competing for public support, and is part of an overall trend toward a systems-planning approach toward management in the business world and in government.

NEW APPROACHES TO PROGRAM PLANNING

These societal trends have had a powerful impact on the approaches used in planning recreation programs. In the past, the most common approach was one in which administrators or supervisors made program decisions based on widely accepted principles, combined with informal observation of what appeared to be popular elsewhere and their own personal views.

In general, it was assumed that certain key activities should be offered because they had "always" been popular.

Occasionally there would be shifts in emphasis, with the gradual development of new program features or the phasing out of less popular ones. However, relatively little systematic planning took place in most agencies, and, while community advisory councils might be consulted, usually it was the authoritarian judgment of the department's administrators or supervisors that prevailed.

Today, a far more complex and systematic approach to recreation planning has evolved. Several distinct models of program development have emerged, including those already mentioned in this chapter as well as others concerned with programming for special populations or with environmental or aesthetic values. There is greatly increased emphasis on assessing the needs, interests, and capability of participants, and relating them to the mission and resources of the sponsoring agency.

Today, as this text will show, program planning involves a number of steps that flow in a logical sequence from the determination of participant or consumer needs and interests, to the objective measurement of program outcomes. Through this process, it is essential that community residents or organization members be meaningfully involved.

Participant Input in Program Planning. Since the very beginning of the recreation and park movement in the United States and Canada, there has been a sustained effort to provide citizen or member input in agency policy making and program development. This was achieved through citizen boards and commissions, and through district or neighborhood councils and advisory committees.

Today, one of the major trends in the management of business, government, and other types of large-scale organizations involves shared decision making and democratic participative management approaches. In the words of John Naisbitt, author of the popular *Megatrends: Ten New Directions Transforming Our Lives*, authoritarian, "top-down" decision-making processes are giving way to "bottom-up" approaches, with widely shared exchanges of views and opinions.[12]

Similarly, Naisbitt points out that decentralization is taking place in many societal institutions. There is a powerful thrust toward having local organizations or citizens' groups make decisions and develop social agenda rather than having them rely on highly centralized federal agencies or the national boards of organizations to determine policy.

In terms of recreation program processes, this means that there is a growing practice of involving participants in the task of determining their own needs and interests, and of enlisting them in significant roles in helping organize and conduct the programs. In part, this stems from fiscal necessity and the major contribution that volunteers can make in operating activities at little cost. However, it also stems from the reality that advisory councils or neighborhood advisory committees are in an excellent position to provide political support and clout, and thus lend real strength to leisure-service programs.

A related trend, also noted by Naisbitt in *Megatrends*, involves the growth of "networking,"[13] which means that, instead of operating independently, many organizations today coordinate their programs closely with others, sharing knowledge, expertise, fiscal resources, facilities, and staff members in joint recreation programs. Each separate agency can maximize its contribution and the public can be most effectively served with needed recreation programs if the full network of potential sponsors is brought into play in a cooperative way.

TODAY'S CLIMATE FOR INNOVATIVE PROGRAM PLANNING

These and a number of other important social trends that influence the shaping of recreation programs today will be illustrated repeatedly throughout this text, with implications for innovative program development.

At this point, however, the reader may wish to say, "Stop! I thought this book was about planning recreation programs. All I've read so far concerns social trends and a lot of abstract-sounding management practices. What about the day-by-day approach to *developing real programs for real people*? When do we get to that?"

The answer is, "Right now!"

But first, the reader must realize that the trends that have just been described, and the new management practices, are not abstract. They represent reality. The day of rule-of-thumb programs, of clichéd justification of activities based on the personal opinion or judgment of the planner, is gone. Today, programs *must* be purposeful and goal-oriented. They *must* include activities that often are nonrecreational in nature. They *must* involve participant input, and they *must* be subjected to careful evaluation and documentation of outcomes. They *must* rely on networking, wherever possible, and they *must* deal realistically with changing life-styles and with the variegated needs of a population that has become strikingly diverse in most communities.

The task of programming is a highly practical one that involves very specific kinds of understandings and skills. As Farrell and Lundegren comment:

> Good programming does not just happen; it is made to happen. Therefore, good programmers must learn their skills. They cannot pick them up at the local department store, ready made and tailored to fit all situations.[14]

Recognizing this reality, this text will attempt to meet the needs of recreation professionals-to-be, both through the content offered in each chapter and through the exercises, class projects, and other learning experiences suggested in the book.

Purposes of This Text: Essential Areas of Knowledge

1. Readers must become familiar with the basic concepts of recreation programming, and with a step-by-step model for planning and carrying out programs in all types of agencies.
2. Readers must understand the exact nature of the eight major types of recreation sponsors, and how their different patterns of sponsorship, funding, staffing, organizational structure and goal-setting influence their program services.
3. Readers will be introduced to a contemporary analysis of the basic values to be derived from recreational participation and to the fundamental needs and interests of participants of different age levels and ethnic, socioeconomic, or life-style backgrounds.
4. Readers must be able to describe the major forms of program service, and the varied categories of recreational involvement, as well as the different formats they take.
5. Readers must also become familiar with the major responsibilities involved in operating programs in different types of specialized facilities, such as senior centers, health clubs, athletic complexes, skating rinks, or facilities serving handicapped populations.
6. Readers must learn essential principles involved in maintaining healthy and safe programs, including risk management and avoidance of possible negligence lawsuits.

7. Similarly, readers must become familiar with techniques used in supervising volunteers or other subprofessional personnel in carrying out programs; in publicizing programs and maintaining effective community relations; in managing revenue sources as an area of program responsibility; and in similar functions related to program management.

8. Finally, readers must learn how programs are to be monitored and evaluated, and how data drawn from such observations are to be analyzed and used to document the worth of recreation as a community service, and to improve future planning and implementation.

Essential Program Planning Skills

It is not enough to know about these major areas of program responsibility in a theoretical sense, or as pure information. This text also has as a key purpose the development of practical skills.

Progressing from chapter to chapter, readers should gain competence in such areas as the selection of appropriate program-planning models, or the formulation of a basic philosophy of leisure service. They should learn to define and develop appropriate program objectives or performance measures, to assess the needs, interests and capabilities of clients, and to analyze program activities in terms of their potential for meeting these needs and interests.

Similarly, readers should develop competence in working with others in program-planning sessions, in developing effective program schedules, in techniques of publicity and community relations, in implementing ongoing programs or special events, and in systematically evaluating program outcomes.

It is important, however, to understand that professionals must be able to do *more* than perform well in a practical, hands-on sense. Many community volunteers are able to lead a group effectively, within a narrow range of activity. They can lead a game or an arts and crafts project, or plan a hike or overnight outing.

However, the task of analyzing the overall leisure-service needs of a community or of the membership of a large organization—such as a YWCA, Fortune 500 company, or armed forces base—demands conceptual and analytical skills that go far beyond the limited practical abilities of such community volunteers or assistant leaders. It requires a level of sophistication and a problem-solving ability that can only be gained through deliberate study, practice, and exposure to a range of realistic situations in different types of recreational settings and agencies.

Given this background, the reader is now urged to explore first-hand the basic concepts of recreation programming, an experience that promises to be challenging and rewarding.

NOTES

[1]Ruth V. Russell, *Planning Programs in Recreation* (St. Louis: C. V. Mosby, 1982), ix.

[2]Christopher Edginton, David Compton, and Carole Hanson, *Recreation and Leisure Programming: A Guide for the Professional* (Philadelphia: W. B. Saunders, 1980), p. 25.

[3]*U.S. Industrial Outlook* (Washington, D.C.: U.S. Dept. of Commerce, 1984), 52–25.

[4]"Old-Line Youth Groups Back in Style," *U.S. News & World Report* (31 January 1983): 75.

[5]John Wilke, "Census Finds Big Changes in the Mating Game," *Washington Post Service* (2 July 1983).

[6]"Keeping in Shape—Everybody's Doing It," *U.S. News & World Report* (13 August 1984): 25.

[7]"Living: TV as the New Fireplace," *Time* (27 December 1982): 70.

[8]"In Pittsburgh: Hacking the Night Away," *Time* (9 May 1983): 13.

[9]See "Swimming and Walking Top Activities in Poll," *New York Times* (29 April 1984): 38; and "Preliminary Findings of 1982–1983 Nationwide Recreation Survey," *National Park Service Report*, 1984.

[10]Alvin P. Sanoff, "Business Gets Healthy from Athletics Too," *U.S. News & World Report* (13 August 1984): 27.

[11]See Howard P. James, "The Industry and the Economy," *Advertising Supplement in Time* (7 May 1984): n.p.; and *U.S. Industrial Outlook* (Washington, D.C.: U.S. Dept. of Commerce, 1984): 52–62.

[12]John Naisbitt, *Megatrends: Ten New Directions for Transforming Our Lives* (New York: Warner Books, 1982, 1984): pp. 121–26.

[13]Naisbitt, Chapter 8.

[14]Patricia Farrell and Herberta Lundegren, *The Process of Recreation Programming* (New York: John Wiley, 1978): p. vii.

QUESTIONS

1. The chapter describes several social trends which are influencing the delivery of organized recreation programs. Which of these are the most significant in your opinion? What are their effects and how should recreation programmers respond to them?
2. Among the most popular recent waves of interest in recreational participation in the United States and Canada are: health and fitness programming, electronic entertainment and computer and video games, and varied forms of outdoor recreation. Which of these do you see reflected most vividly in your family or friends and in what forms? What other trends in leisure interests have you noted recently?
3. Why is it especially important today that leisure service agencies are accountable to the public? What does this mean and how can it best be accomplished?

SUGGESTED READINGS

Reynold Carlson, Janet MacLean, Theodore Deppe, and James Peterson, *Recreation and Leisure: The Changing Scene* (Belmont, Calif.: Wadsworth, 1979), Chapter 1.

Richard Kraus, *Recreation and Leisure in Modern Society* (Glenview, Illinois: Scott, Foresman, 1984), Chapters 1 and 5.

John Naisbitt, *Megatrends: Ten New Directions for Transforming Our Lives* (New York: Warner Books, 1982, 1984), Chapters 5, 7, and 8.

H. Douglas Sessoms, *Leisure Services* (Englewood Cliffs, N.J.: Prentice-Hall, 1984), Chapters 1 and 2.

CHAPTER 2

Recreation Programming: A Conceptual Overview

"Look at these figures, will you, Fred," said Dan Tobias, director of Eastgate Shopping Mall's financial operation.

"Here's our quarterly financial report from all the stores in the Mall—and the Starlight Video Game Arcade has continued to decline. Things looked so good when they came in, just two years ago."

"Yes," said Fred McHale, his assistant. "A lot of video game arcades have gone out of business. But did you notice how the Mountaineer Supply Depot is busting at the seams? They've almost doubled their quarterly sales volume since last year."

Dan Tobias nodded. "Backpacking and camping equipment, skis and scuba gear! Who'd have thought that would be so popular in Eastgate? Who can account for it?"

We will now examine the basic concepts that support and facilitate the program-planning process. The term *concept* as used here is defined as a thought, opinion, or idea—in other words, a form of theoretical analysis as opposed to a purely descriptive approach.

The purpose of this chapter is to provide the reader with a clearer understanding of the nature of recreation programs and the various forms they take, and an awareness of various approaches that have traditionally been used in developing programs. Beyond this, it presents a number of basic concepts that will be useful to the reader in understanding the process of program development in relation to agency structure and community relationships. Finally, it suggests a number of guidelines or principles that provide direction to overall program planning and implementation.

THE MEANING OF PROGRAMS

Starting at the beginning, what does the term *program* mean?

A dictionary definition is likely to include several different elements. A program may be viewed as any of the following:

> A public proclamation, manifesto, an official bulletin . . . a prospectus: a catalogue of projected proceedings or features . . . .
>
> A brief outline or explanation of the order to be pursued, or the subjects embraced, in any public exercise, performance or entertainment; usually, a printed or written list of the acts, scenes, selections, or other features composing a dramatic, musical, or other performance . . . .
>
> A plan of future procedure; as, one's program for the day; the party program . . . .
>
> A doctrine, theory, or system whose validity can be tested only in practical application; as socialism is a program rather than a philosophy.[1]

The essential message found in these definitions is that the term *program* implies both a series of intended activities, events, or presentations, and also an underlying plan or theory that is used to support and justify the activities to be offered. In terms of direct application to recreation, parks and leisure service, Farrell and Lundegren suggest that the word "program" should be taken to mean:

> (1) the activity in which people participate; (2) the facility that enables the activity experience to take place; and (3) the leadership that has been responsible for facilitating this experience.[2]

Similarly, Russell discusses "programmed recreation" chiefly as a form of organized and purposeful activity, designed in an orderly and deliberate way to achieve desirable individual and group outcomes.[3] Finally, Edginton, Compton, and Hanson refer to a program as:

> a purposeful plan of intervention, which is deliberately designed and constructed in order to produce certain behavioral outcomes in an individual and/or group.[4]

PROGRAMS: A BROADER CONCEPT

This text takes the position that the word should have a much broader meaning than any of the definitions cited thus far. The concept of "program" is used to describe the full range of leisure-related activities, services, and other purposeful efforts of an agency that assist and promote all forms of recreational involvement in the community.

For example, a municipal recreation and park department may be expected to provide or sponsor five major types of program services to the public at large: organizing recreation programs, providing facilities, promoting community recreation, educating for leisure, and providing nonrecreational services.

Organized Recreation Programs.   The first and most widely recognized function consists of providing leadership or supervision for direct participation in a wide range of recreational activities. These may include organized playground or day camp programs; sports and games; arts and crafts; music, drama, and dance activities; trips and outings; or hobbies or other special-interest activities. They may also include the sponsorship of regularly meeting youth clubs, senior centers, programs for the disabled, or other groups serving a particular population group.

Provision of Facilities.   The public local recreation and park agency also normally provides a variety of facilities for largely undirected or unscheduled play. These facilities typically include parks, playfields, picnic areas, golf courses, swimming pools, beaches, game rooms, or lounges for self-directed activity.

Such facilities must be carefully designed, constructed, and maintained by the department, and must be supervised to ensure that safety standards and appropriate guidelines for behavior of participants are enforced. Often recreation and park departments make their facilities available by permit to other organized groups. Frequently, too, admission to facilities such as tennis courts, pools, or skating rinks will be subject to schedules that assign people a time to play, or that require a membership card or fee, or have other forms of restrictions. However, the basic form of participation in such settings is likely to be primarily self-directed rather than tightly organized or structured.

Promotion of Community Recreation.   A third important function of many recreation and park departments today is to provide assistance to other community agencies, and to act as a catalyst in the promotion of community recreation. This may be done in several ways:

1. Giving technical help in program planning and development by providing consultants or in some cases lending equipment
2. Making leadership available on a contractual basis to such organizations, or contracting with them to carry on specific programs
3. Cosponsoring programs with civic groups, neighborhood associations, or special-interest organizations
4. Coordinating services with other agencies in terms of joint scheduling, referrals, seeking assistance from their specialists or consultants
5. Helping train personnel, publicize programs, and generally stimulate community concern and support on recreation-related issues

Thus, the public recreation and park department should act as a strong, community-wide representative for recreation, in concert with other civic departments, voluntary, private, commercial, and business organizations, and in cooperation with state and federal funding agencies. The author has written elsewhere:

> The public recreation and park department should act as a catalyst, flagbearer, promoter, mobilizer of public interest, research center, and in any other role that promotes leisure services or related social programs.[5]

Education for Leisure.   Linked to the function of promoting community recreation is the role played by many recreation agencies of all types in helping to educate for leisure.

This task may be carried out in a broad sense by planning activities or events that strengthen and enrich public awareness of leisure needs and values, such as participation in the national "Life. Be In It." campaign. Particularly in agencies that serve special populations, it may also involve providing leisure education or leisure counseling services to individuals or small groups of people, such as those who are reentering the community after a period of rehabilitation, or those who are approaching job retirement.

In any case, it suggests that effective recreation programs must do more than simply provide opportunities for recreational participation. In addition, they must seek to broaden peoples' horizons, and to motivate them for the fullest and most creative use of their leisure.

Provision of Nonrecreational Services.   A fifth important function of many recreation agencies today is to provide other kinds of services, beyond those that are normally thought of as recreational.

For example, a public agency's youth program might include such elements as leadership training, vocational education, job placement, alcohol or drug abuse counseling, legal assistance, family services, and a variety of other forms of social assistance.

Similarly, a program in a senior center might include housing or legal assistance, health service (including dental and medical clinics and glaucoma inspections), hot-lunch programs, seminars or social-action programs on problems of the aging and needed legislation to serve aging persons, and community service projects that enlist older persons as volunteers.

An employee recreation program might be placed within an administrative unit responsible for other personnel services or benefits. Thus, the same staff member who is in charge of planning employee recreation activities might also coordinate car-pool schedules, plan stress-reduction or weight-loss workshops, conduct pre-retirement workshops, or administer a buying cooperative or employee discount program.

The justification for having many recreation programs include such nonrecreational activities and services is that often recreation staff members are *capable* of directing them, and are administratively structured to carry them out successfully.

In addition, there may be a close linkage between recreational activities as such, and the other kinds of services. For example, organizing a low-cost charter vacation flight for a company's employees is very similar to setting up a discount purchasing plan for other types of products. The recreation staff member who organizes a health and fitness program may logically move over into other aspects of holistic "wellness" without difficulty. The therapeutic recreation specialist who plans social programs for mentally retarded young adults is often in an excellent position to assist them in developing independent living skills, or to conduct group counseling sessions about problems of community adjustment.

The director of a leading voluntary agency in this field, Janet Pomeroy, writes about the work of the San Francisco Recreation Center for the Handicapped:

> From . . . 30 years experience . . . with the severely multi-disabled, it is difficult to see how any recreation agency, public or private, can make an effective contribution to the welfare of these persons without recognizing other needs as well. The recreation agency is frequently the first, and often the only, agency with which retarded and disabled people become involved. They bring with them a variety of problems and needs that are not the responsibility of recreation. However, recreation personnel can work closely with social agencies in helping participants and their families to find the services they need. In turn, these agencies can provide valuable consultation services to the recreation staff, to the mutual benefit of the disabled.[6]

Emphasis on Goal-Oriented Programming

Based on these five elements of recreation programming, it must be clearly understood that leisure-service programs today involve more than providing a narrow range of play opportunities carried on for fun alone. Instead, they must be goal-oriented and purposeful, and must satisfy a range of personal and social needs.

This does *not* mean that recreation programs should be grim, or lacking in pleasure as a primary thrust of leadership. Obviously, fun is a key motivation for most participants, in terms of building enthusiastic participation, providing emotional release, and improving the quality of their lives.

Beyond this, recreation programs should be planned to contribute to the physical, emotional, intellectual, social, and spiritual needs of individual participants, and to significant societal or agency goals as well. It must be stressed that if recreation is to receive a full measure of support—whether it be in terms of taxes, approval of bond issues, voluntary contributions by individuals or companies, or membership recruitment in leisure-related agencies—people *must* perceive it as worthwhile.

Goals Based on Agency Purpose.   Each different type of organization is likely to have its own special set of goals or desired outcomes, based on its essential mission or stated purpose. While these are presented in fuller detail in Chapters 4 and 6, several examples are cited here.

Public agencies usually seek to meet overall community needs, and to provide a basic *floor* of recreational opportunities that meet the needs of all residents for constructive and healthy leisure activity. In addition, they often strive to serve the varied needs of different neighborhoods or special populations, and to build a sense of democratic community involvement and favorable relations among residents of different ages, socioeconomic backgrounds, races, and religions.

In contrast, *voluntary agencies* are usually somewhat narrower in their goals, since they tend to serve a more sharply defined population in terms of membership. Often, when the sponsor is a religious organization, nonprofit voluntary agencies focus sharply on character development and spiritual values.

Corporate recreation programs are usually concerned with making the workplace a happier and more appealing environment and giving employees a positive outlook toward their work and the company management. By improving morale and levels of physical and emotional well-being, their ultimate purpose is to reduce absenteeism or accidents, and to contribute directly to employee productivity.

Similarly, recreation personnel in the *armed forces* are concerned with contributing to the physical and emotional well-being of members of military units, and improving morale, personal adjustment, efficiency, and the overall quality of fitness and job performance on the base.

In *therapeutic recreation* agencies, goals may vary widely according to the degree of disability of those being served and the nature of the individual organization. However, recreation may be intended to contribute directly to the therapeutic process or to facilitate the patient or client's adjustment to community life and improve his or her quality of life.

Summing up, although the specific goals of recreation may differ, it is essential that programs be viewed as purposeful and accountable forms of community service or that they contribute in significant ways to the effective operation of organizations that sponsor them.

APPROACHES TO PROGRAM PLANNING

Given this fundamental understanding, it is important to recognize that program planning has traditionally been carried out based on a number of different types of approaches. These approaches include the following:

Traditional Approach.   The traditional program is built chiefly on the basis of what has been done in the past, based on the notion that it has been popular and successful and should be continued.

Current Practices Approach.   In contrast, this approach relies heavily on copying what is being done in other communities—even to the point of adopting new fads in recreation programming. Through the professional literature, presentations at conferences, and observation of programs elsewhere, administrators leap aboard such bandwagons and strive to be in the vanguard of presenting new and novel recreation pastimes or services.

Authoritarian Approach. Here, the administrator and his or her assistants make all programming decisions with respect to activities and schedules based on their personal judgment. Often, this approach results in a uniform set of program activities offered throughout an entire community.

Expressed-Desires Approach. This method relies on surveys, interviews, or interest checklists to have potential participants indicate what they would like to have offered in the program. The assumption is that their expressed wishes will heavily influence the selection of program activities.

Sociopolitical Approach. This approach, which became influential in the 1960s and 1970s, sees community recreation programming as subject to such sociopolitical factors as the demands of pressure groups for facilities and programs, or the varying social needs of different neighborhoods in a community.

Prescriptive Approach. This method, which is found most typically in therapeutic recreation programs, involves deliberate, systematic planning by experts to meet the social or personal needs of participants. It is a form of authoritarian programming in the sense that the selection of activities, counseling, or other services is usually "prescribed" or imposed by the programmer on the participant.

The Cafeteria Approach. This is in direct contrast to the prescriptive approach. Here, a large selection of varied offerings is made available to the potential participant who simply selects the activities that seem most appealing based on free choice.

The Composite Approach

It is probably safe to say that very few recreation departments or agencies rely exclusively on any one method of making program-planning decisions.

Instead, most leisure-service organizations combine reliance on what has proven to be successful in the past with what appears to be currently popular and successful in other communities or similar organizations.

At the same time, as part of a "composite" approach to program planning, the planner's judgment should be supported by a systematic effort to determine community or membership needs and interests. Often, the cafeteria

approach will be found in such settings as public recreation and park departments, voluntary agencies, campus, or armed forces recreation programs, while
human-service or therapeutic agencies make fuller use of the prescriptive
approach.

　　　　In the final analysis, attendance becomes an important means of determining whether programs should be continued or ended. In most leisure-service
organizations, if a given activity draws an enthusiastic group of participants, it is
continued or even expanded. If not, a department or agency may strive over a
period of time to build interest in it if it feels that it has special value or potential.
If this effort is unsuccessful, it is likely to be discarded as a program offering.

OTHER CONCEPTS INFLUENCING RECREATION PROGRAM PLANNING

　　　　In addition to understanding these approaches to program planning, it is
helpful to understand several basic concepts that influence the way in which
opportunities for recreational participation may be selected, structured, and
presented to the public. These concepts include the following:

1. The nature of agency organization for program development on
   several levels, including its structure, scope, and scale.
2. The degree of centralization and decentralization in program planning and implementation.
3. The concept of recreation as a supply-and-demand system, linked
   to an understanding of program life cycles.
4. Networking and the synergetic sponsorship of joint recreation
   programs.
5. The concept of "opportunity models" that provide a floor, or
   essential core, of needed leisure outlets for all potential
   participants.
6. Present-day emphasis on accountability and the documentation of
   program outcomes.

Concept 1: Agency Organization for Program Development

　　　　This concept is concerned with the way in which leisure-service organizations are structured to provide recreation programs and services most effectively. It makes the case that the most productive agencies are those with
precisely defined goals and objectives, and with administrative units and personnel assignments that are geared to achieving these successfully.

For example, the overall task of planning and coordinating programs within a large organization that serves a substantial population is likely to be the responsibility of an agency administrator or program director. This individual normally plays a key role in determining policy, establishing priorities, assigning staff responsibilities, and coordinating various functions related to programming, the maintenance of facilities, fiscal management, and similar concerns.

At a supervisory level, separate divisions are often established to facilitate the planning and conduct of programs. These may be structured in three primary ways, on the basis of program categories or types, community areas, or populations served.

Program Categories. Within a large public recreation and park department, for example, there would typically be several program divisions that are responsible for developing and coordinating programs in such major areas of interest as active sports and games, outdoor recreation or nature programming, creative and performing arts, or aquatics. These are essentially administrative program units that plan and schedule activities, train leadership, and provide direction to programs within each such activity category.

Community Areas. Within such departments, there may also be separate divisions that are organized on the basis of major community areas or districts. Within each such area, there would normally be a district supervisor who is responsible for coordinating all of its facilities and programs, and for promoting program services generally, as well as making sure that the unique needs of different neighborhoods or population groups are met.

Populations Served. A third way of structuring an agency in order to deliver programs more effectively is in terms of populations served. Thus, in a large public department or voluntary agency, there might be a separate program division for different age groups, such as school-age children, teenagers, adults, and seniors. Some departments have traditionally also structured their sports program separately for girls' and womens' sports and boys' and mens' sports. Often, too, there will be a separate program division to serve such special populations as the disabled.

Each such program unit is responsible for planning and carrying out activities within its sphere of activity. For example, an administrative division concerned with the elderly might supervise and coordinate the programs of several senior centers, a city-wide council of elderly residents, or other special events or programs for retired citizens.

A program division responsible for promoting sports will seek to develop instructional classes, leagues, tournaments, and other events within each of the major areas of sports interest. In addition, it might introduce lesser-known sports, promote cooperation among the various athletic organizations in the community, and sponsor leadership training programs, awards banquets, and similar events.

To illustrate the structure of an agency that is geared to serve different leisure interests and population groups, and that is organized for efficient program supervision on a district basis, Figure 2–1 presents a typical organization chart of a public recreation and park department. Figure 2–2 illustrates the structure of an armed forces recreation unit. Figure 2–3 shows how a community-based organization serving the handicapped may be structured.

Obviously, an agency's structure will depend in part on its scope and scale. The term *scope* refers to the range and variety of program elements. Some organizations typically concentrate on a narrow range of activities and populations served while others have a much broader variety of offerings and participants.

The term *scale* refers to the size of the operation (in terms of the geographical area covered), the number of participants, the number of facilities, and similar elements. Both scope and scale obviously influence the way an organization may be structured for effective operation, both in terms of initial planning and ongoing supervision of program activities.

Concept 2: Program Centralization and Decentralization

Within any large organization or federation that has a number of separate branches or service units, there is always the issue of centralization or decentralization. In general, it is assumed that a highly centralized organization lends itself to efficient management and operation controls; however, it may not be fully responsive to local needs and interests. On the other hand, a decentralized program may reflect local conditions well, but may operate in a haphazard or irresponsible manner without adequate centralized direction and supervision.

In examining a recreation agency, one may ask these questions:

Is there a policy of planning all programs in a centralized way, with the expectation that they will be carried out similarly in all locations or local branches? Are there uniform program timetables, schedules, and manuals governing the presentation of activities and events? Or is the policy one of recommending overall goals and appropriate program elements, but of leaving the individual choices of programs and scheduling decisions up to local program directors?

In public recreation and parks, some local departments have imposed uniform schedules of activities on all of their playgrounds, community centers, or other program facilities. For example, the Chicago Park District has established a system under which all local centers are expected to develop programs in a number of major sports and other areas of competition. Based on a uniform schedule throughout the city, competition would be carried on in each such activity area on a local, district, and finally a city-wide level, with common planning dates, deadlines for team registration, periods for final competitions, and other common schedules.

In other communities, there is the practice of generally recommending

FIGURE 2–1 Structure of the Recreation Branch of the Department of Recreation and Parks, Los Angeles

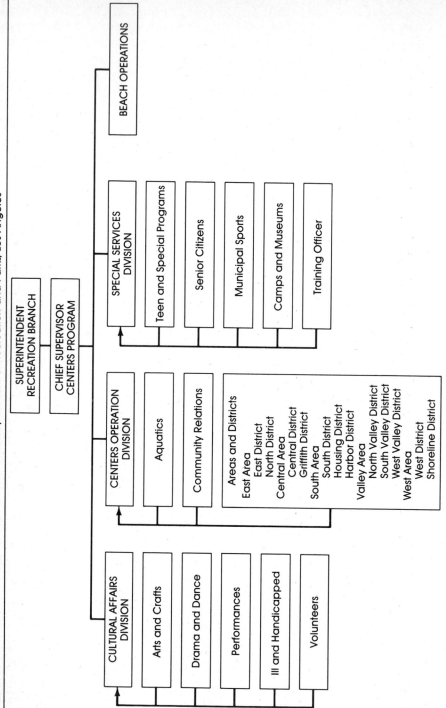

FIGURE 2–2   Structure of the Recreation Department at Naval Air Station, Memphis

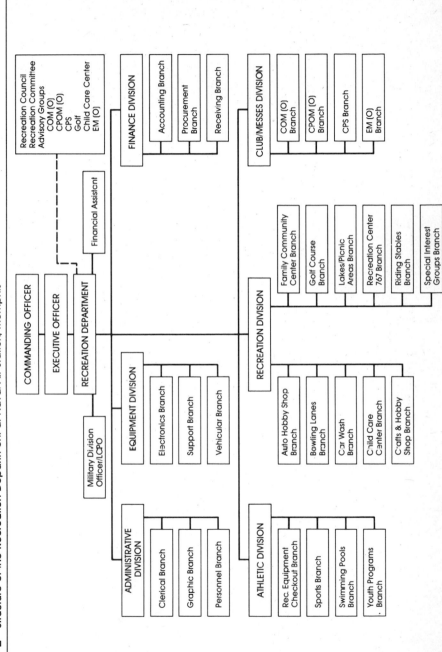

FIGURE 2–3   Structure of Community-Based Organization Serving the Handicapped

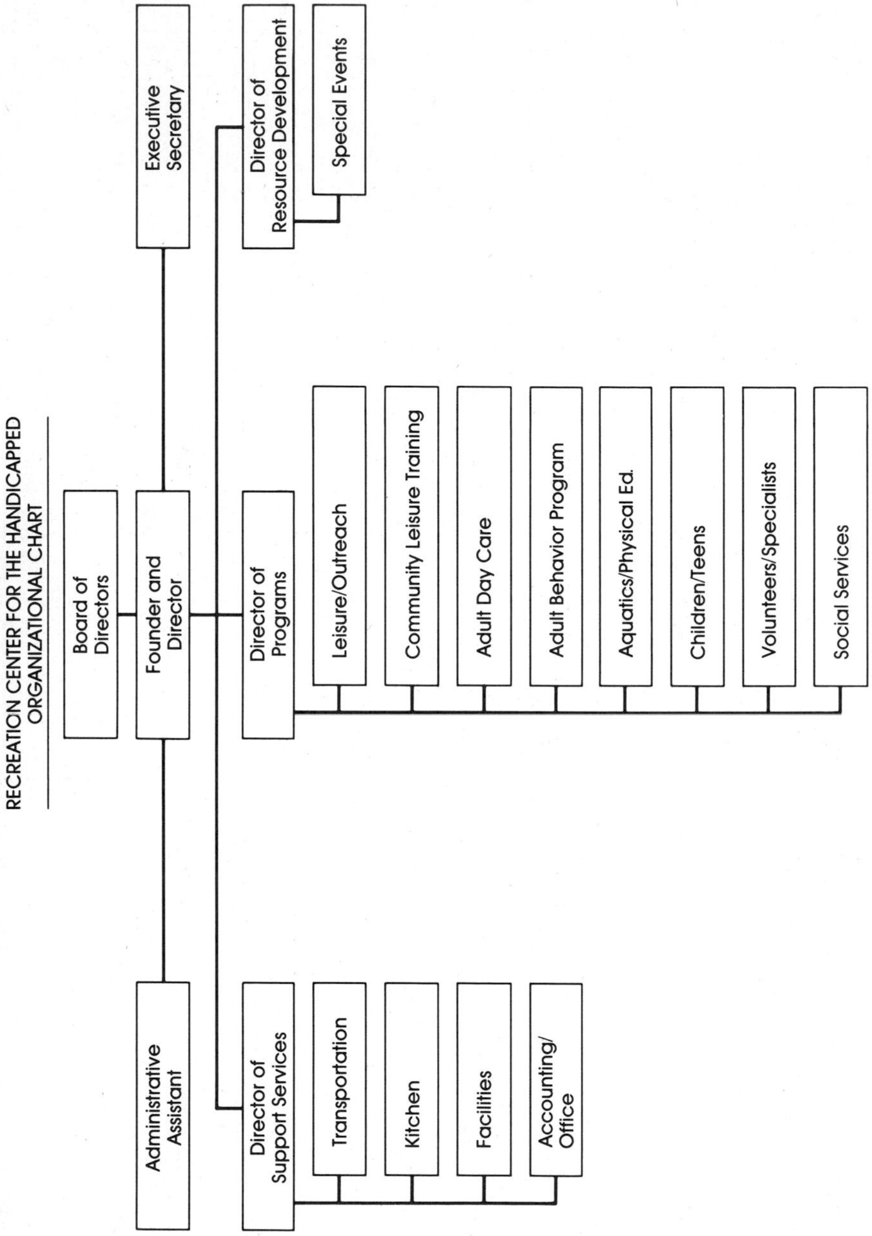

RECREATION CENTER FOR THE HANDICAPPED
ORGANIZATIONAL CHART

Board of Directors

Executive Secretary

Founder and Director

Director of Resource Development

Special Events

Administrative Assistant

Director of Programs

Leisure/Outreach

Community Leisure Training

Adult Day Care

Adult Behavior Program

Aquatics/Physical Ed.

Children/Teens

Volunteers/Specialists

Social Services

Director of Support Services

Transportation

Kitchen

Facilities

Accounting/Office

certain activities and of having the central program office provide assistance, training programs, activity specialists, and similar aids—but of encouraging each local center to develop its own programs based on local needs and interests, potential volunteer leadership, and similar factors.

In organizations such as the YMCA, YWCA, Boys' Clubs, or Girls' Clubs—although there are commonly shared national goals and frequently published manuals which present program guidelines—local branches usually develop their own programs to meet the special needs and interests of their memberships.

In the armed forces, while the Department of Defense maintains a degree of centralization through system-wide policies and personnel practices, separate branches such as the Army or Navy have a considerable measure of autonomy in program development. The program is further decentralized by decisions made at the base level by the officer in charge and the local recreation staff.

Concept 3: Recreation as a Supply-and-Demand System

This important concept is based on the view that leisure involvement represents a competitive supply-and-demand system, which means that there is a large, diversified audience of potential consumers of recreational experiences. They have a given amount of time and money to spend, although this amount may vary according to the degree to which they are motivated to engage in activities, or by other factors such as economic or employment trends.

To meet their need, there is an assortment of public, private, voluntary, commercial, and other organizations that provide a range of leisure activities and attractions, ranging from spectator events or passive forms of entertainment to classes, clubs, competitive sports, travel, tourism, and creative pastimes. This assortment of programs and pastimes can also vary according to the market's needs.

From the supplier's point of view—that is, the agency sponsoring recreational activities—the ideal situation is one in which the agency is providing programs that meet important needs or are very popular and are not provided by other agencies. Since this is rarely the case (with other organizations competing to provide the most popular activities) there is often duplication of programs on the supply side.

However, what also happens is that different types of agencies develop specializations within each area of service—such as the adventure trips organization that sponsors white-water canoeing, or the community arts association that offers fine arts classes. In essence, they develop a domain in which their expertise is recognized and in which they enjoy what is close to a monopoly. Under favorable circumstances, each leisure-service organization is able to

provide those programs and services that it is best able to do and receives
adequate financial support, either through the public's paying of fees or through
some form of subsidy such as tax support or private gifts. Similarly, under
favorable circumstances, each community resident is able to find an adequate
supply of varied recreational opportunities to meet his or her leisure needs at a
cost appropriate to his or her financial status.

In some circumstances, when participants are unable to pay directly for
services or when the sponsoring agency has insufficient funding to provide
needed programs, the supply-and-demand picture is less favorable. While it is
theoretically based on the idea of a large open system in which all people are free
to take advantage of whatever activities are offered, in reality it is often closed
because of economic constraints, with many of the most desirable programs
being offered by commercial, private, or other "closed" sponsors.

Closed Sponsors Within the System.   Many organizations serve
their own memberships and have little or no concern with the leisure needs of the
overall community population.

Employee, campus, armed forces, or private recreation programs illustrate such internal or restricted marketing systems. However, even a membership
organization must persuade its members to use *its* facilities and programs rather
than others that may be available in the community. Even in an almost totally
closed setting, such as a Veterans Administration hospital with patients who in
many cases are not able to use community resources, it is necessary to counsel
and persuade members to take part in scheduled recreation programs. Promotion
of leisure services through advertising, publicity, sales gimmicks, or other
appeals is a constant in our society—particularly when organizations are dependent on having heavy enrollments for fiscal support.

Give-and-Take Within the System.   A second interesting aspect of
the supply-demand system is that, as interest and involvement in one activity
rises, interest and involvement in other activities may also rise or decline as a
result.

In some cases, growing popularity in a given activity may promote
participation in other related pastimes. For example, since World War II there has
been a steady increase in boating as a form of popular outdoor recreation. At the
same time, such related activities as fishing, waterskiing, camping in adjacent
sites, scuba diving, and similar pursuits have continued to grow—all as part of a
complex of interactive water-based recreation.

In other cases, when one activity grows in popularity, others may
decline as a result. To illustrate, when television swept across the country in the
1950s, attendance at movie theaters declined abruptly. When casino gambling
was approved and became popular in Atlantic City, New Jersey, many night
clubs, restaurants, and even horse racing in nearby parts of the Delaware Valley
suffered markedly in attendance.

When video games became a craze in the late 1970s and early 1980s, comparable forms of recreation such as pinball machines were almost phased out. Yet, so volatile are public interests and the ebb-and-flow within the leisure marketing system that the trends were soon reversed. In January 1983, a headline in the Philadelphia *Inquirer* read, "Pinball Industry is Zapped by Popular Video Games." Slightly over a year later, the video game industry had slumped dramatically and the new headline was, "The Revival of Pinball is at Full Tilt."[7]

Numerous other examples of rapidly shifting patterns in public participation might be cited, as in the sharp decline in the purchase of recreational vehicles due to the climb in fuel costs during the 1970s. By the mid-1980s, with the gasoline situation having stabilized, "rec vehicle" sales were enjoying the crest of a dramatic boom. Even in the thriving fitness field, many health spas began to fail by the mid-1980s, thanks to overconstruction and poor management of such facilities.

All recreation attractions must be seen as competing for the time and money of potential consumers. When the supply-and-demand system swings heavily in one direction, other forms of attractions may suffer because their potential audience has been reduced. In many cases, some outside factor rather than the appeal of an activity alone is responsible for the shift in participation. For example, the tremendous boom in home-centered recreation (as evidenced by the dramatic growth in ownership of home video equipment) may reflect the public awareness of danger on the streets and a reluctance on the part of many adults to go out at night. It may also reflect a desire to share family leisure experiences, with the television center or other electronic equipment taking the place of the fireplace or round-the-piano singing of past generations.

The Program Life Cycle.   A third aspect of this overall concept has to do with the understanding that leisure participation is being subject to a typical pattern of involvement known as the *program life cycle*.

Adapted from the broader field of business marketing, this analysis suggests that recreation program activities typically pass through several stages of market acceptance and popularity. Crompton suggests that the life cycle of many recreation activities may be said to have five stages that extend through time:

> The first stage is the introduction, in which consumer acceptance is slow; the second is the take-off stage, which is a period of rapid growth; third, maturity, during which growth rate slows down; fourth, saturation, in which no further growth takes place and consumer acceptance wanes; and finally, decline, resulting either in death, which means removal from the marketplace, or petrification, which is a substantially reduced level of market acceptance remaining constant over a period of time.[8]

In terms of recreation program elements, it is apparent that some program activities, such as the major team sports or individual sports, continue to be durable in maintaining public interest and involvement. On the other hand, many activities which have been seized upon by commercial recreation sponsors—such as the rapid expansion of bowling alleys or indoor tennis centers, slot-car racing, disco dancing and, most recently, video games—swelled rapidly into a dramatic peak of popularity, and then, with oversaturation and excessive competition, declined rapidly.

The specific implications of the program life cycle concept for recreation program planners are discussed at later points in this text. They involve caution in becoming overcommitted to fad-like program activities that have rapidly gained public visibility, as well as useful strategies for prolonging the life of activities that may have lost their original impetus or market appeal, but that are worth continuing.

Concept 4: Networking and Synergetic Program Sponsorship

Earlier in this text, the idea of networking as a powerful trend in modern society was introduced. Naisbitt explains this concept in the following terms:

> Simply stated, networks are people talking to each other, sharing ideas, information, and resources. The point is often made that networking is a verb, not a noun. The important part is not the network, the finished product, but the process of getting there—the communication that creates the linkages between . . . clusters of people.[9]

Naisbitt explains that networks are vital in promoting self-help processes, improving productivity and work life, exchanging information, and sharing resources. In essence, networking represents the opposite of a closed, hierarchical structure, with all communication flowing up and down within a pyramid of administrators, managers, and subordinate employees. It suggests that people throughout a community, or agencies and professionals in different fields can all profit by sharing information, advice, or other technical resources and assistance.

Within the recreation field, networking has become increasingly important in the form of cooperative enterprises in which different organizations or community groups pool their resources to sponsor programs, facilities, or special events and services. The technical name for this process is *synergy,* which refers to combined or cooperative efforts that yield far more than could be achieved through the separate efforts of a number of different sponsors.

Many recreation agencies have in the past developed cooperative relationships with other community organizations, although there has rarely been a serious effort to coordinate all the major leisure-service groups in the typical community. Today, in an era of tight budgets for many public, voluntary, and other recreation sponsors, it has become all the more important that agencies join forces to bring about greater productivity by filling gaps in service and avoiding duplication of effort.

Concept 5: Opportunity Models as a Basis for Programming

A less widely known concept, but one that deserves consideration by all recreation programmers, involves the development of "opportunity models." This represents a planning-standard approach that seeks to answer the question What leisure services should every community provide for its residents?

For decades, no easy answer was available to respond to this question. Typically, recreation and open-space standards sought to provide a planning rule-of-thumb that there ought to be at least one acre of parkland or other outdoor recreation space for every one hundred residents in a community. Other planning standards stipulated that there ought to be different types of recreation facilities, such as playgrounds, small parks, or sports complexes within appropriate distances of all individuals, with service areas based on the distance that participants of different ages might reasonably be expected to travel.

The weaknesses of such approaches were that they were arbitrary and made no allowance for differences among communities. In addition, they dealt only with space and recreation facilities, chiefly oriented to sports and games, and did not relate to other forms of recreational activity or to programming itself.

Instead, a useful approach is to define exactly what all members of a community should have, in terms of available and inexpensive facilities and program opportunities. In effect, there would be an opportunity model that would ensure that all elementary-age children would have the opportunity to engage in different forms of recreational activity—physical, social, creative and intellectual—to meet immediate recreational needs, to contribute to their overall development, and to help them gain useful leisure attitudes, values, and skills for later life. At each later life stage, from adolescence through adulthood and aging, a similar model of basic, needed opportunities would be established.

Through a networking process, different community agencies, including the schools, would share information about the programs they offer and a coordinated plan would be developed to ensure that all community residents would have at least the basic opportunities needed for an adequate core of recreational experiences throughout the year.

If such opportunities did not exist—if, for example, children living in one section of town had no convenient opportunity to swim during the summer, community groups would then identify this as an unmet need of high priority and would develop a plan to meet it. Similarly, if minimal opportunities were not available for other age groups, or for such special populations as the mentally or physically disabled, steps would be taken to meet their needs.

Concept 6: Accountability and Documentation of Outcomes

A final important concept that has emerged dramatically over the past decade involves the need for leisure-service organizations to be accountable— that is, to be able to measure results and to demonstrate the significant values and outcomes of their programs. As indicated earlier, it is no longer acceptable in most communities to speak in glowing but subjective terms of leisure as an ideal, or of recreation as an experience that contributes to mental health or that automatically prevents juvenile delinquency.

Instead, it is essential to document the productive performance of all recreation and park programs in quantitative ways, wherever possible. This means maintaining accurate records of programs and their attendance, as well as the performance of recreation and park personnel. Cost-benefit analyses should be developed, which illustrate the actual financial costs of various program operations, and which juxtapose these with accurate statements of those served and the benefits provided. In order to accomplish this, it is essential that departments establish clearly stated goals and that these be made more specific by having precise objectives for all programs.

In areas such as therapeutic recreation, it is critically important that patient or client needs be clearly identified and that treatment plans have precise objectives, usually stated in terms of behavioral change. Such plans should be developed in cooperation with the treatment team and the program itself should be carefully evaluated in order to measure its effectiveness in achieving stated objectives.

Similarly, every other type of agency must strive to be as accountable as possible in order to gather evidence that justifies its continued support. Beyond this, it is important for the facts of the organization's program outcomes to be effectively presented as part of an ongoing public relations effort that will ensure that the public at large, members, civic officials, or other key executives or governing boards are made aware of its accomplishments.

GUIDELINES FOR RECREATION SERVICE TODAY

In conclusion, this chapter presents a number of important guidelines or principles that should govern the operation of recreation and park departments and other leisure-service agencies. These are adapted from guidelines that have traditionally appeared in textbooks, recreation program manuals, and similar sources. As such, they are framed primarily in the context of government-sponsored, local recreation departments. However, they also apply generally to programs provided by other types of sponsoring organizations, and to the collaborative effort of all such groups in community life.

These guidelines represent opinions rather than statements of fact or the findings of scientific research. However, they are drawn from the views of many recognized authorities in this field and help provide a framework for the development of recreation programs designed to serve the public.

Recreation programs must meet important community needs and promote the values of a democratic society.   By providing constructive, morally sound, and physically healthful leisure activities and opportunities for group involvement, recreation programs make a significant contribution to the community. Thus, they must be viewed as part of the social service field (including education, health, and similar social services). The recreation department should develop a basic philosophy and provide a clear statement of its goals and objectives. It must be prepared to defend these to the community and to civic groups or to its membership, board members, and other involved parties.

Recreation programs should serve all individuals in the community, regardless of age, sex, religion, socioeconomic class, or other factors.   This guide affirms that public recreation and park departments must serve the *entire* community, without discrimination and without slighting the needs of any group or class. While this position is valid, it is *not* valid to say that they must all be served *equally,* as some authorities have held. Realistically, certain age levels (such as children and youth) are much more likely to participate fully and eagerly in the recreation program than those of other ages. It is also true that in many communities, wealthy residents, who belong to country clubs, send their children to summer camps, and in many other ways are capable of meeting their recreational needs independently, are less likely to avail themselves of public services than lower socioeconomic groups. Thus, while the recreation department stands ready to serve all groups, and *seeks* to do so, it is likely to serve different groups in different ways. For some groups of participants, it will provide the major source of constructive recreation. For others, it may meet only some limited or specialized needs.

This guideline must be modified in terms of other types of agencies. For example, armed forces recreation will necessarily be limited to serving members or employees of the various branches of the service and their families. Therapeutic recreation agencies will obviously focus on the needs of certain populations with disability. College and university recreation programs will be geared to serve members of the campus community. However, with such exceptions, it is important that recreation programs be democratic and inclusive in reaching out to all potential participants.

Recreation programs must be realistically planned to meet the individual and group needs and interests of participants.   The primary purpose, both in the selection and presentation of activities, must be on satisfying the important personal needs of participants. These include the universal drives to relate to others, to achieve recognition and a sense of belonging and being accepted, to express oneself, and to achieve. In meeting these needs, the program should emphasize activities and group experiences that are of the highest quality and provide positive interpersonal relationships, creative involvement, and self-fulfillment. At the same time, the program must stress *enjoyment* and must give pleasure and satisfaction to participants.

This guideline raises the question of how the needs of participants are to be identified. Are they to consist of the expressed needs of the individuals themselves or of the needs that a sponsoring agency believes they *should* have? Are their interests to be solely the ones they may express through a recreational interests survey, or would they include the activities that a recreation leader wishes to introduce to them? Such issues are dealt with in later chapters.

In planning programs, recreation professionals should survey existing services and potential resources and should enlist the cooperation and assistance of other agencies in the community. The public recreation and park department's fundamental task is to promote recreation generally throughout the community, filling in gaps, supplementing the offerings of other voluntary or private agencies, and providing a core of recreation opportunity. It should not seek to compete with existing programs that are already meeting public needs, but instead should work with and assist them in a cooperative effort.

It is important to recognize that networking is a two-way process in which all cooperating groups both provide and receive help from others and join together in cooperatively sponsored projects. Particularly in the selection of program activities, public recreation and park agencies should carefully survey the wishes of population groups and neighborhood associations and should work closely with advisory councils and committees.

Recreation program activities should have diversity and balance. In order to appeal to all age groups, both sexes, and a variety of interests, the recreation program must cover a wide range of opportunities. This includes basic offerings in areas such as sports and games, outdoor recreation, hobbies, performing arts, and club activities, as well as other more specialized or offbeat activities, when these can be sufficiently supported. Balance must be achieved between such contrasting extremes as quiet activities and those which are physically demanding; individual and group activities; those which are culturally of a "highbrow" or elite nature, and those involving more "lowbrow" interests; and activities that appeal specifically to a single age group, or sex, or social class. No one type of activity should be permitted to dominate the program, nor should any group of potential participants be ignored in selecting program elements.

Recreation programs should involve challenge, continuity, and depth. *Challenge* implies that the program must provide activities that are new to people, challenge their skills and heighten their motivation. Whereas it is often desirable to start with *known* and *accepted* activities, new skills and interests should constantly be introduced, thus expanding the recreational horizons of participants. *Continuity* means that the program provides activities that continue leisure skills and interests first developed in schools or in youth groups, and makes it possible to carry them on as adolescents or adults. It also means that a person may continue with a hobby or recreational interest year after year, experiencing it in greater *depth* and gaining greater rewards and satisfactions. Thus it is desirable to offer certain activities on several levels: beginner, inter-mediate, and advanced.

Linked to this guideline is the issue of *competition* and *cooperation*. Traditionally, competition has been viewed as an important emphasis of recrea-tion programs—chiefly in sports, but also in other areas of activity where tournaments or competitive festivals might be held. More recently, the win-at-any-cost philosophy governing many sports programs has been sharply criticized on humanistic grounds, with growing numbers of authorities urging that such emphases be limited, and that a healthy component of noncompetitive program opportunities also be offered.

Recreation program activities should be carefully geared to meet the developmental abilities and needs of participants as well as their present and anticipated life situations. To be most successful, activities must be thoughtfully selected, adapted, and presented in order to ensure fullest participation and satisfaction for whatever group is involved. It is especially important to consider the special needs and aptitudes of different age groups. Often, when the term *developmental needs* is used, it is applied chiefly to children and youth. However, we are recognizing more and more that people continue to change and develop throughout their lives as they move from one major life stage to the next.

For example, programs should seek to meet the developmental needs of the aging—not only *after* retirement, but also in the form of *preretirement* programs, workshops, or educational activities that help equip mature middle-aged men and women with skills and attitudes that will help them use their leisure fruitfully in the period that is to follow. Similarly, programs should be specifically geared to serve such special populations as single parents who often have difficulty finding appropriate recreational and social outlets, both for them-selves and for their children, and both as individuals and together as family units.

Recreation programs must be designed to serve special groups in the community, such as the physically disabled or mentally retarded, who have limited leisure resources or skills. This may be done in a variety of ways: (1) by establishing special groups to serve groups with a particular disability; (2) by establishing groups to serve groups with mixed disabilities; (3) by establishing groups to integrate the disabled with the non-disabled; and (4) by ensuring that all recreation areas and facilities are designed or remodeled to permit access for the disabled. It may also involve giving assistance to other community agencies that serve the disabled, or carrying on joint planning to assist individuals who are being discharged from treatment settings and returning to community life.

In many cases, other organizations may develop special programs to serve disabled populations. For example, the Boy Scouts and Girl Scouts frequently sponsor special troops for mentally retarded or physically disabled youngsters. Similarly, Ys, Boys' and Girls' Clubs, and college and university recreation programs may also seek to meet the needs of the disabled.

Whenever possible, recreation activities and events should be meaningfully related to each other. Rather than have each activity provided separately, it is desirable to integrate them. For example, the nature program may also involve experiences in science education, arts and crafts, outings, creative writing, and games. Dramatics activities may involve music, dance, language arts, and arts and crafts. Each experience is thus richer and more meaningful than if it were narrowly approached, and the entire program is strengthened. Often, culminating events such as festivals, fairs, circuses, displays, and exhibitions offer a means of bringing together different portions of the recreation program.

Recreation program activities must be scheduled at appropriate times to ensure maximum participation. Many public or voluntary agency recreation programs are scheduled in fixed, unimaginative ways. Typically, programs are planned for children and youth in late-afternoon and early-evening hours, with adults being served at night, and preschool children or older citizens during the earlier daytime hours.

Obviously, it is necessary to schedule activities and the use of facilities so they fit into time slots that are convenient for participants and that maximize the use of available staff and space. Thus, each group is usually served at a time that is most convenient. However, many individuals have odd working schedules, such as night shifts or alternating shifts, that may free them for daytime leisure programs. Similarly, the alert recreation department or voluntary agency may schedule daytime activities for special groups of adults, such as housewives or househusbands, the unemployed or individuals on strike, or similar potential participants.

It is essential to develop year-long seasonal schedules on the basis of weather and climatic factors, seasonal interests, and the availability of participants at different times (based on school or college vacations, job schedules, family interests, and other involvements). The recreation program should offer opportunities for each person to participate when he or she is able to do so, and should be creatively scheduled to make this possible.

Recreation programs must make the most efficient and imaginative use possible of all community resources and facilities. Whenever possible, the recreation agency should seek to develop its own indoor or outdoor facilities, over which it has full control; these should be designed and built according to professional standards in terms of quality and quantity. They should permit multiple use to meet a variety of recreation interests simultaneously, and should be suitable for different activities at different times of the day or seasons of the year. When necessary, the facilities of other agencies (such as schools, park departments, churches, or Ys) may be obtained by mutual agreement; often this is a reciprocal arrangement, under which each agency uses certain facilities of the other. Even private or commercial facilities—such as bowling alleys—are often used by public departments on favorable terms. Thus, the entire resources of the community are utilized.

Realistically, many organizations are not able to acquire and maintain their own facilities. Scouts, for example, often use meeting places that are owned by other organizations, such as churches, schools, or Ys. Other organizations often operate camps that are situated on forest lands owned by nearby county, state, or even federal land-operating agencies. Such arrangements are essential in making a full range of recreational opportunities available to the public at large.

Qualified professional leadership should be used to fill key positions in recreation and park agencies and programs, and should carefully supervise other, subprofessional employees. It is not realistic to suggest, as some authorities have, that all positions in community recreation should be filled by qualified professional leaders. Many positions are part-time, seasonal, or at too low a rate of pay or level of responsibility to justify hiring individuals who have full professional qualifications. However, if the program is to meet its important goals and objectives, those who hold key positions in administration and supervision, as well as key specialist leaders, planners, and other staff personnel, must be professionally trained and have adequate preparatory experience. They must also carefully guide, supervise, and provide in-service training for all part-time, seasonal, volunteer, or nonprofessional employees.

The term *qualified* implies that an individual has an appropriate level of professional education and experience for the particular role he or she must fill. In therapeutic recreation service, this may be established by requiring the job applicant to be certified at a specific level by the National Therapeutic Recreation Society. In public employment, it may be stipulated that the applicant hold appropriate registration or certification credentials from a state recreation and park society, or meet specific Civil Service requirements for the position. In other types of agencies, such as employee, armed forces, voluntary agency, or commercial recreation, practices vary greatly. Over the long haul, however, as college and university programs of higher education in recreation and parks become more firmly established and widely accepted, it may be expected that the credentialing process will become stronger and more selective, and that this guideline will be widely enforced.

The recreation program should be meaningfully interpreted to the public at large through effective public relations and community involvement. Sound public relations involve much more than just publicity— getting announcements and articles in newspapers, or on radio and television. Staff members must appear before civic groups and organizations and, in effect, fill a responsible role in community life. All elements of the community should be drawn into *planning* the recreation program, or making suggestions for its improvement. When new parks, playgrounds, or other facilities are to be built, community groups should definitely be brought into the planning and design process to determine their needs and wishes. Such involvement is carried out through the establishment of advisory councils and neighborhood center committees, or by working with existing boards and associations. Good public relations depends heavily on the use of effective brochures, printed announcements, and annual reports. Finally, the *best* public relations come about through "satisfied users"—children or adults who have been successfully involved in the program, and who praise and promote it.

In situations where recreation represents one service among many within a large institutional structure (as in the case of recreation or activity therapy in a hospital, or intramural sports programming in a college or university), it is important to carry on effective *internal* public relations efforts.

In the hospital setting, for example, efforts should be made to ensure that the medical, nursing, and other treatment staffs, as well as the hospital administrators, fully understand the goals and methods of the therapeutic recreation staff, and the programs they conduct.

The recreation program must have adequate financial support, and fiscal planning must be part of all program development activities.   Obviously, a key factor in the success of any recreation program is adequate financial support for leadership, facilities maintenance, supplies and equipment, and administrative and other overhead expenses. As outlined in texts on administration, each department executive must do an effective job of planning his or her annual budget so that every item is concisely explained and justified, the per capita costs of various activities identified (using the unit-cost budgeting technique, if possible), and the major categories of expenditure clearly outlined. Then the executive or director must work aggressively to have the budget accepted by the city manager, controller or municipal board (in the case of a local public recreation agency), or other group responsible for budget approval.

There is an increasing trend today toward charging special fees for the use of facilities or enrollment in specific activities. While fees and charges provide a means of added financial support and thus permit recreation and park departments to extend their offerings, they should not be made the sole basis for deciding whether or not new activities or services are to be offered. The fundamental principle is that as many activities as possible should be made freely and easily accessible to all, with special arrangements made if necessary to permit children, the aging, the handicapped, or the economically disadvantaged to take part. At the same time, it must be recognized that many recreation programs are increasingly being required to become economically self-supporting, and that expanded fees and charges are an integral part of the popular marketing approach to recreation management, as we will discuss in Chapter 4.

This guideline also emphasizes the need to consider the fiscal implications of all programs, both in terms of costs and potential revenue, before approving them and setting them in motion. Today, such considerations are essential for recreation and park professionals on every level and in all types of agencies.

The recreation program should be regularly and systematically evaluated.   Most recreation and park agencies tend to accept this guideline in principle, but few carry it out fully and conscientiously. To do so would require that the agency develop detailed and carefully thought-out statements of goals and objectives and that it regularly examine all program activities, experiences, and leadership techniques to determine how successfully these are being met.

For many leisure-service organizations, the chief basis for measuring success has been through counting attendance figures. While this represents one important criterion of performance, it gives only a partial picture. Careful supervision, the planned use of personal observations, periodical written reports or program forms, interviews with personnel and participants, anecdotal records, and analysis of all records and outcomes, all help determine how effective a program has been.

Basic Concepts of Program Planning: Concluding Statement

Summing up, this chapter provides a theoretical framework for the recreation program planning process—particularly the nature of programs and the role of agency structure and goals in planning. The guidelines presented in the final section of this chapter tend to be couched primarily in terms of the needs of major public and voluntary leisure-service organizations, but also have important implications for other types of agencies.

We now move to a very specific consideration of the process of program planning. Chapter 3 presents a traditional approach to carrying out this process, followed by an eight-step contemporary program planning model.

NOTES_____

[1]*Webster's New International Dictionary of the English Language* (Springfield, Mass.: Merriam, 1956, 1977).

[2]Patricia Farrell and Herberta Lundegren, *The Process of Recreation Programming* (New York: John Wiley, 1978), p. 1.

[3]Ruth V. Russell, *Planning Programs in Recreation* (St. Louis: C. V. Mosby, 1982), pp. 6–11.

[4]Christopher Edginton, David Compton, and Carole Hanson, *Recreation and Leisure Programming: A Guide for the Professional* (Philadelphia: W. B. Saunders, 1980), p. 26.

[5]Richard Kraus and Joseph Curtis, *Creative Management in Recreation and Parks* (St. Louis: C. V. Mosby, 1982), p. 159.

[6]Janet Pomeroy, *Annual Report of Recreation Center for the Handicapped* (San Francisco: The Center, 1983), n.p.

[7]See Philadelphia *Inquirer:* "Pinball Industry is Zapped by Popular Video Games," January 23, 1983, 22–K; and "The Revival of Pinball is at Full Tilt," March 13, 1984, 1–A.

[8]John L. Crompton, "Recreation Programs Have Life Cycles, Too," *Parks and Recreation* (October 1979): 52.

[9]John Naisbitt, *Megatrends: Ten New Directions for Transforming Our Lives* (New York: Warner Books, 1982, 1984), p. 215.

QUESTIONS

1. The three organizational charts presented in this chapter illustrate the structure of selected public, armed forces, and therapeutic recreation agencies or services. Compare and contrast them. If you were to develop an organizational structure for a different type of agency—such as campus recreation or corporate/employee recreation—what form would it take?

2. In describing recreation as an interdependent supply-and-demand system, the chapter shows how different activities affect each other, and how interests rise and fall in popularity over time. From your own experience, give examples of such shifting trends in participation.

3. The fifteen guidelines for recreation service at the end of this chapter apply primarily to public recreation agencies. After researching other forms of recreation service, such as therapeutic or commercial recreation, show how these guidelines might be adapted to them. Which guidelines would not apply? Which new ones might you need?

SUGGESTED READINGS

Christopher Edginton, David Compton, and Carole Hanson, *Recreation and Leisure Programming: A Guide for the Professional* (Philadelphia: W. B. Saunders, 1980), Chapter 2.

Patricia Farrell and Herberta Lundegren, *The Process of Recreation Programming* (New York: John Wiley, 1978), Chapter 1.

Ruth V. Russell, *Planning Programs in Recreation* (St. Louis: C. V. Mosby, 1982), Chapter 2.

H. Douglas Sessoms, *Leisure Services* (Englewood Cliffs, N.J.: Prentice-Hall, 1984), Chapter 9.

CHAPTER 3_____

The Program_____
Planning Process:_____
A Contemporary Model___

_____

_____

As they waited at the first green for the foursome ahead of them to tee off, Dean Schuyler asked, "How are plans going for the fall intramural schedule, Jane?"

Jane Barone, Director of Campus Recreation, replied, "They're under control. We've got most of the schedules and assignments made up."

"Have ·you gotten some good help from the Student Advisory Board? They're supposed to review all student activity programs."

"Not really, to be honest," Jane said. "You know, Dean Schuyler, it's awfully hard to get those students to come to a meeting—especially at the end of the summer and in the first weeks of classes."

"Could you have done it last spring, before classes ended?" the Dean of Students asked.

"Well, I just have a lot of trouble getting them to take part and to agree on anything. Frankly, I think it's much more efficient for me to make these decisions myself. And I hire most of them for hourly jobs in the program, so they usually don't complain," said the Campus Recreation Director.

"That's all right then," said the Dean. "Although I do wish we had better participation in the different leagues. It seems to go down every year. Well, there goes that foursome. Time to tee off."

The first two chapters of this text provided a general background to the program planning process by presenting an overview of organized recreation service today and a number of basic concepts underlying program development. We now move on to the actual step-by-step process of program planning.

The term *planning* as used here does not apply only to the initial phase of developing goals and selecting appropriate program activities. Instead, it includes the tasks of organizing and scheduling program activities and services, putting them into action, and supervising and evaluating them.

This chapter begins by describing a traditional four-step approach showing the sequence that may be followed in moving from a broad philosophical position to making procedural decisions in planning a program. This is followed by a more detailed and contemporary eight-stage model that stresses the need to assess participant needs and interests and to define precise program objectives.

TRADITIONAL FOUR-STEP APPROACH

This familiar approach to program planning places a heavy reliance on the judgment and preferences of agency administrators or supervisors. In what might be called the four Ps of program development, programs are evolved through four major steps: *philosophy, principles, policies,* and *procedures.*

These steps offer a means of moving from the abstract and general to the concrete and specific. They tend to be based, however, on staff-centered development of agency priorities and policies rather than on the systematic assessment of participant needs and interests or community recreational concerns. They are presented in a sequence in which each step is briefly summarized and then illustrated, using as a subject a hypothetical community, Elmtown.

Step 1: Establishing a Philosophy

At the outset, it is necessary to develop or adopt a philosophical base for the program. This term implies a broad, interrelated system of thought and belief that expresses fundamental values about the nature of humankind, the role of government or other agencies in community life, and the significance of recreation and leisure.

Illustration: In Elmtown, the recreation director might confidently expect that the community would support him or her in the following views: (1) human life and personality are precious; (2) each person has the right to lead as full and satisfying a life as possible, and to reach his or her fullest capacity as a human being; and (3) government has an obligation to assist the individual by creating conditions or providing services that make this development possible.

The philosophy might also include a number of other fundamental beliefs regarding the specific contributions of recreation, parks, and leisure service in community life, such as its role in helping improve physical fitness or helping create a physically attractive community environment.

Step 2: Principles Stemming from Philosophy

Principles represent somewhat more sharply focused and specific statements of belief or fundamental convictions which provide the basis for more direct program choices and administrative decisions. Thus, principles represent an intermediate step between philosophy and the establishment of policies which in turn give rise to action.

Illustration: In Elmtown, the recreation staff might agree on the principle that creative and aesthetic experiences offer a valuable means of enriching total life experience, and that all individuals should have the opportunity to engage in such activities. Thus, the recreation department views as one of its responsibilities (based on the philosophy that has just been presented), the provision of participant and group opportunities for leisure involvement in creative forms of program activity.

Step 3: Policies Leading to Action

Policies are best described as major operational guides, which define areas of professional or departmental performance, and provide the basis for daily decision making and the allocation of resources.

In many organizations, they are assembled in a departmental manual or printed set of operational rules, which is referred to when decisions must be made. Often such policies or guidelines define the basis for establishing or staffing programs, determining the priority to be assigned to different populations in terms of recreational needs, the arrangements under which facilities may be used by community groups, the rules for charging fees for program involvement, and similar areas of departmental function.

When new policies are evolved or when older ones are discarded, the policy manual is brought up-to-date and all staff members are informed of the change.

Illustration: Based on the principle affirming that aesthetic and creative activities should be made available for all residents, the department has adopted the policy that the visual and performing arts will be widely promoted throughout the Elmtown community. Courses will be offered for a number of age groups in different neighborhoods in such creative and aesthetic areas as arts and crafts, music, drama, and dance. While the success of this will necessarily be dependent on the degree of interest these activities arouse, the effect of the policy is to say that the department commits itself to a strong program effort in this area.

Step 4: Procedures

Procedures are program practices (including direct administrative actions or orders), rules, or steps that must be taken by personnel and that result in services or activities being offered to the public. They represent the actual process of program delivery and define the ways in which it is carried out.

Illustration: In Elmtown, the recreation director, in consultation with staff members and community advisory groups, decides: (1) to offer classes in creative activities (arts and crafts, music, drama, and dance) in several indoor centers, during the late afternoon for children, and during the evening and on weekends for teenagers and adults; (2) to offer other special classes at appropriate times for senior citizens, housewives, handicapped individuals, and other special groups; and (3) to form a civic committee to explore other cultural needs in the community, and tentatively to plan an arts festival.

Specific steps, such as scheduling, public relations, selection or assignment of staff, consideration of fees and charges, and use of facilities, are then taken to translate these decisions into reality. These concrete actions, along with the routine steps taken to promote the activity, register participants, and order materials, are all procedures.

Thus, by moving through the successive stages of *philosophy, principles, policies,* and *procedures,* the basis for a community or agency recreation program may be established. Under the overall philosophy, a number of other principles related to such concerns as health and fitness goals, fiscal management, interagency relationships, or service to special populations, may all be developed. Each in turn will lead to policies which then are spelled out by approved procedures. As presented, this process is carried out through a group planning operation involving the managerial and leadership staff, with little or no direct involvement of participants or other community representatives.

Current thinking in recreation and park management has become much more analytical and systematic in recent years, with the result that the approach just presented—while useful as a way of understanding the program planning process—is no longer fully adequate.

CONTEMPORARY EIGHT-STAGE MODEL

Therefore, the text now presents a more detailed and up-to-date model of recreation program planning. It is visually presented in Figure 3-1, which shows the eight stages that are typically followed in developing and implementing leisure-service programs in various types of agencies.

The remaining section of this chapter explains each of the stages briefly. They are then analyzed and illustrated more fully, with guidelines for carrying them out effectively in the chapters that follow.

FIGURE 3–1   Recreation Program Planning Model

Step 1: Establish Philosophical Framework for Agency

Step 2: Assess Participant/Community Leisure Needs and Interests

Step 3: Determine Program Goals, Objectives and Policies

Step 4: Identify Range of Possible Activities and Services

Step 5: Determine Alternative Approaches to Program Design: Format and Facilities

Step 6: Develop Program Plan

Step 7: Implement Plan

Step 8: Supervise, Monitor and Evaluate Program

Step 1: Establish a Philosophical Framework

The purpose of this initial stage of the process is to provide an ideological base, or system of values and goals, for program planning.

Obviously, any activities that are to be offered should be in harmony with the department's or agency's philosophy and should be geared to meeting specific goals and objectives. This does *not* mean that an elaborate philosophical rationale must be presented to justify each activity. It *does* mean that it should be possible to examine each selected program activity and show that it contributes in a significant way to the agency's goals and objectives.

In some cases, when controversial activities are being considered, the philosophical system may help in the decision-making process. For example, if a public recreation and park department or campus recreation program is considering serving liquor or making use of gambling as a money-raising project, the established value system will provide helpful input.

Similarly, if it has been decided that a given activity should be offered, the philosophical framework may help the program planners decide what degree of priority it should receive and the circumstances under which it should be offered. It it cannot pay its own way through fees and charges, is it a vital enough service to justify being subsidized at the expense of other activities? To what degree should competition be stressed? Should advanced participants rather than beginning players be served? These and similar questions may be answered best on the basis of a consistent and well thought-out philosophy or statement of purpose. In order to develop such a statement, several sources may be employed.

The philosophy may be established by some central authority or administrative body, such as the National Board of the YMCA or the National Girl Scout Council, which, in effect, define goals and purposes for all member units or regional groups.

It may stem, in the case of public recreation agencies, from widely accepted principles that appear in the literature and can readily be restated to meet the particular needs of a given community or group of potential participants.

In some cases, it may be developed with the assistance and approval of a board of trustees, advisory committee, or council. In all situations, it should provide a sense of direction and purpose, which then can be translated into more specific program objectives to achieve agency goals. In terms of its actual format, it may appear as an introductory statement in a set of by-laws or a constitution, or it may take the form of a "mission" statement, a summary of goals and purposes, or a resolution approved by a governing commission or board of trustees.

Step 2: Assess Participant and Community Needs and Interests

The purpose of this second stage of program planning is to ensure that the program is geared to meet the needs and interests of participants, as well as significant neighborhood or community concerns.

Too often we tend to support a statement of this sort without recognizing its complex implications. For example, it implies that we must be concerned both with people as individuals and with entire social groups, age groups, ethnic groups, and, from an overall community perspective, different neighborhoods, districts, or political factions.

At the simplest level, it might mean that a community center director would need to consider the contrasting or even conflicting needs of different age groups or those who are enthusiastic participants in various specialized kinds of activities. At an entirely different level, in state or national parks, it might be necessary to balance the needs of those traveling in elaborate recreation vehicles and who prefer well-developed recreation sites with those backpackers or conservation-oriented park users who would prefer that the wilderness be kept pristine.

Needs and interests may be assessed in several ways: (1) through needs assessment studies or surveys, carried on in the community at large, in specific districts, or throughout the membership of a given organization; (2) through town meetings or meetings of advisory groups or councils; (3) through membership application or intake forms, which individuals may be required to complete when they are admitted to a treatment facility or program; or (4) through reaction forms or program evaluation sheets, which participants fill out at the end of a program or season of activity. In addition, program interests and personal needs may be determined by direct contact between leaders and program participants.

When a considerable amount of such information has been gathered, it must be interpreted. Often, there is a difference between participants' stated or perceived needs, and other unexpressed needs of which they may not be fully aware. In determining the significant needs and interests of members of an organization, is it sufficient to rely on what *they* say their needs and interests are, or should the leader's perceptions or judgment of the agency at large prevail? Often, in assessing the characteristics of a group of participants that influence the appropriate choice of activity, it is necessary to judge the following elements:

1. The past experience of group members, their level of skills in various activities, and their ability to learn new skills;
2. Their stated interests—what they say they would *like* to do, backed up by their demonstrated *readiness* to take part;
3. Their age level—a key factor in selecting activities appropriate to the social, intellectual, and physical development of participants;
4. Their physical and mental capability; obviously, severe physical disability, for example, would require limited or sharply modified games and sports for participants;
5. The numbers to be served, which might permit small-group activities or might require mass programming for large numbers of participants;
6. The sex make-up of participants; while we have done away with a great deal of the restrictive stereotyping that has limited program participation for boys and girls in the past, this is still a factor to be considered in terms of meeting the special recreation interests of *either* sex when they can be clearly identified;
7. Their social maturity and cohesion, including their ability to take on group activities that require decision making or accepting leadership responsibilities.

Beyond this, when assessing the needs and interests of those to be served, it is important not only to survey or examine those who are already members or involved in the program, but those who are *not*. Perhaps they are not involved because nothing in the present programs is attractive to them; it therefore becomes all the more important to determine their interests. Increasingly, present-day surveys of community residents are focusing on nonusers of public recreation and park systems, to be better able to meet their needs.

In assessing neighborhood and community needs, it is essential to carry out a thorough inventory of existing agencies, facilities, and programs. If there are numerous sports programs for youth, but no senior centers or programs focusing on the arts, the implications are obvious. A systematic survey of existing programs will make it possible to identify areas of special needs or high-priority program goals and objectives.

Step 3: Determine Program Goals, Objectives, and Policies

Based on the overall philosophy of the leisure-service organization and on what has been learned about the needs and interests of members of the agency, community residents, company employees, or others who are to be served, it is now appropriate to define specific program goals, objectives, and policies.

These may be presented in terms of several kinds of outcomes: (1) providing certain benefits to the community, such as improving the quality of life, encouraging mainstreaming of the handicapped, or promoting intergroup understanding; (2) promoting interest or participation in a given form of activity, such as sports, the arts, or outdoor recreation pursuits; or (3) bringing about specific changes or behavioral outcomes among participants.

Usually, *goals* represent a broad statement of the purposes that are to be achieved, while *objectives* are considered to be more precise, narrow and measurable outcomes or tasks that are to be accomplished. As indicated earlier, *policies* are operational guidelines or rules which provide direction for a leisure-service agency in striving to achieve stated goals and objectives.

For example, if the philosophy of a public recreation and park department emphasized the value of recreation as a means of achieving physical fitness, and if community surveys showed that a high percentage of people in the community had no opportunity for taking part in organized fitness programs, this might be identified as an area of high priority. A major program goal might be stated that exercise and physical fitness programs should be made available for unserved groups throughout the city as part of a total ''wellness'' approach.

Specific objectives might then be stated to commit the department to establishing a given number of such centers (perhaps one in each area of the community) and successfully involving specified percentages of several target populations in appropriate physical fitness activities.

When program goals and objectives have been stated in a preliminary way, it is important to review them in the light of steps 1 and 2.

Are they in harmony with the stated philosophical purposes of the department or agency? Are there some philosophical beliefs that are not mirrored in the goals and objectives as they should be?

In terms of the participant/community needs assessment, have its major findings been instrumental in framing the new goals and objectives? Have specific group needs been overlooked? Does the statement reflect the total picture of what is available throughout the agency or community, including programs offered by other sponsors?

Finally, a formal policy statement should be developed or revised to ensure that the agency's program is empowered to work toward achieving these goals and objectives. The policies themselves may relate to specific ways of presenting activities and services, involving participants in programs, or assigning priority to high-need areas or individuals. They may also deal with the assignment of facilities, staff members, fiscal resources, or cosponsorship arrangements.

Step 4: Identify Range of Possible Activities and Services

At this point, based on all that has been learned to date, it is necessary to paint in broad strokes the picture of what *might* be offered. This means that the major categories of activity are laid out with preliminary statements of the groups they would be serving and the locations in which they would be offered.

In part, this broad presentation would be based on past programs of the department or agency, including particularly those activities, events, or services that have been highly successful. At the same time, it would include other new program elements that reflect current practices as reported in other leisure-service agencies or that have been requested by participants who have been surveyed.

The recreation staff and group members themselves may then be involved in a brainstorming process to share new ideas for enriching the program. It is important to consider those participants or potential participants in the community or organization who need additional encouragement or activities that will be especially appealing to them. Thus, if there has been comparatively little provision of sports for girls and women in the program, this might suggest an immediate need to provide activities to involve them, whether on a corecreational or single-sex basis. The same should be done for the staff—are all the special talents and skills of leaders being fully used?

In addition to identifying appropriate categories of activities, it is desirable to determine the ways in which they should be presented. In some program areas, instruction might be vitally needed. In others, special interest groups, exhibitions, or leadership training might be the most desirable format.

It should be stressed that this phase of the program-planning process is concerned with identifying possible and desirable activities and services—but not necessarily those that will be included in the final program plan. That determination depends very heavily on their feasibility, which in turn is a matter of the agency's capability for offering them.

Step 5: Determine Alternative Approaches to Program Design: Format and Facilities

At this point, it becomes necessary to determine the feasibility of various program elements, based on the degree to which they might be self-supporting or require subsidy, and on their requirements with respect to staff, space or special facilities, equipment, and similar needs.

Each program activity that has been proposed is examined, in terms of the format under which it would be offered and the number and types of participants who are to be served. Its requirements for leadership (professional or volunteer), for specialized areas and facilities at given times, supplies and equipment, possibly transportation arrangements, and similar logistical needs are carefully defined. It then becomes necessary to decide whether it is feasible for the agency or department to offer the program, considering the possibility of revenues that will help defray these costs, or of special contributions or volunteer assistance from community groups that will facilitate the activity.

In most leisure-service systems, there are normally certain basic programs and facilities that are provided to residents or members of an organization without any sort of special fee or charge. Many others do require such fees for admission, registration, instruction, or the use of materials and equipment.

Particularly when activities require expensive equipment or specially designed facilities, or a high ratio of skilled leadership personnel to participants (for example, in programs for mentally retarded or physically disabled persons), it becomes necessary to ask how such charges will be absorbed.

Will community residents themselves be able to pay such charges for participation, so that the programs can be relatively self-sustaining? Will skilled volunteers be available from the community to provide special leadership when necessary? Will local businesses, foundations, or other organizations assist in cosponsoring activities or providing financial contributions as a gesture of good-will or as part of their own public relations effort? If not, will it be necessary and advisable for programs in some areas to be subsidized more heavily by the overall departmental budget than in others?

In many public recreation and park departments, certain program activities are expected to pay for themselves, or even to earn a small profit, which may then be used to help support other activities or facilities. For example, golf courses and boating marinas frequently are self-sufficient or better, bringing in funds that may be used for other department purposes, assuming that they are not automatically returned to the municipality's general fund. However, many voluntary and private agencies find it necessary to impose fairly heavy membership fees (often on a sliding scale or with consideration for those individuals or families with limited resources). Organizations serving the handicapped may obtain funding from many sources in order to be able to serve participants either without charges or with minimum fees.

In many communities, youth sports programs may be conducted almost entirely by neighborhood sports associations or parents' groups that recruit players, assign them to teams, coach and manage the teams, publicize the schedules, select and assign officials, sponsor award banquets, and carry out all other required tasks—all the while using the facilities belonging to the municipality and acting nominally under their formal sponsorship. Such arrangements make it possible for the sponsoring public department to schedule a wide range of sports with a minimum of staff resources, although they may also sponsor special clinics, workshops, tournaments, and similar events to provide season highlights.

As part of this process, it is necessary to examine the agency's facilities to determine the most strategic locations in which to offer program activities and services. Specialized facilities that have been designed to house sports, aquatics, creative activities, or programs for the handicapped obviously provide excellent settings in which to present such activities. At the same time, it is important that attractive program elements be widely dispersed throughout the community, and that they be offered, where possible, close to the neighborhoods in which the greatest need for them exists. Indeed, many public and voluntary agencies typically develop satellite or dispersed programs or even mobile recreation units to bring needed services close to potential participants.

Summing up, it is in step 5 that programmers determine administrative feasibility and program effectiveness and decide which activities should be presented, in what format, and at what locations. In so doing, they again consult their department or agency's statement of philosophy, goals and objectives, and the thorough assessment of community needs and interests that had been carried out earlier.

Step 6: Develop the Plan

This stage consists of the actual decision-making phase of the program-planning process. At this point, activities to be offered by the department or agency are formally selected. Also determined are the groups that will be served, the format of activities, the use of specific facilities, the assignment of leadership personnel, and the scheduling of programs and events. The plan itself may be evolved in several different ways, including the following:

- Past practices that have been proven workable and are continued with modifications;
- Externally imposed guidelines, which outline the specific activities that should be carried on, the way in which they should be presented, and other elements of leadership or scheduling (as in a city-wide playground manual, which individual playground directors must follow);
- Input from staff members in participative group-planning sessions;
- Possible use of computers to develop schedules that govern participation of and assignment of facilities, teams, and officials (for

example, as in growing numbers of large-scale college intramural programs that employ computers in the scheduling and record-keeping process);
- Use of flow charts or program-planning systems that identify all elements in the process and lay out specific tasks or functions and the dates on which they are to be completed as an aid in carrying out the program.

Typically, a program plan may go through several stages, with a first draft that is developed by district supervisors or program specialists working with a budget director, followed by staff meetings and reviews by administrative personnel. Since it must deal with both short- and long-range concerns, it is likely that it will define immediate tasks or program elements very specifically, in terms of scheduling, staff assignments, and similar concerns, while maintaining some flexibility with respect to program elements scheduled to take place in the future.

In many cases, planning for a specific area of program activity may be coordinated or directed by a specialist who is in charge of that activity. In a large municipal recreation and park department, for example, there might be several specialists (in areas such as sports, athletics, performing arts, arts and crafts, or services for the handicapped) who each formulate program proposals for their own areas and submit these to be considered and incorporated in the total program plan. In smaller departments, a single supervisor or program director may be responsible for the entire process.

In many departments or agencies, when plans are made it is understood that certain activities are scheduled based on adequate enrollment and participation. For example, an evening program of adult classes may typically specify that classes must have a minimal enrollment of twelve or fifteen registrants. If they do not achieve this, they may be canceled. Many popular activities continue to be offered year after year because they are tried and true and well attended. From year to year, some activities may be eliminated from the overall program because they cause serious administrative difficulties, are too expensive, or are in the final stages of the program life cycle. Similarly, each year some new activities are likely to be added to the overall program because of community requests or because they have proven successful elsewhere and deserve a trial.

When the plan has been completed, it should consist of a complete statement (usually in outline or chart form, accompanied by detail sheets if necessary) of all activities, their formats, the age groups for which they are designed, the projected size of the groups (or number of teams in a league), the meeting times (frequencies and duration), budget plans (including both anticipated costs and revenues), the facilities assigned or requested, staff members assigned, and any other elements that should be defined in advance.

Some organizations develop marketing plans as part of their overall program plans, which place heavy emphasis on identifying target populations for program services, developing appropriate pricing levels (where special fees are charged), and preparing hard-hitting advertising or promotional campaigns to ensure good attendance or registration in program activities.

As part of the plan, it is essential to indicate the administrative responsibility for carrying out certain program activities. For example, while teaching arts and crafts on a local playground would probably be part of the responsibility of the assigned leader, conducting a community-wide arts and crafts festival would probably be assigned to a program specialist in that field.

Step 7: Implement the Plan

This stage involves putting the plan into action. It includes such elements as making the actual space allocations and the assignment of personnel to specific locations. Where necessary, it may require staff training sessions or other steps to prepare for the program activity.

Normally, program brochures would be prepared and publicity announcements made or news releases sent out to familiarize the public with the offering. Often, registration dates are set for participants to sign up for teams or for teams to register for league play. If crafts workshops are being held, it may be necessary to inspect equipment to make sure that kilns, wheels, power equipment, or other tools are in good working order. Various other forms of preparation are carried out so the program can get under way with the maximum opportunity for success.

All aspects of program operation are normally governed by a set of policies and procedures that define the correct ways to carry them out. For example, personnel policies should clearly outline the responsibilities of staff members as well as the dos and don'ts of their behavior. If volunteer leaders are being used, they must be recruited, oriented or trained, and properly supervised. All safety and health-related practices must be described in departmental bulletins or program manuals and must be consistently enforced. Procedures related to the collection and transmittal of money, or to other forms of record-keeping must be made explicit and precisely followed.

In some cases, programs are implemented in several stages. For example in a number of major cities throughout the country, it is customary practice to carry out various activities—particularly sports—on three major levels: local, district, and city-wide. If a sport like wrestling were to be introduced, a city-wide committee of leaders skilled in this activity would plan a schedule that included the training or preparation of coaches or instructors, followed by instruction and competition on various weight levels in local recreation centers. Based on this local competition, teams from various centers would compete on the district level. Following this stage, competition would be held on the city-wide level and, in some cases, concluded by intercity competition and ultimately awards ceremonies or banquets.

Normally the program would be carried on during the season that is identified with a particular activity: (1) football during the fall, ice hockey during the fall and winter, and baseball and softball during the spring and summer, or (2) such special activities as marble-shooting contests, kite-flying, or pet shows at any appropriate time. Numerous other examples of scheduling approaches will be shown in Chapter 10.

If the program proceeds successfully, the plan remains in effect. If problems occur, normally leaders and supervisors deal with them directly, based on established departmental policies and procedures. If evaluation of the program suggests that the plan itself was inappropriate in terms of objectives or methods, changes may be made at any point during the implementation stage.

Step 8: Evaluate: Feedback, Modify, Report, and Recommend

Often evaluation is thought of as something that takes place at the *end* of a program or other operation to determine how successful it has been. However, there actually are two types of evaluation: *formative*, which takes place *while* the program is going on, and *summative*, which occurs at its conclusion. Both play an important role in program planning and implementation.

Formative Evaluation.   The formative approach implies that there is a continuing monitoring of the program, to ensure that if there are any significant problems or difficulties they can be attended to directly, while there is still time to improve the operation.

For example, if it were found during the first week or two of an aerobic dance class that the amplification system were faulty, or the hall were not large enough to handle the group attending, it would be reported immediately and adjustments made. Similarly, if it became apparent that the objectives set for a program element were inappropriate or unrealistic, these might be reconsidered. Ongoing feedback of this type ensures that leadership is operating effectively, and that the program design is being carried out as intended.

Summative Evaluation.   In contrast, summative evaluation is carried out at the conclusion of a program. Its purpose is to measure the effectiveness of various elements of the program as well as its overall level of success. Based on this concluding assessment, the decision would be made whether to repeat the program in the future and, if so, give specific recommendations as to its format or direction.

Evaluation should gather input from varied sources:

■ Direct observation by supervisory staff who are not themselves involved in leading the program, but who can observe it objectively and systematically.

- Evaluation reports by participants who may be asked to fill out rating forms at different points in the program to indicate their degree of satisfaction with it or its component parts, or who may be asked for suggestions for its improvement.
- Staff members themselves who may be asked to submit reports regularly, to appraise the effectiveness of the program and whether it is meeting its objectives.
- Outside observers who may be called in to observe the program and in some cases may use a standardized rating form that provides a comparative score for the operation.

The process of evaluation is an important and complex one and should be viewed as an integral part of the program-planning sequence. At the same time, it must be recognized that leaders in particular often view evaluation as a *threatening* experience, and that supervisors themselves may hesitate to carry out searching evaluations because they dislike having to be judgmental and critical of others, even when this may be called for. The solution is to emphasize the constructive elements of evaluation and to make clear that its primary purpose is to gather information that will be helpful in improving programs rather than to damage the reputation or threaten the job security of staff members.

SUMMING UP: APPLYING THE MODEL

All models—including the one that has just been presented—have certain built-in limitations. They usually represent an abstraction of reality; in other words, they offer a simplified depiction of a process that may actually take many varied forms in different real-life situations. Despite this, such a model is useful in that it describes the basic stages that most program planners must go through as they design and carry out leisure-service programs.

The model seems to imply that the process happens all at once, in the sense that the sponsoring agency is starting from scratch. This would be quite rare and would happen only when a new department is put into operation or possibly when a new administrator or board takes over and decides to build an entirely new program.

Recreation programs more typically continue from season to season or from year to year. They usually have an ongoing identity, staff, and structure, and customarily build a certain pattern of service and participation. From time to time, changes in scheduling are carried out. New activities may be introduced and others discarded; new facilities may be opened and others closed. Often, new programs may be introduced at different points during the year. As suggested earlier, if attendance and morale are favorable, it is unlikely that there will be a major revision of the program.

However, if there is a change in administration or if the program is doing poorly, it may require major rethinking. Some organizations deliberately carry out extensive self-studies or have themselves evaluated by outside experts at intervals to determine whether they need to make significant changes in their programming. At this point, a model such as the one presented in this chapter will prove extremely helpful as a guideline to action.

Program Planning on Different Levels

The reader should also understand that programs may be carried out on several different levels. These include: (1) the overall, comprehensive program that is carried on by an agency throughout the year; (2) a seasonal program that may stress indoor or outdoor activities based on climatic factors; (3) a special division of program service related to a particular area of activity (such as aquatics) or population served (such as the aging); (4) a single major program project or continuing element, such as a sports league or regularly meeting club; and (5) a single event, such as a carnival or track meet.

While each such type of program obviously requires careful planning and implementation, the program-planning model presented here applies most meaningfully to the task of developing an overall plan for an agency, comprising many subelements. The task of planning and carrying out a single event tends to be much simpler and is usually broken down into very specific leadership tasks.

Varied Approaches in Different Types of Agencies

Finally, it should be stressed that program-planning approaches vary greatly in different types of agency settings. For example, in treatment settings for physically or mentally disabled persons, there may be several different models of service that stress the use of recreation as a therapeutic element in a medically based model, as a medium of education, or as a time-filler in essentially custodial programming.

In some cases, program-planning approaches may be heavily influenced by national guidelines and directives, as in the armed forces or major youth-serving federations. In others, program planning may be free of all such influences and may be quite free to respond to the individual needs and life-style patterns of those being served, as in retirement or vacation-home communities.

These different approaches to program planning can best be illustrated through a number of philosophical models that give direction to agency goals and objectives. Six of these, ranging from the quality-of-life approach to a hedonist/individualist model of service are described in Chapter 4.

STUDENT PROJECT

Divide the class into small groups, with each group selecting a type of leisure-service agency serving a specific program need or population group. For example, a therapeutic recreation agency serving the mentally retarded, or health spa serving adults.

Then, using the program-planning model presented in this chapter, have each group prepare a brief outline of the planning process it would carry out with its assigned agency, showing how each step would be implemented. The outline should not be done in too much detail, but should present the key elements of each step in preparation for examining them in fuller detail in later chapters.

SUGGESTED READINGS

Reynold Carlson, Janet MacLean, Theodore Deppe, and James Peterson, *Recreation and Leisure: The Changing Scene* (Belmont, Calif.: Wadsworth, 1979), Chapter 12.

Christopher Edginton, David Compton, and Carole Hanson, *Recreation and Leisure Programming: A Guide for the Professional* (Philadelphia: Saunders College Publishing, 1980), Chapter 4.

Scout Gunn and Carol Peterson, *Therapeutic Recreation Program Design: Principles and Procedures* (Englewood Cliffs, N.J.: Prentice-Hall, 1978), Chapter 5.

Donald Weiskopf, *Recreation and Leisure: Improving the Quality of Life* (Boston: Allyn and Bacon, 1982), Chapter 20.

PART 2

Planning, Developing, and Implementing the Recreation Program

People of all ages and backgrounds take part in community recreation. Here, children and their mothers enjoy an exercise class in Vancouver, Canada, while adults take part in a run-for-life fitness program sponsored by the Honeywell Corporation. Other children and their leaders share playground activities in Omaha, Nebraska, and wheelchair participants engage in relaxed horseplay at a summer camp run by the Ontario, Canada, March of Dimes. Other youngsters are introduced to wildlife at an Omaha day camp.

CHAPTER 4

Establishing a Philosophical Framework

Susan Conroy dialed the number and waited a moment or two. "Hello, Mary, is that you? Good," said Susan. "I was wondering if I could come over to your center to talk with you in the next couple of days."

"Of course," said Mary Beattie. "What about?"

"Well, you know the new job I've taken, in the Wabash Community Mental Health Center. I'm going to be in charge of programming for young adult, mildly mentally retarded people who are in a sheltered workshop. And, frankly, I'm not too sure how to handle them."

"How come?" asked Mary. "You've had three years of experience in working with the mentally retarded. I thought you had a pretty good grasp of recreation programming with them."

"That was in a residential center, with more severely retarded individuals. The approach was really custodial," said Susan. "This situation is quite different—it has a lot of expectations and opportunities that I'm not used to. Frankly, I think I'm going to have to develop a whole new philosophy of service in working at the Wabash Center. And that's what I want to talk to you about."

The success of recreation, park, and leisure-service agencies of every type in gaining public support lies in the effectiveness with which they plan their programs and services. Realistically, the most important function of all such organizations is to provide recreational opportunities that will satisfy the needs and expectations of the clientele they serve and will contribute significantly to community or organizational well-being. To do this meaningfully, Chapter 3 pointed out that it is necessary to begin with an ideology or philosophy that provides the basis for goal setting and program decision making. In this context, the word *philosophy* means:

The body of principles or general conceptions underlying a major discipline, a religious system, a human activity, or the like, and the application of it. . . .
. . . . An integrated and consistent personal attitude toward life or reality, or toward certain phases of it, especially if this attitude is expressed in beliefs or principles of conduct.[1]

Applied to the field of recreation and leisure service, philosophy implies a system of human values and beliefs that help shape the program-planning process. This chapter will begin by describing six philosophical orientations that characterize the field today and will conclude by presenting several statements of purpose drawn from representative leisure-service agencies.

SIX PHILOSOPHICAL ORIENTATIONS

Although there has been little deliberate effort to define the different approaches to the provision of organized recreation service that have influenced our program efforts in recent years, six such approaches may readily be identified. They constitute not so much clearly defined philosophies of recreation and leisure as they do *orientations* or *viewpoints* about the important contributions and values of recreation in modern life and the most logical ways in which leisure-service agencies should function in meeting community needs.

These orientations include the following: (1) the quality-of-life or amenity approach; (2) the marketing approach; (3) the human-service approach; (4) the prescriptive approach; (5) the environmental/aesthetic/preservationist approach; and (6) the hedonist/individualist approach.

Each one is based on a number of fundamental assumptions about human and societal needs and about the essential character of recreation and leisure. It should be understood that, as presented here, each one represents an extreme position. In reality, many departments and agencies tend to base their program planning on more than one orientation.

Quality-of-Life Approach

This approach to conceptualizing recreation in society tends to see it as an experience that contributes to human development in a variety of ways and to the quality of daily life. It also is seen as contributing to community betterment by improving mental and physical health, enriching cultural life, helping prevent antisocial uses of leisure, and encouraging community residents to cooperate with each other in varied forms of group play.

The quality-of-life orientation tends to stress the unique nature of recreation as a vital and enriching form of human experience. However, it also stresses the need for recreation activities to be experienced for their own sake rather than as a form of social service. In general, during the period in which this view of organized recreation service flourished—in the 1950s and 1960s—recreation was regarded as activity carried on for its own sake rather than for extrinsic purposes or social goals.

To understand this orientation more clearly, it is helpful to look at the writings of a number of leading authors during this period. For example, George Butler wrote in 1959 that recreation consisted of activities not consciously performed for any anticipated reward, but because of inner desire and the pleasure and satisfaction they yield:

> Recreation is . . . a vital force influencing the lives of people. It is essential to happiness and satisfaction in living. Through recreation the individual grows and develops his powers and personality. As Harry A. Overstreet has expressed it, ''The man who plants his garden or plays his violin or swings lustily over the hills or talks ideas with his friends is already, even though in small degree, investing life with the qualities that transform it into the delightful and adventurous experience it ought to be.''[2]

Other authorities at this time stressed the view that recreation was a fundamental and universal human need. Sapora and Mitchell in 1961 stressed the unique conditions in modern life that made recreation essential for those who wished to maintain emotional health and improve the quality of their lives. They emphasized the changed nature of work in the industrial world, which led to its becoming more highly specialized and monotonous, lacking in creative effort or true sociability. Similarly, they pointed out that such problems as the increase of strain and mental illness in modern life, the threat of juvenile delinquency, and poor levels of physical fitness all made it essential that fuller attention be paid to providing improved outlets for community recreation.

Recognizing the varied contributions made by recreation to physical and emotional health, and the fact that leisure was being increasingly misused, they concluded:

> In seeking a solution it is assumed that there is promise in leisure—that leisure offers a hope and not a threat. . . . It is not known which way leisure is going to take us—whether to new heights of happiness and attainment or to the road that spells ruin for ourselves and our civilization. . . . Education for the healthful, enjoyable, constructive and creative use of leisure has become one of the most pressing social problems of today.[3]

Meyer, Brightbill, and Sessoms commented that community recreation helped build sound physical and mental health and led to the molding of democratic citizenship and character and to the reduction of varied forms of social pathology. Nonetheless, they too concluded that the specific forms that recreation might take stem from a basic urge to serve, gain, express, and create:

> The form which such expression (recreation) takes is conditioned by cultural environment, by physical and intellectual capabilities, by attitudes and habits, and by social influences and interactions. Recreation provides the opportunity

for free expression and thus gives the best chance for creative living, which is its own reward. . . . If recreation has any purpose, it is the enjoyment it can produce and the happiness it can help achieve.[4]

Many of the proponents of this view stress the unique role that leisure plays in modern life—as a means through which all persons may achieve the fullest self-actualization as individuals in a world that has become increasingly dominated by the mass media and other pressures toward conformity. They argue that the freedom and self-choice inherent in leisure and recreation represent their most vital contribution to the lives of participants.

In terms of fiscal support, advocates of this position have tended to assume that recreation should be supported for its own sake as an important area of civic responsibility and that adequate tax funds should be made available for this purpose. In general, this was the case in most American and Canadian communities until the early or mid-1970s. Then fiscal pressures and budget cutbacks began to lead to a business-based or marketing approach in many areas of professional recreation service.

Marketing Approach

This business-oriented approach to providing organized recreation programs and services has evolved rapidly in recent years as a direct response to social and economic pressures on both public and voluntary agencies and is also based on growing awareness of the success of flourishing commercial recreation businesses.

As indicated earlier, there was a steady growth of public and voluntary-agency recreation and park programs during the decades after World War II. With economic prosperity and a generally high employment rate, many communities expanded their parks and open spaces, built extensive new facilities, and hired growing numbers of recreation professionals. During the 1960s in particular, the Land and Water Conservation Act and other federal programs led to a marked growth of outdoor recreation resources in many states.

Period of Fiscal Austerity. In the 1970s, with steadily mounting operational costs and a declining tax base, many cities and states began to cut back on recreation and park budgets as part of an overall fiscal freeze. Federal agencies began to suffer crippling shortages and state park and mental health systems were subjected to severe cutbacks. The most serious budget slashes came in such larger, older cities as New York, Cleveland, Detroit, and Newark—a number of which came perilously close to bankruptcy during this period. At the same time, because of a general economic slowdown, many other types of leisure-service agencies dependent on public giving, such as voluntary youth-serving organizations, suffered cutbacks in their budgets.

In the late 1970s, with California's Proposal 13 and other tax-cutting measures in cities and states throughout the United States, the majority of public recreation and park departments were forced to adopt drastic measures in order to survive. This led to what has been called the marketing approach to recreation and park management.

The marketing approach has several components: (1) imposing expanded fees and charges as added sources of revenue; (2) cutbacks in various aspects of programming, leadership, and maintenance; (3) use of increased concessions, leasing, and contracting arrangements to cut costs or maximize department revenues; (4) new management techniques designed to increase productivity; (5) various other techniques designed to promote community support of recreation and park programs through the use of gift catalogues, sponsorship of parks and programs by companies or community groups, merchandising of leisure-related products, and application for foundation or other grants; and (6) a much more vigorous effort to promote recreation programs and facilities to the public at large, using contemporary marketing techniques.

The marketing approach argues that recreation agencies of all sorts must become much more realistic and aggressive in developing and promoting leisure services that will reach the broadest possible audience and gain the maximum possible income. Crompton, one of the leading exponents of this position, explains:

> In recent years there has been an increasing interest in exploring the extent to which marketing concepts and techniques can be adapted for use by public park and recreation organizations. This interest reflects a growing recognition that marketing is the essential core discipline upon which the success or survival of any agency depends. For a park and recreation agency to carry out its mission, it requires resources and support from citizens. It seeks to obtain these ingredients by delivering services which provide benefits sought by client groups. In *exchange* for services delivered, the agency receives resources in the form of tax dollars and/or direct user charges. Thus, marketing may be defined as a set of activities aimed at facilitating and expediting exchanges with target markets.[5]

Without question, the marketing approach is based on the critical need of recreation agencies to maintain adequate levels of fiscal support and, beyond this, to justify a positive image in the public eye. Too often it has been shown that recreation and leisure rank relatively low on community-wide surveys of the priority attached to different governmental services. Without pleading for support on the basis of social need—which many residents tend not to recognize—the marketing approach seeks to make recreation and park service relatively independent as a form of community service—and able to be competitive with other types of recreation sponsors within the commercial and private spheres.

Issues Raised by the Marketing Approach. At the same time, unquestioning acceptance of the marketing point of view raises a number of important issues in terms of the role that recreation and park agencies have traditionally had. When recreation is viewed primarily as a product to be sold, the issue of social value or achieving positive personal outcomes through leisure involvement becomes secondary. Two illustrations may be found in the strong pressure to have alcoholic beverages become an acceptable part of public recreation center offerings and in the growing reliance on having gambling recognized as a legitimate source of revenue for government in general and also to meet specific social needs.

Without arguing the case on moral grounds, it can readily be seen that public and voluntary recreation agencies—along with other specialized types of sponsors, such as campus, armed forces, or employee services—have traditionally been viewed as socially constructive organizations designed to provide an alternative to more negative uses of leisure. While it is obvious that drinking and gambling may be carried on in ways that are acceptable to the great bulk of the public, it is also apparent that they can lead to extremely destructive outcomes, as is the case with millions of alcoholics or obsessive gamblers.

The philosophical issue is whether recreation professionals can fully accept the marketing approach (which seeks to maximize income by meeting public leisure needs at a profit and which has little concern about social values or outcomes or meeting significant community needs) and at the same time argue that recreation requires a measure of public support as a vital form of community service.

This issue is even more sharply raised in the case of departments that have been forced to raise their fees and charges for a wide range of recreation facilities and services—in some cases moving to the point where half of their operational budgets or more are derived from revenue sources. The question is whether a great number of community residents who belong to special populations (such as the economically disadvantaged, the dependent aging, or children and youth) are being excluded from a large sector of leisure programs and services. While many communities have taken special steps to ensure that such groups are not excluded, the issue is still a matter of serious concern.

Applications in Non-Public Agencies. It should be stressed that the marketing trend and the increased reliance on fees and charges have not applied to public and voluntary agencies alone.

Murphy, for example, describes the action taken in armed forces recreation programs to maximize revenues in order to compensate for lower levels of appropriate funding support. In the late 1970s, for example, the Navy introduced initiatives to its system-wide financial posture. Among these was

> a self-sufficiency concept simply defined as the ability to generate a certain percentage of income from fees and charges within the recreation program to offset some of the expenses incurred. The program became mandatory for all but the smallest and most isolated of recreation funds which received waivers from the concept. . . . With the introduction of fees and charges . . . a more business-like approach to management of a multi-million dollar industry commenced. . . .
>
> The Navy concluded . . . that an overall self-sufficiency level of 70 percent must be attained by all large recreation funds, that a 60 percent level of attainment was mandatory for middle-size funds, and that no minimal level would be required for small, isolated recreation programs.[6]

Similarly, many large voluntary recreation agencies, such as the YMCA, YWCA, and YM-YWHA have been forced to increase their reliance on self-generated revenues, and to move into more aggressive marketing of a wide range of leisure-related programs. In employee recreation services, many companies that had formerly provided substantial subsidies for recreation and fitness programs have reduced their level of support and have required self-generated funding support from employee groups. Even in an area such as the arts, which have traditionally been heavily dependent on voluntary giving, this trend is evident. Frank Hodsoll, Chairman of the National Endowment for the Arts under the Reagan Administration, has urged the necessity for arts organizations to plan on a long-term basis, and to seek more stable long-range financial plans that will assure their continuity. He continues:

> Basically, we want to encourage cultural institutions to become more efficient, taking on some of the best aspects of business in handling their operations.[7]

Many examples may be cited of how different nongovernmental organizations have adopted a marketing approach to recreation service. One of the most striking has been the boom in sponsorship of commercial bingo games by American Indian tribes. Thanks to their exemption from most civil regulatory laws, at least 50 different Indian tribes have established high-stakes jackpot games which draw thousands of players from coast to coast, with millions of dollars in revenue. Profits have been used to pay for medical clinics, day care centers, cultural centers, and college scholarships on some reservations.[8]

Even in the field of therapeutic recreation service, recreation and activity therapy departments in many hospitals and rehabilitation centers have been influenced by the marketing concept. The fact that many such departments have sought to strengthen their funding support by successfully applying for reimbursement under third-party payment plans from insurance companies or Medicaid funds means that they are approaching the programming function with what is essentially a marketing orientation.

Draper points out that the marketing approach extends far beyond simply charging for recreation and leisure services. Instead, it implies that a wide range of new management strategies and techniques that have been drawn from industrial and company-focused research are being used in leisure-service agencies. She asks whether this is a trend that should be accepted as uncritically as it has been:

> Theoretical models and instruments constructed from an industrial standpoint and research findings derived from industrial populations may or may not yield findings that apply to human-service occupations and settings. . . . Research in the area of public recreation and leisure service provision and providers is greatly needed. In the meantime, the adoption and implementation of industrial and business management strategies and techniques must be cautiously considered.[9]

Human Services Model

In direct contrast to the marketing approach is the human services model of organized recreation service. This thrust regards recreation as a critically important form of human and social experience that must be provided in a way that contributes directly to a wide range of desired social values and outcomes.

The human services approach came into being in the United States during the 1960s when recreation programs were generously funded through the Office of Economic Opportunity, both to provide needed summer programs and to offer job training and employment for economically disadvantaged youth and adults in America's ghetto neighborhoods. Niepoth describes the broadened concept of human services:

1. The human services are a collection of agencies, with some characteristics held in common, whose primary functions are to maintain or enhance the well-being of individuals within the framework of societal norms.
2. Human service agencies adhere largely to a philosophy that focuses on the whole person, on the totality and interrelatedness of an individual's needs and desires.
3. The type of delivery system used by human service organizations is based on linkages between agencies to provide a broader base of services than any one agency could supply.[10]

He goes on to point out that in addition to the goal of helping people improve and enrich their own lives through a collaboration of interrelated and interdisciplinary services, human service agencies frequently assume an enabling and helping role within a humanistic philosophy. A particularly strong thrust in the human service direction has come from a number of innovative California recreation and park directors. In a position statement presented at a 1977 California and Pacific Southwest Conference, for example, it was pointed out that among the varied social services that were critically needed—particularly in urban slums—leisure services had a vital role to play:

> The recreation and park movement is not immune to the forces of social change which has altered the consciousness of women, minority groups, to the poor, the elderly, the handicapped and the young. The use of leisure time has important implications for human development, community integration, mental health, conservation of resources and the quality of human existence. However, it is necessary to move beyond recreation activities, buildings and parks and accept the consequences of what we do in terms of making people stronger and improving the quality of community life. Our traditional role of taking care of the parks and offering a program of recreation activities is no longer effective in society's changing social environment.[11]

This approach accepted and extended the arguments of the traditional quality-of-life approach with respect to the social values of organized recreation service. However, it rejected that approach's idealizing recreation as an ennobling kind of experience, carried on for its own sake, and instead urged that recreation must be provided to achieve significant community change and social outcomes, in collaboration with other disciplines and services.

Niepoth points out that this does not mean that recreation and park personnel should seek to *be* health educators, employment counselors, nutritionists, correctional officers, legal advisors, or housing experts. Instead, he writes, they must recognize the holistic nature of the human condition, provide such services when they are able to do so effectively, and cooperate fully with other practitioners in the varied human service fields when appropriate.

As indicated earlier, this often means that recreation practitioners must address themselves to meeting the needs of participants with services that are not recreation. For example, the recreation staff of the Moss Rehabilitation Hospital in Philadelphia has recognized that many of the people it serves are unlikely ever to be able to obtain regular paid employment. However, it also recognizes that they have a need to perform significant kinds of work or to be of meaningful service in the community. It therefore publishes a directory of volunteer opportunities, special classes, transportation services, and similar community resources to encourage its clients to undertake nonpaid community-service tasks. Through leisure counseling, they are helped to make choices and are assisted in making contact with appropriate agencies.

Holism in the Human Service Model.   Linked to the human services model is the fundamental concept of holism in human life and behavior. A leading spokesman for this view, Murphy, makes the case that many aspects of human life have become fragmented and artificially separated by the "calculating, mechanical pace of industrial society."[12]

We have tended to put leisure into an artificial context—seeing it only as free time or as time spent for pleasure or self-enrichment. Instead, Murphy argues, leisure may easily be related to work, family, religion, and education, among other human experiences. Indeed leisure may lead to exactly the same kinds of satisfactions that work yields and may be organized in one's life to be very much like work. Similarly, work may be experienced in creative, self-fulfilling ways. Thus, the arbitrary separation of our lives into different compartments of sharply contrasting kinds of experience is not justified, and recreation and leisure must be recognized as meeting critical human needs and values.

Beyond this holistic viewpoint, many recreation professionals have assumed functions and responsibilities that contribute significantly to human needs that go far beyond pleasure or fun as such. For example, youth programs or senior centers today typically provide a host of special services related to the vocational, health-related, social, legal, or educational needs of their members.

In the field of employee recreation services, many personnel managers today operate extensive fitness and stress-reduction programs, discount purchasing operations, counseling assistance, preretirement workshops, and similar functions.

Public recreation departments may sponsor youth or adult classes in a wide range of educational, vocational, or self-improvement areas, and may also provide day-care programs, special services for the handicapped, roving leader programs for juvenile gangs, environmental projects, and numerous other functions of this type.

Voluntary agencies like the Boys' Clubs or Girls' Clubs of America, the 4-H Clubs, or Police Athletic League tend to combine recreational sports and hobby programs with vocational, drug-abuse, antidelinquency, family-counseling, and a host of other related services for their young participants.

It is obvious that, in its forceful emphasis on the need to meet social problems head on and to achieve beneficial human outcomes, the human services approach to recreation and park programming may at times be at odds with the marketing approach to service. In the marketing approach, efficient management and maximizing revenues tend to represent the bottom line. In the human service orientation, social values and significant outcomes are emphasized.

At the same time, this does not mean that human services cannot represent efficient and cost-effective management procedures. Far from representing an idealistic, ivory-tower concern, human service managers must be highly practical and down-to-earth in their approach to identifying and meeting needs, developing inter-agency linkages, and obtaining needed funding. Gold, for example, describes contemporary recreation planning as the task of translating human needs and leisure behavior into space and services. Within this framework, he writes:

> A human service approach to recreation planning is both necessary and possible. It is the most cost-effective way to cope with the changing nature of many cities and suburbs. This approach requires the integration of recreation planning with other types of functional planning, a broader definition of recreation space and services, and active citizen involvement in the planning process.[13]

He points out that intelligent recreation planning today includes an emphasis on human development, environmental management, recycling developed land into open space, noncompetitive self-programmed activities, and the integration of the arts, senior citizens, day camp, and adult education programs. To achieve this integration, systematic planning is necessary:

> The basic planning task is to inventory, analyze, and project information that relates people (behavior), time (leisure), and activity (recreation) to space (resources) and a geographic area (planning unit), using criteria or measure (performance standards/social indicators) that are sensitive to the changing physical character, social needs, and political priorities of a community.[14]

Within this spectrum, all types of recreation sponsors must cooperate to ensure that important human service needs are met. In many cases, public recreation and park departments have expanded their function to include a range of human service tasks. In others, cities have formed new, umbrellalike municipal agencies in which recreation and park departments are included as service divisions along with other departments concerned primarily with meeting social needs. It is apparent that the human services approach represents an important thrust in recreation and park management and that it offers a major choice to programmers in providing a philosophical base for planning.

The Prescriptive Approach

Of all the possible orientations to organized recreation service today, the prescriptive approach is most purposeful in terms of designating desired outcomes and functions. Far from the original concept of recreation as an activity carried on for its own sake and free of extrinsic purpose, prescriptive recreation is clearly designed to accomplish specific goals.

Examples in Therapeutic Recreation Programs.   Probably the best example of programming that follows this model may be found in therapeutic recreation service within institutions or other treatment settings, where recreation is used as a distinct form of therapy.

Often, such programs follow a medical model with treatment goals providing the basis for diagnosing each patient's or client's needs and determining the role of each type of therapy (including physical therapy, occupational therapy, and other adjunctive forms of treatment).

To illustrate, Wehman and Schleien describe curriculum design in therapeutic recreation service as it is used to develop either an Individualized Education Program (IEP) or an Individualized Habilitation Plan (IHP).

Within each major unit, it would be customary for members of the treatment team to review the patient's or client's level of illness or disability, past recreation, education, other experiences and skills, and current level of functioning. Based on this review, a curriculum would be devised to include the following program components: (1) a program goal; (2) an instructional objective (short-term); (3) a task analysis of each skill; (4) the verbal cue required for instruction in the skill; (5) materials that are required for instruction; and (6) teaching procedures and special adaptations with each skill.[15]

Purposes of Prescriptive Programs.   In some cases, programs may be intended to help patients or clients master important motor skills, improve social behavior, or develop more effective means of communicating with others. Often these represent the primary purpose of the activity. In other cases, the purpose would be to introduce the patient or client to a recreational activity in order to build recreational interest and competence that would be useful in community life. For example, Gunn and Peterson identify a number of "terminal performance objectives" that would be appropriate, measurable, and feasible in an instructional cross-country skiing program:

1. To demonstrate the ability to cross-country ski.
2. To demonstrate knowledge and ability related to maintenance of equipment.
3. To demonstrate knowledge of resources to cross-country skiing opportunities.
4. To demonstrate knowledge related to the purchase of equipment and clothing.[16]

Numerous other examples might be cited of how recreation is used in treatment programs, with the goals and objectives clearly defined, with a careful analysis of activities, group needs, performance assessment, and similar steps. While participants *may* be involved meaningfully in the selection of these activities and in establishing program goals and objectives, often they are not. Instead, the judgment of the treatment team as a whole, and of the recreation therapist in particular, is the basis for prescribing activity.

In effect, the component that is normally an essential element in recreation—free choice because of anticipated pleasure or other personal benefits—is missing within this model. Nonetheless, with the growth of programs designed to achieve specific outcomes and benefits, and because of the need to be able to measure outcomes and thereby document the value of an activity or service, the prescriptive approach is a highly significant one.

Both within the marketing model and the human services approach, it would appear likely to flourish. Within the marketing approach, professional entrepreneurs of therapeutic recreation service may be increasingly able to "sell" their services on a contractual basis to institutions or treatment agencies. These services will often be prescriptive. Similarly, within the human service approach, the specific social outcomes and performance objectives that are designated are also likely to assume the character of prescribed participation rather than fully voluntary or spontaneous involvement.

The Environmental/Aesthetic/Preservationist Approach

This model lumps together three elements that are not precisely synonymous, but that do share a degree of similarity. The environmentalist obviously is concerned with protecting the natural environment and preserving it in as natural and healthy a state as possible. The aesthetic position is one that values the appearance of the environment, both natural and man-made, and which also stresses the inclusion of cultural arts and other creative experiences within a recreation program. The preservationist seeks to maintain the physical environment—not simply out of a respect for nature, but to preserve evidence of an historical past, cultural tradition, or similar concerns.

This approach to recreation planning is more likely to be evident in agencies that operate extensive parks, forests, waterfront areas, or other natural or scenic resources. Thus, one might assume that it would chiefly be found in such government agencies as federal, state, or provincial park departments that administer major parks and outdoor recreation facilities.

However, this is not the full picture. Many urban recreation and park planners are responsible for large, older parks with extensive wild areas. Often they may help rehabilitate or redesign rundown waterfront areas, industrial sites, or gutted slum areas. In many cases, their effort is to preserve or rebuild historic areas of cultural interest that will maintain or increase the appeal of cities for tourism and cultural programming. August Hecksher, a leading authority in this field, has stressed the linkage of environmental and aesthetic approaches in his writings:

> Each city is a place of its own, its uniqueness determined in large measure by patterns created by the alternation of structure and void, of buildings and spaces between. The larger green spaces, parks and parkways, riverbanks and waterfronts, give to a city the coherence that allows the urban dweller to have a feeling for the whole. . . .
>
> The role of open space (enhances) the city's livability. By livability, more is meant than opportunities—crucially important as they are—to play baseball on an accessible field, to find a bicycle path or to go boating. More, too, is meant than the kind of beauty that well-kept lawns and flowerbeds supply.
>
> What is expressed in open spaces is the essential quality of urban life—its casualness and variety, its ability to crystallize community feeling. People find in outdoor meeting places the chance to sense what is going on, to test the mood of the community, to mingle and communicate. Life deprived of these outdoor extensions would lack much of the vitality and savor we associate with city dwelling.[17]

Those who promote an environmental/aesthetic/preservationist approach to recreation planning and programming are not solely concerned with visual or emotional aspects of the leisure experience. Often their purpose is to promote an understanding and love for nature and acceptance of responsibility for its preservation. Knudson writes:

> Perception of natural processes is the component of recreation often derisively referred to as nature study. It is more than watching birds with binoculars. It is more than identifying spring wildflowers. It is the perceiving—the understanding—of the ways in which nature operates. The relatedness of all elements of the environment provides the key to perception. The rhythm of natural changes provides the beat. When man perceives the processes, he understands better the Creation and feels the refreshment of recreation in its deepest sense.[18]

However, such programming approaches cannot be carried out simply through a poetic evocation of the beauty of nature. Instead, Knudson points out that economic and social analyses of visitors, the roles of public and private investment in outdoor recreation, and knowledge of how to deal effectively with different segments of the public are all critical in the programming and decision-making process carried on by modern recreation and park professionals. Scientific expertise also is essential:

Biological principles of recreation area management apply to all types of recreation managers. The more intensively used the facilities—such as in camps and local parks—the more intensive is the need for understanding biological interactions, the carrying capacity of the site, and manipulative principles for managing the site within its natural parameters.[19]

Growing Outdoor Recreation and Environmental Interests. Since the publication of the Outdoor Recreation Resources Review Commission Report in 1962, there has been a powerful thrust toward acquiring additional outdoor recreation and open land. In addition, there has been growing interest in protecting the nation's rich store of cultural resources—prehistoric and historic sites, structures and artifacts, as well as the customs and ways of life of the various immigrations and cultural groups that have contributed to our cultural heritage and diversity. The Outdoor Recreation Policy Review Group pointed out in 1983 that the public's interest in the outdoors has climbed to new heights and is taking varied forms:

> Outdoor recreation represents the conjunction of land and people, of resources and human activities. Most Americans do not work outdoors in a natural or seminatural environment, but many recreate out of doors—they hunt, fish, hike, camp, and participate in team sports. While some recreate through vigorous activity, others photograph wildlife, study nature in its various forms, or explore historic sites and buildings. . . . Outdoor recreation is now seen as one among many uses of leisure time that contribute to physical and mental health, self-identity, and social cohesion.[20]

It seems likely that the environmental/aesthetic/preservationist approach will continue to be influential in the decades ahead. Particularly in the design of new communities and workplaces, it will influence both the nature of the physical environment in which future generations will live and their leisure uses of the environment.

The Hedonist/Individualist Approach

This final approach to recreational programming is concerned chiefly with providing fun and pleasure. It is a highly individualistic form of involvement that is free of social constraints or moral purposes. The term *hedonist* is used to mean one who seeks personal pleasure—often with the implication that it is of a sensual, bodily nature.

Obviously, certain forms of leisure involvement that have grown increasingly popular in recent years fit this mold. The accelerated rate of use and generally freer acceptance of drugs and alcohol by the young and by all classes in society is an indication of the extent to which the search for pleasure and the freedom from earlier religious and legal limitations have invaded the realm of leisure participation.

The social trend responsible for this shift in public values and behavior stemmed from the decline of support for the work ethic and other establishment values that took place in the 1960s, along with the influence of the consciousness-raising and human potential movement of the 1970s. It has resulted in a widespread acceptance of the importance of the individual, the search for self-fulfillment and self-actualization on a highly personal basis, and the rejection of family, community, and other responsibilities and commitments by a growing number of people—particularly the young.

Within the "consciousness revolution," *Newsweek* points out, there was a convergence of modern Western psychotherapy with the ancient disciplines of Eastern religions that sought to put millions more fully in touch with themselves, with others, with nature and—at its most ambitious point—with the "fundamental forces of the cosmos."[21] Millions of people experimented with varied forms of encounter groups, meditation, yoga disciplines, and other programs for self-enlightenment or counter-culture group activities.

Emergence of the "Me" Generation. Gradually a culture of narcissism emerged in which the self came to be perceived as all-important. With the economy booming, many Americans were freed of old anxieties about material success:

> The belief that hard work, self-denial and moral rectitude were their own rewards gave way to a notion, held fervently and misguidedly by some, that the "self" and the realization of its full "potential" were all-important pursuits. . . . Americans came to believe they could have it all—wealth without work, sexual freedom without marital problems, self-absorption without loss of community.[22]

It would be a mistake to assume that the social drift that occurred influenced all Americans. Yankelovich and others have shown that a sizable number of citizens cling to traditional values of hard work, family loyalty, and sacrifice, and decry the new permissiveness. But many others espouse views that would have been heretical only a generation ago:

> They are tolerant about abortion, premarital sex, remaining single, and not having children; they are skeptical about the importance of work, feeling that it does not have to be at the center of their lives.[23]

Impact of New Freedoms on Leisure Participation. As an aftershock of the "Me" decade, there has been greatly increased tolerance toward a wide range of hedonistic leisure pursuits that were formerly viewed either as sinful or morally objectionable and that often were forbidden or tightly controlled by law. Among these pursuits are the use of mind-altering drugs and alcohol, gambling, and sex as a recreational pursuit.

Marijuana, for example, represents a major agricultural crop today, with a street value of $8.5 billion a year. The huge profits to be found in cocaine trafficking are luring more and more middle-class and upper-income Americans to the cocaine trade; in 1982, the United States Drug Enforcement Administration estimated that over $30 billion a year was being spent by cocaine users.[24] In the same year, a Gallup Poll reported that 4 out of every 10 American teenagers drank alcoholic beverages at least occasionally; other reports have shown that as high as 28 percent of teenagers are estimated to be "problem" drinkers.[25]

Similarly, gambling in every form—from card playing to horse-race betting, casino gambling, bingo, and lotteries—has become a craze in modern society. *U.S. News and World Report* has cited federal reports estimating sums

> as high as 32 billion dollars a year for the amount wagered with professional bet takers such as bookmakers and number racketeers alone. Legal gambling now totals more than 24 billion dollars a year, according to. . . . the Public Gaming Research Institute. A stream of recent laws permitting lotteries, race betting and bingo has left only four states—Mississippi, Indiana, Utah and Hawaii—that prohibit all forms of gambling.[26]

In a variety of ways, sex has become a widely available leisure commodity. With weakened religious sanctions and legal restraints, pornography and prostitution have become endemic throughout the society. "Swingers" clubs and conventions, bisexual lifestyles, and homosexuality have all gained a measure of acceptance, all contributing to a way of life that challenges the traditional sex and family roles that have characterized society and emphasizing the right to seek freedom and self-expression without conventional controls.

Erotic video games and cable or cassette television sex films are only the least of these new recreational sex products. Male strippers and dancers who perform before audiences of cheering women illustrate the sex-role reversals found in many leisure pursuits. Sometimes pornography has been combined with brutal violence often graphically depicted.[27]

One major aspect of hedonistic behavior involves getting "high" in other ways—such as through high-risk activities. A growing number of individuals deliberately seek out extremely dangerous pursuits, such as skydiving, hang gliding, mountain climbing, or powerboat racing despite the knowledge that they run an inordinately high risk of serious or fatal injury (Table 4-1).

Those who take part in such activities do not do so in a spirit of grim self-sacrifice, but search for sensations they are unable to find in other activities in life. One racing car driver, Niki Lauda, who slammed his Ferrari Formula One racer into a concrete wall at 140 m.p.h. and lived to race again, despite severe injuries, commented, "I don't want to die. I race for all the pleasure it gives me. When the car responds to me, it's a fantastic feeling." Others talk about the "exhilarating feeling," the "total freedom," or the "ultimate high" they get during free fall sky diving. A psychiatrist who is keenly aware of athletes and their motivations sums up their feelings about extremely high-risk sports in the phrase: "Unendurable pleasure, indefinitely prolonged."[28]

The Search for Individuality. For other participants, the challenge is to be different—and to express themselves as individuals. In a world dominated by the herd instinct and by the mass media, many participants seek to break away from the commonplace. *U.S. News and World Report* comments, "Out of step with your neighbors or co-workers? Don't worry. It's now the heyday of individualism." The director of the "values-and-lifestyles" program at SRI International, a California think tank, sums it up:

TABLE 4-1   Statistics of Participation and Annual Deaths in Selected High-Risk Activities[29]

Activities	Participants	Annual Deaths	Per 1,000
Home-built aircraft	8,000	236	28.2
Horse racing	1,800	23	12.8
Sky diving	30,000	370	12.3
Sprint-car racing	8,500	75	8.8
Powerboat racing	6,500	42	6.5
Hang gliding	30,000	169	5.6
Mountaineering	60,000	308	5.1
Glider flying	18,000	72	4.0
Boxing	55,000	21	3.8
Formula-car racing	5,000	18	3.6
Stock-car racing	26,000	91	3.5
Sports-car racing	11,000	29	2.6
Scuba diving	1,000,000	1,099	1.1
Motorcycle racing	115,000	77	0.7
Ballooning	40,000	24	0.6

The trend is that there is no trend. We're in the midst of a celebration of diversity![30]

One photojournalist, Mark Jury, toured the country, recording an incredible diversity of hobbies and recreational events which illustrate the swelling leisure boom of the late 1970s. Among other activities, he photographed thousands of Americans enjoying trailer camping; backpacking; scuba diving; bar-hopping (a beer-drinking, tavern-to-tavern race); competing in the World Championship Swamp Buggy Race; frying eggs in the World's Largest Frying Pan at the Central Maine Egg Festival; taking part in a Winter Festival with polar-bear swimming and a demolition derby on the ice; enjoying crafts, baseball, snowmobile racing, and skydiving; being part of a Strolling Troubadours company; "marrying" two hermit crabs on the beach at Ocean City, New Jersey; searching for treasure with metal detectors; taking part in traditional Highland Games; volunteering as "mummy dusters" at the University of Pennsylvania Museum; performing as part of a little theatre company; and living as if it were several centuries ago, as members of the Society for Creative Anachronism.

Increasingly, such people are defining their identities through their leisure. While the search for pleasure, novelty, and excitement is part of their motivation, undoubtedly they also are determined to be themselves, and to be *different* through play. Jury quotes a *Life* magazine editorial on Americans at Play:

> The weekend is a state of mind, betrayed by a vacant state, that lasts till Tuesday and an anticipatory twitching that begins on Thursday. We talk fishing at the factory, surfing at the store, skiing in the office, and when we make new acquaintances, we identify ourselves less by what we do for a living than by what we do to loaf.[31]

He illustrates the point by describing a participant at a moto-cross seminar at Pocono International Raceway who indicated that he was in a hurry because his wife was showing their cats at a feline beauty pageant being held at a nearby resort. He had to pick her up and then drive quickly back to Philadelphia to see their daughter compete in a baton-twirling contest. The next day, he would be returning to the Poconos to compete in a motorcycle race, but would have to get quickly back to the city for his regular contract bridge game.

"What do you do in your spare time?" joked one of the cyclists. "I work," replied the man.[32]

While this striking preoccupation with pleasure, novelty, and affirming one's individuality through play is a personal trend rather than a style of programming, the fact is that organizations need to present novel or unusual programs that capture the latest fad or that can compete successfully with the incredible diversity of leisure offerings to capture an audience.

Commercial recreation sponsors in particular seek out novel forms of entertainment, such as women's mud-wrestling, or "bellybucking" championships (a bellybumping contest in which 350-pounders force each other out of the ring). But even public and voluntary recreation and park departments seek to invent or revive zany customs, contests, and celebrations in an effort to gain visibility and attract larger audiences.

Such program orientations are likely to become more popular and to influence the content of other models of program planning. To the extent that individual activities of this type become popular and capture the public imagination and participation, they are self-defeating because those who seek to be different then leave them and move on to the next unique pastime. However, agencies that seek to serve the mass public will undoubtedly be alert to leap onto whatever new bandwagon events and activities appear to be at an upswing phase of the program life cycle.

PROGRAM APPROACHES: NO PURE MODELS

This chapter has presented six different approaches to program planning that emphasize different fundamental purposes and that identify different needs.

The quality-of-life approach probably is the most useful model of programming, particularly for public and voluntary agencies, in that it incorporates positive elements of all the others. It offers programs and services that are clearly attractive to the public at large, and it is able to market them through effective needs assessment, target segmentation and promotion, and use of revenue sources. At the same time, its traditional reliance on meeting important community needs may readily be extended to providing important social programs as part of the human service approach.

However, selected programs and facilities with the overall quality-of-life approach may also use the prescriptive, environmental/aesthetic/preservationist, and hedonist/individualist models. All such approaches may be blended within a single complex program that meets a variety of community or agency needs and interests.

EXAMPLES OF APPROPRIATE PHILOSOPHICAL STATEMENTS

Relatively few leisure-service organizations develop detailed philosophical statements. However, many of them publish brief statements of their basic beliefs, values, or major purposes. In some cases, these are used as an introduction to an organization's constitution or bylaws. In others, they may be presented as opening statements in department manuals, brochures, or annual reports.

To illustrate, several such philosophical statements or summaries of agency purposes are presented. They range from very simple statements of fundamental belief to detailed listings of specific functions and goals.

Public Agencies

The Department of Recreation of the District of Columbia made the following statement of purpose in an annual report:

> Municipal recreation in the District of Columbia is intended to provide a comprehensive and varied program of public recreation activities, services and resources for its citizens at all age levels, from pre-school through senior citizens, in part by the department's desire to provide experiences that are designed to meet constructive and worthwhile goals of the individual participant, the group, and the community at large.[33]

The Recreation and Adult Education Division of the Milwaukee public schools similarly stated its basic purpose:

> In Milwaukee, the Recreation Division seeks to promote the well-rounded development of all boys, girls, men and women, and to meet the needs and desires of all individuals it serves. By emphasizing educational as well as entertainment values of recreation, the varied activities of the different programs conducted by the Recreation Division contribute to increased learning, better social adjustment, and needed relaxation for all participants. Programs are planned by professional recreation personnel, to meet neighborhood interests and needs, providing suitable facilities, adequate equipment, and qualified leadership are available.[34]

Separate programs that are part of larger agency operations may have their own specialized statements of purpose. For example, the Blue Lake Centre, which provides adult leadership training in outdoor recreation, is a special facility of the Province of Alberta, Canada, Recreation and Parks Department. Its philosophy is suggested in the following statement:

> The Blue Lake Centre was created by the government of Alberta for the purpose of developing leaders in outdoor recreation. Blue Lake Centre offers a broad range of outdoor recreation programs to adults who are presently involved, or who are interested in becoming leaders in this field. The centre is organized and administered by the Outdoor Recreation Section, Recreation Programs Branch of Alberta Recreation and Parks.
>
> The Blue Lake Centre believes in experiential learning that is "learning by doing," which is the most effective path to understanding. As man is becoming more urbanized and is given more leisure time, he is turning to the natural world for recreation. It is our responsibility to ensure that, as greater and greater numbers of Albertans are spending more time in our wilderness areas, they have the opportunity to use enjoyable, safe and environmentally sound practices in their pursuit of outdoor experiences.[35]

Voluntary Agencies

Many voluntary agencies that sponsor extensive community leisure-service programs essentially view themselves as character-building or social-action organizations. Often their statement of purpose is extremely broad, involving major social or humanitarian goals. For example, the National Board of the Young Women's Christian Association of the U.S.A. recently issued the following statement of its overall mission:

> The Young Women's Christian Association of the United States of America,
> a movement rooted in the Christian faith as known in Jesus and nourished by
>   the resources of that faith,
> seeks to respond to the barrier-breaking love of God in this day.
> The Association draws together into responsible membership women and
>   girls of diverse experiences and faiths,
> that their lives may be open to new understanding and deeper relationships
> and that together they may join in the struggle for peace and justice, freedom
>   and dignity for all people.[36]

Beyond this, the YWCA identified as its major single imperative the "elimination of racism wherever it exists and by any means necessary." The organization has committed itself to varied programs addressing the status and needs of girls and women in the United States and throughout the world. These include activities related to legal and social rights, career development, combatting sexual harassment, marital and property rights, child care, and other programs designed to assist special populations (native Americans, deinstitutionalized persons, survivors of violence, new immigrants and migrants, and similar groups) in their full integration into community life.

Specifically, the YWCA lists the following purposes with respect to health, physical education, and recreation activities:

Member Associations and the National Board will develop and promote HPER programs for teen, student and adult women, and training for staff and volunteers in the methods and skills needed to carry them out:

- Self-help approaches to promote positive health through comprehensive, holistic education
- Stress management and coping skills related to the pressures of the changing roles of women in society, family and social life, school and work place
- Health education related to sexuality, adolescent pregnancy prevention, pregnancy and parenting, the importance of fitness, nutrition and diet and the dangers of alcohol and substance abuse to potential mothers
- Special programs for pre-natal and post-natal women and their infants which emphasize bonding, coping skills, nutrition and fitness
- Prevention education about the potential hazards of fad diets, tobacco, over-the-counter drugs, alcohol and other drugs and the effects of mixing substances
- Fitness, dance, lifetime sports, individual and team sports and physical activities
- Recreation education and participation in outdoor and indoor activities and programs
- Leisure time counseling for lifetime participation in recreational activities, healthful lifestyle options, family and peer groups
- Education in health, physical activities and recreation, everyday coping skills and techniques for aiding disabled peers, parents, spouses and children
- Development of a clearinghouse for HPER information and programs for teen, student and adult women which will provide a vehicle for sharing knowledge, skills and program guidelines
- Development by member Associations and the National Board of printed safety standards and manuals for YWCA HPER programs to be distributed to all member Associations.[37]

Armed Forces

In the armed forces, recreation is closely attached to morale and welfare functions affecting service men and women and their families. In a recently published manual, the Department of Defense presented the following statement of philosophy and purpose for such activities:

Introduction

Recognizing that quality morale, welfare and recreation (MWR) programs contribute significantly to the quality of life in the military community and directly relate to recruitment and retention of military personnel, the Department of Defense, as mandated by law, advocates a comprehensive MWR program with program activities that:

- Maintain a high level of esprit de corps; enhance job proficiency; contribute to military effectiveness; aid in recruitment and retention by making military service an attractive career; and aid service personnel in the transition from civilian to military life.
- Promote and maintain the physical, mental and social well being of military members, their families, and other eligible members of the military community.
- Encourage constructive use of off-duty leisure time with opportunities for acquiring new talents and skills that contribute to the military and civilian community.
- Provide community support programs, and activities for military families, particularly when the service member is on an unaccompanied tour or involved in armed conflict.

It is the responsibility of military commands to create, maintain, and support comprehensive, quality MWR programs, services, and activities that meet the changing needs and interests of the military establishment; that are flexible to meet unique geographic requirements; and that take into consideration the evolving social and economic environment.[38]

Therapeutic Recreation

Numerous therapeutic recreation agencies have published statements of their overall philosophy and functions. For example, the Children's Seashore House, a treatment center for orthopedically disabled children in Atlantic City, New Jersey, has published the following description of its philosophy and program goals.[39]

Philosophy

The Child
We believe the child is a unique individual.
We believe the child is continuously growing.
We believe the child's needs are holistic in nature.
We believe the child interacts with his environment.
We believe the child's actions have meaning and purpose.

Play/Recreation
We believe that play/recreation is a means of discovery, self-expression and communication for the child.
We believe play/recreation provides a child the capacity to transcend his/her immediate situational demands.
We believe play/recreation is intrinsically motivated behavior which may be extrinsically facilitated.
We believe play/recreation is an energy exchange (release/renewing) between the individual and environment.

Therapeutic Recreation
We believe that therapeutic recreation is a profession dedicated to the promotion of wellness through the use of play/recreation.

We believe therapeutic recreation professionals collaborate with children and
other professionals to plan for the individual needs of the child.
We believe therapeutic recreation is a service with a variety of approaches:
therapeutic activities, general recreation experiences and leisure education.
We believe therapeutic recreation professionals are prepared to educate,
guide, and support the child's independence in or through play/recreation
experiences.

Program Goals
1. To maintain an awareness of the uniqueness of each child, his/her abilities, interests and needs during hospitalization.
2. To engage in communication with other health care professionals to
maximize the T.R. department's effectiveness in assisting the child in
the attainment of the goal(s) of hospitalization.
3. To engage in the evaluation of the TR program and its objectives.
4. To assist the child and family in coping with the hospital experience
through structured and self-directed play/recreation activities.
5. To provide the "natural environment" for the integration and practice of
skills developed through other disciplines.
6. To provide developmentally and situationally appropriate play/recreation
that promotes self-expression and positive experiences with self, family
and staff.
7. To provide opportunities for the development of age-appropriate socialization skills through play/recreation activities.
8. To assist the child in adjusting to limitations, temporary to permanent,
and changes in functional abilities and physical appearance.
9. To enable the child to develop an awareness of leisure values and attitudes, activity skills and knowledge of leisure resources.
10. To assist in making appropriate community referrals.
11. To facilitate and promote independence, wellness, and personal responsibility for the development of a satisfying leisure lifestyle.

A second illustrative statement of program goals and functions in
therapeutic recreation is taken from the staff manual of the therapeutic recreation
program of the Piersol Rehabilitation Center of the Hospital of the University of
Pennsylvania.[40] It shows how the overall philosophy of the service is spelled out
in terms of specific goals and program activities:

Therapeutic Recreation Program
The purpose of the Therapeutic Recreation program is to provide recreational
activities and experiences which are modified to meet an individual's physical,
emotional, mental and/or social limitations and abilities. Activities are aimed at
promoting the functional independence of the individual and aiding in the total
rehabilitation process of the patient.
Recreational activities are directed toward maintaining and/or improving the
physical and mental health of the patient. The overall goals of the Therapeutic
Recreation program are: 1) to facilitate favorable adjustment to treatment and to
the hospital environment, 2) to stimulate socialization and interaction, 3) to

promote optimal psychomotor, cognitive and affective functioning through adapted activities, 4) to provide leisure education, 5) to encourage a constructive, meaningful and independent leisure lifestyle, 6) to prepare the patient for participation in community recreation programs upon discharge. The activities are geared toward teaching skills and hobbies that can be taken back to the home/community environment. The Therapeutic Recreation program works in conjunction with the rehabilitation treatment team, establishing goals that complement the patient's therapy programs in occupational therapy, physical therapy, speech, etc.

Activities are designed to aid in improving, restoring, or developing 1) endurance, 2) gross and fine motor coordination, 3) range of motion, 4) reality orientation, 5) attention span and memory, 6) language skills, 7) intellectual stimulation, 8) positive self-image, and 9) leisure skills which help the patient live a more rewarding life upon return to the community. . . .

Another goal of the Therapeutic Recreation program is to maintain community contact and awareness. Volunteer and community organizations provide many of the evening programs. Another major facet of the program are supervised outings into the community. These trips out of the hospital setting help the patients learn to cope with their disabilities in a "real-life" environment, providing opportunities to practice skills learned in therapy (i.e., P.T., O.T.). While learning how to deal with social and physical barriers in the community, patients are also exposed to accessible recreation programs, facilities, and services. Adjustment to the community is combined with leisure education and referral. Outings are taken to museums, concerts, sports events, restaurants, shopping centers, etc.

The involvement of family and friends in recreational activities is encouraged. Shared recreational experiences promote the maintenance of healthy relationships and structure the satisfying and enjoyable use of free time during the patient's hospital stay.

A transitional program for discharged patients and their families is also offered in the "Alumni Club." This social/recreational group meets monthly to maintain a supportive social network that follows-up on patients' adjustment to community living while meeting some of their leisure needs.

How are such statements of philosophy developed? They often reflect the basic beliefs of a sponsoring organization, board of trustees, or other body of individuals whose views help influence the program's ideology. However, they may also be influenced by the expressed views of citizens within the community or by the professional literature. Staff members themselves should have a voice in framing philosophical statements for their organizations since they should be in agreement with their fundamental tenets if they are to be expected to support them.

Before a philosophy can be translated into a more direct statement of goals and objectives, it is necessary to consider the specific needs and interests of participants, organization members, and the community itself. These must be assessed before goals are precisely defined since they give clear direction to programming efforts. Chapter 5 therefore deals with the next step in the program planning process: assessing participant and community needs and interests.

NOTES_____

[1]*Webster's New International Dictionary of the English Language* (Springfield, Mass.: G. and C. Merriam Co., 1956), p. 1842.

[2]George D. Butler, *Introduction to Community Recreation* (New York: McGraw-Hill, 1958), p. 10.

[3]Allen Sapora and Elmer Mitchell, *The Theory of Play and Recreation* (New York: Ronald Press, 1961), p. 22.

[4]Harold Meyer, Charles Brightbill, and H. Douglas Sessoms, *Community Recreation: A Guide to its Organization* (Englewood Cliffs, N.J.: Prentice-Hall, 1969), pp. 34–35.

[5]John Crompton, "Selecting Target Markets—A Key to Effective Marketing," *Journal of Park and Recreation Administration* (January 1983): 7.

[6]Andrew F. Murphy, Jr., "Military Recreation Takes on Marketing," *Parks and Recreation* (November 1980): 29.

[7]Frank Hodsoll, cited in "The Arts Must Take on the Best Aspects of Business," *U.S. News & World Report* (17 January 1983): 63.

[8]"Indian War Cry: Bingo!" *Time* (2 January 1984): 58.

[9]Debra Draper, "The Adoption and Implementation of Business and Industrial Management Strategies and Techniques," *Journal of Park and Recreation Administration* (January 1983): 59.

[10]E. William Niepoth, *Leisure Leadership: Working With People in Recreation and Park Settings* (Englewood Cliffs, N.J.: Prentice-Hall, 1983), p. 3.

[11]Position statement presented at 1977 California and Pacific Southwest Conference, cited in Niepoth, *ibid.* p. 17.

[12]James F. Murphy, *Concepts of Leisure* (Englewood Cliffs, N.J.: Prentice-Hall, 1981), pp. 33–35.

[13]Seymour Gold, "A Human Service Approach to Recreation Planning," *Journal of Park and Recreation Administration* (January 1983): 27.

[14]Gold: 35.

[15]Paul Wehman and Stuart J. Schleien, *Leisure Programs for Handicapped Persons* (Baltimore: University Park Press, 1981), p. 89.

[16]Scout Gunn and Carol Peterson, *Therapeutic Recreation Program Design: Principles and Procedures* (Englewood Cliffs, N.J.: Prentice-Hall, 1978), p. 125.

[17]August Heckscher, *Open Spaces: The Life of American Cities* (New York: Harper and Row, 1977), p. 4.

[18]Douglas Knudson, *Outdoor Recreation* (New York: Macmillan, 1980), p. 31.

[19]Knudson, p. 8.

[20]Outdoor Recreation Resources Review Commission, *Outdoor Recreation for America 1983* (Washington, D.C.: Resources for the Future, 1983), p. 5.

[21]"Getting Your Head Together," *Newsweek* (6 September 1976), p. 56.

[22]John F. Stacks, "Aftershocks of the 'Me' Decade," *Time* (3 August 1981): 18.

[23]Stacks: 18.

[24]"Crashing on Cocaine," *Time* (11 April 1983): 23; see also *New York Times* (9 August 1982): 15.

[25]Report of Gallup Poll, Princeton, N.J. (7 October 1982).

[26]"Gambling Rage out of Control?" *U.S. News & World Report* (30 May 1983): 27.

[27]Barbara Brotman, "Feminist Protests Against 'Brutal Chic' Are Growing," *Philadelphia Inquirer* (13 January 1980): 5–G.

[28]Don Greenberg, "Unendurable Pleasure, Indefinitely Prolonged," *Philadelphia Inquirer* (16 June 1980): 6–C.

[29]"Death: For Many an Ominous Handmaiden," *Philadelphia Inquirer* (based on analysis by Metropolitan Life Insurance Co.) (16 July 1980): 6–C.

[30]"Life Style of the '80s: Anything Goes," *U.S. News & World Report* (1 August 1983): 45.

[31]Mark Jury, *Playtime! Americans at Leisure* (New York: Harcourt Brace Jovanovich, 1977), p. 40.

[32]Jury, p. 76.

[33]Statement of purpose of Recreation Department of District of Columbia, cited in: Richard Kraus and Joseph Curtis, *Creative Management in Recreation and Parks* (St. Louis: C. V. Mosby, 1982), p. 59.

[34]Kraus and Curtis, p. 59.

[35]*Brochure of Blue Lake Centre*, Province of Alberta Department of Recreation and Parks, 1983.

[36]*The YWCA Looks to the Future* (New York: Communications National Board of Young Women's Christian Association, 1982), p. 1.

[37]YWCA, p. 9.

[38]*Morale, Welfare and Recreation Program Overview* (Washington, D.C.: Office of Assistant Secretary of Defense, March 1982), p. 3.

[39]*Clinical Manual for Therapeutic Recreation* (Atlantic City, N.J.: Children's Seashore House, June 1984), pp. 1–3.

[40]*Therapeutic Recreation Program, Philosophy Statement* (Philadelphia: Piersol Rehabilitation Center, Hospital of the University of Pennsylvania, 1983).

STUDENT PROJECTS

1. The chapter presents six approaches or orientations to recreation program planning. Have the class divide into six small groups and have each group select one of these orientations, and investigate it further through supplementary readings and discussion.

   Then have each group make a presentation before the class on this orientation, in which they: (1) present its strengths and weaknesses; (2) discuss the kinds of agencies it would or would not apply to; and (3) show some of its practical implications for program planning in terms of the kinds of activities and program formats it would probably include.

2. Examples of philosophy statements are given in the chapter for four types of agencies: public, voluntary, armed forces, and therapeutic.

   Have class members divide into small groups in which they prepare similar statements for the four other types of agencies: private, commercial, campus, and corporate/employee programs. If there is disagreement within groups, present alternative or conflicting positions of what the goals of these agencies might be.

SUGGESTED READINGS

Scout Gunn and Carol Peterson, *Therapeutic Recreation Program Design: Principles and Procedures* (Englewood Cliffs, N.J.: Prentice-Hall, 1978), Chapter 2.

Richard Kraus, *Recreation and Leisure in Modern Society* (Glenview, Ill.: Scott, Foresman, 1984), Chapter 15.

E. William Niepoth, *Leisure Leadership: Working With People in Recreation and Park Settings* (Englewood Cliffs, N.J.: Prentice-Hall, 1983), Chapter 1.

H. Douglas Sessoms, *Leisure Services* (Englewood Cliffs, N.J.: Prentice-Hall, 1984), Chapter 3.

_____

CHAPTER 5

Assessing Participant_____
and Community Needs_____
and Interests_____

_____

_____

Don Duval held up a copy of the survey. "This is it, gang. We've got the questionnaire of recreation needs and interests all set, and we're ready to roll!" He distributed the forms and plans for the survey to members of the volunteer committee who were going to help in the planning study.

"We're trying to get a really good cross section of the city covered by working through different PTAs and churches and distributing forms in shopping malls. And each of you is scheduled to interview members of the public in various neighborhoods at different times."

"It looks good," said a committee member. "But, Don, I see that we're not distributing any surveys or doing interviews in the Shawcross area. How come?"

"Those people are just a problem to us," said Don Duval. "They are a very low type. The boys are always hot-rodding around, and half the girls are pregnant before they finish high school—if they finish. They can't tell us anything meaningful about recreation."

"But don't you think we ought to survey them anyway?"

"No," said Don Duval. "Forget Shawcross. Let's stay with the people we can really serve."

A vital ingredient of recreation program planning involves careful consideration of the needs, interests, and characteristics of participants. This second step in the program-planning process may be achieved in two ways: (1) by using what is known about participants to determine appropriate program activities; and (2) by assessing their needs and interests directly, through questionnaires, surveys, and similar techniques.

It is necessary not only to consider the participants, but also to determine overall community or neighborhood recreation needs. Again, this may be done either by arriving at judgments based on careful observation or through the use of surveys or consultation with advisory groups or other community representatives.

First, it is essential to determine just what is meant by needs, interests and characteristics.

The term *need,* when used in this context, usually applies to the emotional, social, physical, or other attributes of participants that create a felt desire on their part for a given type of leisure involvement. An individual may *need* to take part in vigorous physical activity, for example, either to improve his or her fitness or as a release for tension and anxiety. Similarly, he or she may express a *need* to take part in a social program or event, in order to make friends or share social contact with others.

Needs may also represent the judgment of a group leader or therapist who determines on the basis of observation or counseling that a given participant would benefit by taking part in a certain type of activity. In therapeutic recreation programs particularly, the treatment team may identify specific needs of patients or clients, which then become the basis for developing individualized treatment plans. This type of need is externally perceived and the participant personally may not be aware of it.

The term *interests* usually refers more specifically to activities that individuals would like to take part in, or in which they have already had experience. Interests may be determined by having participants or group members fill out intake forms, interest surveys, or similar questionnaires, or through interviews or group planning sessions. Many interest surveys include extensive lists of activities for participants to indicate their choices of activity.

Finally, the term *characteristics* refers to personal traits or group descriptors that are helpful in determining appropriate program activities for participants or potential participants. Examples of group activities include the following: age or life-stage; gender; family status; physical, social, and emotional status; possible ethnic or racial factors that influence participation; educational and socioeconomic background, particularly as it affects one's life-style; size of group; and availability or readiness of access to program activities.

Each of these factors is now explored as the basis for determining appropriate program activities for participants. Following that, specific techniques for assessing individual and group needs and interests are presented.

AGE AND LIFE-STAGE

Traditionally, the single most significant basis for recreation program planning has been the age of participants. Many programs are designated as being for certain age groups, and most youth-serving organizations have established specific membership categories with precise age limits.

While it would be a mistake to assume that all members of a given age group have exactly the same needs and interests, there is no doubt that as people move through the various stages of life, they share many common developmental needs and changes.

Influence of Life-Stage.   Customarily, instead of simply considering the actual age of participants, they are grouped in terms of broad periods of time—referred to as life-stages.

Murphy, for example, identifies six such stages: (a) a generalized stage of childhood, including early, middle, and later childhood; (b) adolescence, when individuals focus on developing a sense of personal identity and autonomy; (c) the early adult years, in which the individual takes a place in the outside world; (d) mid-life, a time for reviewing and confirming one's course in life; (e) the later middle years, in which the person prepares for retirement; and (f) old age, a period of gradual closure and ultimately death.[1] These stages combine with other factors, such as one's individual personality, environment, socioeconomic, and educational status, and other family characteristics, to help create and shape one's leisure life-style.

Four Major Stages of the Life Cycle

To simplify the analysis in this chapter, four major age groupings that are of concern to recreation program planners may be identified:

Children of Elementary School Age: often grouped into levels such as five through seven, eight through ten, and eleven through thirteen.
Teenagers: often divided into younger adolescents, thirteen- to fifteen-year-olds, and older adolescents, sixteen to eighteen or nineteen.
Adults: includes young, single adults, younger married couples, and middle-aged individuals in their forties and fifties; increasingly includes older, unmarried adults.
Seniors: usually implies a minimum age of sixty or sixty-five; in some retirement or adult communities it is used to describe those who are "retired" but who may in some cases be considerably younger.

It should be made clear that each group has a number of subdivisions, and that actually recreation programming may begin well before children reach elementary school age. Many YWCAs and other community centers provide swimming programs for infants before they are able to walk, or gymnastic or creative movement classes for preschoolers. "Mom-and-tot" or "gym-and-swim" programs have become increasingly popular in such settings. Recreation may also be an important service in care settings for the very old or the terminally ill.

It should be recognized at the very outset that guidelines presented in this chapter must not be regarded as hard-and-fast rules. Children, teenagers and adults vary greatly and in ways that may have little to do with chronological age. Indeed, each age group must be viewed as part of a continuous development. One cannot deal with teenagers, for example, as if they existed in a sealed-off time compartment and had no relation to any other age group. They *were* children, and they *will become* adults. In planning programs for younger children, therefore, we must think in terms of the kind of preparation we are offering them for the teenage period that is to follow. Similarly, in working with senior citizens it is helpful to know what their recreational involvement was when they were young or middle-aged adults.

Programming for each age group must be related to the total process of development, in that it provides the opportunity for the individual to gain appropriate skills, meet challenges, or gain satisfactions which are keyed to that stage of the life cycle.

Recreational Needs and Interests of Children

The age group that is most heavily served by most public and many voluntary recreation agencies consists of young children of elementary school age—roughly five- to twelve-year-olds. Why is this so? What are the recreational needs and interests of five- to twelve-year-olds?

First, it should be recognized that children in this age range have a tremendous urge to participate in recreational activities. Play represents one of the most compelling drives in their lives and offers far more than casual or trivial enjoyment. Two leading child psychologists, Gesell and Ilg, confirmed this, "Deeply absorbing play seems to be essential for full mental growth. Children who are capable of such intense play are most likely to give a good account of themselves when they grow up."[2]

Play provides an important laboratory in the lives of children for growing up. Through varied recreational experiences, youngsters gain physical growth and healthy development, and are given the opportunity for emotional and creative expression, and needed group socialization. They explore the environment and learn about their own capabilities in various areas of skill. Finally, through childhood recreation, they develop a variety of interests that may serve them in future leisure and lead to making intelligent vocational choices.

To substantiate the benefits of recreation, Iso-Ahola has cited a number of scientific studies that demonstrate the value of childhood play in developing creativity and effective problem-solving skills. Beyond this, he describes the role of play in helping children gain important cultural norms and values.[3]

Thus, childhood must be seen as the time for widely ranging recreational interests: physical activities, outdoor and nature pursuits, creative pastimes, individual hobbies, and social programs. Intelligent choice of activities for children will be based on full awareness of their physical, social, and mental characteristics. Although there are considerable differences among individuals, it is possible to point out some important common characteristics which describe each developmental stage.

Elsewhere, the author has identified the following typical socioemotional and behavioral characteristics of younger children, ages five through seven:

> At this age level, children tend to be individualistic (''I'' centered), but are learning to participate in group play activities. Generally, they are curious, impulsive and helpful, and enjoy humor.
>
> Emotionally, they are immature in that they are easily upset, having low tolerance for frustration; they need considerable encouragement and understanding. They cry easily.
>
> While children of this age may play with friends of either sex, they are beginning to become more aware of sexual identity, and of sex-role expectations.
>
> They are learning to relate to persons outside their family, and to broaden their circle of acquaintances. They tend to be eager, self-assertive and competitive, but may vary considerably in such responses, depending on the situation.
>
> In terms of play behavior, they tend to be interested in a wide variety of pastimes, but may easily be discouraged in learning skills. They learn best through participation in concrete kinds of tasks. They particularly enjoy repeating activities they have mastered, have active imaginations, and enjoy dramatic play.
>
> They are learning concepts of right and wrong, and are increasingly seeking adult approval. They do not accept criticism well, or lose graciously. While they are increasingly willing to accept responsibility, they often forget or leave assigned tasks. They are easily upset by changes in routines or environments.[4]

Similar sets of characteristics may be identified for each successive age group. For example, eight- to ten-year-olds have more fully developed small-muscle skills, and are ready for more complex eye-hand activity. Because of their longer attention span, they can sustain interest for longer periods of time in each activity. Though their energy level is high, they may tire easily and must be given frequent rest periods. Their interest in belonging to groups is stronger, and club or team activities should be provided.

For each such group, recreational involvement should contribute to the child's overall development. For example, in terms of their growing independence, younger children begin by finding many of their recreational involvements in their homes or immediate neighborhoods. They become involved in group activities sponsored by the Boy or Girl Scouts, the church, or Y programs, and in after-school or recreation department programs. Thus, with increasing age and confidence, children move away from the security of their homes and protected, familiar environments, taking part in activities in community centers, play fields, and other more distant sites.

Recreation is helpful to children in developing a secure sense of their own sexual identification. As described earlier, many recreational activities have tended to be sexually segregated in terms of participation, with girls—for example—being excluded from typically male team sports. Today, such lines are being broken down, as sex stereotyping is questioned by many parents. Younger children usually are not very aware of sexual identification, and will often play freely with each other without concern about being a boy or a girl.

During the years ranging from eight to twelve, the sexes tend to separate themselves sharply and to avoid friendly participation with each other. Then, in the early teen years, boys and girls begin to make peace and to enjoy recreational activities and social programs without the friction of the earlier years.

Such patterns tend to reflect societal or environmental influences, and may not appear in settings that encourage friendly mingling and nonstereotyped leisure participation.

A wide variety of constructive activities should be offered to children of both sexes during the preteen years, with three possible areas of concern: (1) the tendency to provide too much organized activity for some groups; (2) the need to offer activities that do not overstress dating, "going steady," or similar sexually precocious activities; and (3) developing a rational balance between competition and cooperation, particularly in sports and game activities.

Over-Organized Leisure. It is important to provide enough organized recreational opportunity to meet the significant physical, social, and emotional needs of children, but not so much that their time is overly organized and lacking in freedom and self-generated activity.

Particularly for children of middle- and upper-class families, it is common to find boys and girls who are committed to music and dance lessons, ice-skating practice, after-school clubs or sports teams, and numerous other involvements that structure their free time excessively, and leave little opportunity for self-generated play or relaxation. In contrast, many poorer children, without adult direction and encouragement, will often have few structured or purposeful leisure or play opportunities in their free hours, and are likely to spend a great deal of their time loitering, watching television, or in varied forms of antisocial play or gang activity.

Public recreation departments, schools, and other leisure-service organizations should therefore join together to ensure that a healthy range of recreational activities is made available to *all* children, while at the same time insuring that *some* children are not excessively committed in organized play in what should be their free time.

Avoiding Oversophisticated Activities. Similarly, there is sometimes a tendency to encourage younger children to take part in activities that stress boy-girl dating or other forms of recreational pastimes centered around sexually precocious themes and behavior. Given the content of many movies, television shows, and varied forms of popular music, children are constantly being subjected to a barrage of such influences. Ideally, organized recreation programming should strive to help young children remain just that for a reasonable period of time—rather than contribute to their becoming oversophisticated at an early age.

Balanced Competition and Cooperation. A growing concern in recent years has been the degree to which organized sports in particular have emphasized a "win-at-all-costs" approach to competition, and have focused on high-skilled youngsters, while ignoring those with lesser abilities. While there has been an increasing outcry against the high-level competitive approach to sports and games, many have defended these activities as being appropriate preparation for an adult world in which children must learn to compete in many aspects of everyday life.

Iso-Ahola suggests that competitive sports can contribute effectively to the socialization process, to helping children form an orderly view of the social environment, and to gaining useful lifetime skills and values. At the same time, he concludes that excessive competition can also be harmful to young partici- pants, and that there are important values of *cooperation* and *team play* to be learned through sport, which also apply to lifetime needs.[5]

Beyond this, there is growing evidence that, despite the popularity of competitive team sports for many children and youth and the great wave of enthusiasm about fitness programming for adults, we have been neglecting the fitness needs of many younger children. The President's Council for Physical Fitness and Sports points out that there has been a decline in support for physical education programs in elementary schools and that a growing number of younger children are inactive, overweight, and out of shape.[6] Clearly, this should repre- sent an important priority for many public and voluntary agencies serving children and youth today.

Recreation Programming for Teenage Youth

The adolescent age group in our society presents an extremely perplex- ing problem for the recreation program planner. Too often, programs for this age group in voluntary or public agencies are almost completely lacking, in part because they may tend to avoid highly structured or organized programs, and partly because they are difficult to serve.

It is true that certain voluntary agencies, such as the 4-H Clubs, Police Athletic League, Junior Red Cross, and a number of religious organizations like the Catholic Youth Organization have fairly sizable teenage memberships. Yet, many public recreation and park departments have very limited programming for this age group, with the exception of organized sports leagues. Cottrell points out that, although families typically bring their younger children to state, federal, and other campgrounds, only a small percentage of teenagers continue to take part in such family recreation. He writes of the

> alienation of teenagers from our parks and thereby from their parents. There is widespread professional acceptance of the premise that most teens refuse to camp with their families in America's family campgrounds. That the fault may lie with camp programming policy is never entertained.[7]

Awareness of Need for Teenage Programming. In a recent study of recreation needs and programs in the city of Philadelphia, a cross section of community residents of all ages and backgrounds agreed with the professional recreation leaders of the city that teenagers should be given the highest priority for organized recreation service. Yet, it was apparent that programs for this group often failed to attract and involve them.

In many ways, adolescent boys and girls are puzzling and contradictory creatures. They are torn between the dependencies of childhood and the desire to have the freedoms and prerogatives of adulthood, often without being able to demonstrate the mature responsibility demanded of adults. Berger has written:

> The well-publicized conflicts and tensions of the teen-age "transitional stage" stem from the combination of an acceleration in the individual's physical and cultural growth with the continued refusal by society to grant to adolescents many of the rights and opportunities of adults; when sexual desires are more powerful than they will ever again be, sexual opportunities are fewest; obedience and submission are asked of adolescents at precisely the time when their strength, energy, and desire for autonomy are ascendant; responsible participation in the major social institutions is denied or discouraged at the moment when their interest in the world has been poignantly awakened.[8]

What are the psychosocial and behavioral characteristics of adolescents that affect their recreational needs and interests?

> For all adolescents, this tends to be a time for discovering and affirming their identity and independence. For many it is a time of extremely strong feelings and emotions, idealism about the world and introspective searching for self.
>
> Teen-agers often are absorbed in adjusting to their maturing bodies, and to their developing sexual roles. They may show extreme concern about their physical appearance, and worry about lack of popularity, including ridicule or rejection by peer groups.
>
> Moods may change frequently, from defiant and rebellious to cooperative and responsible. As they reach their middle teens, many teen-agers begin to show a high level of responsibility and acceptance of adult values, while others withdraw into a state of chronic (although hopefully temporary) alienation.
>
> Increasingly, adolescents seek support and approval from members of their own social group or conform to its standards. Those who resist or reject their parents' influence may tend to be more open to friendships with other adults, such as counselors or parents.
>
> They may seem to be confident about their own abilities, and act as if they "know it all," while in reality they may be quite unsure about themselves and extremely self-conscious.
>
> They tend to be interested in group games and social activities, and are now capable of a much higher level of physical and intellectual involvement than a few years before. Some teen-agers show a high level of talent in creative activities, or become deeply involved in activities that may become lifetime leisure pursuits, or may lead to vocational choices. They often show a high level of loyalty and devotion to a group or institution, and may be very idealistic about religious values or other social causes or problems.
>
> For a considerable number of adolescents, the desire to be "grown-up" and to resist adult or societal controls, as well as the search for sensation, excitement, or group approval, leads to experimentation with drinking, drugs, and growing sexual permissiveness.[9]

Because this is a period of development which may be extremely destructive for many young people, it is highly important that adolescents be provided with appealing and supportive recreational programs that help build positive social values and support constructive behavior.

Berger, for example, points out that a major factor tending to reduce adolescent rebelliousness is the community youth center, the chaperoned dance, organized sports, extracurricular clubs, and the junior auxiliaries of business, religious, fraternal, and veterans' organizations.

On the other hand, where adult leadership is poor or community facilities and programs limited, where young people see academic advancement and economic opportunity closed to them, high rates of adolescent tension and disorder may be expected.

Defining the Population's Subgroups.   What does this have to say about the design of recreation programs for today's teenagers?

First it is necessary to identify the population's subgroups. There are essentially three types of adolescents, as far as social adjustment and needs are concerned. These are: (1) the large mass of adolescents who are reasonably stable, law-abiding, and positive in their social outlook and behavior; (2) those young people who, because of personal disturbance or family tensions, or because they live in depressed areas where the pressure toward antisocial or delinquent behavior is strong, are "on the fence"; and (3) the comparatively small group that has already become seriously involved in delinquent behavior.

Any recreation department that serves a diverse community should provide three types of programs.

First, there should be programs aimed at the overall youth population— not seen in any sense as social-work or antidelinquency efforts, but simply as attractive, interesting, and constructive activities presented under capable leadership.

Second, there should be programs which involve "marginal" youth, providing desirable *alternatives* to antisocial behavior. The point here is that youngsters in this category are at a turning point in their lives. Unless enjoyable activities specially geared to their needs and interests are provided, it is all the more likely that they will seek out delinquent activity—both for "kicks" and to satisfy personal drives for acceptance, prestige, and peer approval.

Third, for adolescents who are already seriously involved in delinquent activity, or who may be disturbed in a clinical sense, it is necessary to view recreation as a form of social therapy to be carefully designed and closely integrated with other community-sponsored youth services.

Goal-Oriented Programming.   When recreation programs are being developed with the specific purpose of helping to reduce juvenile delinquency, it should be understood that this is a problem that cuts across all social strata and ethnic groups. While statistics suggest that youth crime is a more serious problem in socially and economically disadvantaged urban neighborhoods than in well-to-do suburbs, the fact is that there are also many teenagers in middle- and upper-class communities who take part in antisocial activities. For whatever reasons—their parents' neglect, their "excess" of advantages, or overpermissive adult values—such youngsters represent as great a problem as their inner-city counterparts. For both groups, goal-oriented recreation programming must be carefully planned to have the desired effect.

First, it must provide an alternative to delinquent activities. A teenager's turning to glue-sniffing, drinking, theft, or vandalism simply because there is nothing else that is interesting or exciting to do, or because no one has taken an interest in him, is truly criminal. It is criminal on the part of the adult community that has permitted this situation to exist.

Ideally, the alternative that is provided should appeal to the same drives in teenagers that would otherwise be diverted to antisocial outlets. This implies that the activity must be prestigious and "right" in an adolescent's eyes. If possible, it should have the element of risk, thrill, or glamor to make it attractive. Realistically, many young people engage in activities that violate the law or challenge community social codes—almost as a temporary phase of life. If they do not get into serious difficulty, they gradually discard such behavior as they move toward adulthood.

Thus, the creative recreation leader will discover ways to convert the same drives and interests that might otherwise result in antisocial or delinquent activity into acceptable recreational participation. For example, interest in motorcycling or hot-rodding, which may result in tragic accidents or gang violence, has been shifted in some communities to automobile clubs in which boys learn mechanics and a code of proper road behavior, participate in special programs and events, and actually become responsible and helpful drivers, rather than dangerous menaces. In some cases, public recreation and park departments have sponsored drag-racing, under careful safety controls. In other communities, youth interest in surfing has led to the organization of surfing clubs under the auspices of recreation departments, that serve to control the kind of youth behavior on the beaches that plagues many residents and frequently requires police action.

The effort in such programs must be to provide an environment and adult leadership that can accept the teenager as he or she is, and that will work constructively to build his or her acceptance of adult values and behavioral codes. Far more than other adults, the recreation leader is often in a position to build a strong tie of confidence and trust that is tremendously reassuring and helpful to young people.

Recreation as Social Therapy.   In working with teenagers who live in neighborhoods with a high delinquency rate, or who have already shown seriously antisocial behavior, it may be necessary to view recreation as a form of social therapy. Recreation must be part of a total team approach including intensified and adapted educational services, vocational training and placement, group work programs, family counseling or workshops, improved housing, drug abuse programs, and an adequate agency referral system. Varied public, voluntary and religious agencies share in this task, sometimes assigning "detached" youth leaders to work with juvenile gangs or other problem populations.

It should be stressed that the task of working with problem youth should be only *part* of the comprehensive concern with the adolescent population. Recreation programs should serve the entire range of teenagers with a full variety of leisure opportunities, and should not be regarded solely as an antidelinquency effort. Their aim is enrichment and creative development for all.

Recreational Needs and Interests of Adults

Adults are in a busy and productive period of life. Both men and women are likely to be heavily involved in the business or professional world, and in community affairs. Those women who are married are likely to be raising families and in many cases working as well. In spite of the documented growth of leisure in society, most young married couples tend to have a minimum of real free time when compared with other age groups.

Adults are often involved in community membership groups, such as churches, neighborhood associations, lodges, union groups, service organizations, and fraternal groups. Often, the attraction of such membership groups is that they consist of people of similar social class, interests, age levels, professional status, or religious affiliation. Through them, adults tend to develop their own circles of friends and leisure activity, and are less dependent on community programs for recreational participation than they would otherwise be.

As a group, adults are usually capable of meeting their own recreational needs independently. They tend to be physically capable, mobile, and financially able to purchase equipment, drive to recreation attractions, and in other ways able to satisfy their leisure needs without difficulty. However, for such groups as disabled or economically disadvantaged adults or single parents who must work while also raising a family, time pressures and financial factors may make it very difficult for them to satisfy their leisure and social needs without special programming assistance.

Too often, adults are not involved in community recreation programs because their special needs and interests are not recognized and met in an imaginative way. This is unfortunate because the potential for involving adults in classes in leisure skills, sports, cultural and outdoor recreation programs, and family-centered activities is very great. In order to understand the recreational needs of adults, it is helpful to examine four different segments of this age group: (1) college-age youth, (2) young single adults, (3) family groups, (4) the middle years and later adulthood.

College-Age Youth.   College students, who typically range in age from the late teen years through the early or middle twenties (or even older, in the case of many graduate students), must be regarded as young adults. For them, much recreation centers around the institution they are attending—in college union programs, social clubs, athletic events, fraternity or sorority dances and parties, college entertainment and cultural events, intramural participation, and membership in varied college organizations.

Despite its academic purpose, college life has traditionally also been perceived as an important social experience by many students. Past research has shown that a majority of students have regarded campus social life, including extracurricular activities, sports, and carrying on college traditions as more important than vocational or intellectual goals. It should be noted that although adolescence and the college years are often thought of as a happy, light-hearted time of life, this is not the case for many young people. Indeed, the problem of suicide has been a growing concern for many parents and college administrators who recognize that isolated and withdrawn students often become despondent.[10]

Increasingly, more and more college authorities have developed outstanding programs of constructive and interesting social and recreational activities. In many cases, they are linked to curricular experiences. In physical education, for example, instead of the past practice of requiring a block of courses in gymnastics, fitness activities, swimming, and individual, dual, or team sports, the trend is toward a much freer range of leisure-related courses and clubs. In many colleges, physical education requirements have been abandoned or modified, and students now voluntarily take classes, workshops, or other instructional programs in such activities as: yoga; karate, kung fu or other self-defense activities; and backpacking, hiking, canoeing, sailing, kayaking, scuba diving, wilderness survival, and similar outdoor recreation pursuits.

Young Single Adults.   In the community at large, young unmarried adults represent a group that tends to make minimal use of organized recreation programs, apart from commercial activities—such as those found in health spas or racquetball clubs, singles bars or clubs, rock concerts, and similar forms of entertainment.

A limited number of programs sponsored by churches and synagogues, employee recreation departments, or private "singles" residences meet the needs of this population. A plausible case might be made that public recreation departments should provide more comprehensive offerings of clubs, social activities, sports instruction or competition, outings, and trips that are designed to meet the needs of young adults. Since so many of them are at the point where they wish and need to be part of a congenial social group, and where a "singles bar" does not meet their full need, the department should emphasize this type of program.

In planning programs for adults at this stage, it is necessary to consider their developmental characteristics. Farrell and Lundegren suggest that young adults are usually active, energetic, and flexible in their approach to life, mobile and ready to experiment with various aspects of living and have a strong need for belonging.[11] At the same time that they are consolidating their values and personal identities and affirming their independence, they also tend to be reaching out to be a part of society and to develop significant affiliations with others.

In some cases, community recreation departments have established or assisted special clubs for singles in which the members take the major responsibility for planning programs, assessing dues, and running an ongoing social program. For example, the Denver, Colorado, Recreation Department offers a

Stardusters Club for adults aged twenty-five to forty, and a *Meridian Club* for those between thirty-five and fifty. Both groups provide dance classes, socials, picnics, dinner parties, trips, and other special events. In a number of California cities, clubs with names like *Bachelors and Bachelorettes* are sponsored by recreation departments. In some cases, clubs may even be geared to serve special populations of singles, such as very tall men and women (the *Skyscrapers Club*), or those with special interests, such as skiing, hiking, or tennis.[12]

Some religious organizations have also been active in programming for this population, with churches sponsoring regular social evenings that include discussion groups, special events, dancing, and other forms of entertainment suitable for single adults. National organizations like Parents Without Partners have also sponsored similar social programs, as well as family-oriented activities designed in a self-help cooperative framework to assist single parents and their children.

It should be stressed that many adults today are now single during the middle decades of life, and that this is *not* necessarily just a transitional stage before marriage. Instead, considerable numbers of adults in their thirties, forties, and fifties are unmarried, with a high proportion of individuals who live alone. In addition, there are growing numbers of homosexuals—both men and women—who have become visible for the first time, particularly in larger cities. Such "singles" tend to have their own clubs, special recreational resorts, and vacation settings. However, they obviously share common interests with the rest of the adult population and in many cases are involved in sports, cultural, and other day-by-day programming.

An interesting example of how such special populations have begun to emerge and to take part in overall community recreation involves the famous Mummers Parade in Philadelphia. This unusual New Year's Day spectacle of dozens of brilliantly costumed and cleverly staged marching bands has typically involved representation only from all-white, generally middle-class clubs throughout the Philadelphia area. Future participation in the parade is expected to include black and gay Mummers clubs.

Family Groups.   Despite the growth in the single adult population, the majority of adults in our society do marry and raise families. One of the most important needs in community recreation programs is therefore for more effective and diversified family recreation activities—particularly in view of the high divorce rate that threatens the stability of community life.

Clearly, effective programs of family-centered recreation build ties of unity, understanding, and warmth that are essential for both children and parents. How can the community recreation department strengthen such efforts? It should sponsor a number of activities that appeal to the entire family, such as family evenings, workshops, picnics, theater or music programs, cultural events, hobby centers, or block parties. It should make sure that facilities are designed to be usable by all age levels and, in setting up the schedule for such facilities as swimming pools or skating rinks, should designate certain appropriate periods as "family sessions." When outings are planned, they may be organized and promoted on a family basis. The ingenious recreation director will find many opportunities to promote the family's full participation.

At the same time, it is important to plan recreation programs that will be appropriate for different kinds of family units. Children without a mother or father, or with step-relatives or other adult family friends should be able to participate along with those in two-parent families. It should be noted that the armed forces in particular have made a strenuous effort to promote family-centered recreational activities.

Middle and Later Adulthood.   A vital aspect of adult recreation is that it includes the period of middle age, in which adults may establish leisure patterns that will prepare them for retirement. This is particularly important for health; it is essential that the physical activities carried on at a younger age be continued when medically feasible. Leading cardiologists have stressed the importance of regular exercise in achieving the following benefits: (a) maintaining muscle tone throughout the body, including the heart; (b) providing relaxation by relieving nervous tension and anxiety; (c) aiding digestion; (d) helping control obesity; and (e) improving lung function.

Such activities as formal calisthenics, breathing exercises, bicycling, walking, gardening, fishing, swimming, golf, and tennis are all useful in this regard. In the past, our youth-centered culture has failed to provide encouragement or opportunity for older adults to engage in appropriate physical activities. More recently, as part of the growing awareness of the capability of older persons, there has been a wave of participation by individuals approaching retirement and even their seventies and eighties in jogging, running, and other sports and outdoor pursuits.

However, physical health is only one of the areas of concern for those in later middle age. In addition to conditioning and athletic activities many mature persons today engage in varied social, creative, service, and learning activities. All of these represent an intelligent transition to the period of retirement when the amount of leisure available to the individual increases dramatically.

Carpenter points out that many of our widely held stereotypes about middle age are being questioned today. She comments, for example, that the assumption that the so-called empty nest syndrome is a serious problem for many housewives and mothers when their youngest children move away from home should be balanced by more recent data suggesting that many women welcome the opportunity to pursue their personal lives more freely. Beyond this, she suggests that recreation planners need to be more alert to this age group (as are TV producers, programmers, and advertisers in recognizing them as an increasingly important audience and potential market). Recognizing the changes that are occurring in the attitudes and life-styles of the middle-aged, she writes:

> In the 1960s, it was easy to understand middle age. Everybody in it was 'over the hill' and could easily be dismissed. . . . Now there is increasing appreciation for the 30-plus years, which are middle age. . . .
>
> It is hoped that more (and better) programs and services will be initiated as

recreation professionals become better informed and more creative in their approach to meeting the ongoing leisure needs and diverse expectations of middle-aged adults.[13]

As both work load and family responsibilities decline in the years preceding retirement, there is increased opportunity to take part in enjoyable leisure activities. In some cases, individuals begin to take lengthened vacations or work a lightened schedule in the years immediately before retirement; some industries have provided their older workers with a "three-month sabbatical" for this purpose. Too often, however, the older person works a full schedule until the last moment before forced retirement. He or she is cut off from job responsibilities, a feeling of importance, and a personal schedule and circle of acquaintances built heavily around work. For such persons, retirement poses a serious challenge.

Preparation for Retirement: Learning New Skills and Attitudes. During the period of later maturity, therefore, the intelligent individual should be preparing for retirement. This may involve developing new recreational interests, particularly for individuals who have had limited leisure involvements during the earlier periods of their lives. Skills can often be learned in adult classes in recreational activities that are sponsored in many communities.

Beyond learning new skills, however, it is also important that individuals who are approaching retirement recognize that leisure represents an extremely valuable aspect of their lives—and that it is not simply a matter of filling empty hours with activity. Informal leisure education or leisure counseling experience may help such individuals become aware of how recreation can contribute to their physical and emotional health and provide creative and social satisfactions that will enrich their lives after retirement.

A growing number of companies are sponsoring preretirement workshops that deal with leisure values and attitudes as part of a total approach to preparing for employees' later years.

Recreation for the Aging

Having considered children, teenagers, and adults, we now come to the category of the aging. Generally this group is considered to include all those beyond the age of sixty-five, the commonly accepted time for retirement. However, in many settings the individual in his or her late fifties or early sixties may be regarded as a "senior citizen," and some retirement communities place the age cutoff even lower than that. What are the characteristics and special needs of older persons that make them a subject of vital concern to the recreation profession?

Increasing Numbers.   Older persons are growing rapidly in numbers and as a percentage of the population, due to birth trends and declining mortality rates in recent years.

To illustrate, between 1900 and 1950, life expectancy increased by 17.6 years for men and 20.3 years for women. In the early 1970s, there were over 20 million Americans who were sixty-five and older; by the 1980 Census, there were 25.5 million persons in this age bracket, constituting over 10 percent of the entire population. It is predicted that within about 50 years, one of every five Americans will be 65 or older, and there will be one retired person for every two of working age, compared with one in five at present.

Characteristics of the Aging. Certain basic concepts about the aging have been developed by the National Council on the Aging:

1. Aging is universal, and a normal development process, although it is frequently regarded with fear and aversion.
2. Aging is variable, and no two persons react physically, socially, or emotionally in the same way to this process. The degree to which individuals maintain healthy functioning is heavily based on personal life patterns of activity and interpersonal involvement.
3. Aging and illness are not necessarily coincidental; while there is obviously a greater degree of specific disability with increasing age, much of this can be averted or minimized through intelligent preparation for aging or continuing healthy living habits.
4. Older people represent three generations in that they range from the early sixties to well past 100; it is necessary to identify the variable factors among these three stages of aging.
5. Older people can and do learn. While learning patterns may differ from those of younger people, the capacity is still there.
6. Older people can and do change, and are capable of readjustment to new circumstances.
7. Older people wish to remain self-directing, rather than be governed by the decisions of others.
8. Older people are vital human beings. Although limitations may appear, existing capacities should be used to the fullest extent possible, and stress should be placed on living in the present, rather than in the past.[14]

In a special feature on the elderly, *U.S. News and World Report* points out that with average life expectancy climbing to seventy-four, there is immense interest in the phenomenon of aging, and the lives of older people. The former director of the National Institute on Aging, Dr. Robert Butler, comments that many past preconceptions about aging have proven to be false:

> We used to think that if people lived long enough they would become senile. That's not true. . . . Several studies have demonstrated that decline in intellectual function occurs much less than was reported earlier and is usually caused by a disease—not by the aging process. . . . Quality of life is critical. If you don't keep learning, you don't keep growing; then it becomes less exciting to stay alive.[15]

He goes on to point out the importance of social and psychological factors linked to leisure, in maintaining sharp minds and healthy bodies.

> Social and psychological fitness is as important as physical fitness. Everybody needs a strong social network of relationships and friends. . . . In terms of personal or psychological fitness, you need a goal. That may mean going to every Yankee baseball game, doing community work or starting a new career.
>
> Physical fitness can't be stressed enough. You need a nutritious diet and enough exercise to maintain good heart function and increase bone strength.[16]

Recreation Needs of Aging Persons

Aging persons have certain special needs for recreation, based on their changing life circumstances. Having retired, they have a great deal of time free from work or past family obligations, and need to be able to fill this time constructively to avoid boredom and deterioration. A high proportion of older persons are single and live alone; they have a critical need for group involvement and acceptance. Many are living on sharply reduced budgets, and cannot afford past recreational habits. Often they have problems relating to personal safety, nutrition, health, and housing.

In general, individuals past sixty-five may be categorized on a continuum of health and social capability, ranging from: (1) those who are relatively healthy, mobile, independent, and able to care for themselves with little difficulty; to (2) those who have deteriorated to the degree that they no longer can function independently and must either be homebound, dependent on the care of others, or institutionalized in nursing homes or other treatment or residential-care settings.

The older person with an impressive retirement income or other financial resources can enter one of the leisure villages or retirement homes for the aged in specially planned communities. These villages are usually planned and built by commercial developers, often with expert medical and social consultants. They are intended for retired or semiretired individuals who either rent or purchase a small home or apartment. These communities are usually designed in terms of the varied physical capabilities of the resident population, and may also provide a cluster of medical, housekeeping, shopping, and transportation services as part of the total community plan.

In addition, these communities typically provide an extensive recreation program of clubs, interest groups, modified sports, hobbies, and cultural activities. Often these programs are under professional leadership, and bring in well-qualified specialists to conduct activities. Sometimes older residents who have special recreation skills may plan and direct activities. An important element of such programs is likely to be service activities provided by the retired residents to others in need in the nearby community—in hospitals, other institutions, or homes. Even for such relatively independent retired persons, it is important to provide a sense of self-respect by making it possible to serve others and to be needed by them.

Senior Centers.   This emphasis is also found in many senior citizens' centers or Golden Age Clubs attended by older persons in the community. Such centers often provide a wide range of services for older people. For example, Vintage, Inc., a multipurpose center for senior adults in Allegheny County, Pennsylvania, has the following program elements: (1) educational classes and "enrichment" groups; (2) recreation clubs and social activities; (3) a nutrition program; (4) information and referral program, assisting clients in finding other community resources; (5) an outreach program including in-home meals-on-wheels and housekeeping assistance services; and (6) transportation, counseling, health, and other supportive services.

In addition to sponsoring a network of separate senior centers, many communities also provide city-wide programs that are specially designed to meet the needs and interests of aging persons. For example, the Department of Municipal Recreation and Adult Education of the Milwaukee Public Schools sponsors the following: (1) a golden age club newspaper, which publicizes events and programs of all such centers in Milwaukee; (2) city-wide craft and hobby shops, and an all-city golden age hobby show; (3) a Recognition Week in May to honor senior citizens and their organizations; (4) a series of special lectures and courses for older persons on a city-wide basis; (5) city-wide bus trips, card tournaments, chorus, picnic, concerts, dances, theater parties, musical shows, and outings to sports events.

As another example, the Flint, Michigan, Recreation and Park Board provides the following services to elderly persons:

1. Publication of the *Senior Citizens News.*
2. Sponsorship of the Genesee County Senior Citizen Orchestra.
3. Publication of news releases for all news media regarding aging and senior citizens' programs.
4. Development of a discount card program, giving reduced rates and prices to older persons.
5. Sponsorship of a bicycle club, ecology club and over-80 club.
6. Planning of one-day bus trips and more extended vacation trips for older persons.
7. Sponsorship of other special events, including city-wide dances, parties, luncheons, tournaments and similar programs for senior citizens.

Some cities, like Los Angeles, also sponsor, through their recreation and park departments, a city-wide senior citizens' federation, which unites all older persons in the metropolitan area in an effort to meet their needs in recreation, health, and housing, legal aid, Social Security, and legislation. For the first time, in the 1970s older persons began to organize politically to promote legislation and government action to meet their special needs, through organizations like the Gray Panthers.

Focus on Recreation.   All such programs and services are vitally important to elderly persons in the community. In terms of recreation as a primary focus, it is essential that a full range of leisure activities and programs be offered to help senior citizens meet their varied social, physical, and emotional needs.

Whenever possible, older adults should be involved in constructively organizing, planning, and carrying out their own programs. Simply having senior citizens served by professional or volunteer club leaders does not meet their fullest needs. Because there will be varying degrees of ability among aging persons, those who are most capable should be assigned key roles and tasks. This should apply not only in programs for centers, but also in planning to serve the needs of aging persons on a community-wide basis. Inevitably, while professional social workers, recreation directors, and other social service specialists will take the lead in this process, older persons themselves will have much to contribute and should be well-represented on such planning councils.

Throughout the United States and Canada, there have been state-wide or provincial planning councils assigned to examine the needs of aging persons and to promote effective local services. A number of states and provinces have published useful brochures on recreation for older citizens, and have provided substantial funding with federal assistance to support local programs in this area.

Limitations of Age-Based Planning.   In outlining the characteristics of four major age groupings, this chapter has presented a number of important needs of each group with respect to recreational opportunity. It should be stressed that planning should be flexible, and that individuals should not be rigidly stereotyped because of their age. Today, we recognize, for example, that many older persons can and should take part in a wide range of vigorous, independent activities, such as sports or travel, that they might not have engaged in in past years.

As a unique and amusing example, an organization called Sports Dreams has successfully developed a number of high-priced basketball and baseball training camps, in which successful businessmen and professionals in their forties, fifties, and sixties have had the opportunity to play ball with older, big-league sports stars. While this venture is obviously a form of commercial exploitation, it also illustrates the need of many people to break out of the age-determined mold that typically limits their activity. Paying $2,195 for a week with the Chicago Cubs team of 1969 in one such camp, the players went full-tilt in four-hour daily workouts. Said one sixty-three-year-old pitcher:

> My legs are in shape and my arm feels good. I can still twist off a few curves, pull the string on a change-up, throw a fair knuckleball, and move the ball around pretty good.[17]

Intergenerational Programming.   Beyond this, there is a new and growing interest in intergenerational programming. Some communities and agencies have scheduled activities combining senior citizens and junior high school-age participants, and there is increasing emphasis on family programming which cuts across two or more age levels.

Obviously, intergenerational programming has both potential strengths and weaknesses. Among its positive features are the improved understanding and awareness that it may create between elderly and youthful participants. Often children regard senior citizens with aversion or reflect other negative societal attitudes about the aging, while older people often fear and seek to avoid the young. By helping them make favorable contact as people, members of different generations can share fun together and gain a more positive awareness of each other's positive human qualities and strengths.

Tedrick suggests that one of the advantages of developing intergenerational programs is that greater cooperation between youth-serving and aging-related agencies can mean a shared and more productive use of scarce resources. Staff members may broaden their horizons, rather than concentrate on only a narrow segment of the population. Beyond this, he writes:

> Among the benefits of shared experiences between the old and those younger is the chance to combat agism and stereotyped thinking. Positive role models . . . can be found. The young learn that creativity can be synonymous with aging; the old have the opportunity to view the young, not as discontented or alienated, but as caring persons, eager to share in the fun of recreational pursuits.[18]

On the other hand, there may often be considerable resistance to such programming and leaders must structure situations to ensure that the exposure is brought about in gradual, constructive ways. Elderly persons may help care for younger children, tutor them, or assist in other ways that help build a positive relationship and allow the sharing of recreational experiences and events.

GENDER AND FAMILY STATUS AS PROGRAMMING FACTORS

A number of other important personal factors influence programming needs, including one's gender and family status.

Gender

The sex of participants has traditionally been the basis for much arbitrary limitation in terms of stereotyping programming on all age levels. We have reflected the societal view of appropriate masculine roles by giving fuller emphasis to active sports, games, and outdoor activities for males, and by promoting creative or aesthetic pursuits or activities having to do with homemaking or other domestic roles for females. Today, girls and women are much more actively involved in vigorous and competitive sports and games and, throughout society, are playing a variety of roles formerly assigned primarily to males—such as racing cars or planes, or taking part in other demanding, high-risk activities. Similarly, boys and men are much freer today in taking part in more artistic or domestic pursuits that formerly were viewed as feminine in character.

Nonetheless, it is still apparent that certain kinds of sports and games are predominantly assigned to one sex or another, as in the case of ice hockey for males. A strong case can be made for programming some sex-segregated activities of a social nature, such as clubs or other youth groups which give individuals the opportunity to identify closely with members of their own sex and to be free of the pressures or distractions that often are found in coeducational activity. In general, recreation programmers should be aware of the element of sex, and should seek to meet the special interests of participants of either gender without at the same time overemphasizing their differences or keeping them artificially separated.

An interesting example of current practices in this field may be found in the Little League program. Until 1974, girls were not permitted to join Little League. However, thanks to civil rights suits throughout the United States (including some supported by the National Organization for Women) Little League changed its charter to incorporate girls. However, at the same time, it organized a softball league. Although softball is not legally restricted to girls, today few boys join this program. And, although some girls do play hardball, they are extremely rare. Thus, segregation by gender continues on a voluntary basis, although it is always possible to cross the line.[19]

Family Status.   The family status of participants also plays an important factor in much recreation program planning. In the military, for example, there is considerable emphasis given today to planning events, camping activities, and social recreation that promote family togetherness. It is also critical that the needs of individuals who are *not* members of formal family groups be considered. Some organizations, for example, deliberately schedule activities for single parents and their children, or for nontraditional groups, such as children and adults who live in feminist households, or commune-like extended family groupings. Others program heavily for single adults, particularly in terms of social activities, trips and outings, or other events that meet the unique social needs of these individuals.

In different types of programs, the issue of family relationships may come into play. Often, directors of therapeutic recreation programs serving the mentally ill or mentally retarded in institutions may schedule special family days or get-togethers to promote healthy family ties with the disabled family member. Youth-serving organizations sponsor mother-and-daughter or father-and-son programs, although it is important not to exclude youngsters who do not come from two-parent families.

PHYSICAL, SOCIAL, AND EMOTIONAL STATUS

Beyond the elements of age, sex, and family status, it is necessary to consider other personal characteristics of participants.

Are they physically healthy, active, and vigorous—or do they have special impairments that limit their recreational involvement? Are they within a normal range of mental or cognitive functioning—or are they developmentally disabled or mentally retarded? Or, as an alternative possibility, are they extremely bright and intellectually aware? In terms of emotional status, are they individuals who are stable and reasonably well-adjusted—or do they have emotional difficulties that hamper their recreational participation?

Such issues are important in two ways. First, they provide an indication of what the participants may reasonably be expected to do well, and what might be difficult or impossible for them to do. Although it is certainly true that many disabled persons have been artificially limited in their leisure and social participation in the past, and that they are often capable of far more challenging activities than they have been encouraged to try, it is also true that there are many activities they simply *cannot* carry on successfully. Such limitations must be understood and respected.

The second way in which the possible impairments of participants is significant has to do with their *needs*. If a child, for example, has limited motor skills, it may mean that he or she needs to have a carefully planned, sequential exposure to activities which will *develop* these skills. The teenager who has difficulty relating effectively with other group members may need to have recreational involvements that strengthen such abilities. The adult who has never been able to live independently in the community may need to have assistance through leisure counseling, activities of daily living, and involvement in recreational trip programming that help build his or her confidence and community-living skills.

Program planning for individuals who have such limitations often requires careful assessment of their needs, interests, and experience, and may require joint planning with other skilled professionals, such as medical practitioners, educators, physical or occupational therapists, or social service personnel. Whenever possible, planning should be done *with* the individuals concerned, and the experience should be carefully monitored to ensure that it is psychologically positive and supportive.

ETHNIC, RACIAL AND RELIGIOUS FACTORS

Unlike many other nations which have relatively homogeneous populations, the United States and Canada have diverse societies whose make-up is a patchwork of various ethnic, racial, and religious groups.

What does this have to do with recreation? It is significant first in that people of many ethnic backgrounds often tend to inherit cultural interests, customs, or traditional folklore pursuits that continue to be an important part of their leisure lives. These traditional pursuits add to the richness of community life and should be respected and maintained whenever possible. This can be done by having courses in the folk arts or by encouraging pageants, parades, celebrations, performing groups, art exhibits, or other events that promote and display the ethnic heritage of participants.

Too often in the past, racial minority groups have been sharply discriminated against in terms of education, job opportunities, housing, and recreation. Today there is the clear understanding that all groups must have equal opportunity in terms of leisure facilities and programs and that there should be no artificial barriers that separate or exclude racial groups of any type from the mainstream of participation.

How then should the issue of race be dealt with in recreation programming? Ideally it should play a minor role, although recreation should certainly be used to promote intergroup understanding. Beyond this, it is important to recognize that different racial backgrounds and life-styles should be understood, respected, and even *celebrated* in recreation programming. Unlike past generations that often sought to hide their origins to become as "American" or as "Canadian" as possible—many people of diverse ethnic or racial backgrounds today feel and show their pride in their historical roots.

A number of recreation and park agencies have therefore sponsored events that celebrate the achievements and contributions of various ethnic groups. At the same time, every effort should be made to encourage members of both minority and majority groups in society not to be confined to their own cultural tradition, but to be open to exploring other life-styles and leisure pursuits. This is particularly true when participants may be limited both because of their racial background and low socioeconomic background—as in the case, for example, of black teenagers in an urban "ghetto" who have had extremely limited recreational exposures. Every effort should be made to use recreation as a means for expanding the cultural and social horizons of such groups rather than encourage them to participate in a narrow range of pursuits.

Religion is generally less influential as a factor in influencing recreational tastes and interests than are ethnic and racial backgrounds. Nonetheless, certain religious groups may be linked to national and other cultural traditions that shape the leisure patterns of participants. Such interests must be respected although frequently they are met chiefly by churches, synagogue youth groups, or other organizations that are affiliated with specific religious denominations.

Beyond this, the issue of religion is important in that membership in a particular faith may also influence an individual's values, standards, and judgments about what are appropriate forms of recreational participation. Obviously recreation program planners must accept and respect such values and should provide activities that would not be offensive to them. On the other hand, there is a widely accepted principle that governmental, tax-supported agencies should not promote any particular form of religion, and that such customs as the erection of crêches in a public park or similar site may be highly controversial in some communities.

EDUCATIONAL AND
SOCIOECONOMIC BACKGROUND

The implications of these two related factors are simply that one's education and socioeconomic background usually play a strong influence on one's life-style and leisure participation. For example, men and women who have gone to college or who come from a relatively high socioeconomic background tend to be more interested in cultural or intellectual pursuits than those from more limited backgrounds.

A public leisure-service agency in a highly educated, affluent community would typically be more successful in sponsoring art classes, concert or ballet series, discussion clubs, or other cultural activities than a department in a poorly educated, lower-class community. Such factors must realistically be considered in planning recreation programs. At the same time, it would be a mistake to assume that individuals with limited backgrounds would not be capable of enjoying the arts or other cultural pursuits, or to limit them to recreational programs on the lowest possible level of taste or quality.

Recreation in itself *is* a form of cultural exposure and education and clearly should be used to broaden and enrich the interests and life-style patterns of participants. Every effort should therefore be made to provide a broad range of involvements to all participants and to encourage such exposures for people of every degree of background or socioeconomic class.

NUMBERS AND AVAILABILITY OF PARTICIPANTS

Two final elements that must be considered in program planning involve the numbers of those who are to be served, and how available they are to participate.

In planning a specific program, it obviously makes a great deal of difference if one is seeking to involve several hundred participants compared to a handful of people. It is possible to schedule a wide range of options, ranging from such mass events as large sports leagues, tournaments, huge spectacles, or parades, to small instructional classes with only a few participants.

The size of the group that one is working with affects the degree to which one is able to give individual attention to participants or to focus on the dynamics of group behavior. Particularly in programs that seek to work intensively with individuals in order to achieve specific therapeutic outcomes, it is necessary for participation to be in small groups.

Yet, in many agencies it is important to show a high rate of participation in order to justify program expenditures. This simply means that leaders planning programs should seek to balance both types of activities to provide the necessary numbers and also to achieve desired outcomes with participants.

The issue of availability of programs for participants is another important concern. It would be pointless to schedule attractive programs in the arts, nature activities, or sports clinics in one section of town and expect them to serve the entire community if no provision is made for transportation and if participants are not able to reach these programs independently.

It is therefore essential that basic or core activities be provided in locations where they can easily be reached by participants. In some situations, such as Senior Centers or Golden Age Clubs, a recreation agency or community service organization may assist by arranging car pools or other means of bringing participants who cannot drive and who do not have convenient public transportation to programs.

The problem is particularly acute for the physically or mentally disabled. Many organizations today provide specially equipped buses, some with hydraulic lifts, to transport participants in wheelchairs to recreation programs. Similarly, the issue of architectural barriers must be resolved. All new construction today must be designed and built to permit convenient use by the disabled, in terms of suitable access to buildings, lavatories and similar facilities, along with needed ramps, elevators or entry arrangements. Many outdoor recreation sites today have specially designed play areas for the handicapped, nature trails with specially taped interpretive messages or Braille markers for the blind, or similar aids for those with other disabilities.

A final technique that is useful in providing access to programs for participants consists of mobile recreation units. These include portable pools, nature museums, science displays, libraries, show-wagons, roller skating programs, arts and crafts shops, and other special program features that can readily be transferred from site to site around a community. They make it possible to provide a set period of instruction, such as an intensive period of swimming instruction or carrying out specific projects, before the mobile unit moves on to a new location.

CONSIDERING MOTIVATIONS FOR PARTICIPATION

The elements described thus far in this chapter involve the personal characteristics of participants that are fairly obvious and can readily be used to provide helpful input to the program-planning process. The age, sex, family status, mental and physical condition, numbers, ethnic and racial identification, educational and socioeconomic background of participants can all be considered fairly easily.

What cannot be as easily determined is the underlying motivation for participation. There are a number of obvious reasons that people take part in leisure activities. Some may involve the need for social contact and acceptance by others. They may stem from the desire for physically challenging activities or to build one's health and fitness. Often the creative or aesthetic impulse is at the heart of participation as an individual seeks to express himself or herself in creative or artistic ways. Sometimes it is the search for knowledge or new experience that is the primary motivation. For others, sheer relaxation or escapism may be the underlying need.

Although participants may describe "fun" or "pleasure" as the reason they take part in recreation, often the motivations are more complex. In addition to the purposes just described, they may also seek excitement and risk, a sense of accomplishment, status in the eyes of others, the satisfaction that comes from successfully competing with others or resolving a problem, or even the sense of independence that may come from being able to join a new group, make friends, and function as an individual away from a protected family setting.

Some adults may seek recreational activity that is an extension of their work and involves the same kinds of skills and experiences, like the truck driver who enjoys doing automotive repair or racing stock cars as a hobby. Others deliberately seek leisure outlets that are in total contrast to their work as a complete change of pace from the job. Such motivations and needs cannot possibly be predicted by knowing the demographic characteristics of a group of participants; they are very much a matter of individual personalities, needs, and interests.

The basic point is that, apart from all the characteristics described earlier that provide direction in planning programs, it is important to learn the participants' self-perceived needs and motivations, and to have the participants involved in the program planning process.

ASSESSING PARTICIPANTS' NEEDS AND INTERESTS

How can the needs and interests of participants be measured to assist in program design and construction? There are several ways, which range from using questionnaires or group discussions to determine potential interests to involving participants directly in the planning process.

Questionnaires

Many leisure-service agencies make use of activity-interest questionnaires to determine the potential needs and interests of participants. These may take several forms.

Patient/Client Entry Forms.   Typically, many institutions that serve disabled populations make use of interest questionnaires to determine what kinds of recreational experiences participants may have had in the past, what levels of skills they may have in these areas, and what kinds of activities they might like to take part in within the institution or agency program. For example, Figure 5–1 shows a form used in a treatment setting that combines information provided by the patient or client with additional information and recommendations provided by family members and other medical or treatment personnel.

FIGURE 5–1   Example of Patient Intake Form and Continuing Record[20]

Therapeutic Recreation Clinical Case Study Patient Assessment/Profile Form Patient Activities Department National Institutes of Health

I. Introduction

   A. Introduction of Self

   B. Purpose of Interview

   C. Overview of Patient Activities Department

II. Objective Information

   A. Demographic Information

     Name_____ Referral Date_____

     Nursing Unit_____ Room Number_____ Institute_____

     Residence_____

     Date of Birth_____ Place of Birth_____

     Age_____ Sex_____ Race_____

     Marital Status_____ Number of Children/Siblings_____

     Religious Preference_____

     Education Level_____

     Occupation_____

     Physician_____ Phone_____

     Primary Nurse_____ Phone_____

     Therapeutic Recreation Specialist_____

     Social Worker_____ Phone_____

     Physical Therapist_____ Phone_____

     Occupational Therapist_____ Phone_____

     Other_____ Phone_____

     Projected Discharge Date_____

   B. Medical Information

     Diagnosis_____

     Description of Disease (in laymen's terms)_____

     _____

Treatment Side Effects_____

_____

_____

_____

Limitations/Restrictions

a. Physical_____

_____

_____

b. Mental_____

_____

c. Other_____

_____

C. Social Information

Relationship with Family Members_____

_____

_____

Family/Friends in Area_____

_____

_____

Community Involvement (i.e., Clubs, Organizations, Volunteer Work)_____

_____

_____

_____

Additional Remarks_____

_____

_____

III. Recreation Information

A. Leisure Habits

Patient's Interests Prior to Illness_____

_____

_____

Adaptations to Activities Made after Illness_____

_____

_____

Group Activities with Family/Friends_____

_____

_____

Recreation Resources/Facilities near Residence_____

_____

Hobbies_____

_____

Note: This record is followed by a detailed check-list of activities under such headings as: *Physical Activities (Sports and Active Games); Table Games; Trips and Tours; Arts and Crafts;* and *Creative Hobbies.* These should be checked to indicate whether or not the patient/client has participated in them or would like to learn them now. Following that, the form includes sections to note desired *Goals and Objectives,* a proposed *Patient Treatment Plan,* and *Progress Notes.*

Agency Membership Survey. An organization like a YMCA or YWCA that offers a diversified program of activities based to some degree on the cafeteria model of programming may carry out a survey of its membership, both to determine their views about the programs that are currently offered, and to gather ideas about new types of activities or events that might be popular. It is always possible to use a suggestion box for this purpose, which may yield interesting ideas; however, this does not give a picture of the overall views of the membership when they are asked to respond systematically to a listing of possible program activities.

Community Survey or Feasibility Study. A public recreation and park agency may also use the same technique to learn the views of community residents about its programs and facilities and to get a detailed picture of their suggestions for possible new elements in the system.

This may involve a full-fledged planning study or marketing survey intended to gain detailed understanding of different age groups and neighborhood attitudes, or it may deal more specifically with a single area of programming. For example, the Westchester County, New York, Council on the Arts, in cooperation with the County Department of Parks and Recreation, sponsored a survey of county residents to determine their involvement in varied types of cultural and arts programs, and their potential interest in a county arts center that might host major performing groups and events. Figure 5–2 shows examples of the questions asked.

Guidelines for Conducting Recreation Interest Surveys

Carrying out recreation interest surveys should be done in a systematic and efficient way to ensure that the results are meaningful. The following guidelines will be helpful in conducting such surveys:

FIGURE 5–2   Survey of Arts Interests of County Residents

1. How many cultural events did any adult member of your family attend last month? In Westchester: _____; in NYC: _____; in environs (Rockland, Putnam, Connecticut): _____.

2. Have you ever subscribed to a performing-arts series in Westchester? _____ Which ones? _____ Do you currently subscribe? _____ If not, why did you drop it? _____

3. Have you attended concerts, lectures, films, exhibits related to the arts at Westchester colleges, clubs, libraries, churches? _____ Which ones? _____
_____

4. How would you rate the arts opportunities in your own community (1 to 5)? Outstanding _____ Very Good _____ Good _____ Average _____ Poor _____

Note: This is only a small excerpt from the overall survey.

Developing Representative Sample.   Although it is always possible to conduct a mailed survey or to interview residents or organization members by telephone, these methods tend to be time-consuming and result in a limited response rate. Direct distribution of printed questionnaires or interviews in appropriate locations is therefore often a better means of approaching the public.

Effort should be made to reach as representative a sample as possible by approaching different age groups or other segments of the population at different times of the day or week in a number of different settings. This approach helps ensure that views of a cross-section of participants or potential participants are heard.

Preparing Useful Instrument.   A survey questionnaire or interview schedule should be prepared to ensure that all respondents are asked exactly the same questions. The key topics should be identified; usually these would include both the kinds of activities or facilities people are presently using, their views about them, and the types of additional or new program elements they would like to see added. Several suggestions for developing such a form follow:

1. It is usually best to have closed-end questions to be answered by marking an X or check in boxes rather than open-end questions that may yield responses that will be difficult to tabulate.

2. Questions should be very clear and simple, dealing with one item at a time, and doing so without showing any bias on the part of the interviewer or agency. It is often helpful to give the respondent a range of possible answers, such as Excellent, Very Good, Good, Fair, and Poor, or choices as to frequencies or locations.

3. Questions should deal not only with the current or past recreational interests or involvements of respondents, but also with what they would like to take part in or have the agency sponsor. In many situations, it is also helpful to have them indicate when the most appropriate times for participation would be,

what the best locations would be, and the range of fees that might be acceptable to them.

Administering Survey.

In some cases, where forms are distributed through organizations like Parent-Teachers Associations, churches, or advisory councils, it may only be necessary to provide useful instructions telling the respondent the purpose of the survey and urging him or her to carry it out and return the form.

In other cases where the survey will be carried out directly by interviewers, these individuals should be trained in the process of administering it efficiently and in a manner that will encourage people to cooperate. This process should be carefully supervised, particularly in terms of trying to reach appropriate numbers of target populations in assigned locations, and having completed survey forms promptly turned in.

Analysis and Follow-Up of Findings.

In conclusion, a cut-off date should be set for completion of the survey. In tabulating and analyzing the data, it will be extremely helpful to use electronic data-processing methods. Computers make it possible to carry out statistical analysis of data quickly and efficiently, and to break them down in many special ways according to such factors as age, residential location, relationship of different activities with each other, and similar variables.

When the survey has been completed, its findings should be succinctly summarized in a report. Ideally they should then be publicized (unless the survey was clearly intended for internal purposes only). Recommendations should be formulated and used as input in program-planning processes.

An example of such a study carried out by the author is provided in the appendix. It illustrates methods used to measure both the present involvement of different population groups and their views on programs that should be expanded, as well as other policy issues facing the department of recreation in the city studied.

In carrying out such surveys, it is usually a good idea to do it anonymously, and to assure respondents that their views will be kept private. Questionnaires should be kept simple, avoid highly personal information, and request only information that will be useful. It is usually a good idea to pilot-test a first draft of a survey form to make sure that it is clearly understood and can readily be administered.

Involving Participants Directly.

Another useful technique involves having participants contribute their views directly through group discussions and planning sessions. In public recreation, many recreation and park departments encourage such input on three levels: (1) local advisory committees or councils that are attached to neighborhood playgrounds or community centers and which help plan programs, provide volunteer leadership, and often raise funds to support special activities; (2) district committees or councils that fulfill the same functions on a larger geographical basis and that represent the combined needs of different neighborhoods; and (3) city-wide committees, boards, or councils that may represent either free-standing bodies, appointed by a mayor or city manager or elected on a community-wide basis, or individuals sent by local or district groups to represent them in city-wide planning.

In other types of agencies, similar methods are used. In campus recreation, there may be an interdormitory council or student activity board that has a number of functions, including the approval of policies and authorization of budget expenditures for campus activity programs. In some cases, there may be a college- or university-wide recreation association (with membership representing different classes, schools, or other administrative units) that carries out similar functions.

In employee recreation programs, there are often committees or councils that advise the professional staff on program needs or are directly responsible for the program-planning function. In some therapeutic agencies such as hospitals, long-term care facilities, or physical rehabilitation centers, there may also be patient councils with varied functions, including giving direction to the recreation program.

On a less formal basis, recreation staff members may consult directly with group members and other individuals or plan programs with the groups they are serving. This helps to assure that appropriate decisions are made and encourages participants to volunteer to assume many of the responsibilities involved in carrying out activities.

Individual Counseling and Advisement.   When people enter a program directly—as is the case with adults who sign up for a program at a health spa or a ceramics class—they may not need any form of advice about their own involvement. When children or youth are part of a recreation center or voluntary-agency club or join a sports team, they also have already decided to take part in the activities of that group. However, in many situations where there may be a diversified set of program opportunities, members of an organization or potential participants in a recreation program may need individual counseling or advisement to determine the activities that would be most appropriate and enjoyable for them. The term *advisement* suggests simply that a recreation staff member may point out options for participants and may help the individual make a decision and register in the program.

In some settings, however, participants may require a fuller exploration of their own leisure needs, interests, and capabilities before they are ready to decide. In this process, they are helped to understand their own attitudes and past recreational involvement, and to build positive motivations for participation. In addition, the staff member may assist them in making arrangements to join a group or program, or may make formal referrals to community activities that make the transition easier.

ASSESSING COMMUNITY NEEDS

This chapter has given primary emphasis to the process of determining appropriate recreation program content on the basis of participants' characteristics, needs, and interests. It has shown how community surveys may be conducted to determine the views of representative sections of the population and how advisory councils or committees may provide input to recreation planning.

Beyond this, it is important to recognize that the recreation and park agency itself may have certain goals in mind that participants are not aware of, or that it seeks to promote through program activity. Goals related to physical fitness and mental health, improving community spirit and intergroup understanding, providing a favorable climate for economic development of the community, or reducing juvenile delinquency or other forms of social pathology may help guide recreation professionals in planning programs.

In assessing community needs, recreation and park professionals will also need to gather comprehensive data about the available facilities and programs sponsored by other agencies in different sections of a community. They should confer with other civic officials and department heads, and may also need to carry out comparative analyses of different neighborhoods to determine where recreational priorities should lie.

Based on such information, and with a detailed understanding of what residents themselves want—in terms of program activities and services—it is possible to plan programs that meet needs effectively. A similar approach would obviously be followed in other types of leisure-service settings. In the armed forces, for example, it would be essential to determine the needs and interests of service personnel and their dependents as well as the program capabilities and needs of the overall base or service unit before developing a program plan. The special characteristics of each type of leisure-service organization and their program goals and objectives are described in detail in Chapter 6.

IMPLICATIONS OF PROGRAM PLANNING

Although it is essential to consult community residents or organization members regarding programs, it is not always possible or desirable to follow their suggestions. For example, they may wish to carry on activities that are in conflict with the basic goals or philosophy of the sponsoring organization, or that the sponsoring organization is too ill-equipped with personnel, facilities, or other resources to offer.

In addition, other community sponsors may offer the kinds of program activities they are suggesting, and the sponsoring agency therefore does not feel the suggestions represent a high-priority concern for its program. This is particularly true for public recreation and park departments, which have a general obligation to provide a "floor" of basic leisure opportunities to serve the entire community, but may wish to avoid programs that put them in direct competition with other organizations that are meeting community needs satisfactorily.

Finally, program planners must always strike a balance between individual and group needs. As shown earlier, programs themselves may range from mass activities to other pursuits designed for very small numbers or for individual participation. Most public agencies realistically tend to serve their clientele through mass forms of participation and somewhat impersonal types of program leadership. In contrast, many voluntary agencies, as well as therapeutic agencies and to some extent private and commercial organizations, are prepared to provide more small-group activity and more personalized service.

At this point, we are now ready to move on to the third step of the program planning process—determining program goals and objectives.

NOTES

[1]James F. Murphy, *Concepts of Leisure* (Englewood Cliffs, N.J.: Prentice-Hall, 1981), pp. 111–13.

[2]Arnold Gesell and Frances Ilg, *The Child from Five to Ten* (New York: Harper & Row, 1946), p. 360.

[3]Seppo Iso-Ahola, *The Social Psychology of Leisure and Recreation* (Dubuque, Iowa: Wm. C. Brown, 1980), pp. 98–101.

[4]Adapted from Richard Kraus and Margery Scanlin, *Introduction to Camp Counseling* (Englewood Cliffs, N.J.: Prentice-Hall, 1983), pp. 102–3.

[5]Seppo Iso-Ahola, "Who's Turning Children's Play into Work?" *Parks and Recreation* (June 1980): 51.

[6]"Out-of-Shape Pupils Mark Decline of Physical Education," Philadelphia *Inquirer* (18 May 1984): 1A, 12A.

[7]Richard L. Cottrell, "Teenage-less Campgrounds, A Sad Commentary," *Parks and Recreation* (December 1980): 37.

[8]Bennett M. Berger, "Teenagers Are an American Invention," *New York Times Magazine* (13 June 1965): 12.

[9]Kraus and Scanlin, p. 107.

[10]Jeannye Thornton, "Behind a Surge in Suicides of Young People," *U.S. News & World Report* (20 June 1983): 66.

[11]Patricia Farrell and Herberta Lundegren, *The Process of Recreation Programming* (New York: John Wiley, 1978), p. 18.

[12]For an example of special programs for singles, see: "Westchester County, N.Y., Salutes Singles Thru Get-Acquainted Gala," *Parks and Recreation* (March 1982): 18.

[13]Gaylene Carpenter, "Serving Those in Middle Age: 30–60," *Parks and Recreation* (June 1984): 61.

[14]"Basic Concepts of Aging," adapted from *Centers for Older People,* Report of the National Council on the Aging, 1962.

[15]Robert Butler, quoted in "Today's Senior Citizens: Pioneers of New Golden Era," *U.S. News & World Report* (2 July 1984): 51.

[16]Butler: 51.

[17]"The Boys of Winter," *Time* (7 February 1983): 66.

[18]R. E. Tedrick, "Achieving Age-Integration Through Leisure," *Parks and Recreation* (December 1981): 49.

[19]Kay Raftery, "When a Little Girl's Thoughts Turn to Playing Baseball," *Philadelphia Inquirer* (6 May 1984): 1–N.

STUDENT PROJECTS

1. As an individual or in a group project, select one major age grouping from those discussed in the chapter (children, youth, adults, or the elderly). Research this age group in the literature and/or through personal interviews, and present several priorities for needed recreational programs to serve this population.
2. Hold a debate in class on the issue of whether there should be *no* distinction in recreation programming based on the gender of participants; that is, no separate activities that are designated for one sex or the other.
3. Prepare a questionnaire or personal leisure interest survey form through which to assess the recreational needs and interests of potential participants following the guidelines presented in this chapter. Review and evaluate this form in class.
4. As a follow-up assignment to project 3, a team of students may survey a given population (on campus or elsewhere), using this leisure interest form, and present the findings to the class. (For students majoring in therapeutic recreation, this might take the form of a patient/client needs assessment, resulting in recommendations to be incorporated in a treatment plan.)

SUGGESTED READINGS

Patricia Farrell and Herberta Lundegren, *The Process of Recreation Programming* (New York: John Wiley, 1978), Chapter 2.

Scout Gunn and Carol Peterson, *Therapeutic Recreation Program Design: Principles and Procedures* (Englewood Cliffs, N.J.: Prentice-Hall, 1978), Chapters 5 and 6.

Richard Kraus, *Recreation and Leisure in Modern Society* (Glenview, Ill.: Scott, Foresman, 1984), Chapter 14.

H. Douglas Sessoms, *Leisure Services* (Englewood Cliffs, N.J.: Prentice-Hall, 1984), Chapter 7.

CHAPTER 6

Determining
Program Goals,
Objectives
and Policies

Monsignor Sabatini smiled as he read through the report.

"This is excellent, Father McCray," he said. "I see you've really broadened the CYO program in your parish. You've kept all the sports activities, but you've also added art, music, and some weekend retreats and camping activities. And I like the leadership program you've developed for teenagers."

"Thank you, Monsignor," replied Father John McCray. "We took a chance in adding these new programs, but a lot of the young people seemed enthusiastic about them, and our CYO advisory group was willing to support me. We have a good number of volunteers and I feel we'll be accomplishing a lot this year."

Monsignor Sabatini nodded. "That's the way to do it. I am very pleased with what's happening. I've hoped for a long time that this program would pick up, and it's starting. Maybe we just needed to set our sights higher—to develop some more meaningful purposes."

We now move to a consideration of the third step in the program-planning process—the task of determining agency goals, objectives, and policies. We will begin by defining these terms, and will then move ahead to describe the major types of leisure-service agencies, their program emphases, and their goals.

Following that, the chapter will conclude with a set of guidelines for developing goals and objectives, and will show how policies flow from these two elements.

DEFINING GOALS, OBJECTIVES, AND POLICIES

Obviously, both *goals* and *objectives* represent outcomes that an organization seeks to achieve. However, while the two terms are often used interchangeably, their meanings are quite different.

Goals

Goals are considered to be broad statements of overall purpose that help define the philosophy of organizations in terms of major outcomes to be achieved. They may be *external*, in the sense that they describe the outcomes that the agency seeks to achieve for participants or for the community at large, or they may be *internal* in that they apply to the organization's efforts to mobilize itself for greater effectiveness, or to gain needed support.

Goals may also be either short- or long-range, dealing with immediate plans or needs, or with a projected period of time that may encompass several years. Some national youth-serving organizations regularly develop new goals statements every three or five years.

Objectives

Objectives are defined as narrower statements of purpose that specify the actual outcomes that an organization seeks to accomplish in concrete, measurable terms. As compared with goals, which may be rather abstract, objectives are usually stated in tangible terms and specify quantifiable performance measures whenever possible.

Customarily, objectives are framed on a short-term basis. For example, they may include statements of tasks to be accomplished or outcomes to be achieved within the period of time immediately ahead, such as six weeks or three months. Objectives are typically developed to meet individual needs or achieve specific behavioral changes, particularly in therapeutic recreation programs. Frequently, each goal may have several objectives attached to it, as illustrated in Figure 6–1.

As this example shows, the objectives provide a means of spelling out the goals in concrete terms, and also offer a basis for judging whether they have been achieved successfully. They are frequently stated in terms of performance measures that relate to specific outcomes for participants. In such cases, they are likely to have such quantitative statements as: (1) to be able to swim two lengths of the pool; (2) to conduct six workshops, with an average attendance of 100 persons; or (3) to achieve an average weight-reduction of 15 pounds for all participants over a two-month period.

FIGURE 6–1 Examples of Goals and Objectives of Employee Wellness Program

Goal 1   To improve employees' awareness of basic principles of health and fitness, and of related areas of benefits of exercise, nutrition, and weight control.

Objectives for Goal 1
1. To provide films, demonstrations, and workshops to promote employees' concern and knowledge in these areas, and to reach at least 50 percent of employees with these events.
2. To establish action programs in physical fitness activities and weight-reduction, and to recruit a minimum of 20 employees each in these programs, in a three-month period.

Goal 2   To improve the actual fitness levels of employees, as a means of improving on-the-job performance, and reducing accidents and absenteeism.

Objectives for Goal 2
1. To achieve a significant level of improvement on selected cardiovascular measures for employees taken during the fitness program; and on weight-reduction, for employees taking part in that program.
2. To monitor the personnel records of employees in these programs, as compared to a control group of employees not taking part, to determine differences in selected measures of job performance.

Policies

The third term to be considered at this point is *policies*. As defined in Chapter 3, these represent major operational guidelines or rules that an agency has adopted to define appropriate departmental or professional performance and to serve as the basis for day-to-day decisions and agency actions. Policies must be designed to support the major goals of an organization and to help bring about the attainment of stated objectives.

Since goals, objectives, and policies vary greatly for different types of recreation sponsors, this chapter will begin by presenting an overview of the eight major types of leisure-service agencies. In each case, the nature of sponsorship and a number of the major program elements will be described along with examples of the typical goals and objectives found within the category. Following that, several examples of agency policies and administrative directives related to program delivery will be presented.

PUBLIC RECREATION AND PARK AGENCIES

The term *public,* as applied here, refers to agencies that are a branch of government, rely heavily on tax revenues for their support, and are intended to serve a broad spectrum of population groups with socially constructive recreational opportunities.

There are several levels of government sponsorship of recreation and park programs. On the federal level, such agencies as the National Park Service, the Forest Service, the U.S. Army Corps of Engineers, or the Bureau of Wildlife and Fisheries make a substantial contribution to resource-based outdoor recreation programs. Other federal departments or bureaus provide assistance to state and local agencies, or help support programs serving special populations. On the state or provincial level, numerous agencies operate extensive networks of parks, forests, reservoirs, lakes, and other diversified resources for outdoor recreation. Other state or provincial agencies promote tourism, provide support for special populations, or assist in local recreation planning and the development of technical services.

This chapter is concerned primarily with local public agencies, such as municipal, county, or township recreation and park departments, or special recreation or park districts.

The typical local public agency is a recreation and park department that is legally authorized to acquire and develop properties and other facilities to house recreation activities, and to provide varied programs under leadership and supervision. Usually, it is a tax-supported unit of local government (city, town, village, special district, or county), although its funding may also come from fees and charges, gifts, grants or other supplemental appropriations.

Program Functions of Local Public Agencies

As indicated earlier in this text, local public recreation and park agencies have several major program functions: (1) to provide organized or structured programs of activity under leadership; (2) to provide facilities for unstructured recreation; (3) to promote and assist recreation in the community at large; (4) to provide education for leisure; and (5) to provide nonrecreational services, often of a human service nature.

Under these broad headings of purpose, program services may be organized and developed under several major categories or types, such as sports and games, outdoor recreation, performing arts, or social activities. They may also be structured according to groupings based on the population being served, or major types of facilities, such as playgrounds, community centers, sports facilities, or aquatic areas and other special facilities.

As an example, the Los Angeles Recreation Branch has the following administrative units or sections: (1) a Centers Operations Division, covering five areas with twelve districts, including Aquatics and Community Relations Sections; (2) a Cultural Affairs Division, including programs in the various arts, and an Ill and Handicapped Section; (3) a Special Services Division, with special sections for teenagers, senior citizens, municipal sports, camps and museums, and an in-service training section; and (4) a Beach Operations Division.

In addition to such program divisions, many municipal, county, and district agencies also operate extensive networks of facilities, including parks, golf courses, museums, stadiums, aquatic and athletic complexes, art centers and similar areas.

In many cases, larger communities or county programs have developed highly innovative facilities or services. To illustrate, the Oakland County, Michigan, park system operates a successful wave pool and has also constructed a unique attraction, the Waterford Oaks County Park Waterslide, a giant two-flume waterslide that was named the "Slidewinder" in a public contest, and that attracted close to 100,000 patrons and almost $200,000 in revenue in its first year of operation. With a substantial grant from the federal Land and Water Conservation Fund, it developed an outstanding nature interpretive center at Independence Oaks County Park, and has strongly emphasized platform tennis facilities, bike racing programs, camping, and other popular activities.

Beyond these program elements, it has developed extremely rich recreational opportunities for senior citizens, the handicapped, and other special populations. It has also developed several mobile recreation vans to put special programs on the road, including a Skate Mobile, Puppet Mobile, Sports Mobile, Show Mobile, Nature Discovery Mobile Unit, and Adaptive Recreation Mobile Unit.

As an example of special districts, the Willamalane Park and Recreation District, in Lane County, Oregon, provides numerous programs within each of the major areas of recreation activity, to serve specific population needs. For example, sports, arts and crafts, fitness, hunter-safety, dramatics, backpacking, photography, trips, and entertainment programs are scheduled at appropriate times and in logical formats to meet the needs of *seven* different populations: preschool, elementary age, middle/high school, adult, family, senior adult, and special populations (mentally or physically disabled).

In the health and fitness area, the park district offers fitness evaluation services and individualized fitness programs; aerobic dance on various levels of skills or different age or gender groupings; body sculpture (weight conditioning) classes; bio-feedback and stress management workshops; blood-pressure clinics, and various running and jogging activities and events.

As a third example of innovative programming, the city of Nepean, Ontario, Canada, has developed a number of programs designed to meet the needs of different age levels and other special populations.

Several programs are designed for younger children, including Little Duffer Doo Time, a diversified play group program serving over 875 preschoolers in eight different community centers. As part of this program, parents must provide volunteer leadership and must assist in fund-raising events to assure the program's success. Other play programs, including family swimming activities, ice-skating classes for "moms and tots," and a Saturday morning playgroup for fathers and preschool children, encourage family participation. There is a Sports Learning Center, which offers sequential instruction in play, fundamental sports skills, and applied skills in the most popular sports for children in four age groups ranging from three to twelve years.

Other special features, such as a Magic Workshop for Children, a basic and advanced-skill hockey camp, Leadership Development Program for Youth,

March Caper (a week-long intensive workshop in twenty-four
e activities, ranging from a superstar challenge to kite-making,
ribbean Fun Day to Small Craft Safety), reflect the variety of
es offered. There is an extensive program of social activities for
s elderly residents, and other groups for adults who have been in
psychiatric treatment programs and are being reintegrated into the community,
and for orthopedically disabled adults.

Goals and Objectives of Local Public Agencies

These examples of current programming in several communities in the
United States and Canada help illustrate the goals and objectives of local
recreation and park departments today.

The primary goal is to meet the need of the public at large for constructive and enjoyable leisure activity within a wide range of different interests and
varied types of physical, creative, social and outdoor recreational pastimes.
Many local agencies today place heavy emphasis on serving special population
groups, such as children, teenagers, the aging, families, or the handicapped.
Growing emphasis is being placed on providing health and fitness activities and
other human service functions.

Beyond this major purpose, local agencies also have a number of related
goals, having to do with promoting cooperative relationships in community life
and maintaining positive community morale, improving intergroup relationships,
helping reduce antisocial forms of play, and contributing to neighborhood stability. Finally, in a broad sense, they have the goal of educating for leisure and
helping promote positive and constructive forms of recreational involvement for
all community residents.

VOLUNTARY, NONPROFIT ORGANIZATIONS

A second major form of organized recreation service in the United
States and Canada is provided by voluntary agencies and organizations. These
are nongovernmental in nature, and are financed primarily by contributions,
community chests, fund-raising drives, annual memberships, and fees charged
for participation.

The term *voluntary* is sometimes misinterpreted to mean that such
organizations are staffed by volunteers. This is not the case, since they obviously
have many full-time, paid professional employees. Instead, it refers to the fact
that they represent the voluntary efforts of citizens' groups to meet important
public needs, *beyond* programs that are sponsored by government. Such organizations tend to be of several different types, including:

1. Nonsectarian youth-serving organizations, many of which are structured on a national level, with regional districts, and local chapters, councils, clubs or troops;
2. Sectarian youth-serving organizations or other recreation programs, sponsored either by major religious denominations or by individual churches or synagogues;
3. Community centers that meet a variety of recreational, educational, and related social needs for different age groups, which are independently formed and supported by organizations of local residents; a number of these are identified as antipoverty programs which are specifically designed to serve socially disadvantaged residents;
4. Special-interest organizations, which seek to promote, either on a local, state, or national level, interest and participation in a single type of activity or to serve the needs of a particular population, such as the mentally retarded, or the aging;
5. Fraternal organizations, lodges, or service clubs within the community, which promote recreation programs on a nonprofit basis, usually to meet social needs.

The policies and programs of voluntary organizations are determined by their own boards, officers, or professional administrators, thus making them flexible and able to respond quickly to changing community needs. In some cases, particularly in a number of major Canadian sports or cultural organizations, they may receive operational subsidies from federal or provincial government agencies. A number of different types of voluntary agencies are described in the pages that follow, with examples drawn from the United States and Canada.

Nonsectarian Youth-Serving Organizations

These include a wide range of organizations with memberships that number in the millions, such as the Boy Scouts, Girl Scouts, Camp Fire, The Police Athletic League, Boys' Clubs, Girls' Clubs and 4–H Club Youth. They are nonsectarian, in that they are not attached to any single religious organization, although in some cases they may promote spiritual values or concepts, and may use the facilities of churches or other religious groups.

Some are found only in a single country, while others are international, with chapters in as many as forty or fifty other nations. Usually, they attempt primarily to "build" character (implying responsible citizenship and other forms of social behavior or competence). Within this effort, they give heavy stress to recreation, camping, and other social activities and programs. Carlson, MacLean, Deppe and Peterson state that:

> Most of these (quasi-public agencies) would describe themselves as health, education, social services, or welfare agencies rather than as recreation agencies. . . . Tax-exempt yet not tax-supported, independent yet in varying degrees related to government, these organizations evolved to meet needs that were not met by government.[1]

Religious Organizations Meeting Recreation Needs

Many religious denominations, as well as individual churches or synagogues, provide extensive programs of recreation, primarily for youth, but also for single adults, couples, families, and for the elderly. They do so in recognition of leisure and recreation as important aspects of modern life and related directly to the spiritual well-being of participants on all age levels.

Among the categories of activities widely found in locally sponsored programs of church or synagogue-centered recreation are the following:

1. Camping and similar outdoor activities, including family camping, conferences and institutes, or retreats emphasizing religious education programs—programs that frequently place heavy stress on recreational activities of all types through the day and evening, including various forms of "inspirational" events, such as campfires, vesper services, singing, dramatics, and rhythmic worship
2. Similar to the above are day camps, play schools, or summer Bible schools, which are conducted by many religious agencies and usually involve many plan activities, along with more formal educational content
3. A year-round program of social recreation activities, including family nights, picnics and outings, covered-dish suppers (where each family brings a special dish), game nights and carnivals, bazaars, dances, and informal community singing and dramatics
4. Special interest groups in the arts and crafts, or in the performing arts of music, drama, and dance that may involve religious pageantry and drama, or secular plays, choruses, choirs, and instrumental groups
5. A network of clubs or fellowship groups for various age levels, which meet regularly and have both social and spiritual emphases in their programs and may include youth groups, couples' club, Scout groups, service groups (which perform volunteer service activities in the community) and golden age or senior citizens' clubs
6. Sports activities, in the form of bowling or basketball leagues, or less structured participation in other sports
7. Discussion groups that deal with current events, literature, religious themes, and similar subjects

In terms of direct program involvement at the local level, many churches and synagogues have developed special parish halls, community center buildings, or wings of buildings with all the types of facilities, meeting rooms, and equipment that are needed for well-rounded recreation programming. Often these are connected to religious education; they may also be provided as separate social facilities.

In addition, each of the major faiths in our society maintains a number of national organizations serving youth and adults with varied social, educational, spiritual and leisure-oriented programs. Examples of these are the YMCA and YWCA, the Catholic Youth Organization, and the YM-YWHA, as well as numerous other youth associations sponsored by specific Protestant denominations.

Nonsectarian Community Centers

Particularly in large and medium-sized cities, there may also be one or more community centers or settlement houses designed chiefly to meet the needs of disadvantaged residents. Viewed as part of the total social welfare structure of such communities, these centers are voluntary in nature and usually independent of any larger organization or sponsorship, although they may be linked to community councils or associations of neighborhood agencies.

Financially, they usually depend on fees, charges, and direct contributions, and on sharing income from civic fund drives, such as United Way or Community Chest campaigns. Since the 1960s, many such organizations have also contracted directly or indirectly with the federal government to provide special services for youth, the aging, or other populations in need.

Other Types of Voluntary Organizations

In addition to the examples just provided, several other types of voluntary, nonprofit community organizations provide or assist recreation programs and participation, including special-interest and fraternal organizations and service clubs.

Special-Interest Organizations.   These are national, regional, or local organizations that are founded to promote interest and participation in a given area of leisure activity, such as cultural pursuits, hobbies, outdoor recreation, or sports.

For example, there are literally hundreds of sports organizations, such as the Amateur Athletic Union of the United States, Amateur Softball Association of America, American Bowling Congress, Babe Ruth Baseball, Ice Skating Institute of America, National Field Archery Association, National Jogging Association, National Rifle Association, National Shuffleboard Association, Pop Warner Junior League Football, United States Figure Skating Association,

United States Golf Association, United States Lawn Tennis Association, United States Ski Association, and the United States Volleyball Association.

These organizations promote interest in a great variety of recreational activities. In some cases they directly sponsor activities, promulgate and enforce rules of play, and enfranchise district operations. In others, they seek primarily to publicize their area of interest, and to promote widespread public participation. Usually they are financed through their own membership fees, contributions, and endowments, although a number have the support of private manufacturers who are interested in assisting their efforts.

Fraternal Organizations and Service Clubs. A final example of voluntary organizations that assist or provide community recreation opportunities consists of fraternal orders or lodges such as the Benevolent and Protective Order of Elks, the Loyal Order of Moose, the Independent Order of Odd Fellows, and the Fraternal Order of Eagles. Other civic groups, such as the Kiwanis and local businessmen's or businesswomen's associations, also provide recreation and related services, particularly for youth and the handicapped.

A number of similar organizations have been established to provide recreation programs for handicapped children and youth. Some, like the Easter Seal Society, tend to serve a variety of special populations with essential social services. Others are geared to meeting the needs of a single population, such as the visually impaired, the deaf, the orthopedically disabled, the mentally retarded, or those who have diabetes or muscular dystrophy, with educational, vocational, and recreation programs.

Goals and Objectives of Voluntary Nonprofit Organizations

The goals of voluntary agencies vary considerably, but generally focus on meeting important social needs, or with promoting desirable religious or social values. Their purposes may include helping reduce delinquency and crime; helping girls and young women function more effectively in society; providing needed educational, counseling, or health-related services; encouraging participation in outdoor recreation or other special-interest activities; and generally helping participants develop richer and more positive life-styles.

While recreation is not usually perceived as the primary thrust of such nonprofit organizations, it often represents one of the major services they offer.

COMMERCIAL RECREATION ENTERPRISES

A third major type of leisure-service agency in modern society consists of commercial recreation enterprises. These are businesses that offer programs, facilities, and products to the public at large for profit. Such recreational offerings far outweigh all the combined efforts of government, voluntary and religious agencies, therapeutic, industrial, armed forces, and other goal-oriented types of recreation sponsors. Carlson, MacLean, Deppe, and Peterson write:

> Commercial recreation is recreation for which the participant pays and from which the supplier intends to make a profit. It is one of the most important and fastest growing aspects of American culture today.[2]

Several major categories of commercially operated recreation programs include the following:

Travel and Tourism.   This is probably the largest single category of commercial recreation enterprise. It includes the operation of motels, hotels, commercial campgrounds, amusement complexes and theme parks, as well as the management of tours, cruises, airline charters, and similar ventures.

Travel and tourism involve immense expenditures in terms of both domestic and foreign trips and pleasure-seeking outings. Many states and regions depend heavily on this form of commercial recreation to support their economies, and millions of men and women are employed in various aspects of travel and tourism, ranging from travel agencies and tour guides to the operation of resorts or other tourist destinations.

Outdoor Recreation.   This form is closely related to travel and tourism, in that people frequently take trips to engage in outdoor recreation. However, it is different in that it focuses on particular types of outdoor recreation activity, such as camping and backpacking, skiing, boating, ice skating, riding, hunting, and fishing as the primary motivations for participation, as opposed to travel and tourism, in which travel for its own sake or being exposed to a new environment are generally the key motivations.

Entertainment.   This includes commercially operated theaters, indoor and outdoor movies, concert halls, sports stadiums and events, circuses, amusement parks, race tracks, bingo halls, gambling casinos, television and other forms of electronic entertainment.

Sports and Fitness Centers.   This category includes racquetball courts, bowling alleys, billiard centers, health spas and fitness centers, commercially operated swimming pools or aquatic centers, riding schools, and centers for instruction in karate, judo, and other forms of self-defense. It is also closely linked to schools or studios that give instruction in varied forms of dance, music, or other recreational skills.

Companionship Centers.   This includes clubs, bars, or similar businesses, singles organizations, dating or escort services, and other leisure programs that are designed to promote sociability and companionship.

Manufacturers and Suppliers of Recreation Goods.   Many recreational activities pursued in the home or neighborhood do not require special facilities or instruction, but do involve the purchase of needed equipment or materials. Thus, musical equipment (phonograph records and players, tape recorders, instruments and sheet music), toys, games, gardening equipment, books, magazines, radio and television sets, special clothing for play, barbecue equipment, and numerous other products all represent forms of commercial recreation enterprise.

All of these forms of activities, facilities, equipment and services make possible a vast amount of leisure participation by people of all ages.

Goals and Programming Approaches in Commercial Recreation

As indicated earlier, the primary motivation of commercial recreation is to make a profit by providing recreation programs, facilities, or products to the public. However, many profit-oriented organizations meet important public needs related to fitness, creative development, cultural involvement or family-centered activity in a highly constructive way.

In terms of program content, often commercial recreation simply provides a form of passive entertainment for its audience. In such situations, there is relatively little programming as such. On the other hand, other commercial leisure-service agencies require complex program planning and operations.

For example, a successful health center may need to provide far more than simply exercise equipment, a pool and sauna, lockers, and a running track. To make a go of it in a highly competitive environment, the health and fitness center may need to identify a number of potential audiences, and determine exactly what types of program activities will appeal to each group—and at what time, and in what format. Varied forms of activity (such as racquetball or squash, weight training or use of exercise machines, running or jogging, swimming or use of the sauna, individualized exercise regimens, aerobic dance, or Jazzercise) must all be combined so that they appeal to the greatest number of different participants—and keep them continuing as enrolled members.

Successful commercial recreation planners investigate the possible motivations and needs of their potential clients—including those they may not recognize for themselves, or acknowledge fully. For example, the ostensible purpose of a health club is to help people achieve the maximum level of personal health and fitness. For some individuals, however, this may take a cosmetic form—in that they are more interested in how they *appear* to others, than they are in fundamental health outcomes. For some clients, the fitness program may be intended to reinforce their weight-loss efforts; others may want to take part in exercise because of its positive psychological outcomes. Still others may join a health club primarily because it provides a good place to meet others.

Therefore, in a facility such as a health spa, it is necessary to consider and provide for each of these motivations. In many other types of commercial recreation centers, complex forms of recreation programming and leadership may be called for. In resort hotels or on cruises, for example, recreation directors must frequently plan side trips or tours, parties, shows, card playing, table-game contests, tournaments, exercise sessions, or other forms of entertainment.

Much of the programming that is carried on by commercial recreation entrepreneurs is intended not only to satisfy current clients, but to attract new ones. For example, the promotion of a major sports team or sports stadium may involve inviting local organizations and clubs to attend on special nights; having "giveaways" of jerseys, caps, or other prizes; having special contests during halftime; having performances before and after games; and a variety of other tactics designed to make the sports event more appealing and entertaining.

The primary thrust, therefore, of commercial recreation agencies is to attract and satisfy their members or patrons with a high caliber of efficiently managed and appealing recreation activities and facilities. To a great degree, their emphasis is on competing successfully within the supply-and-demand system described earlier in this text. In so doing, they must develop innovative programs and services, and market them effectively through carefully designed advertising, membership campaigns, and other promotional efforts.

It should again be stressed that, although commercial recreation organizations emphasize the profit motive, many of them offer healthful and positive programming, and contribute significantly to the overall spectrum of community recreation activities.

PRIVATE-MEMBERSHIP ORGANIZATIONS

A related type of leisure-service agency is the private-membership organization that provides various forms of recreational activity for its members.

The most obvious forms of such groups are country clubs, tennis clubs, golf clubs, or yacht clubs, which are established for social and recreational purposes. Such organizations have tended historically to be socially exclusive, with their memberships drawn from the wealthy and elite; frequently their admissions policies have rejected members of ethnic, national or religious minorities. In addition to the types of clubs just listed, there are also hunting and fishing clubs, athletic clubs, luncheon clubs, and similar groups.

Private social and recreation clubs tend to be of two types: (1) those organized by a corporation or other private sponsors as a business, with control of policies and membership in the hands of the organizers; and (2) organizations that exist as independent, incorporated associations of the members themselves who elect their own officers and boards, and hire paid employees to carry out the actual work of maintenance, instruction, operating dining facilities, or similar tasks.

The first category is very much like most commercial recreation organizations. One version of it may be found in real estate developments that include extensive recreation facilities as part of their sales package, and as continuing opportunities available to those who purchase or rent living units. Such real estate ventures may include large apartment complexes, private-home developments, condominium conversions or other developments with swimming pools, tennis courts, health and fitness spas, clubs and social centers, and similar facilities.

A special type of recreation service connected with real estate is found in retirement communities. These are usually privately operated developments primarily designed to serve elderly and retired individuals and couples. Many of these are commercially operated by corporations, although some are sponsored by religious organizations or other nonprofit, voluntary agencies. Customarily, they provide facilities for indoor and outdoor recreation for their residents, and also sponsor a range of recreational, social, cultural, and educational activities.

Goals of Private-Membership Organizations

Like commercial recreation businesses, private-membership organizations are chiefly concerned with attracting and satisfying members, and with providing enjoyable and efficiently operated programs and facilities. Since their memberships are usually sharply defined in terms of socioeconomic class, special interests, or residence, recreation is often perceived as a social lubricant that draws people together. It is a commodity that is offered as an amenity to promote real estate sales and similar ventures. The goal then is to make it as attractive a sales element as possible.

RECREATION IN THE ARMED FORCES

A major area of recreational service today lies in the facilities and programs provided by the federal government to millions of members of the armed forces and their dependents.

Before World War II, military recreation tended to be extremely decentralized and lacked both adequate fiscal support and professional leadership. However, in the decades that followed, armed forces recreation programs expanded rapidly.

In a recent report, Baumgardner summed up the present scope of military recreation sponsored by the United States armed forces. This program serves approximately nine million individuals, including active-duty, reserve, and retired military personnel; civilian employees; surviving spouses of military personnel who died on active duty; and dependents. Morale, Welfare and Recreation (MRW) programs are provided on virtually all of the 923 Department of Defense Installations in the United States, and 363 installations in 29 foreign countries and U.S. territories.[3]

Within each of the major branches of the armed services, there is a different pattern of recreation program. The U.S. Army recreation service, for example, offers seven core programs, including arts and crafts, dependent youth activities, library, music and theater, outdoor recreation, recreation centers, and sports for both soldiers and their dependents. Recently, these programs annually involved 125 million units of participation, at an average cost of about $.80 per unit.

In the Navy, recreation is provided by the Recreation and Physical Fitness Branch of the Bureau of Naval Personnel. Most naval installations ashore have indoor and outdoor sports facilities, swimming pools, hobby shops, and movie theaters. An outstanding example of U.S. Navy recreation may be found at the Great Lakes Naval Training Center. This 1,600-acre base with twenty different commands is located forty miles north of Chicago on Lake Michigan. Each year 30,000 recruits complete basic training and 30,000 technical people are trained at Great Lakes. The military personnel, civilians, and dependents who are attached to the base create at Great Lakes the recreational needs of a small city.

To serve this population, ranging from seaman recruits to admirals, the Great Lakes Special Services staff employs thirty-eight full-time civilians, fifty-five part-time employees, and sixty-four military personnel. In a recent ten-year period, the recreation program expanded from a limited number of intramural sports and bowling to include the following:

> Intramural sport competition, including bowling, football, basketball, volleyball, softball, golf, and sailing
>
> Family activities with an indoor roller rink with rental skates, 8 outdoor and 3 indoor tennis courts, 2 billiard parlors, a trap-shooting range, and an indoor miniature golf range
>
> A library with 32,000 volumes, complete loan equipment for camping, fishing, and winter sports, and a recreation building with a pleasant social center with reading lounges, billiard and ping-pong tables, color TV, and a music room
>
> Organized tours and low-cost tickets for cultural and sports activities in Chicago
>
> A Child-Care Center to care for infant, preschool and school-aged children of Navy personnel, along with a summer day camp program
>
> An Auto Hobby Shop with 28 stalls and varied tools for car repair; also an Electronic Hobby Shop for repair and building of video and audio equipment; a Woodworking Hobby Shop, Arts and Crafts Hobby Shop, and Ceramic Hobby Shop[4]

Similarly diverse programs are found in the Air Force and Marine Corps. Depending on its location and the make-up of those on the base, program emphases differ, ranging from physical fitness or adventure programming, to services designed to improve family stability, reduce and promote emotional well-being.

In a recent (1982) policy statement of the Department of Defense, it was made clear that high-quality Morale, Welfare, and Recreation (MWR) programs contributed significantly to the quality of life in the military community.

Summing up, this Department of Defense statement stressed that

> It is the responsibility of military commands to create, maintain, and support comprehensive, quality MWR programs, services, and activities that meet the changing needs and interests of the military establishment; that are flexible to meet unique geographic requirements; and that take into consideration the evolving social and economic environment.[5]

Goals of Military Recreation

Armed forces recreation programs provide a useful example of the two types of goals presented at the beginning of this chapter—external and internal.

Their external goals represent outcomes they seek to achieve for the morale and welfare of the armed forces. These include improving the overall quality of life in the armed forces, contributing to the recruitment and retention of military personnel, maintaining a high level of esprit de corps, and promoting physical, mental and social well-being of all members of the military community.

Internal goals in armed forces recreation are primarily concerned with maintaining a highly effective and well-supported operation. This may be illustrated in terms of policies and procedures related to the financing of MWR programs.

Self-Sufficiency and the Marketing Approach. An important trend in military recreation has been the strong push toward self-sufficiency in the marketing and financing of armed forces programs. The financing of armed forces recreation is derived from two types of sources: *appropriated funds,* which are part of the Department of Defense budget and derived through taxes, are generally used to pay for military and Civil Service personnel assigned to recreation, as well as travel, facilities, equipment, and maintenance expenditures; *nonappropriated funds,* representing money derived from military exchange and motion-picture services, are used to pay for non-Civil Service personnel, consultants, part-time enlisted personnel on off-duty assignments, and other miscellaneous expenses such as supplies, materials, portable or fixed equipment, and payment for awards and prizes.

Murphy points out that through the 1960s and early 1970s, appropriated funding sufficed, when augmented by Navy Exchange resale profits, to meet the financial needs of diversified recreation programs.[6] However, in the late 1970s, gradually reduced tax-support funds coupled with shrinking Exchange profits, compelled the Navy to introduce a new policy designed to improve the system's financial operation. This policy, which has been paralleled in other branches of the armed forces, meant that a higher level of fees and charges were expected to yield revenues from many formerly free programs. In addition, emphasis on increasing revenues meant that other aspects of marketing recreation programs had to be stressed. These included more creative planning of products (program elements), systematic pricing procedures, vigorous promotion of programs, and carefully planned placing of programs.

Thus, as in many other types of leisure-service agencies, internal goals concerned with maintaining the viability of the organization may have an important effect on overall program planning.

CAMPUS RECREATION

Another major form of specialized recreation service serving many young men and women in our society today consists of campus recreation—the games and sports, social and creative activities, clubs, fraternities, outings and cultural programs sponsored or conducted under the general supervision of college and university administrators. Such programs have expanded steadily in recent years, with many departments of student life or campus recreation operating huge student unions, physical recreation centers, and similar facilities.

Leisure programs in colleges and universities are carried out under a variety of administrative arrangements. They may be sponsored by campus recreation offices, intramural departments, student unions, residence or dormitory staffs, or other administrative offices. Typically, they are under the overall direction of a Dean of Students or Dean of Student Life, although physical recreation (including intramurals, sports clubs and outdoor recreation activities) frequently is sponsored by a department or school of physical education and recreation, or by the institution's office of athletics.

Funding is usually provided by a campus-wide activities fee, or by the allocation of other funds to support overhead expenses and maintain key staff personnel. Certain activities, such as concerts, trips, special courses, or dances will typically be supported by fees on a self-sufficiency basis.

In some institutions, a student recreation organization is established to hold full responsibility for organizing, financing, and staffing the entire recreation program. For example, at San Diego State University in California, the

> Associated Students Organization sponsors a remarkable range of films, concerts, recreational and athletic programs, legal services and other activities. This multi-million dollar corporation, funded by annual student fees, operates the Aztec Center, the college's student union building. In addition, it runs a highly successful travel service, intramurals and sports clubs, special events, leisure skills classes, lectures, movies, concerts, an open-air theater, a large aquatics center, a campus radio station, a child-care center, a black students council, a general store, a campus information booth, and many other services and activities. Within this spectrum, the bulk of the leisure activities on the San Diego campus are operated directly by the Recreation Activities Board, a unit within the overall Associated Students Organization.[7]

In many cases, other organizations, such as religious societies, may sponsor programs on a college campus. For example, the Christian Association of the University of Pennsylvania recently sponsored an unusual but popular program of classes and activities as part of a Health and Wellness Project:

> *Basic Massage and Healing.* An introductory course in which students will obtain basic competence in Esalen massage and an introduction to shiatsu, reflexology, gestalt therapy, visualization and guided fantasy, postural diagnosis, acupuncture, and oriental diagnosis.
>
> *Psychodrama, Gestalt, and Bodywork.* Methods employed in this course will include the empty chair, visualization and guided fantasy, role-playing and role-reversal, pillowtalk and bodywork.
>
> *Friday Night Meeting: Dances of Universal Peace.* "The Watcher is the prayerful devotee, but the dancer is divine." The dances will bring people together in a social and spiritual context and will also include breath and walking exercises, and singing and reading from a wide range of spiritual teachers.
>
> *Oriental Diagnosis and Massage Therapy.* Students will learn diagnostic theory and methods stemming from three perspectives: acupuncture, massage and Gestalt therapy; and will gain proficiency through in-class and assigned out-of-class exercise.
>
> *Life Drawing.* A direct experience of the body exploring its structure and movement, and the interconnection of its form and providing an opportunity to improve figure drawing skills, while enriching and complementing your bodywork and massage.
>
> *Training Group.* A training group for healing practitioners and people considering a serious commitment to healing will be formed as interest occurs.

Obviously, this program represents a very specialized orientation to recreation programming, much of it derived from the human potential movement, and various encounter-group or other holistic treatment approaches. However, it illustrates the wide range of interests and approaches that may be found in many campus activity programs.

Why have many colleges and universities assumed the responsibility of providing comprehensive recreation programs on their campuses today? There are several reasons, linked both to the traditional roles of higher education, and to the practical needs of such institutions in modern society.

Parental Role.   In the past, colleges and universities were often expected to act *in loco parentis* (in a parental role) in overseeing the lives of young men and women entrusted to their care. This expectation typically applied to maintaining control over the behavior of students with respect to activities such as drinking, drug use, gambling, sexual involvement, and similar behaviors that might involve a risk to health and safety.

In addition to establishing campus-wide rules and restrictio[n]
institutions of higher education recognized the need to provide alternat[e]
of play that might appeal to students and that would encourage them t[o use]
leisure in healthy and constructive ways. Thus, it became accepted practice for
colleges of all types to develop networks of intramural programs and sports
clubs; theater, dance, and music organizations; varied types of social clubs and
special-interest groups; film series and radio stations; and other recreational
programs.

Cocurricular Enrichment.   Often leisure-related activities on campus serve to extend interest and skills that are first experienced as part of the
formal curriculum. For example, journalism majors may sharpen their skills by
working on the campus newspaper or yearbook, while majors in the performing
arts become part of campus productions. In numerous other ways, cocurricular
activities contribute to the academic life of the institution.

Enhancing the Institution's Image.   Campus recreational opportunities contribute positively to the total institutional image, just as outstanding
buildings, an attractive campus, and impressive academic achievements do. At
the same time that many college administrators are struggling with problems of
campus drinking, which has become an increasingly serious challenge at many
institutions, it is helpful to be able to point out positive forms of campus social
life sponsored by the institution.

In an era of diminishing enrollments, having a lively and colorful
panorama of campus life—including recreational traditions, clubs, and events—
is part of the recruitment appeal for many colleges. Similarly, to maintain
enrollment and strengthen a sense of belonging and loyalty to the institution,
numerous cocurricular activities help build satisfaction and a positive campus
image. Finally, in the sense that campus life is just that—life—and should
represent a whole experience, recreational involvements serve to provide a
rounded education, and the continuing opportunity for physical, emotional, and
social development that all college students must have.

Goals of Campus Recreation

Briefly stated, the goals of campus recreation are to provide satisfying
and enriching leisure programs that extend the academic function of the college
or university by offering opportunities for a wide range of experiences linked to
academic subjects. Beyond this, campus recreation serves to keep the institution's spirit and morale high, and to enhance its image in terms of recruitment
appeal to potential students.

CORPORATE RECREATION PROGRAMS

Another specialized form of recreation sponsorship consists of leisure-service activities carried on in business concerns for employees and their families. Formerly called *industrial recreation* because it tended to be found in large manufacturing companies, today such a wide variety of companies provide recreation services—including banks, insurance companies, airlines, high-tech firms, publishing companies, and others—that the broader term *employee recreation* was generally adopted. The professional organization representing this field, the National Industrial Recreation Association, recently changed its name to the National Employee Services and Recreation Association, reflecting concern with a fuller range of employee services than recreation alone.

The term *corporate recreation* has begun to come into use, and has been adopted by a number of major companies. Since it makes clear that all levels of personnel are involved in programs—including management—rather than the lower-level ranks who are typically thought of as *employees,* this term is coming into increased favor, and will be used in this text.

Several examples of successful leisure-service programming in large corporations follow:

Union Carbide.   This company, in South Charleston, West Virginia, runs one of the country's largest hunting and fishing ranges. In other plants, Union Carbide places heavy emphasis on travel, with the Recreation Association sponsoring a travel club that shows travel films, brings in guest speakers, and charters jet flights for vacation group trips.

Lockheed-Georgia Company.   The Recreation Association operates an outdoor recreation facility, Long Hollow, on Lake Sidney Lanier, about fifty-five miles from the company plant. Using land purchased by the company and waterfront access rented from the Army Corps of Engineers, employees have built beaches, docks, floats, roads, launching ramps, campsites, cottages and other facilities which are used heavily throughout the year by various employee clubs.

Minneapolis Honeywell.   During the 1960s this company completed a huge recreation park, including a casting range for fishermen, a ski tow, and a thirty-six-hole golf course.

Nationwide Insurance.   The home office of the Nationwide Insurance Company, in Columbus, Ohio, sponsors an activities association with a staff of professional supervisors hired and paid by the company as part of its personnel department. Activities are planned and carried out by several employees' councils, established in such areas as sports, social activities, community service, and cultural activities.

Today, as indicated earlier, recreation tends to be closely linked with other personnel services, rather than regarded as a separate function. To illustrate, in a recent study of 221 Fortune 500 companies, Taylor and Weiner found that employee services and fringe benefits included a wide range of practices:

> Of the 221 respondents, 98 percent (N = 216) offered some kind of employee service or fringe benefit program for their employees. The most popular programs were tuition refund programs (98 percent, N = 216), pre-retirement education (52 percent, N = 115), adult education (46 percent, N = 102), and discount cards (43 percent, N = 93). Other employee services included various recreation clubs, family stores, season theater passes, annual health examinations, counseling, YMCA memberships, cafeterias, credit unions, trips and tours, etc. . . . Fifty-seven percent (N = 125) of respondents had organized recreation programs for their employees.[8]

In some cases, recreation may be structured as a single element within a larger cluster of employee services. As an example, the Employee Services Department of the Connecticut General Insurance Company, which later merged into the Cigna Corporation, provided or sponsored such facilities as an employees' store, a library, "general stop" (which handled various types of repair and cleaning services), a cafeteria, beauty salon, and barber shop. Other services included a bowling alley and leagues, transportation assistance through commuter buses serving the Hartford metropolitan area, varied sports facilities, a childcare program, and varied vending services and bill-paying arrangements.

Patterns of Sponsorship

Since companies vary so greatly in their policies, no single pattern of sponsorship may be identified in corporate recreation programs. Several alternative arrangements are found:

1. The company takes complete responsibility for an organized recreation program, providing facilities and leadership, and maintaining control of the operation. There may be a fee system for participation, and there may be an advisory council of employees.
2. Facilities, or a capital outlay for developing areas and facilities, are provided by the employer. Management and employees, however, share responsibility for operating the program, usually with a fee system for participation and an employee's council to determine policy.
3. As a variant of the above, the employer may provide the facilities, ranging from clubrooms to gymnasiums or ballfields, but the employees are in total charge of the program.
4. In some companies, an independent employees' association has complete responsibility for the recreation program and uses facilities that it has developed *away* from the plant.
5. When a union operates a program of employee recreation, it may make use of plant facilities, but, more commonly, will use union-

owned buildings, campsites, or other facilities for the program. In some cases, the sponsoring agency may be a union local that includes membership from several companies operating in the same field.

6. The program may involve cooperation between the company and the surrounding community or adjacent municipality. In some cases, under contractual agreement, the recreation program may make use of public facilities but provide its own leadership. In others, the company may provide *all* public recreation within the area.

A common arrangement is to have recreation participation based on voluntary employee membership in an employee club, association, or athletic association. When the company itself takes the responsibility for the program, it usually is made a function of an industrial relations or personnel relations division.

Goals of Corporate Recreation

There are several reasons that so many large companies have sponsored or assisted in the development of corporate recreation programs, including the following.

Recruitment Appeal.   It is known that potential employees today desire cultural and recreational opportunities when they consider joining a new firm, both for themselves and their families. Thus, an attractive employee recreation program has significant recruitment appeal. As an example, a recent advertisement seeking to recruit skilled machinists for a major airplane manufacturing concern stressed the "livability" of the plant's environment, near Seattle, Washington:

> Enjoy the relaxed life-styles and the unspoiled beauty of the Pacific Northwest in the "Nation's Most Liveable City." Discover skiing just 90 minutes from work. Hike in abundant forests, catch a salmon or set sail for scenic islands over the weekend. Swim or water ski in nearby lakes.[9]

Employer-Employee Relations.   Traditionally, many of the company-sponsored recreation programs that dated from an earlier period when there was considerable friction between management and labor had as a major purpose the establishment of harmonious relations within the plant.

Even today, in a period of comparative labor peace, corporate recreation programs serve to strengthen the loyalty and improve the morale of workers. In this sense, it is comparable to employee councils, profit-sharing, flex-time, health benefits, retirement plans, and similar incentive-building policies.

Promoting Esprit de Corps. As in the military, many business leaders regard company recreation programs as a useful means of establishing a sense of belonging and unity within the organization. For example, Ken Leonard, Corporate Manager of Recreation for the National Semiconductor Corporation in Northern California states:

> National Semiconductor has grown from a small company to a large one in a relatively short time. A recreation program will foster communication to create and maintain a small company atmosphere. It will improve interpersonal relationships by allowing people at all levels and from different cultural backgrounds to get together on an informal basis. It will enable employees to exercise and release tension whether it be in a physical or emotional way to achieve a healthy attitude and a better work environment. The management is concerned with the quality of life and is striving to improve that which we have.[10]

Employee Efficiency and Productivity. It is believed that recreation within an industrial concern—just as in a community—promotes physical and emotional well-being. Absenteeism is a major concern of American business today. Each day, an estimated 3,500,000 employees fail to show up for work because of "illness," representing a direct cost to U.S. industry of $13.6 billion a year in wages, salaries, and benefits, with many other indirect costs. Leading authorities in industrial management are convinced that major factors in absenteeism are boredom and emotional illness; studies have recognized the value of recreation programs in reducing absenteeism of this type.

Particularly with the growing awareness of problems related to stress and employee burnout, employers are concerned with providing services that will help reduce tensions and provide work satisfactions, as well as specific group programs that will build positive employee morale and on-the-job performance.

Closely linked to this is the function of improving employee health through physical fitness programming. Each year, a growing number of large companies are building elaborate exercise facilities, pools, jogging tracks, and similar facilities designed to promote cardiovascular fitness and counteract the stresses and pressures that so often affect management personnel in particular. Thus, the goals of corporate recreation are varied, and include elements drawn from several of the models presented in Chapter 4 of this text.

THERAPEUTIC RECREATION SERVICE

The final type of leisure-service agency to be described here is a form of specialized programming rather than a type of administrative sponsorship.

Therapeutic recreation service, as a distinctive area of professional practice, is concerned with programs designed to meet the needs of the mentally and physically disabled, the dependent aging, the socially deviant, and other special populations in modern society.

Although this field of service has been known in the past under varied titles (including "hospital recreation," "recreation for the ill and handicapped," or "recreation for special populations"), today it is customarily referred to as *therapeutic recreation service.*

In recent years, interest in this form of leisure service has grown rapidly. Many specialized curricula provide professional preparation in it, and it is represented by a strong national organization, the National Therapeutic Recreation Society, as well as many active state or regional associations.

Expansion of Service Focus.   During the earlier decades of this century when recreation was provided as a special service for the ill and disabled, it tended to be done chiefly in hospitals or other institutional settings, such as psychiatric hospitals or special homes or schools for the mentally retarded. Today, therapeutic recreation programs may appear in many different types of settings:

> Hospitals under varied sponsorship (Veterans Administration, military, public health, state, county, municipal, voluntary and proprietary), dealing with a variety of patient populations (general, chronic disease, psychiatric, pediatric, and others)
> Schools or residential centers for those with specific physical disability (including the blind, deaf, orthopedically disabled, or neurologically involved), or those with mental deficiencies or retardation
> Penal institutions for adult criminals, or custodial institutions or special schools, reformatories, remand centers, or camps for youth who are socially maladjusted or committed because of delinquent acts
> After-care centers for discharged mental patients or those who are not hospitalized, but are receiving day clinic services; institutions serving drug addicts under treatment; or other centers serving those who require continuing special services in the form of counseling, training, psychotherapy, and sheltered or guided social experiences
> Nursing homes, extended care or health-related facilities, chiefly for geriatric patients who either require intensive nursing and medical care, or who are unable to live independently in the community

In addition to providing recreation services in such settings, there has also been a marked expansion of programs serving special populations living in the community itself. Several factors gave rise to this development, including the following: (1) fuller awareness of the number of ill and disabled in society, and of their needs and potentialities; (2) changing attitudes toward disability, and acceptance of greater and more humane responsibilities toward the disabled;

(3) government leadership, through both legislation and court decisions, in affirming the rights of the disabled, and providing programs for them; and (4) the "deinstitutionalization" movement, which sought to prevent institutionalization for the disabled, linked to a powerful thrust toward "mainstreaming" them in integrated programs with the nondisabled.

Recreation and the Needs of Disabled Persons

What are the important needs of disabled persons that are met by recreation programs and services? In the early stages of the therapeutic recreation movement, these tended to be thought of primarily as treatment needs, and the question asked would have been How does recreation contribute to the treatment of illness or the restoration of function?

Basically, the aim of therapeutic recreation, like that of the overall rehabilitation process, was conceptualized as helping the ill, disabled, aged, or retarded individual achieve the fullest physical, mental, social, psychological, and economic life possible within the limits of his or her illness or disability. Specially designed recreation programs were intended to promote broad goals of adjustment and socialization that would return a happier, more productive, and better adjusted human being to community living or, short of this, to help him or her live as fully as possible in some type of sheltered environment.

Attempts to define the field of therapeutic recreation service were made difficult by the growing number of community-based programs which served disabled persons living at home, such as local chapters of organizations serving the mentally retarded, or wheelchair sports or Special Olympics programs. Should programs for such clients be regarded as therapy?

NTRS 1982 Philosophy Statement

In an effort to resolve the difficulties imposed by these varied images and functions of therapeutic recreation service, the National Therapeutic Recreation Society (NTRS) undertook a process of redefining the field. This resulted in the Statement of Philosophy of Therapeutic Recreation Service, which was formally published in 1982.

The statement identifies three services that should be offered as part of a comprehensive approach to therapeutic recreation: *therapy, leisure education,* and *recreational participation*. It held that therapeutic recreation specialists should be prepared:

> to provide all three services. The decision as to where and when each of the services would be provided would be based on the assessment of client need. Different individuals have a variety of different needs related to leisure utilization. For some clients, improvement of a functional behavior or problem

(physical, mental, social or emotional) is a necessary prerequisite to meaningful leisure experiences. For others, acquiring leisure skills, knowledge, and ability is a priority need. For others, special recreation participation opportunities are necessary, based on place of residence or because assistance or adapted activities are required.[11]

All three services should be viewed as interdependent parts within a total range of services, rather than separate entities. Often they may be seen as part of a continuum of service in which given clients and patients are initially provided with needed therapeutic services, and gradually move, with the help of leisure education, toward more independent recreational involvement.

Goals of Therapeutic Recreation

Today, five major types of populations may be identified as recipients of therapeutic recreation service, in both institutional and community settings. These include: (1) the mentally ill; (2) the mentally retarded; (3) the physically disabled; (4) the dependent aging; and (5) socially deviant individuals. Within each group, a specific set of goals of therapeutic recreation may be defined— although these too may vary somewhat according to the philosophy of the agency offering the service, or the specific needs of the group being served.

Generic Goals in Treatment and Community Settings

The following tend to be the most important generic goals in that they represent key concerns for all populations and in all settings:

1. To provide constructive, enjoyable and creative leisure activities—a general need for persons of all ages and backgrounds.
2. To improve morale and a sense of well-being and interest in life, as opposed to depression, disinterest, or withdrawal.
3. To help individuals come to grips with their disabilities and build positively on their existing strengths and capabilities.
4. To help individuals gain security in being with others and develop healthy, outgoing social relationships and a feeling of group acceptance.
5. To emphasize positive self-concepts and feelings of individual worth, through successful participation in activity.
6. To help individuals gain both skills and attitudes that will assist them in using their leisure positively and constructively as opposed to negatively and pathologically.
7. To help hospitalized patients build bridges for the successful return to community life, or to help those clients who may be living in the community to function more independently.
8. To contribute a sense of community and cooperation in institutions or other community residential settings and to promote an atmosphere which encourages progress toward recovery.[12]

Goals of Therapeutic Recreation with Specific Populations

Stated in terms of the specific needs of different types of disabled populations, the following goals may be identified:

1. For psychiatric patients, to provide a positive means of relating to others constructively, coming to grips with reality, expressing aggression or hostility harmlessly and gaining leisure interests that will contribute to their mental health.
2. For the mentally retarded, to promote physical, social and intellectual functioning, to assist in developing social independence, and to promote confidence and the ability to function in the community or at work.
3. For the physically disabled, to provide new skills and interests that compensate for lost functions or abilities, to provide practice in self-care skills and to assist in reintegration in community recreation programs.
4. For the socially maladjusted, to assist in developing effective social relations with others, to use leisure constructively, to learn to accept the rules and values of society, and to encourage values of good sportsmanship and fair play.
5. For aged persons, to provide creative satisfactions, meaningful social involvement and the opportunity to be of community service.[13]

In addition to having specialized goals based on serving different kinds of populations, the nature of the facility may also affect program goals, objectives, and policies. In the Clinical Center of the National Institutes of Health, a five-hundred-bed research hospital in Bethesda, Maryland, for example, all therapeutic recreation activities are influenced by the special mission of the institution, which is devoted to carrying on biomedical research. Patients constitute an extremely diverse population of all ages and from many countries; each one is on a research protocol. Often special adaptations are required to serve individuals. As a single example:

> Any planned activity must accommodate intravenous trolleys, sweat studies, Laminar Air Flow units, meticulously controlled diets, and many other appurtenances of medical research. The Laminar Air Flow units, for example, present special problems to the therapeutic recreation specialist. Patients are isolated in these rooms because they must live in a sterile environment. Since everything that goes into the unit must be sterile, the recreator not only designs appropriate activities for the patient, but must find out if the materials—crafts, games, books, musical instruments—*can* be sterilized, and then make sure that these materials *are* sterilized.[14]

Summing up this discussion of therapeutic recreation, it is apparent that within each category of disability, and within many different types of treatment or program service settings, recreation may be used to achieve certain important goals related either to treatment of rehabilitation of the individual, or to helping him or her achieve a fuller and happier life.

Having concluded this analysis of several major types of organized recreation service, we now move to an examination of how goals, objectives, and policies are formulated and applied.

DEVELOPING GOALS STATEMENTS

Chapter 4 presents philosophical statements drawn from the specialized areas of public recreation and parks, voluntary agencies, armed forces, and therapeutic recreation.

How are such statements developed? Depending on the structure of the agency itself, there may be several possible approaches.

First, many leisure-service programs are conducted under the overall guidance or direction of a central board or policy-making authority. For example, the Young Women's Christian Association, as shown earlier, operates under the leadership of a National Board which periodically reviews and restates its national priorities. Similarly, the Catholic church, or such nonsectarian organizations as the Boy and Girl Scouts or 4-H Clubs, typically issue national goals statements and guidelines for program development from time to time.

In some cases, as in armed forces recreation, central goals and policies may be established to provide the direction for leisure-service programming. However, if a particular organization is not part of such a system, and operates in an autonomous way, it must develop its own goals statements.

For example, the newly hired director of an employee recreation program in a large manufacturing concern may discover that his or her predecessor has never attempted to formulate a specific statement of goals for the program. In this case, he or she may draw on a number of sources to develop a specific statement of philosophy, goals, and objectives. These sources may include: (1) similar statements found in the general recreation literature or in publications dealing with corporate/employee recreation and related services; (2) philosophical or "mission" statements published by appropriate professional societies; or (3) statements or goals that have been issued by other companies in the same field or within the region. To these, he or she should add goals statements that reflect the particular needs or characteristics of his or her own organization—as expressed by company administrators or executive officers, members of recreation advisory groups, or rank-and-file program participants.

All of these sources should yield a number of basic ideas that can be welded into clear, expressive statements of purpose, with realistic and realizable outcomes. As indicated at the outset of this chapter, and as shown in the examples that have been cited, they should be rather general in nature and should clearly reflect the philosophy of the organization and the views of its key administrative officers.

This goals statement may then be submitted in draft form for review by administrators, personnel officers, and members of the employee group. Based on their comments and suggestions, it should then be revised as necessary and placed in final form. It then provides the basis for developing more detailed and specific program objectives which delineate the action-oriented measurable outcomes that the director will seek to achieve.

Policy Development

Along with the development of goals and objectives, it is essential to develop policies that are based on these statements, but which also provide concise guidelines or rules for the operation of programs. Policies may be used to determine appropriate priorities for different kinds of recreation program activities, or to decide when and how they are to be offered. Policies may relate to the assignment of leadership, the recruitment of volunteers, the use of facilities, the setting of fees and charges for program participation, or many similar concerns.

To illustrate the nature of policies, several examples of policy statements of different types of recreation agencies and membership organizations are provided.

Girl Scouts of the U.S.A.   This organization has certain membership and governance policies which apply to all councils, troops and camps in the nationwide Girl Scout movement. These include:

> *Admission to Troops.* A girl who meets or can meet membership requirements shall not be denied admission to a troop because of race, creed, nationality, or socio-economic factors.
>
> *Place of Religion in the Girl Scout Program.* Girls are encouraged and helped through the Girl Scout program to become better members of their own religious group, but every Girl Scout group must recognize that religious instruction is the responsibility of parents and religious leaders.
>
> *Political and Legislative Activity.* Girl Scouts of the U.S.A. and any council or other organization holding a Girl Scouts of the U.S.A. credential may not, nor may they authorize anyone on their behalf to, participate or intervene directly or indirectly in any political campaign on behalf of or in opposition to any candidate for public office; or participate in any legislative activity or function which contravenes the laws governing tax exempt organizations.
>
> *Permissions for Commercial Endorsements.* Permission to endorse commercial products or services or to give endorsement of such by implication must be obtained from Girl Scouts of the U.S.A. and shall be granted only when such endorsement is in keeping with Girl Scout principles and activities.[15]

Nassau County, New York, Department of Recreation and Parks.   This public agency's administrative directive handbook provides a variety of operational policies specifying the exact procedures that must be followed within a wide variety of areas of responsibility. Examples include:

> *Responsibility for Inspections.* It is the responsibility of all levels of administration to conduct regular inspections to ascertain the level of efficiency of this organization, and its ability to perform its assigned mission. All inspections which are made by personnel who are not indigenous to a park administration will be accompanied by the Facility Supervisor or his designee, whenever possible.
>
> At the conclusion of informal inspections, a memorandum should be for-

warded to the Facility Supervisor concerned, listing any discrepancies or exemplary items noted. Copies of this memorandum are to be sent to the appropriate Unit Supervisor and Division Head. It is important that suggestions be given, through constructive criticism, as to how any noted discrepancies should be corrected.

Receipts. A receipt is required for each individual petty cash expenditure. Any material purchased requires a vendor's receipt, indicating the vendor's name, the total expenditure, and a description of the commodity. Expenditures for services require receipts (handwritten, if necessary). If toll charges for a County vehicle are paid with petty cash, a receipt must be secured and the license or vehicle number must appear on the receipt.

Responsibility for Training. Division Heads are responsible for providing the American Red Cross Standard First-Aid Course to members of their staff who have occasion to be in direct contact with the public in the normal course of their responsibilities. It is advisable that shop and crew foremen, maintenance mechanics, etc., who, although they may not come in direct contact with the public, should be given first-aid training in case of accidents to their staff.

A program to keep first-aid certification current will also be established within each Division. First-aid training is to be provided at the earliest possible time after appointment of new personnel. Periodical refresher courses will be established; primarily before the commencement of peak operating seasons.

Releasing Personnel from Duty Due to Inclement Weather. In cases of inclement weather where part-time and/or seasonal personnel are involved, Facility Supervisors may offer assignments other than the normal duties of the personnel concerned. (Such as laborer assignments in the case of lifeguards, etc.) If these personnel do not desire to accept assignments of this nature, they may so indicate to their supervisor and be allowed to sign out for the period of time on a non-pay basis and without prejudice.[16]

Policies of this type might also be referred to as administrative directives, in that they provide very concise statements of practices that must be observed throughout the agency's administrative operation. Several such directives are usually clustered together in given functional areas, such as supervisory procedures, money-handling, or safety and accident prevention.

Napa, California, State Hospital.   A final illustration may be taken from the Rehabilitation Therapies Manual of the Napa State Hospital in California. This shows how *policies* and *procedures* may be seen as comparable to *goals* and *objectives;* procedures are used to spell out and implement policies, just as objectives are used to translate goals into action. For example, a policy directive dealing with Off-Grounds Field Trips is as follows:

Policy. Napa State Hospital will provide patients/residents with the opportunity of leaving the hospital grounds on social, recreational and/or educational field trips as often as clinically desirable and economically feasible.[17]

Several sets of procedures, dealing with different aspects of field trips, then serve to spell this policy out in concrete terms, just as objectives serve to specify goals in narrow, measurable units. One set of procedures follows:

Planning and Preparation

1. The coordinator of the trip will orient all other employee participants as to plans, responsibilities, geographical consideration, hazards, resources, and accountabilities in advance.
2. Procedures for handling and storing medications are to be explained to the escorts by responsible personnel prior to the trip.
3. Staff should know which patient/resident each is responsible for at all times.
4. All staff should know how to contact the medical and law enforcement agencies nearest the outing site before leaving the hospital grounds.
5. Before leaving on Class II or III trips, notify hospital telephone operator of trip destination and the name of the trip coordinator.
6. An emergency medical first aid kit shall be taken on all outings other than Class I trips.
7. Adequate plans for food and equipment shall be carried on all Class II and III trips (see instructions and forms—Nursing Manual and Food Manual).
8. On arrival at the outing site, the coordinator shall again orient staff as to boundaries, individual patient/resident supervision and potential hazards.
9. Outings near water hazards (as determined by the Program Director), require one staff member trained in life-saving techniques and holding a current Red Cross Life Saving Certificate. If swimming is planned, this member is not to be held responsible for escorting, (during the swimming time) but is to devote himself only to lifeguard duties.
10. On campouts, 24 hour watch is required.[18]

Many other recreation agencies develop handbooks or manuals which outline policies and procedures governing program planning and implementation. Typically, such manuals begin with statements of goals and overall missions, and then outline program elements, administrative structures, and policies that provide a structure for the day-by-day operation of the program.

NOTES

[1]Reynold Carlson, Janet MacLean, Theodore Deppe, and James Peterson, *Recreation and Leisure: The Changing Scene* (Belmont, Calif.: Wadsworth, 1979), p. 163.
[2]Carlson et al, p. 194.
[3]Walter H. Baumgardner, "The 'Perimeter'—Will Military and Civilian Programs Continue to Cooperate?" *Parks and Recreation* (June 1983): 31.
[4]Lt.Jg. Carol Couvaris, USNA, "Recreation for 30,000 Sailors," *Recreation Management* (November 1975): 10–13.
[5]*Morale, Welfare and Recreation Program Overview* (Washington, D.C.: Office of Assistant Secretary of Defense, March 1982), p. 5.
[6]Andrew F. Murphy, Jr., "Military Recreation Takes on Marketing," *Parks and Recreation* (November 1980): 28–29.
[7]See *Break Away,* Recreational Guide to San Diego State University, San Diego, Calif., Spring 1979.

[8]Frances W. Taylor and Andrew I. Weiner, "The Status of Recreation and Fitness in Fortune 500 Companies," Research Presentation, NRPA Congress, Minneapolis, 1981.

[9]Personnel Advertisement of Boeing Corp., in *Philadelphia Inquirer* (12 March 1978): 20–D.

[10]See *National Semiconductor: Inter National News,* Santa Clara, Calif. (May 1979): 2.

[11]*Philosophical Position Statement* (Alexandria, Va.: National Therapeutic Recreation Society, 1982).

[12]Richard Kraus, *Therapeutic Recreation Service: Principles and Practices* (Philadelphia: Saunders College Publishing, 1983), p. 74.

[13]Kraus, pp. 74–75.

[14]*Therapeutic Recreation Program of the Clinical Center, NIH* (Bethesda, Md.: U.S. Public Health Service, n.d.), p. 7.

[15]*Leader's Digest of Official Documents, Policies and Procedures* (New York, N.Y.: Girl Scouts of U.S.A., 1973), p. 8–10.

[16]*Administrative Handbook of Nassau County Department of Recreation and Parks* (Eisenhower Park, Nassau County, N.Y.: n.d.).

[17]*Rehabilitation Therapies Manual* (Napa, Calif.: Napa State Hospital, September 1981, Policy No. 764).

[18]*Rehabilitation Therapies Manual.*

STUDENT PROJECT

Chapter 6 describes eight major types of leisure-service agencies. To get a fuller picture of each type of agency, have the class divide into eight smaller groups, with at least two or three students in each group. Have each group identify, make contact with, and visit one such agency, examine its program, interview staff members, and gather relevant information on its goals, objectives, policies and administrative structure. Have groups report to the class, emphasizing the purposes, population served, and programs of each agency studied.

SUGGESTED READINGS

Reynold Carlson, Janet MacLean, Theodore Deppe and James Peterson, *Recreation and Leisure: The Changing Scene* (Belmont, Calif.: Wadsworth, 1979), Chapters 4–10.

Scout Gunn and Carol Peterson, *Therapeutic Recreation Program Design: Principles and Procedures* (Englewood Cliffs, N.J.: Prentice-Hall, 1978), Chapters 8 and 9.

Richard Kraus, Gaylene Carpenter and Barbara Bates, *Recreation Leadership and Supervision: Guidelines for Professional Development* (Philadelphia: Saunders College Publishing, 1981), Chapters 8 and 9.

Ruth V. Russell, *Planning Programs in Recreation* (St. Louis: C. V. Mosby, 1982), Chapter 4.

CHAPTER 7

Recreation Program Elements: Activities and Services

The Harcourt Corporation's Recreation Council members sat around a long table in the employee lounge, reviewing suggestions for the company's recreation programs.

"Well," said Alice Greenberg, "I think we've got some very good ideas here. The co-ed volleyball league is bound to be successful, and the theater ticket discount program sounds excellent. Based on past performance, the Glee Club tour should be a highlight. But what about this teenager job clinic?"

"That's my suggestion," said Bill Washington. "But I talked about it with a number of other people, and they like it."

"What would it be?"

"Well, we would identify a whole bunch of jobs that teenagers who are members of families of Harcourt employees can do. Jobs like house cleaning or lawn maintenance, baby-sitting, messenger service, snow removal, and so on. Then we'd run some simple clinics on these skills and set it up for those who take the clinics as a job placement service. We'd advertise their availability. I bet a lot of youngsters could get good part-time jobs through this."

"But I thought we were supposed to be serving the company employees with recreation," objected Alice mildly. "Should we be running this kind of operation?"

"Read the bylaws of our organization," said Bill. "They're pretty broad. And I know this is a service that people would appreciate. Let's do it!"

We now move to the fourth step in the program-planning process by examining the full range of leisure pursuits and services that are sponsored by various types of recreation agencies today. In so doing, the following elements will be considered: (1) the major types of recreation activities that may be provided; (2) the different formats that activities may take; (3) the development of special facilities which house related clusters of leisure activities; and (4) the presentation of other program services, such as the coordination of other community-based programs or leisure education functions.

Recreation program textbooks customarily provide an overview of a number of important categories or classifications of leisure activities, giving numerous examples of each type. This text will also offer a number of specific suggestions as to the particular values or administrative advantages found within each category of activity, as far as planning recreation programs is concerned. It should be noted that no effort is made to document these values; instead, the chapter merely presents widely held views regarding their worth. A number of studies of the actual outcomes and benefits of recreation participation are summarized in Chapter 12.

This text does not seek to be an encyclopedia of recreational activities, nor does it give detailed descriptions of different games, songs, dances, or nature projects. These may be found in other readily available sources that are listed in the bibliography, or in this book's companion volume, *Recreation Leadership Today*.

The major types of recreation program activities that will be described in this chapter include the following: (1) active sports, games, and physical fitness activities; (2) outdoor recreation activities that are normally carried on in a natural environment; (3) swimming and other forms of aquatic activity; (4) arts and crafts, and related hobbies; (5) performing arts, such as music, drama, and dance; (6) social recreation, including clubs, parties, and other special events; (7) activities based on communications skills, such as discussion groups, writing workshops, or activities involving film, television, or radio; (8) other activities related to self-improvement or developing useful coping skills or self-enrichment activities; and (9) other types of social-service functions, such as health-related, counseling, or referral services.

ACTIVE SPORTS, GAMES, AND FITNESS ACTIVITIES

Without question, this category represents a major form of program activity in almost every type of leisure-service agency. Organized sports represent a major interest of people young and old in every nation of the world, and it has been estimated that they represent about two thirds of *all* participation in public recreation programs.

Examples of Active Sports, Games and Fitness Activities

Active sports are usually classified in one of two ways: team sports, and individual or dual sports. Examples include:

Team Sports

Baseball	Basketball
Football	Hockey
Lacrosse	Soccer
Volleyball	Softball

In addition to these major team sports, there are many popular variations, such as touch or flag football; field, floor, or street hockey; or slow-pitch softball.

Individual or Dual Sports

Archery	Badminton
Bowling	Boxing
Fencing	Golf
Horseshoes	Handball
Judo	Karate
Platform Tennis	Racquetball
Shuffleboard	Table Tennis
Tennis	Track and Field

While these activities customarily involve competition of one player against another, or two players against two players, as in tennis or badminton doubles, they may also be played as team contests, with one boxing team competing against another, on different weight levels.

Active games include vigorous playground contests within such categories as kickball, tag, dodgeball, and relay or lead-up team games that involve modified forms of the major team sports.

Fitness activities might conceivably include any active sport or outdoor pastime, but usually are regarded as including the following: jogging or running as a conditioning exercise; gymnastics; varied forms of aerobic exercise, such as aerobic dancing, Jazzercise, or use of the trampoline; swimming laps; weight training or use of exercise machines; and racquet sports such as handball or racquetball.

Values and Administrative Advantages

Active sports, games, and fitness activities have numerous values and administrative advantages as program activities in recreational settings. First, they are extremely popular; even those who do not take part regularly in such activities often follow them as fans, and watch sports events regularly in person and on television.

Because they are highly competitive, sports are said to represent significant societal values, and to be an important means of training children and youth in such areas as effective team play, self-discipline, good sportsmanship, acceptance of rules, and commitment to group tasks and goals. This represents a controversial issue in that many argue that we have overstressed the goals of winning in sports and have given far too much attention to the highly skilled player at the expense of the ordinary or less-skilled participant. Others argue that cooperation should also be stressed in sports play, and that noncompetitive games, such as those used in New Games program, should be stressed.

When properly presented, sports can satisfy varying levels of interest and ability, and can be used to involve a wide range of participants. Today girls and women actively engage in many forms of sports, active games, and fitness activities. Similarly, older persons who might never have taken part in strenuous activities in past years today are becoming increasingly involved. Finally, sports can effectively be used with handicapped persons, including the blind, deaf, orthopedically or neurologically impaired, and similar populations.

From an administrative point of view, sports are an excellent activity in that they may be used with small groups or large, and are capable of maintaining interest over a sustained period of time. They offer exciting spectator activity for nonparticipants, easily obtain colorful publicity, and represent a key link between recreation and park management functions (since so many sports use outdoor play facilities). In addition, sports are an excellent means of developing community involvement; parents' clubs or volunteer sports associations help coach and manage teams, raise necessary funds, maintain facilities, and operate many programs with a minimum of paid professional leadership.

More than most other types of activities, sports can also be used to develop contacts and working relationships among different groups. For example, in a large city teams may compete in a local center, a district or neighborhood, and on a city-wide competitive level. Different Boys' or Girls' Clubs may compete with each other, or different Catholic Youth Organization centers may take part jointly in track meets, gymnastic events, or numerous other joint programs.

Active games are useful as developmental activities in that they promote strength, speed, agility, endurance, team-play, and other desirable physical and mental attributes. They are useful lead-up activities for team sports, but, probably most importantly, they are fun to play and often are extremely popular activities on playgrounds or school yards, in camps, or other recreation settings.

Sports are often thought of as a major component of public recreation and park department programs. However, they also are popular elements in many youth-serving and adult voluntary agencies, in campus recreation programs, and in corporate/employee recreation actvities. They may also be widely found in programs serving the handicapped, such as Special Olympics and wheelchair sports competitions.

OUTDOOR RECREATION ACTIVITIES

Outdoor recreation involves activities that are carried on outdoors and that relate in some way to the natural environment. To illustrate, basketball played on an outdoor court would not normally be thought of as an outdoor recreation activity, since it might just as readily be played indoors, and does not depend on the natural environment in any way. In contrast, fishing would normally be regarded as an outdoor recreation activity because it is heavily dependent on the natural setting for much of its appeal and character.

Examples of Outdoor Recreation Activities

Examples of outdoor recreation activities include any of the following:

Backpacking	Bird walks
Camping	Coasting or Tobogganing
Gardening	Hiking
Hunting	Ice boating
Ice skating	Kite flying
Mountaineering or rock climbing	Nature study or nature projects Orienteering
Outdoor cooking	Skiing (downhill or cross-country)
Picknicking	Snow tracking
Snowshoeing	Target shooting (rifle or pistol)
Surfing	Trap-shooting (shot gun)

Other activities might include those that make use of such off-road vehicles as snowmobiles, dune buggies, motorcycles, gliders, or such high-risk pursuits as hang gliding, free-fall parachuting, or small plane piloting. Scuba diving, waterskiing, sailing, and canoeing might also be considered forms of outdoor recreation, but are classified here under the heading of aquatic activities. Bicycling and horseback riding in its various forms, ranging from trail riding to jumping or dressage, are also forms of outdoor recreation.

Values and Administrative Advantages

Like sports, outdoor recreation activities are also immensely popular; indeed, many of them might well be classified *as* sports since they represent competitive events, such as skiing, sailing, target shooting, or riding. However, they are also commonly enjoyed simply as pastimes without the element of competition. Beyond this, they provide exposure to the outdoors, and bring participants in contact with woods, fields, streams, and the great beauty of nature. They offer a tremendous range of experiences, including the quiet discovery of nature and its living creatures, or the excitement and daring of high-risk activities.

They also have great appeal because they may be carried on by people of all ages, ranging from a tiny infant on a camping trip to elderly participants who enjoy quiet nature hobbies. Today, more and more handicapped persons are being involved in outdoor recreation—even in such relatively difficult experiences as skiing. Such activities may be approached on very simple levels, or as extremely advanced projects. Most outdoor recreation interests can therefore represent lifetime interests, whereas many competitive sports today tend to be engaged in primarily by younger persons.

Ideally, all outdoor pursuits should be presented to build respect for the environment, and to avoid pollution or other forms of ecological harm. Many of the activities that formerly were taken for granted in camping and backpacking programs, such as cooking with fire, collecting wild specimens, or lashing camp equipment or tools, are no longer appropriate except in quite wild surroundings, and even then with great care and awareness of environmental values.

Swimming and Other Aquatic Activities

Obviously swimming and other water-based activities might either be classified as sport—which they are—or as outdoor recreation activities since they meet the criteria of either type of recreational pursuit.

They are presented here as separate forms of activity chiefly because they are such a popular area of leisure involvement with many different pursuits all linked by the dependence on the aquatic setting, and also because they are often set aside as a separate administrative area in camping programs or other recreational agencies.

Examples of Aquatic Activities

Examples of aquatic activities include the following:

Boating (canoeing, power-
    boating, rowing, and
    sailing)
Fishing
Swimming for the
    handicapped
Skin and scuba diving
Synchronized swimming

Water games
Diving
Life-saving classes
Water safety classes
Swimming and bathing
Surfing
Water polo
Water skiing

Values and Administrative Advantages

Swimming and related water-based activities are clearly among the most popular activities of Americans and Canadians young and old, partly because they involve sunbathing, family outings, and other pleasurable uses of leisure. However, swimming is also an outstanding form of exercise that lends itself to other specialized forms of play, such as scuba diving or surfing.

As Chapter 8 will show, aquatic activities may be organized in many different kinds of formats to serve different population groups. Obviously, they require very careful supervision and safety measures, because of the risk of drowning. However, with adequate supervision, swimming should be a thoroughly safe activity that appeals to all age groups and many special populations as well. Swimming may also be provided in many different settings, ranging from natural rivers, lakes or beaches, to indoor or outdoor pools. It may be completely relaxed and noncompetitive, or may lend itself to races or large-scale swimming meets as well.

ARTS, CRAFTS, AND RELATED HOBBIES

These represent a major type of recreation program activity, including so-called fine arts activities as well as craft pursuits. Many hobbies also involve construction or building projects that have a strong element of craft about them.

Examples of Arts and Crafts

Fine arts activities are usually considered to be creative pursuits that are intended to yield not useful products, but decorative objects that result from emphasizing aesthetic experience and personal expression. They include:

Drawing and Sketching
Sculpture (clay, metal, stone or wood)
Graphics (includes various types of print-making, such as lithography, etching, silk-screen or wood-block printing)
Oil Painting
Watercolor Painting

Craft projects may also involve a high degree of skill and personal expressiveness, and well as attractive designs, colors, and textures. Today they are often viewed as comparable to so-called fine arts activities, as far as aesthetic worth is concerned:

Basket making	Beadwork
Carving (wood, soap, bone, or plastic foam)	Ceramics or ceramic sculpture
	Jewelry
Furniture refinishing	Macrame
Leather working	Origami
Metalcraft	Printing and book making
Photography	Calligraphy
Weaving	Woodworking

Many craft-like activities may also include varied forms of hobbies that involve construction, such as making model planes, cars, or trains, or various science hobbies that involve making displays or carrying on experiments. Hobbies also include collections of all types (autographs, coins, dolls, matchbooks, stamps, and numerous other kinds of objects), and other pursuits that may require artistic or craftlike presentations.

Values and Administrative Advantages

Arts and crafts are extremely useful activities for organized recreation programs, in that they have a wide range of appeal, and may be presented on several levels, including instruction, special-interest groups, and exhibitions. Many individuals who are not interested in sports or vigorous outdoor pastimes are able to take part in arts and crafts; they are particularly appropriate for working with handicapped populations. Although some crafts may require expensive or elaborate equipment, such as kilns, presses, or weaving looms, others may be carried out with a minimum of special tools or equipment.

Another important advantage of arts and crafts is that they may appeal to beginners on the simplest level of participation, with such simple activities as fingerpainting, drawing with crayons, or modeling with clay—or on extremely advanced levels of creative expression. Some recreation and park departments or voluntary agencies maintain entire art centers with ceramics shops or sculpture and painting studios and employ highly qualified professional craftsmen, craftswomen, or artists as instructors.

Although people often think of arts and crafts as a "one-shot" activity, they also provide the opportunity for continuing growth and more advanced involvement. For example, one might take a macrame class and make a key chain. Later, one might take an advanced class and learn additional knots; in time, the same individual might join a special interest club, or even become an instructor in the activity.

In terms of their unique values as forms of leisure activity, arts and crafts involve personal creative growth and aesthetic appreciation. They may result in products that can be displayed in shows or exhibits, thus contributing to the participants' sense of satisfaction and accomplishment, or to the community's awareness and appreciation of the agency's program. They are usually noncompetitive and lend themselves to programming in special-interest groups that often have a highly cooperative and friendly social atmosphere. They may even create products that can be sold at art fairs, bazaars, or auctions as fund-raising activities to support agency programs.

Hobbies are somewhat more specialized as a form of recreation programming. They do not usually involve regular instruction, but may provide the basis for hobby club meetings, "swap" sessions, displays, and exhibitions. Often, hobbies may be explored on neighborhood playgrounds, with different adult or youth hobbyists coming to show their own interests, and ending with hobby fairs or shows.

PERFORMING ARTS: MUSIC, DRAMA, AND DANCE

The performing arts are unique in that they represent a form of artistic expression in which no product is created, except for the sound or visual effect of the performance in time and space. Music, drama, and dance are all extremely popular forms of cultural activity in modern society, as they have been for many past centuries.

As forms of artistic expression, they appeal to the sense of beauty and design in participants and spectators, and can be used to communicate emotions and themes of every sort. The performing arts have throughout history appealed both to the nobility or highly cultured classes and to the lower socioeconomic classes as well. Each one takes many forms and may also be approached on social or recreational levels as well as creative, performing-arts levels. For example, while ballet is usually thought of as a prestigious, high-level art form, it may also be enjoyed as an appealing form of exercise or hobby activity by the adult participant who takes a weekly class in elementary ballet technique. Vocal music may involve world-class operatic singers on the stage of the Metropolitan Opera House, or may consist of barber shop quartets or folk singing around a campfire.

Examples of Performing Arts Activities in Recreation

Listed under each heading for the performing arts are both *art* forms and *social* or *recreational* types of participation.

Music

Chamber music groups	Choruses
Community singing	Creative music and rhythmics
Drum and bugle corps	Folk singing

Glee clubs   Instrumental instruction
Jazz bands   Opera or operetta
Rhythm bands   performances
Symphony orchestras   Rock-and-roll music

Drama
Adult theater   Charades and dramatic games
Children's theater   Creative dramatics
Experimental theater   Marionettes, puppets and
One-act plays   mask-making
Storytelling   Play reading groups
Variety and talent shows   Theater parties

Dance
Ballet   Tap and clog dance
Ethnic dance   Creative dance for children
Jazz dance   Folk, square, and round dance
Rock-and-roll dance   Modern dance
Disco dance   Social or ballroom dance

As indicated earlier, varied forms of exercise-based dance, such as aerobic dancing or Jazzercise, are often featured in fitness programs. Other types of dance, that are temporarily popular, like the Charleston, Big Apple, or most recently break dancing, may be popular for only a few years before being replaced by another fad.

Values and Administrative Advantages

Like arts and crafts, the performing arts may be presented at many levels of proficiency. They often are highly social activities and lend themselves to regular group classes or performing groups that meet regularly, week-after-week, and year-after-year. They are ideal corecreational activities, and by definition must normally have participants of both sexes and varied ages—particularly in various dramatic programs in which play casting requires such diversity.

Performance-oriented groups have additional values, in that they usually require many other participants beyond those who are actually performing to carry out such tasks as designing and building scenery for the stage, selling tickets, doing publicity, and making costumes. They can be used to raise money and often are highly successful. They are also visible and attractive ways of getting public attention and support. A key factor in developing any type of performing arts program is the leadership involved. A skilled choral director, dance teacher, or play director is the key to developing enthusiastic participation!

As far as personal outcomes are concerned, the performing arts provide depth and richness to one's leisure. They contribute to one's confidence and creative potential and, as indicated earlier, provide rewarding social outlets. Although they are usually thought of as cooperative forms of activity, they may also be presented within a competitive format, as in play or choral festivals that involve judges who award prizes. There have been numerous ballet competitions and it is common for associations of music teachers to take part in large-scale contests, with their pupils competing on different skill levels.

Unlike sports or outdoor recreation activities that are often restricted by season and climatic factors, the performing arts can usually be carried on successfully throughout the year. They do not customarily require special meeting places, though appropriate halls or studios are necessary for some dances and performances. However, they can also be adapted to other environments, and simple outdoor performances of music, drama, and dance are often scheduled.

SOCIAL RECREATION

Social recreation may be defined as the type of recreational program that stresses the informal mixing of people and the enjoyment of casual, noncompetitive socializing activities that are often traditional or folk-like. It includes various types of events, such as parties, carnivals, or bazaars. It may also involve specific types of groups that meet regularly for social recreation purposes. It may also be considered to include the forms of activity that lend themselves to social-recreation programming. Each subcategory of social recreation is illustrated in the following section.

Examples of Social Recreation Events

Social recreation may include both small-scale events carried on as a weekly program feature on a neighborhood playground or in a community center, and ambitious large-scale events scheduled as annual celebrations or money-raisers. Examples include:

Banquets	Barbecues and picnics
Card parties	Carnivals
Clambakes	Father-and-son or mother-and-daughter parties
Fun nights	Campfires and marshmallow roasts
Las Vegas nights	Potluck or covered-dish suppers

Play days   Progressive parties (from place
Scavenger hunts or   to place, or activity to activity)
treasure hunts   Athletic exhibitions
Talent shows   Water shows

Numerous other special kinds of parties, based on holidays, anniversaries, seasonal themes or similar ideas, may be planned.

Examples of Social Recreation Groups

Groups that are organized and meet primarily for social recreation purposes include:

Coffeehouses or canteens for   Married couples' clubs in
teen-agers   churches
Parents Without Partners clubs   Single adult clubs
for single parents
Senior Centers
Golden Age clubs

In some cases, such groups are not sharply defined by membership, but simply consist of an open lounge or community-center that welcomes participants for social recreation activities, dancing, or similar activities.

Examples of Social Recreation Activities

Many of these activities are drawn from other categories and are simply adapted to the social recreation setting. They include:

Charades and informal dramatics
Community singing
Icebreakers, stunts, and mixers
Table games, cards, chess, and checkers
Folk and square dancing
Group games, such as guessing games or quizzes
Social dancing
Refreshments

Typically, many of the activities might be based on a particular theme, with songs, games, dances, refreshments, decorations, and publicity all designed to promote this idea or subject.

Values and Administrative Advantages

Social recreation is particularly useful in meeting the leisure needs of specific population groups—such as teenagers, single adults, the elderly, or the handicapped—who usually need and welcome social outlets. All people have a need for social companionship, and such programs provide the opportunity for fun, informal friendship, and assuming appropriate social roles. Social recreation normally should be inexpensive, noncompetitive, welcoming rather than exclusive, and informal.

A special feature of social recreation is that it should be planned and carried out by participants themselves, rather than professional leaders, as much as possible. This represents an administrative advantage in that the group members take a major responsibility for their own programming, usually under staff supervision. It also means that the participants gain management and interpersonal skills. Particularly for young people, learning to make group decisions, do publicity, plan budgets, purchase supplies and refreshments, and carry out all the other tasks involved in sponsoring special events contributes greatly to social growth in later years.

Small-scale parties, contests, celebrations, or shows help provide excitement and interest to ongoing recreation programs, and serve as culminating activities that conclude program units or activities. Large-scale or community-wide carnivals or parades may contribute in a major way to the recreation agency's image in the community, and its relationships with numerous community groups. In addition, they help build a sense of sharing and being part of community life for such groups. Civic celebrations, ceremonials, and shared rituals have traditionally helped strengthen community morale and intergroup relationships, and social recreation at this level contributes meaningfully to this function. Craig summarizes the impact of such special, one-time programs:

> The value of special events often extends beyond the event itself, providing the community with a vast array of benefits, including: community revitalization; public recreation department program visibility; tourism stimulation; a unique way to initiate or end seasonal programs; a context in which to recognize community leaders, services or facilities; stimulation of community support and interest in city-sponsored programs; enhancement of the quality of life; and mobilization of various community (commercial, public, private, and industrial) resources for one common good.[1]

MENTAL, LINGUISTIC, AND COMMUNICATION ACTIVITIES

This program category usually includes quiet activities of a mental nature, often involving the exchange of ideas through group discussion or other means of communication. While many such activities are obviously part of daily life, or the business or professional world, they may also be approached as enjoyable leisure activities. In some cases, they are carried out as regularly meeting clubs; in others, as special program features or as occasional activities.

Examples of Mental, Linguistic, and Communication Activities

Examples of mental, linguistic, and communication activities include the following:

Book club
Current events discussion group or forum
Magic tricks
Leisure counseling or other personal discussion groups
Paper and pencil games
Puzzles
Computer club
Video-taping club
Creative writing club
Foreign-language study group or conversation club
Mathematics tricks
Mental games
Poetry club or workshop
Radio club or radio station
Spelling bee
Writers' workshop

Like social recreation, such program elements may simply be activities that are plugged in as part of other programs, or may involve regularly meeting groups that pursue a given interest and carry out a variety of projects.

Values and Administrative Advantages

Programs of this type tend to be found in campus recreation programs, corporate/employee settings, or voluntary agencies that place stress on forming special-interest groups, rather than public or commercial settings. Hospitals and other treatment centers frequently have newsletters that are written and edited by patients, and encourage other activities of this type—particularly for individuals who have sustained serious physical trauma or functional losses and need to develop new skills and interests. Some large Veterans Administration hospitals, for example, have patient-run radio stations, discussion groups, and similar programs.

The personal values of such program activities are that they help build the mental capabilities of participants and develop their knowledge and skills in varied areas of cognitive performance. They serve to underline the point that recreation is not only sports and games, but also many kinds of cultural and intellectual pursuits as well. Computers and video games, for example, which have become extremely popular forms of activity in recent years, may lead directly to an interest in computer programming and other areas of career development for young people.

Apart from this type of value, it is simply a fact that mental games, tricks, challenges, and puzzles are intriguing to many people. In addition to contributing to knowledge or to one's thinking and reasoning skills, they also are fun! The amazing popularity of the table game *Trivial Pursuit* in the mid-1980s was testimony to this appeal.

From an administrative point of view, such activities are useful in that they do not usually require any special equipment, and the programs themselves may often be planned and directed by participants. In addition, group members may often volunteer to assist with the administrative tasks of the agency that are related to public relations, communications, and preparing reports.

OTHER TYPES OF SELF-ENRICHMENT ACTIVITIES

Many leisure-service agencies sponsor classes, workshops, or other learning experiences that are designed to contribute to the personal growth, coping skills, or self-enrichment process of participants. While these might appear to be educational, they are not directed toward such formal educational goals as earning a diploma or degree, and are not provided by formal educational institutions. Instead, they are obviously forms of leisure participation that have somewhat more serious or goal-oriented motivations than other types of recreation—but which are recreation nonetheless.

Examples of Self-Enrichment Activities

Classes and workshops of this type fall under many headings. They may be designed to build competence in personal investments, home management skills, health and fitness, interpersonal relationships, personal grooming, vocational development, or other community roles and areas of individual growth. A number of examples drawn from the brochures of an urban YM-YWHA and a suburban YWCA include the following:

Aerobic exercise and bodytone
Calligraphy
Childbirth education
Cooking, gourmet
English as a second language
Home repair—survival in a mechanical world
Lifesaving
Self-defense skills
Weight-reduction program
World service committee
Assertiveness training workshop
Career counseling
Dynamics of Jewish history
Divorced and separated discussion group
House plant workshop
Mother-toddler play workshop
Travel agents training course
Women and finance

Again, such activities reinforce the idea that recreation is more than fun and games, important as those may be. Instead, public, voluntary, corporate, armed forces, and other recreation agencies are in a position to offer programs within this category that are directly relevant to meeting the important life needs of participants and that, in many cases, also provide other important leisure values.

Values and Administrative Advantages

Most self-enrichment programs are typically offered in class-like settings, over a period of ten to twelve weeks, and with a fee that makes each course or workshop economically self-supporting. In terms of staffing, self-enrichment activities are usually led by outside specialists who are paid on a per-session or per-course basis, and agree to direct a class based on its having a sufficient pre-enrollment to justify being offered.

Self-enrichment classes or workshops are often held in local schools or college buildings, and are sometimes cosponsored by a municipal recreation or park agency and a public school system. Some communities offer an extremely impressive catalogue of adult education and recreation programs each year, with hundreds of different classes located in several different schools, community colleges or recreation centers. An important advantage of such activities is that they are particularly geared to meeting the needs of youth and adults who often are not heavily involved in public recreation programs.

From the participant's point of view, self-enrichment activities of this type are not only enjoyable and help meet social needs, but also contribute directly to one's competence in dealing with different areas of challenge or difficulty. In that sense, they vividly illustrate the value of recreation from the quality-of-life perspective.

SOCIAL-SERVICE FUNCTIONS

A final program area of many recreation and park agencies is providing services that meet specific nonrecreational needs of participants. As described in Chapter 3, in the discussion of the human service model, these functions may relate to health, nutritional, vocational, legal, housing, educational, family, and other areas of social need.

Although they are *not* recreational in nature, social services are often provided or coordinated by leisure-service professionals who direct multiservice programs. Recreation practitioners often come into close contact with youth, the elderly, or other special populations that are in need of such services, and are therefore likely to provide social services or refer their clients to other appropriate settings. In other types of settings, such as corporate programs or armed forces MWR units, such responsibilities become an assumed part of the overall role of personnel workers.

Examples of Social-Service Functions

Social or human service functions provided or coordinated by recreation professionals in different types of agencies include the following:

Career or vocational counseling
Discount purchasing plans
Health clinics, such as glaucoma screening or dental services
Nutritional (free lunch or meals-on-wheels programs)
Preretirement workshops or courses
Stress-reduction programs
Weight-loss programs
Day-care programs to assist working parents
Drug and alcohol abuse programs
Legal assistance and referral services
Physical fitness programs
Roving leader services for youth gangs
Tutoring
Educational counseling

It should be stressed that recreation leaders may not be qualified to conduct programs that require special training or certification. Glaucoma testing or other medical services provide an obvious example. In such cases, they may work in cooperation with agencies that can provide such expertise, or may hire part-time specialists to assist with such functions. In some situations, as in many therapeutic recreation programs, recreation specialists may receive special training and supervision that qualifies them to conduct group therapy sessions or such special services as "sensory training," "reality orientation," or "remotivation" sessions.

Values and Administrative Advantages

The values in having such services as part of a recreation program are obvious. Many individuals are assisted in these problem areas of their lives in a convenient and effective way, whereas if they had to search out such forms of assistance elsewhere they might well not do it. In addition, it strengthens the overall contribution of the leisure-service agency when it meets such needs, and helps support a higher level of respect for recreation and park organizations based on their making significant contributions to community life. From an administrative point of view, in such areas as armed forces, campus, or corporate recreation, it is helpful to be able to combine a number of related functions in one service unit.

Further, such program activities reinforce the view of recreation as a holistic kind of experience. Recreation programs can function best when participants are physically and mentally healthy, and when they are free of other social or pressing economic concerns. By assisting in these areas of life along with more obvious leisure services, recreation professionals are able to provide a fully rounded experience to participants.

Examining Motivations for Participation

Listing and categorizing different types of recreational activity are important first steps in helping one begin to select appropriate program activities from the broad range of possible pursuits that might be offered.

However, it is not enough simply to list activities. It is also important to analyze activities in terms of the nature of the experience they provide, the motivations they satisfy, and the formats in which they can be offered to the public. For example, in terms of the kinds of behaviors they involve, recreation activities have been classified under a number of major headings that cut across the categories that have been presented thus far in this chapter. These include the following:

Types of Recreation Involvements
  1. **Socializing behaviors**—activities such as dancing, dating, going to parties or visiting friends, in which people relate to each other in informal and unstereotyped ways.

2. **Associative behaviors**—activities in which people group together because of common interests such as horseback riding, car clubs, or stamp-, coin-, or comic book-collecting groups, or similar hobbies.
3. **Competitive behaviors**—activities including all the popular sports and games, but also competition in the performing arts, or even in outdoor activities in which individuals struggle against the environment or even against their own limitations.
4. **Risk-taking behaviors**—an increasingly popular form of participation, in which the stakes are often physical injury or possible death.
5. **Exploratory behaviors**—in a sense, all recreation involves some degree of exploration; in this context, it refers to such activities as travel and sightseeing, hiking, scuba diving, spelunking, and other pursuits that open up new environments to the participant.
6. **Vicarious experience**—much modern recreation consists of reading, watching television or motion pictures, viewing the art works of others, listening to music, or attending spectator sports events.
7. **Sensory stimulation**—behaviors which center about hedonism and the stimulation of the senses as a primary concern include drinking, drug use, sexual activity, and such visual experiences as light shows and rock concerts, which may blend different kinds of stimuli.
8. **Physical expression**—many activities, such as running, swimming, dancing, and yoga, may involve physical expression without emphasizing competition against others.
9. **Artistically creative behaviors**—activities which involve aesthetic expression, either in the areas of arts and crafts or in the performing arts.
10. **Intellectual behaviors**—involving experiences in the realm of ideas, including discussions, philosophical analysis, or certain forms of writing.
11. **Volunteer service**—although not always recognized as forms of recreation, acting as a volunteer in community programs is an enjoyable and rewarding leisure experience for many individuals.
12. **Spiritual involvement**—certain forms of leisure activity, such as retreats, varied kinds of Eastern exercise and meditation processes, or involvement in the outdoor, have clearly spiritual motivations and outcomes.[2]

Recognizing that all human beings have important needs for such experiences or emotions as affection, companionship, physical release, escape from boredom, or a sense of accomplishment and creative expression, it is important to provide program activities that meet the perceived needs and motivations of participants. For example, if a participant has a strong need for successful accomplishment and for receiving the approval of others, he or she should be helped to select those program involvements that are likely to provide such outcomes.

APPLYING PHILOSOPHICAL CRITERIA

Should a recreation agency seek to meet all expressed leisure needs or recreational motivations of participants? One category of motivation in which this question is particularly relevant deals with risk-taking behaviors. Obviously, this has become an extremely popular form of recreation in recent years, with such activities as hang gliding or mountain climbing growing steadily in participation. Many agencies hesitate to sponsor risk activities because of the danger of injuries and lawsuits. Beyond this, they might wish to weigh the desirability of providing high-risk pastimes from a philosophical point of view.

Increasingly, it would appear that the *idea* of danger, risk, and fear is becoming fascinating for its own sake in many recreational pursuits. As an example, following a major tragedy in a New Jersey amusement park in the spring of 1964 which took eight lives, attendance did not fall off in the park. Experts in the field were surprised that attendance did not go dramatically up.

> "Usually, attendance increases if someone has been killed," muses one representative from a company that makes roller coasters for amusement parks. "It's awful, but it's true."[2]

The very idea of fear itself seems to be alluring, and is built into the design of roller coasters. Thus, some companies produce roller coasters designed to look rickety, although they are actually very sturdy. Creaky sounds are amplified to make the ride more frightening; a ride that isn't terrifying simply isn't appealing.

Should leisure-service agencies sponsor programs that satisfy potentially dangerous urges? The answer is that sponsors must judge their suitability in terms of their stated philosophies; the goals they have evolved must provide the basis for programmatic decisions.

Simply to reply, "This is what people want, and we must therefore supply it to them; we are not in the business of making moral judgments," begs the question. No agency could ever meet all of the possible leisure needs and interests of the public. It must therefore make intelligent choices when selecting program activities based on its mission and level of capability.

THE COMPLEX NATURE OF ACTIVITIES

In examining the broad range of recreational activities, it is also essential to recognize that many pursuits are not as simple or as easily defined as they might appear to be at the outset. Often we do not recognize the complexity and full potential of such leisure activities.

For example, if most people were asked to describe the game of American football, the adjectives that would be likely to appear would be "highly physical," "aggressive," or "violent." Yet the game of football is also highly mental in that players must learn a tremendous number of plays and strategies and to respond to game situations in split seconds. It is a creative game, in terms of making decisions and solving problems, and it is certainly a highly disciplined sport with a strong element of team cooperation underlying success. Finally, although it is not commonly thought of as an artistic experience, it certainly has an aesthetic quality—as do all sports—which is attested to by paintings, drawings, photographs, and sculpture of players in action.

Football is not simply rough-and-tough; it has a number of other dimensions and values. Similarly, although one might tend to think of art as delicate, sensitive, or poetic in nature, many forms of art can be heavy, brutal, and harsh. A sculptor who welds huge metal shapes or carves statues from great blocks of granite illustrates this aspect of fine art.

As another example, the popular pursuit of gardening represents a very complex activity, which is difficult to classify under any one heading of leisure involvement. In the first place, one might question whether it should be considered recreation at all, if its primary purpose is to yield fruits and vegetables for sustenance. Recognizing however that most people engage in gardening primarily for the pleasure that it provides, one might conclude that it should be thought of as a hobby.

Obviously, this would be correct—but could not gardening also be considered a form of outdoor recreation which brings the participant closely in touch with nature? Or should gardening be considered an artistic experience, since so much of it has to do with the blending of forms and colors, and with the designing of gardens and displays for flower or horticultural shows?

In another sense, gardening might be thought of as a scientific experience, with distinct connections to botany, biology, chemistry, and the skills involved in plant propagation, insect control, and similar tasks.

Finally, shouldn't gardening be thought of as a social activity, with garden clubs, outings and tours, hobby groups, and friendships based on sharing a common interest?

The point is that many recreational activities are complex and should be carefully analyzed to determine their program potential and how they satisfy the needs and motivations of participants.

ACTIVITY ANALYSIS AND PRESCRIPTIVE PROGRAMMING

Particularly in the field of therapeutic recreation service, there has been a systematic effort to analyze different recreation activities in order to define the precise demands they make of the participant or learner and to use them most meaningfully in the treatment process. Gunn and Peterson point out that the therapist must seek to identify the physical, cognitive, affective, and social components of an activity. This process, they write:

> has many applications in therapeutic recreation programming. If the program is instructional in nature, the process of activity analysis, combined with the functional assessment of a person with a disability, allows the instructor to know exactly what modifications of the activity are needed to accommodate that person. For example, an analysis of the front crawl in swimming compared to the functional ability of an individual with cerebral palsy would indicate the exact areas needing adaptation, i.e., the kick, or the coordination of arms and breathing.[3]

Beyond the physical demands of an activity, which may be clearly identified in kinesiological terms, it is also important to understand its cognitive requirements. This may involve understanding the basic rules and purpose of a game, as well as its strategy and other key elements. Other activities have important social-interaction requirements which also must be matched to a client's present abilities and overall treatment goals. For example, Avedon has carried out a systematic analysis of the social structure of games, showing how they involve various types of intra-individual and group relationships.[4] These in turn may be used to facilitate different types of learning experiences or social involvement for participants as part of the therapeutic or rehabilitative process.

When considering an activity for possible inclusion in a program, it is necessary to determine whether it will require modification to be suitable for the population to which it will be presented.

More difficult than assessing the participant's needs and interests (and offering program opportunities based on them) is designing the recreation experience to achieve precise social and behavioral outcomes. The design must specify the criteria to be used when assigning the participant to given tasks, and rating his or her success or failure at every stage of the process. If recreation is as free and voluntary an experience as we believe it to be, and if it is to be characterized—like leisure—by a sense of freedom and personal choice, one must ask whether activity analysis that leads to a prescriptive approach is desirable as a form of programming and leadership.

The obvious answer is that programming of this type does not really constitute recreation as such, but rather the use of recreational activities to achieve treatment goals. However, such prescriptive approaches and carefully directed and monitored learning experiences may help the patient or client achieve the needed skills and positive attitudes toward involvement that will later lead to voluntary, enjoyable participation in leisure activity, at which point participation becomes truly recreational.

OTHER PROGRAM SERVICES AND FUNCTIONS

The bulk of this chapter has been concerned with activities that involve direct participation and are recreational. It is important to recognize, however, that they are not all fun and games. Many involve important areas of personal growth and creative achievement. Some involve a high degree of risk, discipline, and commitment for continued involvement. Others consist of human service programs that help enrich an individual participant's life, or which deal with problems of community adjustment, family cohesion, health, or vocational development.

Beyond these services, as Chapter 2 makes clear, many leisure service agencies provide other important program elements. Typically, public recreation and park departments provide indoor and outdoor facilities for play, which may be used by many other community agencies or by individuals in unstructured forms of leisure activity. In many cities, the bulk of organized sports programming that is carried on using sports fields owned by public recreation and park departments is actually conducted by community sports associations, youth clubs, and similar organizations.

As an example, in the city of Philadelphia, many sports clubs offer a wide range of athletic activities for children and youth. These groups recruit participants, coach and direct teams, help maintain community recreation facilities, and serve as a means of uniting neighborhoods in a common interest; in one area alone, such clubs serve almost 10,000 children.

In addition to such organized play, a great deal of outdoor recreation such as hiking, boating, picnicking and bicycling, is carried on in an unstructured or unsupervised way in parks, by community residents young and old.

Another important responsibility of public recreation and park departments is to promote recreation and leisure values generally in the community, and to help promote and coordinate varied forms of recreational involvement throughout the year.

How is this done? First, such departments should accept the principle that they have a meaningful responsibility for providing such leadership. While commercial, private, therapeutic, employee, voluntary and other types of organizations have an important role to play in meeting leisure needs, the fact is that they tend to serve specialized segments of the overall community population— and that they also tend to specialize in terms of the activities they offer.

In contrast, the public recreation and park agency is the one organization with an overall responsibility for meeting varied leisure needs of all groups within a wide range of activity. Thus, the public department should consider carrying out any of the following kinds of functions designed to promote recreation in the community:

Sponsor "Leisure Awareness" Events. These may involve such special events as "Life. Be In It." celebrations, or playdays, program exhibitions, film showings, holiday parties, or other activities designed to upgrade public awareness of leisure values and oppportunities. These may be keyed to a particular theme, such as fitness, historical traditions, environmental quality, or similar subjects, or may focus directly on recreation as a vital aspect of public life.

Assist Other Community Agencies. This function may take several different forms. Public recreation and park departments may offer leadership training or certification programs, provide facilities for their use, or publish newsletters or directories that publicize their programs. Public departments may also assist in developing master schedules of recreation activities and events, and may work closely with the public schools in cosponsoring activities and supervising the use of school facilities by community groups.

As an example, in White Plains, New York, the public Department of Recreation and Parks accepted responsibility for assisting a nonprofit Community Chest Day Camp for families of working mothers, in the following ways: (1) printing and distributing applications for the camp; (2) issuing news releases and other publicity; (3) screening and interviewing staff applicants; (4) later providing training for day camp staff, along with members of its own playground staff; (5) offering a special summer swimming program for all campers; (6) assisting with supervision; (7) helping plan and put on special programs and events; and (8) lending the day camp needed equipment.

Similarly, the Hartford, Connecticut, Department of Parks and Recreation freely lends such equipment as camping materials, field line markers, portable scoreboards, and fishing equipment to its residents. It lends public speaking lecterns, trash barrels, tables, and chairs to neighborhood groups sponsoring community festivals, and distributes varied other "Recreation Bank" materials, using a van to reach areas in need.

Promote Leisure Education. In addition to the kinds of leisure awareness programs mentioned above, public departments may also offer leisure-counseling services or adult education classes in leisure skills.

They may help to sponsor professional meetings that deal with issues of recreation sponsorship and concerns, and may enlist varied community groups in the process of developing support for leisure programs. They may work with major companies in sponsoring preretirement workshops, and may develop special groups that work with discharged mental patients or other groups with disability that have been referred to them for sheltered program services.

Although these have been described as functions of public departments, all types of recreation agencies have an important stake in promoting leisure as an important community concern—and in working together to sponsor needed programs. Later chapters will provide examples of synergistic programming, in which two, three, or more different organizations join efforts to achieve such results.

PROGRAM EMPHASIS BASED ON AGENCY GOALS

All of the activities and services which have been briefly described in this chapter represent a vast pool of possible program elements.

Ideally, each agency would probably wish to provide a broad range of activities and services, and to encourage participants to engage in highly diversified pursuits, in order to achieve a full and rich leisure life. However, it is obvious that no one type of leisure-service organization is likely to be able to offer all kinds of program activities with equal levels of support. Federal, state, and county park systems, for example, are much more likely to be able to offer extensive programs in outdoor recreation than other types of agencies, simply because of the resources they possess, and the traditional role they have played. Beyond this, each different type of leisure-service agency or program is likely to have a somewhat different set of goals and program emphases, based on its sponsorship, philosophy, and population served.

Based on this, the actual selection of program activities will vary markedly from agency to agency. Each leisure-service organization offers activities that are appropriate for its stated goals and resources. Armed forces recreation programs are likely to offer a heavy component of sports, fitness, hobby, and social programs, but may offer little in terms of artistic and cultural activities. Voluntary agencies serving senior citizens will give heavy emphasis to social recreation and to other types of human services that meet the needs of their clientele, but will probably offer few sports or outdoor recreation pursuits.

SELECTING FORMATS TO MEET PROGRAM NEEDS

Every type of recreational activity may be offered in a number of different ways, based on the needs and interests of participants and on agency resources. In planning programs, for example, it is not enough to say that the program will sponsor fitness activities. Instead, it is necessary to determine the exact form they will take and the way in which they will be presented to the public—or to the organization's membership—for participation.

The varied formats that may be used, as well as their particular advantages and limitations, are described in detail in Chapter 8. This analysis is accompanied by an overview of several different types of leisure facilities along with their implications for program development. The reader is presented with a number of alternative choices that can be used directly in program planning and implementation.

NOTES_____

[1]Dee Wayne Craig, "Successful Special Events: The Rochester Formula," *Parks and Recreation* (March 1983): 48.

[2]Adapted from James F. Murphy, et al. *Leisure Service Delivery System: A Modern Perspective* (Philadelphia: Lea and Febiger, 1973), pp. 73–76.

[3]Scout Gunn and Carol Peterson, *Therapeutic Recreation Program Design: Principles and Procedures* (Englewood Cliffs, N.J.: Prentice-Hall, 1978), p. 157.

[4]See Elliott M. Avedon, *Therapeutic Recreation Service: An Applied Behavioral Perspective* (Englewood Cliffs, N.J.: Prentice-Hall, 1974), pp. 162—70.

STUDENT PROJECTS

1. The chapter describes nine major categories of recreational activity or program service which may be provided by a leisure-service agency. It then identifies twelve types of motivation for taking part in recreation. Divide the class into several small groups. Each group should examine one major category of activity in terms of the kinds of motivations it is able to satisfy. Groups should present their conclusions to the class for discussion.
2. Individual students may read appropriate chapters on activity analysis and prescriptive programming in Gunn and Peterson, and then analyze a specific form of activity in terms of the needs of a group of clients or patients in a therapeutic setting. Then present the findings to the class for discussion.

SUGGESTED READINGS

Reynold Carlson, Janet MacLean, Theodore Deppe, and James Peterson, *Recreation and Leisure: The Changing Scene* (Belmont, Calif.: Wadsworth, 1979), Chapter 11.

Patricia Farrell and Herberta Lundegren, *The Process of Recreation Programming* (New York: John Wiley, 1978), Chapter 5.

Scout Gunn and Carol Peterson, *Therapeutic Recreation Program Design: Principles and Procedures* (Englewood Cliffs, N.J.: Prentice-Hall, 1978), Chapters 10 and 11.

Richard Kraus, Gaylene Carpenter, and Barbara Bates, *Recreation Leadership and Supervision: Guidelines for Professional Development* (Philadelphia: Saunders College Publishing, 1981), Chapters 5 and 6.

Ruth V. Russell, *Planning Programs in Recreation* (St. Louis: C.V. Mosby, 1982), Chapter 5.

CHAPTER 8

Alternative Approaches to Program Design: Formats and Facilities

A woman in the back of the auditorium got up to speak, at the end of the monthly Recreation Commission business meeting, which was open to the public.

"I'm Mrs. Ginny Daley," she said. "And I want to complain about the township's sports program."

"What's wrong with it?" asked a member of the commission. "All the leagues are going great guns."

"Well, I feel it's too limited," said Mrs. Daley. "My sons don't seem to be good enough to play in these leagues—so they've given up on them. But they enjoy sports. And my daughter can't really find any good sports for girls in the program."

"Well, we do have over three hundred boys and girls involved in the leagues," said the commission member. "Isn't that good enough?"

"Not really," replied Mrs. Daley. "There are 1800 teenagers altogether in the junior and senior high schools. Aren't there some other ways we could involve the rest of them—like nonleague play, or open times at fields or in gyms? Or sports clinics to teach skills, or some other games for kids who aren't great athletes? Could we take a look at these possibilities?"

"Yes," said the commission member. "I guess we could."

Having established a philosophical base for our program, assessed the recreational needs and interests of participants, determined program goals and objectives, and identified the full range of possible activities, we are now ready to complete the fifth step in the program-planning process.

Our task is to consider the possible ways in which various program activities may be built into our agency's overall program plan, both in terms of their desirability and the kinds of agency resources they will require to be successful. In so doing, we will examine: (1) the different kinds of formats that program activities may take; (2) several types of physical settings or locations in which recreation may be offered; and (3) the questions that must be asked in putting together the best possible mix of activities, formats, locations, and participants for our final product—a recreation program.

EIGHT USEFUL FORMATS FOR ACTIVITY

It is not enough to say, "We will schedule basketball as a teenage program activity." Does this mean that we will provide instructional sessions or clinics in basketball skills, that we will allow free play in a gym for all visitors, or that we will schedule organized leagues or basketball tournaments?

The term that is used to describe each of these choices is *format*. It means the form that an activity takes in the planning and scheduling process to meet a particular need as it fits into an overall program of activity. There are at least eight possibilities that may be selected, including: (1) instruction; (2) free play or unstructured participation; (3) organized competition; (4) performances, demonstrations, or exhibitions; (5) leadership training; (6) special-interest groups; (7) other special events; and (8) trips and outings.

INSTRUCTION

Instruction is one of the most common formats in many categories of activity. It includes classes or practice sessions in many different sports, aquatic activities, outdoor recreation skills, creative activities, and even hobbies.

In addition, many self-improvement or life-enrichment activities are usually offered in an instructional format, that is, classes meeting regularly over a period of time. Typically, in recreation, the classroom approach to teaching is less formal and more spontaneous or fun-oriented than most school-centered instruction. However, it still represents a teaching process, geared to the participant's level of skills and interest.

Instruction may take other forms; it may consist of casual instruction in sports skills, arts, and crafts or other program activities on playgrounds, in community centers, or other settings. It may also include special workshops, clinics, or seminars on advanced levels of participation.

FREE PLAY OR UNSTRUCTURED PARTICIPATION

This format implies participation without formal instruction or direction in an informal setting. Examples are children or teenagers playing games or sports activities on an athletic field—without organized teams, leagues, or schedules—or playing table games in a youth center's lounge in an unstructured way.

Many other activities may be approached in the same way. The family that takes a casual walk through a park or visits a neighborhood swimming pool, an elderly person completing a crafts project while enjoying sociable conversation at a senior center, or a middle-aged person practicing a golf swing at a neighborhood driving range are all taking part in recreation on a free-play basis. It is important to note that this format may involve general supervision being given to an area. However, direct leadership is not provided in an organized way. Other examples of the unstructured use of open facilities might include family or group picnics, attendance at a concert, recreational library visits, or using a center's arts and crafts facilities to take part in self-directed hobbies.

ORGANIZED COMPETITION

A much more structured format for play consists of organized competition. Usually this is thought of in terms of sports participation, with teams being formed and games being scheduled, either in ongoing play throughout a season, or formal leagues or tournaments. However, many other kinds of recreational activities may involve organized competition.

Youngsters taking part in a 4-H club fair may compete by showing animals they have raised or produce they have grown, along with other types of projects or handicrafts. Musicians and dancers may compete for awards, and photographs and paintings may be judged against each other. Even in the program activity area involving mental, linguistic, and communication activities there may be spelling bees, essay contests, or poetry awards.

PERFORMANCES, DEMONSTRATIONS, OR EXHIBITIONS

A fourth important format consists of putting on shows or performances of some type. This might involve gymnastic or dance demonstrations, art exhibitions or hobby shows, or performances of choruses or drama groups. Almost any type of recreational activity may lend itself to a demonstration of some type.

Such events are usually scheduled at the end of a program that has extended over a period of time to show the results of instruction and participation. They are particularly valuable in that they heighten the motivation and interests of those taking part and also serve to make others aware of the various program activities that are offered. Thus, they are useful publicity tools and may also be used for fund-raising purposes.

LEADERSHIP TRAINING

While it should not be called a form of recreational participation in a strict sense, leadership training represents a way of promoting or providing a recreational activity within an overall program. For example, many organizations provide courses in life-saving or water safety. Others may sponsor clinics in coaching methods, officiating, or teaching skills in different recreational areas.

While this may appear to be another form of instructional programming, the distinction is that it is concerned with promoting community recreation and assisting other agencies by providing leadership training—as opposed to simply teaching participants how to take part in activities.

Programs of this type tend to be offered by large agencies, such as county or park district departments, and may serve numerous local recreation departments or voluntary agencies that are too small to be able to provide their own leadership training or inservice education programs. For example, many such departments offer two- or three-day recreation leadership training programs before the summer season, which are used to prepare young leaders with basic recreation skills and principles, as well as first-aid and safety information. In some cases, special workshops may be sponsored in areas such as arts management, dance teaching methods, or similar leisure-related skills.

SPECIAL-INTEREST GROUPS

Another way of providing or assisting participation in a given program activity area is to sponsor a social club or special-interest group based on involvement in the activity.

For example, recreation agencies may form archery clubs, camping clubs, square dance clubs, hiking clubs, poetry groups, theater groups, and numerous other special-interest groups of this type. Such clubs usually plan a variety of events and activities based on their interests in hobbies or other leisure pursuits. However, they often tend to become social clubs as well, sponsoring parties and other informal get-togethers.

OTHER SPECIAL EVENTS

In addition to demonstrations or exhibitions, which usually are intended to display a given activity or its products, it is also possible to schedule other parties, carnivals, play days, or celebrations linked to a given activity. One very common event is an awards day or banquet, or father-son or mother-daughter party involving those who are regular participants in a given activity. Such events must, however, be carefully designed not to alienate participants unnecessarily, in this case, for example, providing for children from nontraditional households.

TRIPS AND OUTINGS

Certain special-interest activities lend themselves to trips and outings that help promote or enrich the overall recreational experience.

For example, a nature-study club might obviously take a hike or visit to an environmental center, to see nature close-up. A local theater club might plan to visit a nearby city to see a popular play or repertory company. An antique collectors' club might travel to a large antique show in a convention hall at a distance, and students in an adult painting class might visit a famous museum to see an art show of particular interest.

OTHER SERVICE FUNCTIONS

A final way in which a recreation agency may deal with any type of leisure pursuit—although not a format for participation—is to promote and coordinate it on a community-wide basis.

In some cases, the public department may assume a responsibility for cosponsoring programs with various community groups. While this does not represent a unique format for activity, it does illustrate a way in which leisure-service agencies may help present needed programs and thus promote overall community involvement.

DIVERSITY OF FORMATS WITHIN A SINGLE ACTIVITY

Obviously, every type of recreational activity may not be appropriate for all kinds of formats within the typical leisure-service programs. However, the creative programmer will soon discover that he or she is able to serve a recreation audience in many diversified ways, simply by exploring possible formats that have not been tried before.

Possibilities in a Swimming Pool

As an example of format diversity, one might cite the different kinds of uses to which swimming pools may be put. The author of this text served as a consultant on programs to the Director of Recreation in the New York City Department of Parks, Recreation and Cultural Affairs. At that time, such major facilities as golf courses, tennis court complexes, and swimming pools were the administrative responsibility of the Division of Maintenance and Operations, rather than the Recreation Division of the Department.

In a discussion with the author, the Director of Maintenance and Operations of one of the city's five boroughs argued strongly that this arrangement made sense. After all, he said, running a swimming pool was chiefly a matter of maintenance, rather than programming. "Why do you need recreation leaders or planners to operate a swimming pool?" he asked. "We can hire and train lifeguards just as well through Maintenance and Operations as through Recreation. What else do people do at a pool, besides swim?"

A quick review of the kinds of activities that are often found at different kinds of swimming pools—including community, school, or private pools—revealed the following 15 activities:

1. *Casual swimming* in a relaxed way.
2. Simply *lying around,* lounging on the side of the pool, sun-bathing and occasionally playing in the water—probably the most common pool activity, particularly for family groups.
3. Swimming for *exercise and fitness,* either individually by doing laps, or through an organized class or group, in some cases combined with other exercise programs.
4. *Instruction* in swimming skills, on several levels of competence, ranging from complete beginner to advanced swimmer.
5. *Competitive swimming,* either through informal races or by having a swimming team that represents the pool in inter-pool competition, or by scheduling a major swimming meet at the pool.
6. Instruction, competition, or free-play use of *diving* boards at different heights.
7. Use of pool for *practice with small craft,* such as canoes or kayaks; learning paddling strokes, or overturning craft and re-entering.
8. Instruction and practice in *scuba* diving, prior to field trips.
9. Special swimming programs for *handicapped groups,* such as the physically disabled or mentally retarded; these may or may not require special facilities, such as lifts or movable pool bulkheads.
10. Large-scale *water shows* or *carnivals,* with a variety of aquatic events, such as races, exhibition diving, clowns, stunts and other novelty entertainments.

11. Smaller *parties,* in which a pool is used as a setting for a picnic, barbecue or other program, including pool games for general participation.
12. *Synchronized swimming* (sometimes called water ballet) instruction and practice, usually with a regularly meeting special-interest club.
13. Using pool to teach *life-saving* and *water-safety,* or to train other types of aquatic officials or leaders.
14. Playing *water polo* or other active group games in the pool.
15. Holding a *fishing derby* in the pool; some recreation departments do this at the end of the swimming season, after permitting the chlorine to die down, as a fund-raising event or novelty program.

Obviously, not every recreational swimming pool will lend itself to all of these program possibilities. However, in order to encourage maximum participation and use of the facility, several of them are likely to be successful. Developing *policies* as to which activities should be offered or given priority over other possibilities is obviously a recreational concern since it deals with the fundamental goals and objectives of the agency and should be based on an analysis of community and participant needs and interests.

Often a pool director may develop a "tie-in" with other organizations, such as a "mothers-and-tots" swim-and-exercise club or a lunchtime exercise program in which the pool is taken over by a nearby company for its employees on a regular basis. In scheduling its own activities, the pool staff should consider programming for different age groups, and should also seek to build links between activities, with advanced swimming classes leading to competitive swimming interest or life-saving courses. If the pool is operated by a YMCA or YWCA with a summer camp on a lake, the year-round staff may use the pool to teach scuba diving or introductory small-craft skills during the winter months for those groups who will be going to camp during the summer.

FORMATS TO FIT AGENCY ORIENTATION

Each leisure-service agency is likely to select and use program formats that are appropriate to its particular orientation.

For example, the recreation and park department that subscribes to the quality-of-life model will generally select those activities and formats that help contribute pleasure, fun, and family togetherness.

The organization that bases its operation on the marketing orientation will concentrate on programs that yield revenue in one form or another, including rental of facilities to outside groups. A good example would be a public department that operates an ice-skating rink that is used to serve not only general skating sessions, but figure-skating classes and practice sessions, private parties, or hockey team practice and games—all for added revenue.

The agency that bases its program on the environmental/aesthetic/ preservationist approach will select activity formats that do least harm to the environment and have limited energy demands, or on those that enrich public taste and awareness of historical or aesthetic values.

Ideally, different formats should be consciously used to fulfil a number of the programming principles presented in Chapter 2 of this text. By using appropriate ways of packaging activities, balance, depth, variety, and continuity of participation can be achieved. Beyond this, program formats can be intentionally designed to meet the individual or group needs of participants. If their interest is in gaining a sense of achievement or meeting risks and challenges, a highly competitive format may be appropriate. If it is for companionship and acceptance by others, special-interest groups involving social interaction are likely to be effective. If they are seeking to broaden and enrich their leisure involvements or to gain greater competence in living independently in the community, instructional programs may be most valuable.

Whatever the agency orientation or the needs and interests of participants, formats may be chosen that will fulfil the program's goals and objectives, through an intelligent process of planning and implementation.

DESIGNING PROGRAMS FOR SPECIAL FACILITIES

Having considered the different types of formats through which activities may be presented, we must now deal with the question of facilities as they affect program planning.

Some settings, such as playgrounds, parks or community centers, may lend themselves to a wide variety of program elements. Others are much more special in nature, and designed primarily for one type of pastime. This chapter will now consider the element of facilities, as they influence the kinds of programs that are evolved. Although most of the kinds of facilities considered here might appear to be appropriate for public recreation and park departments, many are also operated by other types of leisure-service agencies.

To begin, the initial planning of any facility, as well as its actual design and construction, should be done with full awareness of its programmatic functions. Those who are to manage the facility should have input in this process. Too often, architects who may have a highly developed aesthetic sense and awareness of engineering and construction principles have a very limited understanding of the uses to which a facility may be put. Therefore, it is essential that the recreation professionals responsible for future programming of a facility be drawn into its initial planning.

ROLE OF PROGRAM PLANNERS IN FACILITY DEVELOPMENT

The task of determining the need for any leisure facility and deciding the precise program functions it should satisfy is a complex one. To illustrate, Downs has described the process of planning a modern recreation center and sports complex, designed to meet the aesthetic and practical needs of family members of all ages and backgrounds with a wide range of programs, events, and activities. The challenge today is to do more than "questimate." Instead, Downs writes, the program planner must develop a comprehensive plan to analyze:

- Site location with respect to population, transportation, utilities, and physical properties of the land.
- Area future trends, including population growth estimates, market planning, and economic stability.
- Employment centers, their growth within the community, their effects on the project, and local sources of income.
- Present and future needs, including adequacy of present recreational facilities, existing competition, and need versus market size.
- Size and type of design for the purpose intended.
- Income levels and economic capabilities of families in the area, need and desire for recreational facilities, and resultant financial support to the project.
- Complete costs of the project.
- Costs of operation based on local conditions, as well as analysis of income from all sources.
- Methods of financing and debt reduction.
- All factors determining whether the project will be self-liquidating or self-supporting in the future.[1]

Obviously, program planners should play a key role in helping interpret such logistical concerns. Based on this, they should be an integral part of the planning team in terms of the design of different program areas, the relation of one part of the structure to another, and the development of an attractive and efficient structure that permits convenient access and supervision, that can be economically maintained, and that is relatively vandal-, crime-, and accident-proof.

Facility Maintenance. Recreation program managers also have an important stake in the way a facility is maintained in terms of its appearance, efficiency, and safety. Particularly in the case of a natural, outdoor facility, the quality of maintenance will have a great deal to do with the respect that people have for a site, and the kinds of uses to which it may be put. Owens makes this point eloquently:

> When you go to visit a park and find an inviting entrance—verdant, well-kept lawns; full, vigorous shrubs and trees that complement the landscape; buildings

that are proportional and painted in harmonious colors; clear, wide, smooth, and direct walkways and roadways; convenient, accessible parking areas; automobile barriers confining traffic to roadways and parking areas that are readily seen; pleasing signs for location and direction; attractive, accessible, and adequate receptacles for refuse; and neatly dressed employees who are informed and answer questions courteously—then you know that management has recognized the important role that maintenance holds.

If further observations inside buildings where recreational programs and activities are underway reveal clean windows, walls and ceilings, and unlittered floors (orderliness even though there is a bustle of activity) then we know that management has effected cooperation between maintenance and program personnel.[2]

TYPES OF RECREATION FACILITIES

Today, new technologies and imaginative designs are being used to create facilities that offer innovative leisure experiences to participants. Combined with a careful analysis of the needs and potential involvement of target populations as part of systematic feasibility studies, they have resulted in many new types of multi-use facilities. In many public departments, the trend has been to construct facilities that will yield substantial fees and charges, and thus will be relatively self-sustaining or even capable of paying for their construction costs over time.

A comprehensive list of the types of facilities, both indoor and outdoor, that are operated by different categories of recreation sponsors, would include the following:

Playgrounds.   These may range in size from small tot-lots to large play areas for children and youth—sometimes with attached buildings and sports fields. The majority are constructed in a traditional mode, with such fixed equipment as slides, swings, jungle gyms and sand-boxes, but a growing number have more innovative or exploratory kinds of equipment, sometimes based on special themes.

Community Centers.   These have traditionally been buildings with indoor and outdoor facilities for a variety of sports, social, creative and other group activities. In addition to the general type of recreation center, today they may include youth centers, senior centers, or multiagency centers meeting different human service needs.

Facilities for the Handicapped.   These may include recreation centers that are specifically intended for use by physically or mentally disabled individuals; they may also include other types of facilities, such as playgrounds, small parks, or nature trails that have been designed for such uses.

Nature Centers.   Nature centers are customarily located in settings that provide an assortment of different natural environments, such as older forests, fields, streams, marshes, and similar resources. Often there is a rustic building with displays, crafts and hobby areas, and other facilities for environmental education. Such facilities may be operated by recreation and park authorities in cooperation with school authorities, although usually all ages may use nature centers.

Art Centers.   Many recreation centers include special rooms that are set aside for art activities or craft shops. However, some communities today operate one or more facilities designed to house arts and crafts programs specifically. Not infrequently, old mansions have been converted to such arts centers, and various community special-interest groups, such as a Weavers' Guild or Ceramics Club, may use them as their home base.

There are also performing arts centers that house programs or special groups that sponsor music, drama, and dance activities. Usually they are not large enough to house performances before large audiences, but instead offer studio-type or small theater-in-the-round settings for performance.

Civic Arenas and Auditoriums.   A growing number of cities today sponsor civic auditoriums, with halls of various sizes that are useful for music, dance, or theatrical performances, or community meetings. In some cities, large arenas can house expositions, "home" shows, hobby shows, camping shows, boat shows, and similar events. Complexes of this type often serve as convention centers and are heavily booked throughout the year for conferences, trade shows, and similar programs. In some cases, they provide large seating sections that are suitable for entertainment events, such as rock concerts, circuses or wrestling shows.

Sports Complexes.   Recreation agencies of all types today are likely to have one or more sports complexes that house popular athletic activities. In some cases, these may be primarily fields for varied types of outdoor play, such as baseball, softball, soccer, lacrosse, or football. They may include separate golf courses or tennis complexes. They may be indoor facilities with gymnasiums, courts, and other special rooms to be used for games such as basketball, volleyball, badminton, floor hockey, wrestling, boxing, judo and karate, racquetball and other popular indoor activities. Often such facilities also have pools, indoor tracks, weight rooms, and sometimes even bowling lanes.

Stadiums.   A number of city or county governments today own stadiums that house outdoor sports, as well as occasional concerts or other large-scale performances and events. In some cases they are operated solely by the public recreation and park department, while in others they have been built in partnership with private enterprise or with long-term lease arrangements with the owners of professional sports teams.

Swimming Pool Complexes. Swimming is one of the most popular recreational pursuits for the entire family today in countries around the world. Pool complexes may range from relatively small, simple outdoor pools operated by smaller units of government, camps, or other sponsors to much larger and more complex natatoriums. Colleges and universities, voluntary agencies, private membership organizations, the armed forces and even employee recreation programs may operate swimming complexes with two, three, or more different pools designed for different uses (recreational swimming and sunbathing, exercise laps, diving, or competitive swimming). In some cases, they combine indoor and outdoor structures with movable covers to adapt to seasonal or climatic changes. With the invention of "wave pools" and other forms of innovative technology, pools today may present entirely new kinds of leisure experiences.

Health and Fitness Centers. Health and fitness centers have become extremely popular in the United States and Canada over the past two decades as a result of the tremendous surge of interest in physical fitness. Sponsored for the most part by private enterprise—sometimes in large franchised chains with many units—they also may be operated by public departments, voluntary agencies, colleges, the armed forces, private membership groups, and employee recreation associations. The key facilities tend to be rooms with exercise machines and weights, although many health spas also include swimming pools, saunas, racquetball or squash courts, indoor or outdoor tracks, and rooms for aerobic dance.

Game Rooms, Lounges, and Video Arcades. In past decades, a popular form of commercial entertainment was visiting a pool or billiard parlor, or a chess or table tennis center. While many of these still exist, they have been replaced to a degree by commercial video arcades with many new electronic games, catering chiefly to a young audience. In some cases, such centers also offer pinball machines or other mechanical amusements. Many colleges and universities have also developed such game rooms, chiefly as a means of raising revenues to support other programs. Voluntary agencies like Boys' and Girls' Clubs also operate game rooms, although these games tend to be less mechanical, and more in the realm of table tennis, billiards, and such table or board games as Skittles, Nok-Hockey, or Monopoly.

Sportsmen's Centers. Two of the most popular outdoor recreation activities—chiefly engaged in by men, but with a growing number of female enthusiasts—are hunting and fishing. While these normally require fairly wild tracts of land or streams or lakes in a natural environment, and therefore tend to use sites managed by public recreation and park agencies, they are in some cases owned by private groups. A growing number of local, public departments today operate sportsmen's centers that offer related activities. These may include indoor and outdoor shooting ranges, trap-shooting or skeet facilities, archery ranges, bait-casting pools, and similar facilities. Often they are used for practice or competition by hunting and fishing clubs, rifle or pistol associations, law-enforcement groups, and other outdoor enthusiasts.

Skating Rinks.   There are two types of skating rinks; one for roller skating and one for ice skating. Roller skating may be carried on using any smooth, flat surface, indoors or out, with specially designed skates that do not damage hardwood floors. Ice skating is obviously more demanding, and may involve either natural or artificial ice arenas. In colder northern climates, recreation agencies may clear and maintain skating areas on lakes or streams, or may flood playgrounds or school yards for outdoor skating. In warmer climates, and to ensure a longer period of high-quality ice, indoor skating rinks have become popular. Because of their high energy and maintenance costs, artificial ice rinks must be heavily marketed to ensure maximum usage and revenues from a variety of different types of recreational users.

Ski Complexes.   With the development of technological devices that made downhill snow skiing feasible for relatively warm climates, many commercial developers have built outstanding ski centers in recent years. These may range from impressive complexes in Colorado, Utah, or Vermont, with several long runs at high altitudes, to small, close-to-home facilities in the Mid-Atlantic and Great Lakes regions—or even in North Carolina or Tennessee. Such ski facilities must rely on artificial snow for much of the season. Usually they operate mechanical tows or chair lifts, and may also offer toboggan runs, ice skating facilities, cross-country ski trails, and similar winter sports facilities, along with lodges, restaurants, and entertainment centers.

Marinas.   Both public and commercial developers have built boat basins, marinas, launching ramps and other facilities to serve the millions of recreational boats in the United States and Canada today. Power-boating, sailing, and other small-craft activities are extremely popular, making it feasible even for municipal authorities in large cities that border on rivers, lakes, or the ocean to build economically self-sustaining marinas and related boating facilities. In many cases, residential developers have built extensive condominium or other vacation-home complexes attached to marinas, some with each home having its own water frontage and boat-launching or mooring site.

Riding Centers.   Another popular outdoor recreation activity is horseback riding. Again, this may take many forms, including so-called Western trail riding, or Eastern-style riding, which involves more intricate skills of horsemanship, including jumping, varied gaits, and dressage for advanced riders. Typically, a number of recreation and park departments today operate stables with exercise rings, in conjunction with networks of riding trails in larger parks. In some cases, this is done through concession arrangements with private stable operators who own the horses and provide programs of instruction and trail riding, using the public department's facilities.

Campgrounds.   Campgrounds represent one of the most widely found and heavily used types of outdoor recreation facility. They are operated by many different types of sponsors, including: (1) federal, state, provincial and other large land-managing agencies that usually operate a network of different parks with campgrounds for overnight campers; (2) commercial campground owners who offer similar facilities, often close to lakes or other recreational sites; (3) voluntary agencies, armed forces, or even colleges or universities that may combine camping and outdoor education programs on natural sites at a distance from their campuses; and (4) residential camp operators with more elaborate facilities, including cabins, dining halls, offices, infirmaries, and extensive sports and other recreational areas for extended use, chiefly by children and youth.

Theme Parks.   Evolving from traditional amusement parks that were situated close to cities in the earlier decades of this century, but that outlived their appeal, theme parks have become a major new thrust in popular entertainment, tourism, and travel. Cleverly designed and marketed to attract family audiences to a sparkling clean, upbeat environment with many new kinds of technological attractions, these parks combine brief excursions into cleverly created, exotic environments, thrill rides, colorful buildings and vistas, and exhibits and games, along with attractively packaged shops, restaurants, and accommodations. Their themes may range from storybook or fairyland characters to different foreign nations, jungle or Wild West environments, world tours, to trips into the future, into the past, or into various novel settings.

There are many other types of settings or special facilities for public recreation use, including botanical gardens, zoos, discotheques, bars, clubs, bowling alleys, and a host of similar examples. However, the 18 major types that have just been briefly described represent a good overall sampling of the most common types of facilities that offer recreation program opportunities.

As indicated earlier, recreation personnel should have an influential voice in the planning and design of all such facilities. While they may not be as knowledgeable about the engineering or structural factors involved as an architect, they should certainly be able to contribute knowledge about what "works" in terms of the layout of different areas, the best materials to use, appropriate dimensions of facilities, and similar concerns.

Once a facility has been constructed, it will be the responsibility of recreation program personnel to run it. This may include direct authority over the maintenance task, or this may be an administratively separate function. In either case, it is important that the recreation practitioner understand the maintenance plan and be in a position to make recommendations for carrying it out effectively, and to request and supervise the repair and replacement of damaged equipment. He or she should be familiar with other procedures that may affect the health and safety of staff and participants.

PROGRAM PLANNING IN DIFFERENT FACILITIES

The primary emphasis of this chapter is not on the physical management of recreation facilities. Instead, it is to show how different types of facilities typically permit or encourage varied program activities and formats, and to show trends in the design of certain major types of facilities. Four major types of facilities will be examined more fully: playgrounds, recreation centers, swimming pools and aquatic complexes, and facilities serving the disabled.

PLANNING PLAYGROUND PROGRAMS

In most communities, playgrounds continue to represent a key responsibility of municipal recreation and park departments. Wuellner points out that the combined public and private playground equipment market is estimated to be between $110 and $135 million, with an annual growth rate of 7.5 to 10 percent.[3]

The traditional functions of neighborhood playgrounds were to serve the play needs of children of preschool or elementary school age with free-play areas and equipment (slide, swings, seesaws, sandboxes, wading pools, and showers), and organized programs of arts and crafts, music, dance, dramatics, games, sports, and hobbies.

It must be recognized that many playgrounds today do not have regular, year-round leadership, and that their success depends very much on the potential appeal of the area's layout and equipment for self-directed play. A number of studies over the last decade have indicated that traditionally conceived playgrounds, with standardized, fixed equipment, are *not* successful in attracting participants for frequent or sustained periods of play.

Limitations of Traditional Playground Design

Wuellner, for example, points out that studies have shown that children typically visit conventional playgrounds for only an average of fifteen minutes a day, and that play apparatus tends to be unused for close to four fifths of the time. Despite these findings, he also reports that playground equipment accidents have ranked high on the Consumer Product Hazard Index, with about 118,000 persons each year receiving hospital emergency room treatment nationwide for injuries related to playground equipment. He concludes:

> This indicates that a child may become bored by using conventional equipment in conventional ways and jeopardize his safety with new ways of using the equipment. This hazardous adaptation might be characterized as either a form of arousal seeking, or a means of developing new areas of competence.[4]

Wallach illustrates the point by pointing out that when children learn to use play equipment and become bored with it, they seek additional, challenging learning experiences, which adults regard as "misuse." For example, the child who has gone down a slide several times in the approved way, then seeks new excitement by coming down head-first on his or her stomach, or in tandem with other children. Attempts to prevent such behavior by more rigid supervision or by designing "safe" equipment are often ineffective. Wallach writes that

> the more safeguards we provide, the lesser the challenge, the sooner the boredom. . . . High risk activities have become exciting play experiences for adults—upon whom children model their play. Grownups today sky-dive, hang-glide, balloon, and rock climb. Television shows children how exciting and satisfying these adventures are. Is it any wonder that children create high-risk situations at play?[5]

New Playground Concepts and Designs

One approach to dealing with this problem has been to design new types of playgrounds and playground equipment. Today, there is a strong effort to provide such facilities with the opportunity for self-directed play and exploration. Generally, they are of three types: (1) theme playgrounds; (2) architect-designed playgrounds; and (3) adventure playgrounds.

Theme Playgrounds.   These often are based on new kinds of play equipment that have been designed and marketed to challenge the child's imagination and promote creative play. Typically, such playgrounds feature huge animals made out of concrete or metal, as well as ships, space rockets, or other structures which are usually brightly colored and designed in contemporary style. Often, such playgrounds are designed to represent a particular theme of history, storybook characters, or world travel. For example,

> Sunnyvale, California, has four such facilities: *a space age* playground, with "craters of the moon," space ships, rockets, and satellites; a *prehistoric park,* dinosaur climbers, a Stone Age spray pool, and a cave in a sandbox; a *southwestern* playground boasting a Spanish galleon and Spanish-style fort, and a *Mississippi River* park, complete with riverboat, riverside "town," and even a muddy flowing stream. Other communities have developed playgrounds based on comic characters, such as "Dennis the Menace," other themes of children's fiction, or world history and travel.[6]

Architect-Designed Playgrounds.   These innovative, one-of-a-kind facilities usually involve varied terrain and construction features, with mounds, walls, tunnels, labyrinths, ropes, and overhead walkways for climbing and crawling. They represent a philosophy that children's growth is heavily dependent on the ability to explore and to create experience, and that children's play can be designed by the participants themselves. Such facilities often do not include areas for sports and games or other leader-directed activities, although in some cases, a "creative play" area may be attached to a larger playground with facilities for traditional playground programming as well.

Adventure Playgrounds.   These represent a unique thrust in playground concepts and originated in a number of European nations where, after

World War II, children were observed to play freely and creatively in bombed sites, often building their own structures and using available objects in free and experimental ways. These led to the development of so-called junk playgrounds, in which used tires, discarded furniture, boulders, timber, and other improvised materials were used as the basis for play.

Gradually, such areas came to be known as "adventure playgrounds." This type of play facility was defined by the British National Playing Field Association as:

> a place where children of all ages, under friendly supervision, are free to do many things they can no longer easily do in our crowded urban society; things like building—huts, walls, forts, dens, tree-houses; lighting fires and cooking; tree climbing, digging, camping; perhaps gardening and keeping animals; as well as playing team and group games, painting, dressing up, modeling, reading—or doing nothing. For it must also be a place where children just meet and talk in a free relaxed atmosphere.[7]

In a description of adventure playgrounds in Vancouver, Canada, Clark points out how children organized themselves independently for activity:

> Within a week, the playground bully was instructing the five-year-olds how to hammer nails. Once the children realized the playleaders would not interfere in their personal relationships unless absolutely necessary, they quickly established their own social order. A monetary system based on pine cones was established, and the opening of a post office by the playleaders paved the way to the construction of a hotel, a Holiday Inn and a McDonalds. With the nucleus of a community established, fort building began in earnest. Interest in gardening was low during the first weeks, but by the conclusion of the programme, flower and vegetable gardens were lovingly tended by almost all children. Dogs were borrowed from the nearby SPCA centre and cats from the centre were regular visitors, much to the delight of the children.[8]

The adventure playground approach illustrates how facilities and program planning are closely linked. Traditional playgrounds make use of standardized equipment in stereotyped ways, and also rely heavily on leader-directed participation in organization and structured forms of activity. Leaders in adventure playgrounds obviously encourage children to learn from their own experiences; they play much more of an enabling role without scheduling formal program elements in advance or teaching activity skills as such. The important question of safety and risk, as it relates to this type of play environment, is discussed in Chapter 10.

RECREATION CENTER PROGRAMS

A second major type of facility operated by many public and voluntary recreation agencies is the recreation center, or *community center* as it is sometimes called. These include: (1) community centers with facilities for athletic, cultural, leisure, educational, and other recreation programs; (2) civic centers, which often have auditoriums, libraries, and government offices; (3) cultural centers, including museums, art galleries, theaters, studios, and workshops; (4) day-care and play centers for younger children; (5) fitness centers; (6) recreation centers, which are generally restricted in purpose to recreational activity, with a heavy emphasis on sports and games, social programs, and arts and crafts; (7) senior centers for elderly persons living in the community; and (8) teen centers, serving chiefly adolescents in the community.

In addition to public departments, many voluntary organizations, such as Ys, Boys' and Girls' Clubs, Police Athletic Leagues, and other nonprofit youth-serving organizations, operate center buildings that often are multipurpose.

Planning Considerations. In building a new community center building in Costa Mesa, California, with funds derived from various federal and local sources, it was necessary to ask:

> Whom do you need and want to serve and how will you respond? Will you be serving the senior population? Will you need an (outdoor) site for activities? Do you plan to provide a space for business meetings, receptions, and entertainment to generate revenues? Or will you benefit the greatest numbers by creating a multipurpose center?[9]

Depending on the answer to these questions, a public or voluntary agency that is planning to build a center will be able to determine the essential purpose of the center, the population it should serve, the most appropriate location, and the kinds of program activities that should be featured. In designing the new Costa Mesa center, in addition to serving the city's senior citizens club during the day, the building was planned to accommodate reasonably priced conventions, conferences, banquets, community meetings, and wedding receptions. Kitchen facilities, seminar and banquet rooms, a large hall with a stage and dressing rooms, portable bars, and a portable dance floor all lend themselves to this type of use.

Other centers have incorporated the revenue-raising emphasis found in the Costa Mesa center, but with a wider range of facilities and program features. The Fairfax County, Virginia Park Authority has constructed four major self-supporting indoor recreation centers, for example, and has plans for the construction of four additional facilities and the expansion of two existing sites. In terms of facilities, Downs writes:

> These centers provide swimming pools (25- or 50-meter), saunas, locker rooms, exercise/weight rooms, video and table game areas, lounging space, concession/food service, handball/racquetball/squash courts, darkrooms, nursery rooms, dance rooms, meeting/class rooms, and arts and crafts space. In addition, one center houses an ice rink and a Jacuzzi; another encompasses an indoor gymnasium. All facilities are accessible to persons with disabilities.[10]

Fairfax County's four recreation centers' annual operating costs are approximately $2.7 million, balanced by $3 million in revenue generated by user fees. These fees are reviewed semiannually and compared with those of other privately and publicly owned facilities offering comparable programming and facilities. A quarterly *Leisure Fitness Pass* entitles the holder to unlimited use of the swimming pool, sauna, locker rooms, and weight rooms at any of the four sites. Classes in swimming, physical fitness, dancing, photography, pottery, skating, sports, fine arts, crafts and other special hobby interests bring in a total of about $750,000 in fees annually, and video game rooms have generated about $100,000 in profits each year.

In addition, rental of the center facilities by organized sports groups, ranging from the Washington Capitals hockey team to local swim teams and ice-skating clubs, assures constant use of special facilities during nonpeak hours. So detailed is the effort to market the facilities effectively that swimming pools rent out lanes, leaving space available for classes as well as "drop-in" swimmers at the same time. Local business and government agencies such as military bases account for much of the daytime use of the Park Authority's facilities. Obviously, these centers represent an excellent example of the "marketing" model applied to the operation of special recreation center facilities.

Specialized Types of Centers: Senior Centers

In addition to multiuse facilities serving different age groups with varied activities, many recreation centers are designed to focus on a particular type of activity or recreational use, or on a given type of population. Senior centers represent an example of the latter category.

There are several thousand senior centers and Golden Age clubs in the United States today, and a proportionate number in Canada. Senior centers are considered to be agencies that meet for substantial periods of time—usually during the day—several days a week. Operating under professional direction, they usually offer several different types of services and program activities (Table 8–1). Usually, they operate in their own facilities, and may be sponsored by different kinds of agencies, such as municipal recreation and park departments, housing or welfare agencies, or religious federations. In contrast, Golden Age clubs are usually social or recreational clubs for older persons, operating under volunteer or nonprofessional leadership, and meeting much less frequently.

TABLE 8–1 Average Hours Per Month of Activities Offered in Senior Centers[11]

Activities/Services	Hours per month	Percent of total
Active recreation	22	.05
Creative activities	58	.14
Sedentary recreation	61	.15
Nutrition counseling	15	.038
Education	22	.05
Counseling	34	.08
Information and referral	50	.12
Other services (employment, health)	40	.10
Meals on premises	64	.16
Governing activities	10	.02
Leadership development	11	.02

Typical recreation activities in senior centers include arts and crafts, informal conversation, Bingo, dance and drama activities, hobbies, table games and modified sports, group singing, outings, and other social recreation pastimes. In addition to these leisure activities, many senior centers offer varied social services, such as the following, which are drawn from the program of the South County Senior Center in Edmonds, Washington.

Hot Lunch Program	Adult Basic Education
Legal Aid Service	Vision Care and Glasses Repair
Religious Education	Hearing Aid Repair
Food Stamp Certification	Senior Power and Political
Seminar on Issues Affecting	Discussion Group
the Aging	Nutrition Consultant
Income Tax Service[21]	

Too often such programs are accepted as a fact of life or as the benevolent gift of a municipal government or other social agency. What is not realized is that it often requires the concerted effort of many community groups—including senior citizens themselves—to have a facility constructed and to develop a high-quality program.

Example of Community Process: Buena Park Senior Center

To illustrate, a determined group of senior citizens in Buena Park, California, were the moving force in an effort that took several years of campaigning and planning and finally resulted in a $1.2 million, 18,129 square-foot facility with outstanding facilities and programming elements to serve the community's elderly residents.

Beginning in 1975, when the idea was first proposed to the city of Buena Park Parks and Recreation Commission, studies were conducted, sites were considered, and fund-raising sources were explored. The culmination of these efforts was an outstanding facility with the following program areas:

> The center has three large dining/meeting rooms, which seat 896 assembly style and 418 banquet style. There are two classrooms, two meeting rooms, one game room, one adult day care center, one gift shop, one nurses station, one conference room, two administrative offices, one reception area, two kitchens, one kiln room, one passive outdoor recreation area, and one active outdoor recreation area.
>
> The active outdoor recreation area has two shuffleboard courts, two horseshoe pits, and picnic tables with embossed checker and chess boards on the top . . . . The building is uniquely constructed to allow versatility in the large dining and multi-purpose area. The room can be divided, by electrically operated partitions, into as many as five separate rooms or used as one expansive area with a total of 6,283 square feet. In addition, there are other classroom facilities should a group need the entire multi-purpose room.[12]

Programs include numerous social, artistic, and game activities as well as discount-purchase plans, free physical examinations, a nutrition and meals-on-wheels program, a branch library in the center, a unit of the Retired Senior Volunteer Program (RSVP), and a special day care center open five days a week from 8 A.M. to 5 P.M. for individuals who have been moderately disabled by stroke, heart disease, hearing or visual impairments, and similar conditions, and who require special assistance to be able to continue to live in the community independently.

The key point of this illustration is that directing such a center involves far more than simply planning and carrying out a selection of recreation activities. Instead, it requires a creative, responsive approach to meeting the needs and interests of elderly persons, plus the ability to coordinate and work closely with individuals and agencies representing a variety of interests and special disciplines.

SWIMMING POOL PROGRAMS

We now examine a third type of special facility: swimming pools. As earlier chapters have shown, swimming is one of the most popular of indoor and outdoor recreation activities throughout the United States and Canada, with estimates showing that approximately half of the total population takes part in it at least occasionally.

Until recently, almost all pools were constructed with the purpose of satisfying two primary needs: competition and instruction. They were typically designed as rectangular structures deep at one end and shallower at the other (but still deep enough to continue to swim from end to end). Mackie comments, "rarely, until very recently, [has] a pool's potential as a non-competitive, recreational facility [been] given proper consideration."[13]

Recreational Approaches to Swimming Pool Design

We have gradually become aware of the need to recognize other popular uses of swimming pools. For example, Henry Wong, a Canadian recreation planner, comments that he regards himself as a "passive recreator" who does not like to swim laps, but wants to relax and have fun when he goes to a pool. Speaking for millions of others, he writes:

> We want sun—plenty of sunshine, water, fountains, waterfalls, free-form pools, palm trees, nature, music, splashing, a cool gin-and-tonic, deck chairs, umbrellas, take a nap, noise of waves, cool breeze, people . . . . plenty of deck space to lie down on or lounge on. . . .[14]

Jasulak points out that in the three leading countries in Western Europe in the field of indoor swimming pools—Great Britain, Germany, and the Netherlands—planners have come to realize that new design features are necessary to provide appropriate leisure activities for the majority of pool-users, and for the family as a unit. He summarizes research carried out in Holland on the needs and behavior patterns of visitors in existing conventional, rectangular swimming pools:

> Only 11 percent of those attending came for physical exercise. Eighty-nine percent viewed their visit to a swimming pool as a way to combine leisure activity and physical exercise, with the emphasis on leisure activity. Swimming by itself did not appear to be essential. The stay and the play in and around the pool were the desired elements.[15]

He goes on to describe the observed behavior of people vacationing at holiday resorts around the Mediterranean, in Italy, France, and Spain; they usually spend whole days in and around the hotel swimming pools, relaxing under the palm trees, or at the beach, playing in the waves and at the same time doing little swimming. Jasulak writes:

> In their home countries . . . these same people rarely go to their local swimming pools. The question is, why? Of course the warm climate and the sun play a very important part. The attractiveness of the hotel swimming pools was enhanced by a number of things—the free form of the pools, water temperature, wide and spacious pool decks with sunbathing facilities, subtropical flora, such as palm trees, color, and other elements.[16]

Many of these elements have been incorporated in leisure-oriented swimming pools, including whirlpools, slides, wave machines, and pyramid and dome structures with transparent or translucent materials that admit as much sunlight as possible. In many of the newer pools, restaurants have been placed with a view of the "beach" area, along with adjacent areas for recreational indoor activities like squash, racquetball, table tennis, bowling, or chess, or special playrooms for children and youth. Such pools have been constructed by both public and commercial agencies with great success.

The key point is that, both from a quality-of-life and a marketing perspective, analyzing user needs and interests can lead to radically new kinds of designs. This does not mean that there is no place for conventional pools, but rather that new formulas are needed for pools that are intended to serve primarily as leisure centers, and to appeal to the majority of potential users.

Water-Play Parks.   As a dramatic extension of this concept, and based on much of the new technology that has been developed over the past fifteen years, a number of public commercial sponsors have developed large-scale water-play parks. These are facilities which require a minimum site of five or six acres, with a minimum of eight to ten additional acres for parking. Shedlock writes that, although there are now about thirty such parks in the United States, Canada, and Mexico, they are still sufficiently uncommon to be unfamiliar to most people:

Fundamentally, a full-scale water-play park consists of a major swimming pool equipped with wave-making machinery, one or more activity pools, often featuring diving platforms, pulley slides, and small "waterfalls;" and a number of body flumes and slides. This often is augmented by special play areas for small children, and by non-water-play activity areas. A reasonable proportion of space allocated to rest and sunbathing also is vital.[17]

Although most such water-play parks have been commercially developed, one highly successful public one, Point Mallard Aquatic Center in Alabama, continues to grow in attendance year after year. Shedlock comments that the long-term popularity of such facilities seems assured. Much in the way that Disneyland changed the image of the amusement park into an acceptable form of family entertainment, he writes, the water-play park has begun to transform the experience of going to the beach into something which is both safer and more fun for the entire family!

SPECIAL FACILITIES FOR THE DISABLED

Another important type of facility to consider from a programming point of view is the recreation center, park, playground, or other special facility designed for use by handicapped groups. With an estimated 60 million persons in the United States who are suffering from some significant degree of disability, and with a comparable population in Canada, there is growing awareness of the need to provide adequate recreation programs and facilities for such individuals.

The issue of facilities access may simply require removing architectural barriers that prevent entry and participation, and providing needed ramps, wide doors, accessible toilet facilities, and similar elements. It may also involve the special design of equipment and areas to involve and challenge the disabled, or to make participation more enjoyable and successful.

For example, a number of organizations have designed and constructed special playgrounds, small parks, nature centers, swimming pools, and entire recreation centers designed to serve the disabled and in some cases their families. While the problem might appear to be one of modifying areas to serve the physically disabled, some facilities have also been designed to be specially appropriate from a learning point of view for the mentally retarded or learning disabled. In this sense, it is not simply a matter of providing access to a facility, but of designing program opportunities that are as enriching as possible in terms of motor learning, cognitive, social, and environmental awareness development.

Playgrounds and Small Parks for the Disabled.   As an example, an unusual playground was developed for disabled preschool children at the New York University Medical Center's Institute of Rehabilitation Medicine. Designed by a well-known architect, it includes a ladder leading to a tree house (which may also be reached by ramps), a waterfall, tabletop sandboxes, and other forms of equipment that contribute to the development of participants. Similarly, a special playground for disabled children has been developed by the Child Study Center in Fort Worth, Texas, and other cities and leisure-service organizations have planned experimental facilities of this type.

Storage and Bowers point out that a few playground equipment manu-facturing companies have designed special play facilities to meet the creative play needs of severely disabled children. At the same time, they comment, these facilities afford a challenging and exciting place to play for nondisabled children. Design segregation of play facilities, they write,

> is not generally desirable. The integrated design context, consequently, is the optimum concept for our future parks and playgrounds. . . . [They] are con-structed to increase the possibility of children meeting and interacting with a variety of people with differing physical and social characteristics.[18]

Other communities have developed special types of outdoor play facilities that go beyond the routine purpose of providing areas for recreational use to promote a full range of developmental and growth experiences. For example, the Town of Hempstead, New York, has constructed an Environmental Resource Center on the Atlantic Ocean at Lido Beach Town Park. This facility was designed to serve both disabled and nondisabled children, youth, and adults for the town's ANCHOR Program (Answering the Needs of Children with Handicaps through Organized Recreation), an organization with about 750 par-ticipants. The Environmental Resource Center utilizes:

> large garden plots worked by the participants, nature trails related to the ecological systems of the seashore, three camping areas for platform tent camping, a large center building, outdoor shelter areas, beach access at three locations, special curbing and sitting walls to guide the blind, hard-topped game areas and pathways and a playground designed as a progressive obstacle course.[19]

Among the specific program activities provided at this center have been music, arts and crafts, physical exercise, field and court games, aquatics, special events, field trips, home economics and health-related activities, horticulture, animal husbandry, and outdoor recreation skills—all based on the environment, wherever possible.

Recreation Centers for the Disabled

A number of communities have developed special centers for the dis-abled. Probably the outstanding facility of this type is the Recreation Center for the Handicapped, in San Francisco, California. Established in 1952, this organ-ization today serves 1600 severely disabled individuals ranging from infants to adults, with numerous recreation programs and related services that include camping and nature-oriented activities, a day-care operation, referral, social-

service, and educational activities, as well as extensive outreach activities and
transportation assistance using 17 vehicles that average 38,000 miles per month.
It has 80 full-time paid employees and involves 150 volunteers each week.

In addition to programs operated at its main facility, the Center also
conducts programs in satellite facilities in senior complexes, public playgrounds,
church basements and YMCAs and YWCAs. In terms of the populations served:

> The Center is the primary provider of socialization programs for the adult
> mentally retarded who have spent many years in institutions, and is a major
> factor in their successful adjustment to community living.
> A Day Care program serves profoundly retarded, multi-disabled young
> adults, who would otherwise vegetate in their homes or require hospitalization.
> A pre-school program is provided for severely disabled infants and children
> ranging from one to three years of age.[20]

Other populations involved include children and teenagers enrolled in
school, school graduates, physically disabled adults, and senior citizens.

The cooperative relationships that have been developed by the San
Francisco Recreation Center for the Handicapped include several kinds of involvements. Funds are raised by the Board of Directors from individuals, civic
and fraternal organizations, and special shows, benefits, and rummage sales. In
addition, the San Francisco Recreation and Park Department, the Community
Mental Health Service, and the municipal Department of Social Services sub-
sidize a major portion of the center's budget. It has also received as many as five
federal grants at a time to provide care for previously institutionalized, mentally
retarded persons, and to support a physical fitness program serving all participants. In addition, the center has worked closely over a period of more than thirty
years with numerous community organizations who continue to assist it financially. These include foundations, men's and women's fraternal associations,
service clubs, the Parents' Auxiliary, private individuals, and corporations with
"community involvement teams."

In addition to its in-house programming, the San Francisco Recreation
Center for the Handicapped has developed an extensive outreach program serving over 900 individuals. These include the following kinds of services:

> One-to-one visits for those who cannot leave their homes due to the severity
> of their disability, their inability to socially interact in a group, or who are afraid
> to go out.
> Small travel groups for physically disabled seniors, mobile severely retarded
> who are in transition to a group situation, and the mentally ill who live in Board
> and Care Homes.
> An infant stimulation program for. . . severely disabled children from the
> day of birth until progress makes a day care place possible.
> A group socialization program for seniors in 18 Housing Authority apartment
> complexes.
> Socialization and resocialization programs for the elderly in 17 small residen-
> tial care homes.[21]

Clearly, this agency provides an outstanding example of the human-
services approach to recreation program development. Perhaps the most impor-

tant point that it illustrates is that recreation must respond to real needs, as a form of community service—but that, when it does so, it is possible to call on immense resources and forms of assistance in carrying out significant programming.

Selection of Program Activities and Services

This chapter has shown how the wide range of available recreational activities and services that were described in Chapter 7 may be organized and presented within several different types of formats, and in specialized kinds of facilities that impose certain challenges and program needs.

Initially, the underlying philosophy and program goals of the recreation agency are used to screen those activities that are appropriate for program inclusion. Based on the age, sex, socioeconomic and educational backgrounds of participants along with their physical and emotional characteristics and expressed needs and interests, a further determination of desirable activities is made. If the setting is a hospital or other rehabilitative agency, it is likely that activity program planning will be carried out on an individualized basis, and will reflect the results of a thorough assessment of patient/client needs, as well as the recommendations of other members of the treatment team.

At this point, program planners are ready to make firm decisions about the age levels that are to be served or about other ways of grouping or attracting participants. It is now possible to decide what formats the activities will take, and where they will be offered.

Questions of possible fees and charges or cosponsorship arrangements must all be resolved at this time. Ultimately, the task of evolving a final program plan becomes one of providing the activities that are most likely to yield the greatest attendance and most positive benefits in terms of participant outcomes within the framework of the organization's realistic capability. The specific process of laying out the program plan, developing staff assignments, and determining schedules for various activities is presented in Chapter 9.

NOTES_____

[1]Joseph P. Downs, "Planning and Marketing: Two Keys to a Recreation Center's Success," *Parks and Recreation* (October 1983): 31.

[2]Rhodell E. Owens, "The Role of Park Maintenance in Community Preservation and Beautification," *Parks and Recreation* (February 1983): 37.

[3]Lance Wuellner, "Forty Guidelines for Playground Design," *Journal of Leisure Research* (1st Q., 1979): 5.

[4]Wuellner: 5.

[5]Frances Wallach, "Play in the Age of Technology," *Parks and Recreation* (April 1983): 37.

[6]See Richard Kraus and Joseph Curtis, *Creative Management in Recreation and Parks* (St. Louis: C. V. Mosby, 1982), p. 141.

[7]See Christopher Edginton, David Compton, and Carole Hanson, *Recreation and Leisure Programming: A Guide for the Professional* (Philadelphia: Saunders College Publishing, 1980), p. 194.

[8]Terri Clark, "Creative and Adventure Playgrounds in Vancouver Area,"' *Recreation Canada* (April 1978): 35.

[9]Jon Ribble, "Before You Build: A Check List of Community Center Considerations," *Parks and Recreation* (October 1983): 38.

[10]Downs: 30.

[11]"Senior Centers: Report of Senior Group Programs in America, 1975," in Max Kaplan, *Leisure: Lifestyle and Lifespan: Perspectives for Gerontology* (Philadelphia: W.B. Saunders, 1980), p. 104.

[12]Sue Williams, "A Victory for Seniors: A Center Under One Roof," *Parks and Recreation* (October 1983): 35.

[13]Bill Mackie, "Swimming Pools: Is Biggest the Best?" *Recreation Canada* (June 1980): 14.

[14]Henry Wong, "Recreation Facility for the Passive Majority," *Recreation Canada* (June 1980): 7.

[15]Neil Jaskulak, "European Swimming Pool Designs Cross the Atlantic," *Parks and Recreation* (March 1983): 45.

[16]Jaskulak: 45.

[17]Robert E. Shedlock, "Water-Play Parks on Public Land: A Revenue Source and a Public Benefit," *Parks and Recreation* (March 1983): 39.

[18]T. W. Storage and Louis E. Bowers, "Playgrounds of the Future," *Parks and Recreation* (April 1983): 33.

[19]See Ray McGrath, "Environmental Resource Center—Making the Outdoors Available to the Handicapped," in Larry Neal, ed., *Leisure Today: Selected Readings* (Washington, D.C.: American Association for Leisure and Recreation, 1975), p. 92.

[20]*General Fact Sheet* (San Francisco, Calif.: Recreation Center for the Handicapped, 1983), n.p.

[21]*General Fact Sheet*, n.p.

STUDENT PROJECTS

1. This chapter uses swimming pools as a special example to show how many different activity formats may be found in a single type of facility. As a brainstorming exercise, consider other types of facilities or major program categories like arts and crafts or outdoor recreation and have the class suggest a wide variety of different program formats for these facilities or activity categories.
2. The chapter identifies 18 different types of facilities, and describes four of them in detail (playgrounds, centers, facilities for the handicapped, and aquatic complexes). Have the class divide into small groups, and have each group select one type of facility, excluding the four already covered. Have them examine the literature or visit selected sites, if possible, to identify trends in the design and construction of such facilities, and their implications for program development.

SUGGESTED READINGS

Christopher Edginton, David Compton and Carole Hanson, *Recreation and Leisure Programming: A Guide for the Professional* (Philadelphia: Saunders College Publishing, 1980), Chapters 6 and 7.

Patricia Farrell and Herberta Lundegren, *The Process of Recreation Programming* (New York: John Wiley, 1978), Chapter 3.

Richard Kraus, Gaylene Carpenter, and Barbara Bates, *Recreation Leadership and Supervision: Guidelines for Professional Development* (Philadelphia: Saunders College Publishing, 1981), Chapters 11 and 12.

CHAPTER 9 _____

Developing the _____
Program Plan_____

_____

_____

_____

Myra Polanski, director of the High Falls Senior Center, smiled at the group of center members who had stayed after the regular session to meet with her. She was going over the spring schedule activities with them to get their reaction.

"Most of these activities," she said, "are things we've done before. The only thing I'm wondering about is this idea of a spring carnival that we would run jointly with three other senior centers in town. I understand the purpose would be to raise funds to assist the handicapped children's program at the Ward School. That's a very nice idea, but do you think we can really handle it?"

"Why not?" asked an elderly man sitting in the corner. He was new to Myra, and had only been coming to the High Falls Center for the last few weeks.

"Well, it will be a lot of work," she said. "Contacting the other centers, developing different booths, planning a budget, and so on."

"I'd be willing to help," said the newcomer. "And I'm sure others would pitch in."

"We'll need a chairperson to head it up," Myra said. "Would you be willing to do that? And do you think you'd be able to handle it?"

"Yes, I would," said the man. "I've got a lot of free time. And I'm sure I could do it. I used to be the head of a big company; I'm pretty capable."

We have now arrived at step 6 of the program-planning process. It is time to develop the plan itself, by making a number of key decisions about programs, including the population groups that we plan to serve, the activities we will offer, the formats they will take, and the locations where programs will be provided. Such decisions, along with specific plans for scheduling activities at various levels of participation, are all part of the program-planning process.

We will now review and discuss each part of this process to gain a better understanding of the forms a program plan may take and how it can enable an agency to provide an efficient and successful range of leisure services and opportunities to the public at large or to a more sharply defined audience.

NATURE OF THE PLAN

First, what *is* the plan? It usually consists of a carefully worked-out, comprehensive statement of the program activities and services that the agency plans to offer over a specific period of time. It normally includes a seasonal breakdown of program elements along with relevant information about the population groups to be served, the assignment of staff members to program responsibilities, the facilities where activities will be offered, and similar factors.

A simple plan for a relatively small program may be provided on a page or two, or on a bulletin board or other graphic presentation. The plan for a much larger or more complex agency may fill a large manual, including detailed projections of attendance, budget breakdowns, and other details. Obviously, it will not always be possible to predict all program events or services that will be offered during the year. However, all major divisions of service and all important functional areas should be outlined at this point.

It should be understood that *not all* agencies formulate a precise written plan as just described. In many cases, they may simply describe major program areas in which activities are to be offered, as well as overall program goals, and then permit those in charge of districts of a city, or of specific areas of program activity, to define the precise activities to be sponsored.

In this chapter, primary emphasis is given to overall agency programs—rather than to planning of separate components of activity, such as youth activities, or drama programs. And, while a number of references may be made to planning for individual clients or patients, this is not a major thrust of the chapter.

STEPS INVOLVED IN DEVELOPING THE PLAN

This process involves making a final decision regarding the activities and services that will be offered in the program as well as other decisions with respect to the format in which they will be presented, the location in which they will be offered, the nature of the agency's sponsoring or cosponsoring role, and the actual schedule that will be followed.

It is highly desirable to involve participants in this phase of the planning process. Rather than simply ask them what activities they would like to see

FIGURE 9–1   Steps Involved in Developing the Plan

1. Selection of appropriate activities, based on:
   a. agency philosophy, goals, objectives, and policies
   b. expressed desires of participants, clients, members or community advisory groups
   c. staff views, expressed through participative management and cooperative goal structuring process
   d. consideration of budgetary factors
2. Design of selected activities, including:
   a. selection of program formats for different activities
   b. determining levels of involvement (beginner, intermediate, advanced, leadership roles)
   c. age group, developmental needs, and gender groupings
3. Nature of sponsorship or cosponsorship roles
4. Preliminary determination of major program elements:
   a. scheduling (seasonal, monthly, weekly, daily)
   b. determination of staff assignments, appropriate locations for activities, and similar factors

offered, surveys may explore the degree of priority or importance they assign to different program elements, as well as their attitudes on fees and on the facilities, activities, and leadership provided.

Decision-Making Process

As described in Chapter 2, there are several different approaches to decision making in the program-planning process, including: the traditional, expressed desires, authoritarian, current practices, sociopolitical, prescriptive, and cafeteria approaches.

In actual practice, many organizations use a composite approach that combines several of these elements. In some types of agencies—such as armed forces or corporate/employee recreation units—it is probable that greater emphasis might be placed on authoritarian or current-practices approaches. In others, such as therapeutic recreation, prescriptive programming would be favored.

The decision-making process in program planning must obviously be based on the agency's stated philosophy, goals, and objectives. If clear-cut policies regarding program priorities and scheduling have been established, these must be followed. Beyond this, two key elements should be the expressed desires approach, which was stressed in Chapter 5, combined with the management technique known as "cooperative goal structuring."

Cooperative Goal Structuring.   This simply represents a form of participative management. Little points out that for any organization to be effective, its members must behave in a manner that supports organizational goals. Since problem solving, implementation of decisions and performance of complex tasks all require cooperation, using cooperative procedures should enhance the successful operation of an entire leisure-service agency. She writes:

> The leisure service manager serves an important role in articulating congruency between organizational and employee goals. To structure goals

cooperatively, managers should present a task or problem to everyone in the organization who affects or is affected by it, establish group ownership of the task, design nonthreatening ways to exchange information and ideas, develop problem-solving groups based on individual strengths, and reinforce successful completion of each step through feedback.[1]

Applied to the program-planning process, this means that there should be a systematic and widespread effort to get the views of participants regarding program plans for the coming year or season. This would include careful review of evaluation forms for programs that had been carried out in the past, as well as the use of interest surveys to have participants rate past, present, and possible future activities. It might also involve planning sessions with representatives of special-interest groups, neighborhood associations, center advisory councils, or similar bodies.

The wishes and recommendations of such groups would be carefully recorded, or presented directly at staff meetings. At this point, all agency personnel who have a stake in program development should have the opportunity to present their recommendations for program changes—including the addition of new programs, the modification of existing programs, and the deletion of past, unsuccessful programs. Attendance records would be carefully reviewed, to fill out the picture.

At this stage, the concepts and principles presented in the preceding chapters of this text would be applied.

> Will the program elements that are being considered support the basic philosophy and goals of the leisure-service agency?
>
> Will they serve diverse populations—of different ages, genders, socioeconomic backgrounds, ethnic, and life-style interests—equitably?
>
> Will they meet important community needs and help promote desirable values of a democratic society—or other specific values of the sponsoring organization?
>
> Will they make appropriate use of available community or agency resources?
>
> Will they have diversity and balance, and will they offer challenge and depth to participants?
>
> Will they be suited to the developmental abilities and needs of participants, and will they be designed to serve such special populations as the physically or mentally disabled?

Application of External Guidelines.   In addition to using such program-planning criteria, planners may also need to consider standards or requirements that come from other sources.

For example, in the field of therapeutic recreation service, the National Therapeutic Recreation Society has developed a set of Standards for Practice that deals with such elements as the orientation of clients, program development and implementation, program content, leisure education, interdisciplinary activities, and the scheduling of services. In most therapeutic recreation settings, the effort would be made to adhere to these standards or to other professionally mandated practices.

Many recreation agencies that are funded to carry out programs do so under very precisely worded guidelines or contractual agreements that define the services they will provide. As an example, colleges and universities that sponsor summer youth sports programs funded by Congress through the National Collegiate Athletic Association know that their programs will be evaluated according to a specific set of standards, and plan their programs in accordance with these standards.

Budgetary Considerations.   A key consideration at this point involves budgetary factors. What will it cost to operate a given program, and how will it vary according to the number of participants, the number and type of staff members, the location, and similar factors?

On the other side of the ledger, what revenues might be derived from fees and charges for this activity or service, and how would this affect probable participation?

Would it be possible—and desirable—to operate a given program on a subcontracting basis, with an outside group conducting it for a fee? Could it be converted to a concession-run activity, and what impact would that have on the agency's mission within city government or as part of another organization?

If the program is being carried on in a corporate/employee setting, how much of it will be subsidized by the company, and how much of its financial support will have to be derived from participant fees?

If it is being conducted in a hospital or other treatment setting, will its costs be paid for through a reimbursement plan, through third-party payments from insurance companies or Medicaid funding?

In a voluntary agency, can certain programs receive special support from Community Chest, United Way, or similar funding sources?

Such factors must be carefully considered, and may be sharply defined through a cost-benefit analysis that measures both costs and varied benefits and outcomes as precisely as possible. Although a given activity may be relatively costly and may yield little or no revenue in return, it may have such a high priority of social value that it *should* be supported. On the other hand, it may be necessary to seek outside sponsors or cooperative sponsorship arrangements, to offer such activities and services.

Kemp and Feliciano write that many recreation managers are seeking ways to maintain existing programs and even provide additional services, without requiring more departmental budget support. The latest buzzword, they write, has to do with "leveraging" public services.

> Experimenting with this leveraging factor has occurred primarily in the cultural and recreational service areas. It involves the use of volunteers and part-time employees to provide a greater level of service at a minimal cost. Additionally, as user fees and charges are increased, public officials are providing a "safety valve" of increased fees in an effort to accommodate those citizens who

cannot afford to pay the added cost. "Free days" and "free times" are quickly becoming a political fact of life.[2]

Other Fiscal Strategies. Many leisure-service agencies are exploring the avenues of cosponsored or specially funded programs, to help reduce the financing problems involved in supporting certain activities. Similarly, every possibility for having other agencies or organizations provide needed community services—without cost to the agency—should be explored. Kemp and Feliciano describe the practice of having varied community organizations use the Seaside, California, recreation center, without charge, to provide numerous programs and services:

> Examples of social services provided to the public at no expense to the taxpayer include rehabilitation education for disabled persons, a senior nutrition program, an alcohol awareness program, a vegetable brown-bag program, constituent times for elected state officials, estate planning course, life savings courses, and a host of other social programs for senior and disabled citizens. About 50 social programs are provided by various community organizations at little or no expense to the taxpayers.[3]

Such approaches are not restricted to social-service programs, but may also include many clearly recreational activities. In the same center, drama, dancing, youth excursions, swimming lessons, teen dances, card games, square dancing, clogging classes, ballet, modern dance, body movement, flower arranging and even bingo sessions are provided by outside groups, at little or no cost to the recreation department or the taxpayer.

Selection of Program Formats

At the same time that decisions are being made about the activities that are to be offered, it is also necessary to make related decisions about their formats, the groups they will serve, and appropriate scheduling arrangements. Rather than simply ask participants what activities they would like to see offered, surveys may explore such issues as their motivations for taking part in activity, the importance they assign to different types of programs, attitudes toward fees, and opinions regarding the facilities, activities, and leadership provided.

For example, a pilot study of user preferences was conducted at three indoor campus recreation facilities at the University of Michigan. Over 400 users—including undergraduate and graduate students, faculty and staff members, alumni, guests and spouses—were surveyed regarding their choices and preferences of activity, and their reactions to different possible cost-cutting strategies in the program. Table 9–1 shows their responses to one section of this survey, yielding information of considerable value to campus recreation program planners.

Frequently, such studies or surveys will provide helpful information in determining which activities to offer, and in what type of format. Obviously, certain kinds of activities lend themselves almost automatically to certain kinds of formats. For example, arts and crafts tend to be best suited to instruction, free play or unstructured participation, and to exhibitions or demonstrations. Nature and environmental programs often lend themselves to instructional activities, trips and outings, and community-service projects.

Rossman carried out a study of recreation participants, and determined that the kinds of satisfaction they reported were clearly related to different types of activity formats:

> Satisfaction with social enjoyment appears to be least likely to be realized in instructional classes and most likely to be realized in special events. Similarly, satisfaction with leisure programs for the opportunities they provide for family escape seems least likely to be realized in leader-directed programs and open-facility operations.[4]

TABLE 9–1   Frequency of Participation and Budgetary Priorities of Campus Recreation Users[5]

1. How many times per week do you use the facilities for recreational purposes?

Number of Times:	1–6	6–10	11–15	16 or more
	67%	29%	3%	1%

2. If the Recreational Sports Department was short of money and had to cut back or eliminate some services, which would you propose they do first, second, and third?

	Increase Fees	Cut Hours	Cut Programs
First choice:	44%	11%	59%
Second choice:	35%	33%	24%
Third choice:	21%	56%	17%

3. What is the maximum fee you would be willing to pay per year?

$5	$10	$15	$20	$25
29%	31%	14%	9%	17%

4. Which hours would you prefer to see eliminated?

	Morning	Extended Noon Hour	Late Afternoon	Early Evening	Late Evening
First choice:	53%	11%	11%	4%	21%
Second choice:	19%	16%	26%	6%	33%
Third choice:	1%	30%	17%	13%	39%

5. Which of these programs would you eliminate first, last, or not at all?

	Intramural Program	Sports Club	Special Interest	Drop-In Hours
Cut first:	24%	54%	62%	7%
Cut last:	31%	29%	25%	16%
Not at all:	45%	17%	13%	77%

Note: this is only a *partial* selection of the survey questions.

In planning programs, it is important to provide formats that "connect" with each other in logical ways and help to enrich the overall program. Instruction will logically lead to organized groups, competition, and exhibitions. Special-interest groups may be interested in doing performances, taking trips, or other formats that help them explore their interests further and at the same time involve social contacts.

OTHER WAYS OF ORGANIZING PROGRAM ACTIVITIES

In addition to planning different types of formats to meet the needs of different age groups or special populations, it is necessary to plan activities at different levels of involvement.

Levels of Involvement

For example, in a community art center, *beginners, intermediate,* or *advanced* classes might be offered in oil painting, ceramics, or other arts and crafts program areas.

In an aquatics program, participants might be classified as *nonswimmers, beginners, intermediate* or *advanced* swimmers, or on successive levels of leadership skill or certification.

Organizing program groups in this way makes it possible to lead or instruct activities efficiently—presenting learning tasks or other forms of activity involvement that are appropriate for participants at their present stage of ability, rather than having to adapt lessons and challenges to a wide range of abilities.

In addition, it provides the opportunity for participants to progress from one level to more advanced ones, thus helping to maintain their interest and motivation and bringing about the fullest possible personal development.

Groupings Based on Age Categories

It is also common practice in recreation to develop groups based on age categories. In many cases, this ties in directly with level of ability. For example, in Little League baseball, each successive age group, beginning with 8-year-olds and extending through the minor and major leagues for older players, will be marked by a higher level of playing ability.

Many activities are more acceptable to participants if they are organized on an age-group basis. For example, adults will feel more comfortable in a ballet or modern dance class if their fellow students are adults or older teenagers, rather than children—even if the children have a high level of dance expertise.

Elderly individuals often prefer to be in programs with other senior citizens, although some successful inter-generational programs have been developed. With the growing number of older persons in our society and the need to improve communication and understanding between them and other age groups, increasing support is being given to such efforts, and recreation program planners should consider the possibility of cutting across age-defined lines in selected programs.

Developmental Needs

Still another way of organizing groups is based on the developmental needs of participants. This approach is commonly found in therapeutic recreation programs serving the developmentally disabled or mentally retarded. Here, it is common practice to carry out a process of activity analysis, which identifies the social, psychomotor, cognitive, and other elements of specific program activities, and to make use of these to achieve specific behavioral-change objectives among participants.

Within activities such as roller skating, music, or swimming, various learning tasks are identified at successive levels of complexity, and clients are introduced to them based on a treatment plan that establishes learning objectives that build on previously mastered skills. In such settings, functional levels of participants would normally be diagnosed, and they would be assigned to groups based on reasonably comparable levels of developmental need and capability.

Grouping Based on Gender

Traditionally, much recreation program participation tended to be based on sex grouping, with separate programs of athletics for boys and men, and with a tendency to design a number of activities in such areas as the arts, dance and music, or homemaking-related activities, chiefly for women.

As described in Chapter 5, sex stereotyping has recently been challenged in many settings. In terms of the activities themselves, girls and women have successfully entered many areas of sports activity, outdoor recreation, or similar programs that were formerly thought of as exclusively masculine domains. Boys and men have begun to feel freer about engaging in activities that were formerly considered to be essentially feminine in nature.

In some cases, organizations themselves that had been entirely masculine or entirely feminine in their membership and service orientation have moved into a joint-gender orientation. Many formerly all-male Boys' Clubs or all-female Girls' Clubs have now become Boys' and Girls' Clubs. Years ago, the Jewish youth center movement formed joint Young Men's and Young Women's Hebrew Associations, and both the Young Men's and Young Women's Christian Associations today, although separate organizations, have substantial numbers of members of the opposite sex.

Basis for One-Sex Groupings.   In general, it is desirable to prevent sex-role stereotyping that excludes either sex from activities that they would like to engage in, and that might represent an unfair form of discrimination. Indeed, many educators and recreation program administrators hesitate to make any distinctions between various kinds of participation based on sex, fearing to be accused of prejudice and discriminatory practices.

It would, however, seem clear that some program activities are either more appropriate for one sex than another, or have substantially more appeal for one sex. Realistically, most people would agree that boxing, wrestling, and tackle football are more often suited to male temperaments and physiques than to females. Although it may reflect past stereotyping practices and a narrow view of the sexes, certain artistic or creatively expressive activities tend to continue to be more attractive to girls and women, than to boys and men. Yet, even these kinds of distinctions based on gender are beginning to break down. Often they are patently absurd; for example, although we tend to think of cooking and sewing as feminine activities, the great chefs of the world and most high-fashion clothing designers have been men.

An argument can be made that, particularly during the latency (pre-adolescent) period of human development, one-sex groupings will be helpful to many boys and girls in establishing their own sexuality and sense of security in sex-related roles. It can also be argued that children are often encouraged or pressured to ''grow up'' too early, in a social sense, and that by maintaining single-sex groupings in appropriate activities, this can be avoided to a degree.

NATURE OF SPONSORSHIP ROLE

A final factor to consider before moving directly to the process of program scheduling concerns the nature of the sponsoring agency's role with respect to program activities.

In the past, it was assumed that the most appropriate role was simply one of having full responsibility for planning, organizing, and carrying out each program activity, and for providing leadership, equipment, and facilities as needed.

Today, with limited resources and with greater awareness of the values of cooperative sponsorship, many public and voluntary agencies have moved into shared sponsorship functions. For example, many public departments offer programs with the assistance of community groups, such as Parent-Teacher Associations or other parent groups, sports associations, neighborhood clubs, and similar bodies. These groups may provide leadership in the form of coaches, managers, instructors, or officials; may raise funds for equipment; may assist with scheduling and planning; or may help with publicity and other managerial tasks.

Examples of Cosponsorship Practices

Numerous examples of cosponsorship arrangements between different types of leisure-service agencies may be cited. These include: (1) cooperative programs involving military bases and other recreation agencies; (2) programs sponsored with the assistance of major corporations; (3) public-commercial joint ventures; (4) programs operated with the assistance of private or volunteer community groups; and (5) programs involving cosponsorship practices between religious and other agencies.

As an example of cooperation between armed forces recreation agencies and other leisure-service groups or community organizations, the Seymour Johnson Air Force Base near Goldsboro, North Carolina, participates actively in many community programs. Volunteers from the base provide leadership in a local Boys' Club, run a Special Olympics program, work with other handicapped

TABLE 9–2 Examples of Armed Forces Cooperation with Community Groups[6]

| | Seymour Johnson AFB | | Community, State, Private Agencies | |
	Provides	Uses	Provides	Uses
Pools	●	●	Seyboro Swim Team	Seyboro Swim Team
Golf Course	●			High School
Ball Fields	●			Junior High School
Gyms		●	Junior High School	
Bleachers	●			Goldsboro P&R Dept.
Chairs		●	Goldsboro P&R Dept.	
Toy Repair	●			Salvation Army
Water Safety		●	Red Cross	
Entertainment	●			Senior Citizens
Nature Trails	●			Boy Scouts
Interns		●	Colleges & Universities	
Hospital	●			Special Olympics
Hobby Shop	●			Wayne Community College
Classes and Seminars		●	Wayne Community College	
Big Brothers/Big Sisters	●			Elementary Schools
Theater Arts		●	Community Arts Council	
Running Track		●	Junior High School	
Recreation Center	●			N.C. Recreation & Park Society
Volunteers in Education	●			Local School System Society

groups, assist senior citizens programs and conduct numerous other special programs. Reciprocally, service personnel and their dependents take part in numerous city-run programs, and make use of varied private, state and community agencies for their programs (Table 9–2).

Numerous large corporations have developed national programs in cooperation with municipal recreation and park organizations. Among the leading examples have been the Wham-O Corporation, which has conducted the National Hula Hoop Contest and the World Junior Frisbee Contest; Kids' Dog Shows, cosponsored by the Ken-L-Ration pet food company and the National Recreation and Park Association; and the popular Hot-Shot Basketball Contest, supported by the Pepsi-Cola Company.

An outstanding recent example has been the Wells Fargo Gamefield Fitness Campaign, America's largest privately funded outdoor fitness program. This program has been promoted in conjunction with the National Recreation and Park Association and the President's Council on Physical Fitness and Sports, to assist park and recreation agencies and schools in designing, funding, promoting, and programming a uniform and cohesive network of fitness facilities in over 5,000 communities across the United States.

Public-commercial joint ventures have bridged the gap that traditionally existed in our thinking about these two types of leisure program sponsors, which Crompton described as a false dichotomy. He pointed out that "public" and "commercial" enterprises are complementary rather than mutually exclusive institutions. Federal and most state laws require that commercial recreation facilities be open to the general public, making them as "public" as those operated by government agencies. At the same time, government agencies are sponsoring more and more fee-charging, profit-making programs, such as indoor tennis facilities, golf courses, and skating rinks.

Despite these differences, there has often been a marked gap between public and commercial recreation agencies. Howard and Crompton write:

> Often the most serious obstacle impeding public agency-commercial enterprise joint ventures is the attitude of one party toward the other. The public agency frequently views commercial motives with distrust and suspicion, whereas the commercial operator often regards public agencies negatively as incompetent bureaucracies which try to frustrate the legitimate goals of the businessman.[7]

Gradually, such barriers are being overcome. Among the leading examples of public-commercial cooperation in recreation-related projects and programs are the numerous stadiums, marinas, ski centers, and other facilities that have been constructed recently by government, with long-term leases to private operators, or by private companies with substantial subsidies or other forms of assistance from governmental agencies in order to encourage tourism and assist the local economy of communities or regions.

Allen describes the advantages of such arrangements in an era of austerity in public finance. He writes that one alternative to funding cutbacks is to create a climate whereby private enterprise becomes an integral part of a community's provision of good recreation and park facilities and services. . . . The concession or lease arrangement approach to cooperation in particular has several advantages to it. It provides revenue-producing park facilities without capital improvement expenditures and without operation and maintenance costs. It produces non-tax funds which can be used to help support other non-revenue-producing park units. The concession concept allows private enterprise to lease public facilities for general public use. It can be used on any facility on which fees and charges can be levied.[8]

Numerous local recreation programs are carried out today with the direct assistance of local community organizations and volunteer groups. These groups may sponsor youth sports leagues, organize cultural arts classes or performing groups, or take the lead in promoting services for the handicapped. They may also act as sponsors for local parks and playgrounds, provide rehabilitation or maintenance efforts to keep outdoor facilities in good shape, or carry out major environmental clean-up projects.

There is an immense fund of latent goodwill in the community at large, in terms of potential support for recreation, parks, and environmental programs, despite the widely held belief that the public considers recreation as unimportant. Many of the potential resources that exist in the community have not yet been explored, however. Epperson, for example, points out that despite the very widespread activity by churches and other religious agencies in leisure-service programming, there has been relatively little interchange and cooperation between church-related sponsors and public recreation and park organizations.

Summing up, it is highly desirable that all such possibilities for pooling community resources through such cosponsorship arrangements be explored in developing a recreation program plan and organizing specific groups and activities.

OUTLINING THE PLAN

We are now ready to lay out the actual plan. As indicated, this may be more or less complex, depending on the size of the agency and the population that is being served.

In a large public recreation and park department, there may be dozens of different facilities, each one with a separate program of activities for different age groups. In contrast, the program of a small nursing home might have one or two hobby or social activities each afternoon, and programs of entertainment on two or three evenings a week.

Essentially the plan should contain a breakdown that includes the following elements: (1) which activities are to be offered, in what formats, and in what locations; (2) an analysis of different populations—either in terms of age groups or other demographic factors, or residential areas—and how they are to be served; and (3) the specific time frame in which activities will be carried on.

THE SCHEDULING PROCESS

Recreation program scheduling is an extremely vital aspect of program planning. If an activity is presented at the wrong time, or too infrequently, or with insufficient time to carry it out, it obviously will be severely handicapped. On the other hand, intelligent scheduling means that an activity is offered at the most appropriate time of the year, week and day, and in combination with other attractive program elements that are designed to meet the needs of participants. Several factors enter into scheduling: *organizational sponsor, physical location,* and *time*.

Organizational Sponsor

This refers to the structure of the organization itself, and the fact that different units or divisions may operate different types of programs. Thus, in Milwaukee, Wisconsin, the Department of Municipal Recreation and Adult Education divides its programs into two major categories: *neighborhood programs* and *city-wide programs*. The first unit includes daily playground activities for children from about five years of age through the mid-teens; children's social centers for youngsters of elementary school age operating during the afternoons; and evening social centers, termed "Lighted Schoolhouses," which serve both youth and adult needs. The second unit involves a network of adult centers offering more specialized or highly developed programs in the arts, nature activities, adult education, and senior citizens' programs, as well as municipal athletic leagues and sports instruction. Based on this breakdown, a given activity might be presented in several different forms, under different department units.

In a large voluntary agency, such as a YWCA, YMCA, or YM-YWHA, there are also likely to be several program divisions dealing with specific activity categories, or with different membership groups who are to be served. Here too, it is necessary to decide which program division should take responsibility for sponsoring a particular activity.

Sometimes the same activity may be presented in different formats in different divisions. For example, a teen social club program might produce a one-act play production as a club project, while adults might join a theater club that attends professional performances, and a children's summer day camp program explores creative drama activities, all as part of a YWCA activity program.

Physical Location

Next, it must be determined which locations will provide which programs. Obviously, in playgrounds, athletic facilities, ice rinks, swimming pools, or similar areas, the nature of the facility itself tends to determine the activity that it will house. However, a leisure-service agency must often decide where it should locate specialized programs such as performing arts classes, special services for the disabled, adult classes or other activities that may be put in different places, but cannot be provided in all possible settings.

One major consideration is obviously based on need or demand. Clearly, a senior citizens' program should be located in a neighborhood where there is a substantial number of older residents, and where they will have convenient and safe access to the facility, just as a youth sports program should be established where a large number of young people will be able to use it easily.

Physical location is also a matter of the adequacy of facilities. It is obvious that you can only really operate a swimming program where there is a swimming pool, or that a theater program will be most successful in a well-equipped modern theater. However, not all decisions as to location are this obvious, and in many cases facilities must be carefully examined to see if they have the potential for successful use before placing a given activity in a desired location.

Finally, location of program elements depends heavily on what is already in a given district or neighborhood of the community. If a Boys' Club, Police Athletic League or YWCA is already providing a rich arts and crafts program in a certain neighborhood, the public recreation and park department might be well justified in looking elsewhere to present special arts and crafts activities.

Often, the decision to place an activity in a given location will heavily influence those who take part in it. For example, in a study of participation in urban and suburban public recreation programs by minority-group residents, it was found that a very high percentage of those who took part in such combative sports as boxing, were black youth and adults. However, this reflected the program-planning policies of the public agencies involved, which tended to locate such programs chiefly in black neighborhoods and in so doing tended to discourage whites from attending.[9]

Support Capability. Within a ''marketing'' orientation, where a department has developed the policy that the bulk of program activities must yield substantial revenue—either a full ''pay-as-you-go'' policy in which they must bring in enough revenue to pay for all their administrative or leadership costs or a given percentage of it—the factor of potential fiscal return must be considered in selecting physical locations for program activities.

For example, a sportsman's center which will provide target-shooting, trap-shooting, archery, fly-casting or similar activities at fees comparable to what private or commercial facilities might charge, should be located in an area that is reasonably convenient or accessible for such a potential audience.

To make such determinations effectively may require feasibility studies or interest surveys, in which various neighborhoods or potential locations are examined. These explore the interest and financial capability of residents in an area with respect to a given activity or facility, and also the existence of competing facilities within a given geographical area.

It is possible to do analyses that will determine within reasonable levels of certainty how far people will travel to take part in given activities; such studies are extremely helpful in making decisions with respect to the placement of special program activities or facilities.

Ingenious program modification may make it possible to offer activities that might otherwise not be feasible. For example, some leisure-service agencies offer skiing during the early fall months by giving pre-ski exercise programs or dry-land skiing sessions, and then by sponsoring trips to ski centers. With the development of new plastic surfaces for practice skiing or even ski-jumping, and also the use of skiing on grassy slopes, it is possible to improvise further in such areas.

Often a department that does not possess a given type of facility may rent it from another agency, or work out a cooperative or cosponsorship arrangement with them. The public or voluntary organization that wishes to offer car hobby activities or an auto maintenance workshop may find that there is a public-spirited garage or service station operator who is willing to let his or her facility be used for such purposes on an off-hour schedule. And, as indicated earlier, many employee, military, and similar leisure-service programs rely heavily on the fields, gyms, and pools of nearby recreation and park agencies or college and university athletic facilities to conduct their sports activities.

Time Scheduling

This is the chief consideration to be dealt with in recreation activity scheduling. All programs, with the exception of special events that occur just once or at infrequent intervals, are normally broken down according to the following time categories: seasonal, monthly, weekly, and daily schedules.

Seasonal Schedules

Seasonal program planning reflects climatic factors, since certain activities, such as swimming, outdoor sports, or ice hockey, depend heavily on climate. It also reflects the school year, in that children in most communities are on vacation during the summer months, which justifies a sharply expanded summer playground or vacation day camp program. Seasonal planning also reflects school or college terms, since many recreation and park departments divide their programs into fall, winter, spring and summer sessions. This means that activities normally played in a given season—such as football in the fall or baseball in the spring—would logically be fitted into that season.

While many program activities are scheduled *within* specific seasons, others may be carried on *throughout* the year. For example, a strong basketball program might begin in the fall, continue through the winter, and end with city-wide or even inter-city tournaments in the spring. This imposes the need for careful scheduling. The Chicago Park District, for example, makes up a detailed annual schedule for all sports and physical activities. This gives the exact dates when all activities are carried out, including: (1) meeting of planning committees; (2) skills workshops or instructional clinics; (3) progressive competition on the local, area, and city-wide levels; and (4) submission of final reports. This program involves complex, overlapping scheduling, with some activities getting under way as others are in the middle or at the end of their sequence. The entire schedule must be carefully backed up by thorough committee assignments and publicity to announce beginning dates and registration for activities throughout the city.

Monthly Schedules

Some agencies or groups which have a considerable number of special events are likely to plan programs on a monthly basis and to send out schedules to their membership, which show programs for the month ahead. It would be impractical for such groups to publish annual schedules, since many activities are planned or arranged on relatively short notice. On the other hand, it would be difficult and expensive to publish daily or weekly schedules. Therefore, the monthly newsletter approach, which reaches the organization's thousands of members in the last week of the preceding month, informs them of upcoming events shortly before their actual dates, but in sufficient time for making inquiries or registering to take part.

Monthly schedules usually are based on a structure in which certain activities are offered regularly, at the same time and place each week. Others are one-time events or activities that are offered only at certain times during the year. The Valley Forge, Pennsylvania, Chapter of Parents Without Partners offers a wide range of *family activities* (such as roller-skating events, parties, nature walks, horseback rides, swim parties, and similar programs); *social events* for single parents (including social dancing, bridge parties, choral groups, potluck dinners, and discussion groups); and *service programs* and *educational sessions* (including speakers, symposiums, counseling and work projects). These events, along with meetings of committees and organizational work-groups, are all listed in a detailed monthly calendar, in which each day or evening throughout the month has at least three or four, and as many as eight or ten different events. As an example, a single Sunday in January, 1985, included the activities listed in Figure 9–2.

FIGURE 9–2 Example of Parents Without Partners Program Activities for Sunday, January 20, 1985, Listed in Monthly Calendar[10]

FAMILY SQUARE DANCE/DINNER. We are at a new place and we want to see how much fun we can have here. Bring a main dish to share and when we have eaten everything in the place we will "do-se-do". We will be in the Royersford area. Dinner will be at 4:30 p.m. and the dancing will begin at 6:30 and continue until 9:30 p.m. Cost will be $2.00 per family. For reservations and directions call Karl or Harry.

FAMILY ROLLER SKATING at Radnor Rolls at 6:30 p.m. Join us for an evening of fun. Radnor Rolls is located in the Villnova area. Show your PWP membership card and sign in at the desk. This is an event for PWP members only. Guests are treated the same as the general public and do not sign our PWP sign-in sheets and pay directly at the desk. Member adults $1.50 and member children are FREE accompanied by an adult member. Price includes admission and skates. For reservations and directions call Karen or Harry.

KING OF PRUSSIA/NORRISTOWN FRIENDSHIP CIRCLE at 7:30 p.m. at Peg's. Let's forget about the January chill and concentrate on having a great evening with PWP friends. We'll sip wine and enjoy creative snacks as we welcome Peg back as chairperson for the King of Prussia Friendship Circle. For information on what to bring, call Peg or Ruth. Cost $2.00/$6.00.

DISCUSSION/WINE & CHEESE at Grace's in North Wales at 6:30 p.m. Morris Glatt moderates THE POSITIVE SIDE IN RELATIONSHIPS. Too often friendships or involvements end, because we focus on what's wrong, rather than on what's right or good. Do you see a glass as being "half-full" or "half-empty"? Let's examine relationships, past or present, and see if we're focusing on the positive or the negative side. We will begin with wine and cheese at 6:30, discussion at 7:30. Cost $2.00/$6.00. For reservations and information call Grace or Morris.

PINOCHLE PARTY at Shirley's in West Norriton at 7:00 p.m. Let's play Pinochle, all levels welcome. "Favorite Snacks or Dessert Night", please bring along your favorite appetizer or dessert to share tonight at cards. Limited to 5 tables. Tables and chairs will be needed. 48 hour reservation deadline. Beginners' tables will be marked. For reservations and directions, call Shirley or Tom. Cost $3.00/$8.00.

SUPER BOWL PRIME TIME PARTY in West Chester. Come before kick-off and cheer your team to victory. Snacks will be served so BYOB. Cost $3.00. Call Nancy or Irene for reservations.

TNT SUPER BOWL SUNDAY—Let's meet at Millie's in Lafayette Hills before kick-off for some friendly carousing. Come on ladies, you know how this game is played. Don't let the men enjoy the day alone. Bring snacks and beverages (enough to last through the game). If your team wins we'll turn it into a post-game PARTY. Cost $3.00 plus extra if we have to send out for food etc. Call Millie, John or Kay for reservations and directions.

Weekly Schedules

Customarily, most community recreation agencies offer a weekly schedule that is composed of two elements: (1) certain activities that are scheduled on a regular, daily basis throughout the week; and (2) other special events, classes, or activities that are offered at less-frequent intervals or at special times throughout the week.

For example, a suburban YWCA would be likely to schedule the following types of activities throughout the week: (1) senior citizens' program during the morning or afternoon, meeting daily; (2) preschool group, "tot" swimming program, or other activities serving mothers with young children, either daily or once or twice during the week; (3) classes in business education or vocational education for adults, which might be held daily, during the day, as a regular intensive course, or on a weekly basis at night; (4) other classes or swimming or exercise programs for adults during the day, usually scheduled around the lunch hour to permit breaks for working personnel; and (5) a full range of evening and weekend classes, special events, and social programs for all age groups.

Public recreation and park departments also normally schedule their playground or community center programs on a weekly basis. This involves following a daily schedule of activities, while adding certain elements to the weekly program. For example, each week a different sports or games tournament might be conducted on the playground. This would be introduced on Monday, and carried out during the week, with the final competition being held on Thursday. Also, an "Emphasis of the Week" (a special program theme, activity, or event) would be introduced on Monday, with sessions devoted to it throughout the week. The culminating event, which might consist of a performance, an exhibit, a display, or other special program, would be held on Friday.

In many playground programs, part of one morning a week might be set aside for a leadership workshop for leaders and aides. This serves to improve their professional performance, offers a briefing session for events and activities in the city-wide program, and may also give technical assistance in conducting activities scheduled for the week ahead. Usually such sessions are scheduled on a Monday. On Friday afternoons, special staff tasks include preparing the playground bulletin board for the week ahead, and making out attendance and other reports. In many playground programs, additional features are scheduled on a once-a-week basis, to provide variety to the regular schedule of daily activities. These include such activities as visits by playground specialists who do brief workshops in music, dance, or storytelling, or by mobile units which set up roller skating programs or science shows. Other examples of weekly programs are typically found in scheduling swimming pools or ice rinks for varied groups.

In many recreation programs, weekend scheduling is relatively light, although it is obviously a time when many schoolchildren and adults have greater amounts of leisure time. The question of weekend scheduling is particularly critical in such residential treatment centers as physical rehabilitation or psychiatric hospitals, where patients typically have a number of therapies scheduled during the week, but where there may be almost nothing of interest to do on weekends. In some such settings, special efforts have been made to schedule weekend recreation programs, with staff members being placed on alternate work schedules so that they would be "on duty" every third or fourth weekend, to plan and carry out programs.

Daily Schedules

The process of planning daily schedules in such settings as playgrounds or recreation centers normally involves dividing the available time period into time blocks during the morning, afternoon and evening hours. Then, on the basis of the availability of participants, the nature of each activity, and the amount of stress that is to be given to it, and such other factors as climate, degree of interest, and effective use of leadership, activities are assigned to time blocks.

A good illustration of program planning on a daily basis may be found in the departmental handbook of the Parks and Recreation Department of Phoenix, Arizona (see Figure 9–3). It shows how certain types of activities may be carried on concurrently or in sequence on a summer playground, and also shows how leaders, aides, or volunteers can be involved.

Example of Basic Daily Playground Program.   A good program should be based on a sound daily plan that includes time for supervisory or management activities, self-directed program activities, leader-directed activities, and assignment of leadership to specific tasks. The specific assignment of leaders and the number of time blocks used for directed activities will depend on the number of available leaders and participants, and special program facilities and areas.

Another way of planning daily programs would be to begin by outlining the major time blocks and choices of activities available on the playground. Then separate columns would be drawn for each of the age groups attending the playground, for example: *six- to eight-year-olds, nine- to twelve-year-olds,* and those *thirteen and older.*

Then a program would be developed for each age group, within each time block. For example, during the first morning time-block, the youngest children might be doing arts and crafts while the middle group is involved in self-directed games and the older children are practicing sports skills. In the next time block, the youngest children might have a storytelling session while the middle group takes part in sports and the older children begin practicing a drama situation. The purpose of this type of programming is to ensure that each age group is given a diversified program appropriate to its needs, and that the use of the playground facilities, as well as the attention of staff members, is fairly distributed among them. At certain points, of course, all of the age groups might join together in a common activity, such as a playground carnival, songfest, or trip.

Flexible Daily Schedule

The preceding examples tend to be tightly structured in terms of regularly assigned time blocks and to be based on having regular groups that take part in program activities. In some settings, where participants come irregularly

FIGURE 9–3 Chart of Basic Daily Playground Program (Phoenix, Arizona)

A.M. *Time Block*	*Activity*	*Person Responsible (Name)*
	Open area; inspection tour for condition of area, safety of equipment	Leader
	Get equipment out and set up (tetherball, bases, table games, etc.)	Leader, Aide, or Volunteer
	Start self-directed activities for early arrivals or those not involved in sports (table games, 4-square, tetherball, various ladder tournaments)	Aide or Volunteer
	Active team sports or tournaments (while it's cool)	Leader or Aide
	Start or check self-directed activities for those not participating in activities below	Aide, Volunteer, or Leader not involved in next activity
	One or more special-interest group activities involving direct leadership (arts and crafts, music, dance, nature-science, games, or "emphasis of the week")	Leader and/or Aide or Volunteer
Prelunch Lunch Hour	Self-directed activities, conversation, general supervision, meetings, lunch	All
P.M. Time Block	Indoor Activities (hot part of day)	Person Responsible
Afternoon	Start self-directed activities (table tennis, teen canteen, table games)	Leader, Aide, or Volunteer
Two or More Time Blocks	Special-interest group activities involving direct leadership (arts and crafts, music, dance, nature-science, clubs, etc.)	Leader, Aide, or Volunteer
Predinner Dinner Hour	Self-directed activities, meetings, preparation of reports, general supervision, dinner	All
P.M. Time Block	Indoor-Outdoor Activities	Person Responsible
Evening	Start or check self-directed activities	Aide, Volunteer, or Leader
Early Evening	Teen program slanted toward self-directed activities, some equipment may be reserved for them at this time—table tennis, game courts, etc. Corecreational activities	
	Teen Clubs	Leader or Aide
	Sports—Leader circulating as much as possible on area with one Leader	Leader
	Check on supplies, inspect area, lock up	Leader, Aide

Planning check list:
1. Are program activities based on interests of participants and designed to meet their needs?
2. Are boys, girls, adults served? Major age groups? Varied interests?
3. Is the work load evenly distributed?
4. Do Leader and Aide have some time to think, plan, and prepare?

or at widely varying times, it is not feasible to plan such regularly scheduled activities. Instead, it is necessary to accommodate participants at their convenience.

Programming in Fitness/Health Spas. In a commercially operated fitness center or health spa, for example, the bulk of the program may consist of the free use of such facilities as the swimming pool and sauna, the track, the weight-lifting or exercise-machine room or similar areas throughout the day and evening.

Other services, such as the use of racquetball courts, or sessions with a masseur, physical therapist, or other fitness consultants might be scheduled by appointment. Finally, there might be a few regularly scheduled activities, such as aerobics or Jazzercise classes, or special events with films or guest speakers, or social activities for members. However, the bulk of participation would be on a free and unstructured basis, as indicated.

Scheduling in Limited Time Frames. In other types of agencies, scheduling may have to be carried out within a tightly restricted time frame. For example, many companies that provide organized recreation programs for their employees will do so only after work hours, in the late afternoon and evenings, or on weekends. However, some such companies will deliberately schedule activities during the middle of the day, with exercise programs or swim-and-jog activities taking the place of lunch, and with a modified work schedule to make this possible.

With the growing use of flex-time schedules in which employees are able to vary their work hours within a total block of available time, it is possible to schedule recreation activities during the day. Obviously, in the case of chartered vacation trips, employee recreation programs fit these into appropriate periods, when sufficient numbers of interested employees would be able to be away for an extended period of time.

In therapeutic recreation agencies, it is usually necessary to schedule recreation programs around other treatment services—such as medical or nursing care, or other adjunctive therapies such as occupational or physical therapy. However, in some treatment settings, where recreation is employed in a prescriptive way to carry out specific therapeutic procedures, it will be scheduled during the morning or early afternoon hours when such programs usually take place.

In some cases, the specific nature of the program dictates the time frame in which activity will normally be carried on. For example, at Children's Village, a home and special school for disturbed and dependent youth in Dobbs Ferry, New York, recreation takes several forms: (1) instruction in basic recreation skills, which takes place during school hours as normal curricular activity; (2) involvement in organized group activities by living unit or by special assignment, during the late afternoon, in which the skills learned during the earlier sessions may be practiced; and (3) free choice of campus-wide recreation activities or special events, during the evening hours.

In military recreation programs, as in employee recreation, recreation must also be scheduled around the participant's assigned or on-duty schedule. In such settings, as in public recreation and park programs, it is essential to be creative in scheduling and to ensure that all groups' needs and work patterns are considered. For example, in many larger communities, there are large numbers of night workers, such as people on night shifts in factories, police or fire department personnel, security employees, and similar groups. Often there are very limited opportunities for such individuals during the daytime hours, and the ingenious recreation program planner may be able to set up special fitness programs or other activities during the day that meets their needs perfectly.

Use of Computer in Scheduling

One of the newer trends in scheduling recreation and park facilities and programs involves the use of computers to determine availability of resources or reservations, or to plan complex programs efficiently.

Some large state park systems have introduced computer-based reservation systems, through which campers may reserve campsites by telephoning a centralized office set up for the purpose. Similarly, reservations for performances, hotel or motel lodgings, or similar tourist activities are increasingly being handled by computer. Probably the best example of computer use in recreation is in intramural sport scheduling. Holley has described how a large sports program can be handled efficiently and quickly by computer, including the scheduling of league or tournament contests, scheduling of playing areas, assignment of officials, maintaining game records, and similar uses. In terms of scheduling itself, the computer assigns each team to compete at appropriate times and with the correct opponents in a round-robin tournament format. Specifically, it does the following:

> The computer will check eligibility. If the team is eligible, it will be scheduled.
> If a team fails to show up (forfeit), the computer will drop the team from further play. . . .
> The computer prioritizes teams according to the number of games they have played and schedules first those teams with the fewest games played.
> If, when scheduling a league, the computer runs out of facilities, it will then assign byes to all other unscheduled teams and put them on priority for the next schedule.
> Printouts . . . produced for posting on campus . . . have the following information:
>> One team versus another team
>> Each team's won/lost record
>> The facility in which they have been scheduled
>> The time and day they will play. . . .
> The scheduling program has a variety of capabilities. It can schedule on a weekly, bi-weekly, or an entire semester basis.
> The computer recognizes a team's identity and will not schedule any two teams to play each other more than once, as in a round robin tournament.[11]

As a second example of the use of the computer in program scheduling, a number of summer camps have begun to use this approach. For example, Kamp Kohut, a private boys' camp located in Oxford, Maine, has for the past ten years employed a computer to develop programs for up to 200 boys and 80 staff members. The computer is fed the basic structure of the camp's program and is informed of the activities available to campers, the skill level of boys in certain key activities, and the skill capabilities of staff members. Activity preferences of all individual campers are plugged in, and the computer is also informed of the number of campers various activity areas can accommodate at any given time.

> From this information, a complete camp schedule, a cabin schedule and individual camper's schedule, and the staff's schedule can be printed, either on paper or on a screen. Variations in schedules can be made because of a person's illness, the weather, an overnight hike, or the unavailability of a ball field. The computer accepts change easily.[12]

Schwartz points out that the computer accomplishes this entire task quickly, taking about ten minutes to schedule all campers into 30 activities over a five-period day. The computer program can be set up so that it can be operated by a clerk with no special computer training or knowledge. While relatively few camps have adopted this approach, it may become a more widely used method of scheduling, particularly in larger or more complex camps.

In contrast to such approaches—which involve large numbers of participants, program activities, staff members, and facilities in a complex schedule of games or other activities—some scheduling is relatively simple and done on a small scale in recreation centers or similar facilities.

Whatever approach is used, it is essential that the schedule permit the maximum number of high-priority activities to be offered within a given period of time, under conditions that encourage favorable enrollments or participation totals.

VISUAL PRESENTATION OF PROGRAM

Once they have been fully planned, recreation programs may be summarized or presented in various kinds of visual formats, both to provide guidance to participants and to assist staff members in organizing and carrying out activities.

Typically, many programs are presented in detailed lists or chart-like forms in newsletters or brochures. Often departments that offer a considerable number of special-interest groups or courses for youth and adults print voluminous brochures, which are sometimes distributed as inserts in local newspapers. Sometimes activity schedules may be summarized on a single sheet or printed on a chart or bulletin board, in order to give visitors to a center an idea of weekly and daily activities.

Use of Flow Charts

To assist staff members in their work, flow charts may be used. These show individual projects or programs laid out over a period of time, with each operational task (such as initial planning and approval, facility and equipment requisition, publicity, registration, completion and final report) given dates on which they are to be carried out. These are a common tool in business management and are particularly useful in that they identify deadlines that *must* be met and thus facilitate efficient supervision of the program planning and implementation function.

Community-Wide Maps of Program Activities

Useful chiefly for public recreation and park agencies, these involve mapping all major facilities and accompanying the map with a diagram listing program activities and showing where they are being carried on. Different types of facilities and programs may be color-coded or indicated by special symbols or pins on the map. This type of visual presentation is particularly helpful in terms of showing the overall distribution of varied community program activities and possible under- or over-provision of leisure opportunities on a geographical basis.

Program-Activity Diagraph

A third type of visual presentation, which is particularly useful to agency supervisors in coordinating varied programs, is the program-activity diagraph. As described by Recreation and Park Commissioner Joseph Curtis of New Rochelle, New York, this is a visual presentation that combines elements of a diagram and graph to show all events and continuing program activities in a convenient and easily understood form:

> it consists of a 1/4-inch-thick rectangular board, 4 feet by 6 feet, consisting of two skins of white gloss paper separated by fine styrofoam and weighing approximately 3 pounds. The program-activity diagraph is mounted in a staff planning room, to provide a work board for program conferences. Twelve vertical columns represent the months of the year; the activities themselves are organized under three types of headings: scheduled sequences (short-term courses or other series); sustained sequences (long-term activities); and special events.[13]

To organize the diagraph, a data-collection process is carried out in which all programs are identified, cross-referenced, and labeled with dates, staff assignments, and locations. All scheduled and sustained programs are applied horizontally, using color-coded tape, on the 12-month format, covering the exact time periods. Special events are depicted by bright yellow disks of adhesive tape placed at the date they occur.

> The program-activity diagram can be used for budget-planning sessions, and to provide information for current maintenance, repair, and construction programs. At a glance, it gives information about: (1) variety of programs offered; (2) programs of greatest time extension; (3) months of greatest and least time congestion; (4) conflicts among special events; and (5) areas of needed program service.[14]

Each of these three forms of visual presentation of programs provides a useful means of showing the diverse leisure opportunities offered by an agency in an organized and easily comprehensible way.

Getting the Program Under Way

In conclusion, this chapter has examined the process of developing an effective program plan, based on shared staff decision-making and the systematic assessment of the needs and interests of participants.

It shows how agency goals, objectives and policies are used, along with other professional guidelines, in examining possible program activities. Budgetary considerations and strategies are reviewed, with respect to the selection of program formats. Various levels of participant involvement are described, along with the process of structuring program groupings based on age, developmental needs and special capabilities, and gender. Different types of sponsorship arrangements are considered, including the use of cosponsorship practices with other agencies, businesses, or neighborhood groups.

Finally, the scheduling process is presented, with guidelines for developing seasonal, monthly, weekly, and daily programs, and with a consideration of the selection of sites and locations where programs are to be held. The use of the computer in this process is described, with special application to sports programming.

The final result is a program plan that presents all the major activities within key program areas, and which describes the formats in which they are to be presented, the locations, the arrangements for fees and charges, and the schedules when they will be made available. Obviously, this plan is not etched in stone, but can be changed, added to, or cut back during the course of its operation, according to the way the public responds to it, or other circumstances that occur as it is being carried on.

The task of program implementation is described in Chapter 10. It deals with several important phases of the process, including the assignment of personnel, the development of procedural manuals or operational guidelines, program publicity and promotion, and control procedures to prevent accidents and maintain a healthy and safe environment for play.

STUDENT PROJECTS_____

1. Divide the class into small work groups. Have each group select a type of program, such as a senior center, armed forces recreation unit, or corporate/employee program. Based on materials presented in earlier chapters, develop an overall program plan for each of these settings.

    Indicate in this plan what activities will be offered, and in what format. Show how the program breaks down, in terms of seasonal activities or major units of involvement, as well as special events or other short-term activities. Indicate also how a typical week will be scheduled.

2. Prepare a large visual presentation, making use of one of the approaches suggested in the chapter, of a seasonal recreation schedule in a large leisure-service agency (flow charts, community-wide maps, or program-activity diagraph should be used).

SUGGESTED READINGS_____

Christopher Edginton, David Compton, and Carole Hanson, *Recreation and Leisure Programming: A Guide for the Professional* (Philadelphia: Saunders College Publishing, 1980), Chapter 9.

Patricia Farrell and Herberta Lundegren, *The Process of Recreation Programming* (New York: John Wiley, 1978), Chapter 4.

Richard Kraus and Joseph Curtis, *Creative Management in Recreation and Parks* (St. Louis: C. V. Mosby, 1982), Chapter 10.

Ruth V. Russell, *Planning Programs in Recreation* (St. Louis: C. V. Mosby, 1982), Chapter 7.

NOTES_____

[1]Sandra Little, "Cooperative Goal Structuring," *Leisure Today, Journal of Physical Education, Recreation and Dance* (April 1982): 43.

[2]Roger Kemp and Marty Feliciano, "The Creative Management of Recreational Services," *Parks and Recreation* (October 1982): 54–55.

[3]Kemp and Feliciano, pp. 54–55.

[4]J. Robert Rossman, "The Influence of Program Format Choice on Participant Satisfaction," *Journal of Park and Recreation Administration* (January 1984): 48.

[5]Sally A. and William Hammitt, "Campus Recreation Users: Their Preferences and Administrative Priorities," *Leisure Today, Journal of Physical Education and Recreation* (April 1980): 37.

[6]Stephen H. Moler, "Military and Civilian Cooperation: A Case Study," *Parks and Recreation* (June 1983): 35.

[7]Dennis R. Howard and John L. Crompton, *Financing, Managing and Marketing Recreation and Park Resources* (Dubuque, Iowa: Wm. C. Brown Co., 1980): 111.

[8]Stewart E. Allen, "Public-Private Cooperation," *Parks and Recreation* (July 1980): 44.

[9]Richard Kraus, *Public Recreation and the Negro* (New York: Center for Urban Education, 1968), 48.

[10]*Newsletter of Valley Forge Chapter* (King of Prussia, Pa.: Parents Without Partners, January 1985).

[11]Bruce Holley, "Computer Coordination for Campus Intramurals," *Leisure*

Today, Journal of Physical Education and Recreation, (April 1980): 50–52; and Gerald M. Maas, ''Intramural Sports Scheduling: The Computer vs Instant Scheduling,'' *National Intramural and Recreational Sports Association (NIRSA) Journal* (October 1981): 26–30.

[12]See Stu Schwartz, ''Programming Your Program,'' *Camping Magazine* (February 1981): 16.

[13]Richard Kraus and Joseph Curtis, *Creative Management in Recreation and Parks* (St. Louis: C. V. Mosby, 1982), pp. 184–185.

[14]Kraus and Curtis, p. 185.

CHAPTER 10

Program Implementation___

Sue Perry looked over the budget plan of funds being allocated to support recreation activities on the base, which Major Garcia had just given her. "This is pretty tight," she said. "And I'm somewhat concerned about not having enough staff members to supervise all programs."

"You're going to have to get volunteers for some of that," said the major. "And I think you can get some college students from Eastport College to do field work here. They have pretty good skills."

"What about these fees for equipment rental and registration charges?" Sue asked. "They're higher than last year."

"Yes," agreed Major Garcia. "We don't have any choice about that; we're being required to raise a much higher percentage of our operating budget from program revenues this year."

"Well," said Sue, "it means we're going to have to target our markets a lot more thoroughly, and be very aggressive about promoting our programs. And we'll have to boost registration in some of these activities, and cut those that aren't doing well."

"Right," said the major. "Can you do it?"

"We'll have to," said Sue Perry. "It'll work out."

Having followed the program-planning sequence through its first six steps, we are now ready to move into the action phase, and to set the program in motion.

This involves a number of specific tasks, including: (1) assigning personnel to leadership responsibilities; (2) preparing procedural manuals or operational guidelines; (3) developing a coordinated plan for program publicity and promotion; (4) having an ongoing plan for supervision of programs; and (5) maintaining needed control procedures to prevent accidents and maintain a healthy and safe recreational environment.

Each of these functions is described in detail in the body of this chapter. Others are not analyzed as separate functions, but are dealt with in the concluding plan for carrying out a swimming meet, which illustrates many of the most important tasks of program implementation.

In describing each task, the author has provided a number of practical and realistic suggestions. These are not presented as absolute guidelines, since agencies and program elements vary so widely. Instead, they are presented as suggestions, with a number of examples that illustrate the most appropriate approaches.

ASSIGNING LEADERSHIP PERSONNEL

One of the key elements in program implementation involves the assignment of leadership personnel. Typically, in a large municipal or voluntary leisure-service organization, there is a staffing plan that indicates the specific assignment of each full- or part-time staff member and shows which facilities have regular leaders and which do not. It also shows the hours of coverage. For example, in many communities only larger playgrounds with indoor centers are assigned regular staff coverage during the colder months of the year while much fuller coverage of all facilities is provided during the late spring and summer seasons.

Depending on the format of activity, there may or may not be assigned leadership. Obviously, instructional programs require skilled teachers, and many free-play activities must be supervised by qualified personnel. However, many organized competitive activities may be directed by their own volunteer coaches and managers and special-interest groups often have their own officers and activity specialists.

In another type of setting, such as a hospital or other treatment center, personnel are customarily assigned on the basis of patient/client groups and are made responsible for directing programs for a given ward or section of a facility. They may also be assigned to specific activities with other groups, such as accompanying them on trips, conducting crafts sessions, or assisting in special events.

Specific assignments are usually worked out on a master schedule of programs that ensures needed coverage at important times, and also allows times for team meetings and planning sessions, preparation of reports, and other administrative tasks.

The assignment of personnel in commercial recreation settings may vary greatly. In some situations, such as health and fitness spas, their tasks may include work at the front desk or in the office, interviewing potential enrollees, conducting activities such as aerobics or other exercise classes, or acting as lifeguard in the pool. In others, such as ski centers, an instructor may do nothing but teach classes or individuals on a regular basis. In major complexes like large theme parks, individuals are usually assigned to a very specific task connected to a ride, entertainment area, or other attraction, or to other roles connected with maintenance or beside-the-scenes operations. On higher levels of responsibility in commercial recreation settings, leaders may also become involved with managerial tasks or responsibility for generating special projects, or for supervising other program personnel.

Each type of leisure-service agency has a characteristic way of assigning personnel to programs. What is important is that there be a clear understanding of the expectations of leaders or other staff members in terms of their responsibilities and the way in which these should be carried out. To accomplish this, orientation sessions, staff-training courses or workshops, and ongoing supervision all are essential.[1]

Use of Part-time or Seasonal Personnel

Despite the past assumption that recreation groups should always be directed by professionally qualified leaders, most face-to-face group leadership today is not carried on by full-time, year-round, professionally trained personnel. Instead, in many agencies, program activities are directed by part-time employees or skilled specialists who work on a session basis, by subprofessional recreation assistants, or by seasonal or volunteer leaders.

In assigning individuals, it is important to select leaders who have the basic skills, attitudes, and personal qualities that make for successful performance in leisure-service programming. The entire subject of leadership is dealt with at length in the companion volume to this text, *Recreation Leadership Today,* and will not be dealt with here—other than to state several key principles with respect to program implementation.

Leaders must be aware of the basic goals and objectives of the programs they are directing, as well as of the needs, interests and personal backgrounds of the groups they are directing.

They should be thoroughly familiar with the policies and practices of the agency in which they are employed. Typically, many departments prepare manuals to assist leaders in carrying out programs within special areas of activity, such as athletics, arts and crafts, or special events. Examples of such procedural guidelines for working with special populations or in special settings are presented later in this chapter.

It should be stressed again that leaders in recreation situations are not solely concerned with presenting or directing group activities. In addition to leading games, or arts and crafts, or special events, they are working with people. The group experience, the growth and development of each participant, and the development of constructive recreational attitudes and skills are important goals that they must work toward.

In addition, they must serve in other leadership capacities—as counselors to group members, as disciplinarians when necessary, as spokespersons for the group, as advocates for its needs, and as public relations representatives in working with other community agencies or the news media. As earlier chapters have shown, those responsible for recreation programming in employee, armed forces, or campus leisure-service settings must often carry out other personnel functions or direct other types of activities.

Such concerns must be carefully considered when assigning personnel to program responsibilities. It should also be understood that the assignment of leaders to groups or facilities is often not totally in the hands of agency supervisors. In some large public recreation and park departments, for example, leadership personnel may request assignment to specific job openings and often it may not be possible to transfer or assign them arbitrarily to other locations, without risking union grievances or similar obstacles.

Often leaders tend to be placed in the same assignment year after year and to become highly knowledgeable in carrying it out effectively, making constructive community contacts, and building active and successful programs. Against this pattern, one must contrast those leaders who fall into a rut, become bored, and put their time in doing little innovative work. For such leaders, job rotation or rearranging an entire system of job assignments may make good sense.

PROCEDURAL MANUALS OR OPERATIONAL GUIDELINES

Often recreation leadership tends to be thought of chiefly in terms of the personality and enthusiasm of the leader, or his or her competence within the area of activity that is being presented. However, leadership involves many very specific kinds of principles and group-management skills. In addition, program leadership in various types of settings or activity areas often is described very precisely in procedural manuals or operational guidelines that have been developed by the program sponsor.

Such manuals usually define the specific responsibilities of the leader, as well as rules or suggestions which indicate how activities are to be carried on. They may indicate precise procedures for handling problem situations, such as accidents or disciplinary infractions, as well as the sequence in which program activities are to be presented.

To illustrate, a set of guidelines illustrating effective program leadership on playgrounds sponsored by public recreation and park departments might include the following:

Guidelines for Program Leadership in Playgrounds

1. *Seek out ways to develop activities in sequences of interest.* Storytelling may lead to informal dramatics, and from there to puppetry, drawing, costume making, or stage design. A nature scavenger hunt may lead to setting up a nature museum or playground display, or a pet show.

2. *Group activities around logical themes and special events.* Coordinate games, stories, crafts, music, dance, and other activities around common themes, and involve them all in special events and programs, as weekly or culminating activities.

3. *Teach games or prepare areas children can use by themselves.* Teach game skills or lay out game areas that children can use without adult leadership or supervision, for such activities as quoits, miniature golf, hopscotch, apparatus games, table tennis, lawn bowling, and horseshoes.

4. *Encourage the "game" way of learning and practicing skills.* Use games—inventing them if necessary—to have children learn basic skills like running, throwing, catching, batting, serving, or jumping; and use "lead-up" games to teach basic concepts or strategies of sports to be learned later.

5. *Increase program variety by expanding leadership capability.* It is possible to add to the number of different activities being presented by making full use of junior leaders, parent or teen-age volunteers, neighborhood residents or similar helpers and by recruiting, training, and supervising them effectively.

6. *Plan special events carefully—and make them interesting.* Special events add adventure, fun and interest to the playground. They must be carefully planned for maximum participation, and should be carefully publicized. Plan for the unexpected, the novel, the surprising!

7. *Chart your program in advance.* Make sure that your schedule of activities is carefully laid out on a calendar available to all staff members or helpers. This is more than a daily schedule posted on the bulletin board; it includes full dates, deadlines, responsibilities, report-due days, and similar details.

8. *Explore your neighborhood*. Get to know the community—its storekeepers, parents, police officers, church leaders, and all its other human and physical resources. Get people interested in your program, and find out how they might be able to help you, or how you might be able to assist them. Make the neighborhood part of the program.

9. *Encourage children to do as much planning as possible*. Have children play a meaningful role in planning daily programs and special events—and make sure that they do the background work needed for these activities (making props or costumes, doing posters, etc.). It will increase their interest and personal involvement.

10. *Use sign-up sheets*. Don't rely on word of mouth and memory to involve children in activities. Have them sign up for tournaments, classes, clubs, or special contests, to make sure participation is carefully recorded in advance.

11. *Promote activities with ''carry-over'' possibilities*. Ideally, your program should include many activities which children can use at home with their families, or in later life. The playground leader is a true educator for leisure.

12. *Recognize, accept, and work with so-called problem children*. It is a constant challenge for those in charge of programs to involve problem youngsters successfully—for example, the shy nonparticipant, the aggressive or hostile child, the disinterested or one-track youngster. The answer lies both in understanding leadership and providing the right activities.

13. *Have emergency activities ready*. Although your day's program or special event may be fully planned, it is helpful to have different activities ''up your sleeve'' if there are emergencies, or you need to replace activities that are not working out well.

14. *Challenge makes for interest; recognition makes for pride*. As earlier guidelines suggested, people of all ages enjoy challenge that is reasonably within their grasp, rather than ''too-easy'' activities. Provide awards, ceremonies, honor rolls, or parties to acknowledge success. Try to have every child successful in at least some areas of activity.

15. *Involve custodian or maintenance personnel in planning*. Get the park foreman or playground custodian involved in planning all major schedules or special events—not just in cleaning up after-

ward. Their advice will be helpful, and their cooperation more fully assured.[2]

Obviously, having such guidelines appear in printed form in a department or agency manual does not ensure that leaders will follow them effectively. However, the guidelines may be used in staff-training sessions, or as the basis for conferences between program leaders and supervisors, in which the various recommended approaches or procedures are reviewed and discussed.

OTHER EXAMPLES OF PROGRAM GUIDELINES

Numerous other examples of guidelines dealing with other special program areas might be cited. Of these, the following section includes four fairly typical areas: (1) guidelines for camping for senior citizens; (2) guidelines for carrying out a sports competition; (3) guidelines for developing specific curriculum elements in therapeutic recreation; and (4) guidelines for trips, outings, and picnics.

Camping for Senior Citizens

As more and more programs are being developed to serve the elderly in society, one area of interest that has gradually been growing in scope is camping for senior citizens. In many respects, their needs are much like those of other age groups. However, certain special arrangements or modifications of the camp setting will help make the camping experience even more successful for the elderly.

To illustrate, the Senior Adult Committee of the Board of Christian Education of the United Church of Canada has suggested the following guides for overnight camping for this age group. First, it is important to carefully review camp accommodations to insure the physical health and comfort of the campers. Privacy is important; if larger than two-bed cabins are used, dividing screens or curtains help. Generally speaking, each older camper likes to be assigned his or her own bed, a place to hang clothes, and the washroom to be used immediately upon arrival at camp. He or she likes to keep the same place at the table throughout. It is recommended that camps for older adults provide:

> Level ground between place of sleeping and eating with no great distance between the two. Minimum of stairs, with banisters. Cabins for sleeping with not more than two beds in a room—some single rooms—with easy access to bathroom facilities under same roof, and with electricity.
>
> Plenty of bedding—hot water bottles, flashlights, extra pillows for those who sleep propped up, rubber sheeting for beds. Chair beside each bed. Plenty of seating accommodation in various spots around the grounds out-of-doors.

Arrangements for some special diets—salt-free, skimmed milk, etc. Campers on similar diets might be seated at one part of table. Arrange for nurse to discover needs of each camper for toilet facilities, medical services, and to clear diets with the cook.

Books, and games, both active and quiet, such as Scrabble, checkers, chess, horseshoes, etc. Provide garden tools, materials for crafts, outdoor painting, etc. Have writing materials, stamps, pens available. Provide music—piano, record player, etc.

Tags for each piece of luggage with names in big print to eliminate anxiety, and persons available to carry luggage. Have an electric kettle handy for making coffee at any hour, day or night. Have an extra supply of sweaters, shawls, flannel nightwear, raincoats.[3]

In addition to such general recommendations, any agency that sponsors such programs is likely to develop a number of other policies or procedures that apply specifically to its own camp operation. These may have to do with transportation practices, emergency procedures, preliminary health screening of campers, or program activities to be carried out during the camping session.

Guidelines for Carrying Out a Sports Competition

Procedural manuals for conducting sports competitions, such as tournaments, meets or other athletic contests may vary greatly. Some deal with the overall process of setting up the event, inviting participants, and carrying it out over a period of time, like the example of the swimming meet that is included later in this chapter. Others may be highly technical, in terms of precise guidelines that deal with such elements as eligibility of contestants or teams, levels of competition, rules for play, basis for appeals of officiating rulings, awards, and similar concerns.

The guidelines for such competitions are often precisely described. The Pepsi Challenge/National Basketball Association Hotshot Competition for example, clearly defines the levels of competition, awards, and contest rules.[4] This program (in which a major soft-drink manufacturer, a top sports league, and thousands of recreation and park agencies join forces) is a national basketball skills program for boys and girls, nine to eighteen years of age. It also has precisely detailed rules for eligibility and scoring opportunities from six points on the basketball floor. The levels of competition include Playground Competition, Youth Service Organization Championships, Area Playoffs, Area Finals, Division Championships, Conference Championships, and National Championships.

Similarly, sports competition sponsored by organizations such as the Police Athletic League, the Catholic Youth Organization, or various branches of the armed forces, typically have detailed rules manuals that structure the way in which contests must be carried on.

Program Design in Therapeutic Recreation

As earlier chapters have shown, many therapeutic recreation agencies today follow a program design format in which the patient or client's involvement is based on a careful assessment of his or her needs, resulting in a detailed, sequential treatment plan. Referring to this process as curriculum design, Wehman and Schleien identify six stages that constitute the activity planning process:

1. A program goal
2. An instructional objective (short-term)
3. A task analysis of each skill
4. The verbal cue required for instruction in the skill
5. Materials that are required for instruction
6. Teaching procedures and special adaptations with each skill.[5]

Wehman and Schleien give a number of examples of games, hobbies, sports, and similar activities in which core skills are identified and presented in a logical developmental sequence appropriate for each learner's level of functioning. As a specific example, they describe the process of teaching a multiply handicapped woman to take a photograph of another person, a skill she had never been exposed to before, including a number of tasks involving social interaction, physical manipulation of the camera, and timing.

Guidelines for Trips and Outings

Numerous other examples of recommended procedures for carrying out different types of recreation program activities might be cited. As a last example, the following section includes guidelines for planning and conducting trips, outings, and picnics, which are appropriate for the programs of public recreation and park departments.

The Phoenix, Arizona, Parks and Recreation Department sponsors varied trips and outings for Phoenix residents of all ages; it provides the following rationale for this type of program activity:

> Adventure Trips are expeditions of exploration and discovery. They may lead to far places . . . or take place within the community and its outlying areas. Far away places are beyond the reach of most of us, but there is much to explore close at hand that is exciting and fun, as well as leading to discoveries about the community in which we live.
>
> The trips suggested here are adventures of interest to children, youth, and adults, including Senior Citizens. Age is no limit to interest . . .
>
> Trips may be taken any time of the year. For children and youth in school,

late afternoons, Saturdays, and school vacations (summer and winter) are times for planning excursions. For the retired, any time is right.

Values in adventure trips lie in the fun and excitement of going to a new place (or revisiting a favorite), growth in knowledge and understanding, awareness of the variety and complexity of community enterprises, and the socializing factors in planning and sharing experiences in a group. For young people, adventure trips can have vocational overtones, with glimpses into different kinds of work. Trips can emphasize and stimulate interest in volunteering, through visits to hospitals, etc.

Emphasis on exploring and discovery, coupled with enthusiastic leadership, make trips "adventures" for participants. There is something in everyone that responds to adventure—to going places, doing something new, finding out.[6]

Among the types of trips scheduled or organized by the Phoenix Parks and Recreation Department are the following: art museums; children's theater; public library; communications centers (newspaper, radio and television stations); government buildings (county hospital, fire department, state capitol building, civil defense office, Air National Guard, U.S. post office); historical museums; manufacturing and processing plants; outdoor and nature science centers (botanical gardens, mineralogical museums, planetarium, bird sanctuary); and service centers and transportation centers (railroad terminals and roundhouses, bus terminals and airports).

PROGRAM PUBLICITY AND PROMOTION

A third important function of program implementation involves carrying out needed publicity and promotional efforts. Before any program is put into action, it must normally be publicized to attract participants and to continue to keep the public aware of the agency's operations. Promotional efforts may be carried out in a number of ways, some based on the use of publicity releases or announcements, and others through linkages with community groups and a comprehensive system of sound public relations.

It is worth making a distinction between the two terms—*publicity* and *public relations*. Some have clarified the difference by suggesting that "public relations is publicity with a conscience."

Put another way, *publicity* is primarily concerned with making members of the public aware of a program by using various media to call it to their attention. Public relations is a broader process concerned with the organization's image and the role it plays in the community, as well as its relationship with various groups and social programs. In this text, we are chiefly concerned with publicity as a means of encouraging public awareness of program opportunities and events.

Internal and External Publicity.   Each recreation agency is likely to have its own approach to promoting program activities and developing a positive picture of enrollment and attendance. Some organizations, such as armed forces recreation or employee recreation programs, are responsible for serving only those individuals who are part of their own system. Therefore, their publicity is largely internal and may be carried out through newsletters, posters, announcements on public address systems, notices placed in lockers, and similar approaches.

Often a great deal of such publicity is by word-of-mouth, on a person-to-person basis, and often the development of teams or other special-interest groups is generated by participants themselves. In order to take part in an activity, they must either arouse sufficient interest in it to have it sponsored, or to form a group that then provides the vehicle for entering the program.

In contrast, a public recreation department essentially must depend on external publicity. It must reach the surrounding community by making use of bulletin boards, posters, handbills and fliers, announcements in newspapers or on radio or television, or similar media. In so doing, it may work through citizens' groups or other organizations, such as local stores or businessmen's/women's associations, Parent-Teachers Associations, churches and synagogues, advisory groups, or neighborhood or block associations.

In addition to spreading the word about program activities, which is essentially a one-way process, effective public relations should stress two-way communication. If community residents have been consulted about program plans and needs and have shared in the planning process or are involved as volunteers, they will help promote it and build participation.

Still other organizations must rely on both *internal* and *external* publicity. Such organizations as the YMCA or YWCA normally have fairly large memberships who can easily be reached through posters, announcements, or membership mailings. However, Y's often seek to reach outsiders who are not interested in full membership, but may be attracted to special events or other program activities or series; they must therefore also use publicity outlets that reach the overall community.

Use of Shotgun and Rifle Approaches.   In carrying on promotional efforts as part of the program implementation process, agencies make use of both shotgun and rifle approaches. The shotgun approach to publicity usually tries to reach a large, undifferentiated audience or public with a broad message about the overall program. The rifle approach seeks to inform a very specific group about a particular program that they should be interested in.

In doing publicity, some groups may have several different publics that they must seek to reach. In a therapeutic recreation setting like a large Veterans' Administration hospital, for example, program publicity may need to be directed to members of other adjunctive therapy staffs (such as occupational or physical therapy), medical and nursing personnel, hospital administrators, families of patients, and the patients themselves—in order to achieve awareness and understanding of the program.

It has sometimes been said that the best means of publicity is a good program. Certainly this is true; however, it is also essential that any leisure-service agency take necessary steps to ensure that the public *knows* about its program successes, and that ingenious and creative publicity techniques be used to ensure this awareness and appreciation.

Example of Creative Programming Leading to Publicity.   Often, creative programming can result in special events or other activities that attract a wave of favorable publicity. As an illustration, a New Jersey Catholic Youth Organization scheduled a fund-raising event in which its volunteer coaches played in a basketball game against members of the Philadelphia Eagles football team. The program gathered considerable publicity, in addition to a highly successful fund-raising outcome. Similarly, Camp Confidence, an outstanding camping program for the mentally retarded in Brainerd, Minnesota, has sponsored many unique special events, including major celebrity tournaments designed to attract large numbers of spectators and participants and to raise funds to support programs.

Sometimes outstanding publicity may be derived simply from happenings within a program that are of unique human-relations interest. As a single example, when a young man who had undergone double-leg amputations succeeded in meeting Explorer Scout requirements in a suburban Pennsylvania scouting program, the resulting news stories provided a rich understanding of the philosophy and positive outcomes of present-day scouting.

However, because the use of such stories *may* be controversial, and may arouse negative reactions on the part of the public, there should be a policy that all special efforts to get publicity (such as news story releases, interviews, press events, or radio or television features) should be reviewed and approved by a responsible agency administrator. Public relations efforts must be coordinated and cannot be handled loosely by all members of the staff in a random or haphazard way. In the case of recreation programs in larger organizations, such as the armed forces or a large business concern, normally publicity ventures are cleared through a public information officer for the overall organization.

ONGOING PROGRAM SUPERVISION

A fourth key element in successful program implementation consists of effective ongoing supervision of program elements. This means that the task of implementation is not over when a program has been set in motion. Instead, it normally requires continued monitoring and care to ensure that things are going well and that the plans and managerial decisions that were made in developing the activity were sound.

Such supervision is carried out in several ways. Typically, those responsible are normally expected to submit regular program reports—usually weekly. Such reports must include accurate registration or attendance figures and must summarize activities over the period, including descriptions of any special events or new activities; accident reports or other incidents, such as disciplinary action taken; and possible recommendations for program changes or modifications.

Beyond this, agency supervisors may also meet regularly with leadership personnel. In many departments, division heads may meet once a week with center directors, activity specialists, or other leaders to review past activities and plan for future ones. At such times, program problems may be discussed and solutions sought.

In addition, supervisors also should observe programs in action. This can be done in a number of ways: (1) through planned or scheduled visits, either while routine activities are being carried on, or when a special demonstration or exhibit is being offered; (2) through surprise visits in which the supervisor drops in to observe programs in action without preliminary notice; or (3) simply by eyeballing, in which the supervisor may drive by to observe activity casually, without actually visiting the program or meeting with staff members or participants.

Too often, the supervisor may be perceived in a threatening light; when he or she observes a program in action, leaders may be apprehensive about their reactions. This is an unfortunate distortion of the true purpose of supervision. It is the supervisor's task to establish a constructive climate of human relations and promote favorable work attitudes on the part of employees toward their job, each other, and the organization itself.

Supervisory Functions. The supervisor must interpret and apply company or agency policies and work orders, train new employees, counsel and discipline employees (where necessary), initiate or recommend personnel actions, and plan and put into action time and work schedules, subject to limitations on his or her authority:

> Thus the supervisor may be viewed as a leader and trainer of others, an implementer of fresh ideas and approaches, a superior to lower-level employees, a co-worker with others, and an aide to top management. He or she must be able to understand and effectively express and respond to the needs of those on all levels and, where necessary, help to mediate employee complaints or requests, or enforce overall management policy.[7]

While most descriptions of supervisors' roles in leisure-service agencies tend to focus on their personnel-related functions, it should be understood that they also play a key role in guiding and directing program activities. They should help leaders be innovative in developing attractive program ideas, and should assist them in becoming better teachers of activity, or in other functions on the playground, in the recreation center, or in other special program areas. In a sense, they function both as coaches and as counselors in this effort.

PROGRAM SAFETY AND RISK-MANAGEMENT PRACTICES

A final important phase of program implementation to be dealt with in this chapter consists of maintaining effective safety, accident-prevention, and risk-management practices. This is a key concern, particularly in certain sports or outdoor recreation pursuits that have a high potential for injury or death. However, accidents can occur in many types of recreation settings. As indicated earlier, over 100,000 children are taken to the hospital each year because of injuries sustained on neighborhood playgrounds; hundreds of fatalities each year are incurred in the country's national park system.[8]

Every leisure-service agency seeks to prevent such occurrences, both to avoid the possibility of costly lawsuits for negligence, and as a matter of responsibility to program participants. Typically, accident prevention may be approached in a number of different ways.

In many departments, safety and accident prevention are made the responsibility of all supervisors and leaders, and guidelines for supervising play activities and inspecting all equipment and areas to eliminate unnecessary hazards are prepared. It is recognized that all accidents have causes, and that every effort should be made to prevent them before they occur. All recreation staff members should know their own responsibility and degree of liability with respect to accidents as well as the agency's liability. In addition, correct procedures for handling accidents and injuries should be made clear to all staff members, and carefully enforced.

Specific Safety Practices. Beyond such general principles, specific safety practices should be prepared for each type of recreation situation, ranging from arts and crafts sessions to white-water canoe trips. A set of illustrative guidelines for playground supervision might include the following rules:

1. Prepare, post, and enforce simple rules of safety for your playground or other facility.
   a. Prohibit climbing on fences, buildings, or other structures not intended for this purpose.
   b. Prohibit bicycle riding on the playground, and restrict the use of skateboards, scooters, roller skates, jump ropes, and similar equipment to specific areas.
   c. Prohibit climbing on apparatus when it is wet and slippery.
   d. Prohibit rough-housing, unnecessary pushing, and throwing of sticks, stones, or other objects.
2. Inspect all equipment, grounds, and facilities daily, and carry out the following measures:
   a. If any piece of equipment or apparatus is not in working con-

dition, place it ''out-of-order,'' and notify the maintenance department immediately.

b. Keep play areas and sanitary facilities clean at all times.

c. Keep all pointed or sharp-edged tools out of reach when they are not in use.

d. Restrict play activities in areas where surfaces are slippery or not suitable for use.

e. Keep animals off grounds, except when they are part of organized playground activities, such as pet shows.

f. Establish ''safety zones'' around areas such as swings, giant strides, or merry-go-rounds, so children can move past them safely.

g. Locate active games involving batted or kicked balls in areas where they will not interfere with or endanger ''tot'' playgrounds or other quiet activities.

h. Generally, keep play areas free of congestion.

3. In carrying on active games, sports, gymnastics or similar activities, observe the following guidelines:

a. See to it that children have proper conditioning or preparation before engaging in strenuous activity.

b. Require physical examinations before organized competition.

c. Require children to have suitable equipment and uniforms (such as batting helmets in baseball) for specific activities.

d. Exclude children who are recognizably ill from activity, and stop activities before fatigue sets in.

e. Gear activities to the physical capabilities and skill levels of groups.

Koslowski has cited a number of examples of municipal recreation and park agencies being found liable because of negligence in not adequately supervising such activities as a playground game of ''crack the whip,'' or permitting dangerous foreign objects such as broken glass to remain in a play area. In addition to preventing such instances of negligence, it is essential that leisure-service agencies develop appropriate follow-up procedures providing first aid for minor injuries, or emergency measures in the event of more serious accidents. For example, when a serious injury occurs, the following steps should be taken:

1. Make the injured person as comfortable as possible, covering him or her to provide warmth. Do *not* move an injured person because this may aggravate the injury.

2. In the event of severe bleeding or stoppage of breathing, apply emergency first aid measures. Do not apply any other treatment; do not probe injuries, test the movement of limbs, or attempt to set fractures.

3. Immediately call for appropriate medical assistance if the injury appears to be of an emergency nature:
   a. In some departments, the procedure is to call the police or sheriff's office directly, to have them call for an ambulance.
   b. In other departments, the procedure is to call a special police emergency squad that normally transports individuals to hospitals after giving expert first aid.
   c. In other situations, the recreation leader must call the ambulance directly.
4. Call parents or guardians immediately. In some departmental guidelines it is required that this be done *before* sending for medical assistance, so that parents can make needed decisions. If the injury is extremely severe, or if it is not possible to contact parents, the recreation leader must send for an ambulance first.
5. Notify the recreation department of the accident, and fill out a report form, giving full details of the incident. Meanwhile, other participants should be encouraged to continue with the recreation program.

Recreation leaders must be familiar with precise guidelines with respect to follow-up procedures after such incidents, including: (1) securing signed statements from all witnesses; (2) appropriate procedures for discussing the accident with anyone other than appropriate departmental or municipal officers; (3) remaining at the location until medical help has come and investigating officers have gathered all necessary information; (4) follow-up telephone calls or visits to the injured persons and family; and (5) reinvolvement of the injured participant in the program, after recovery.

An example of questionable follow-up procedures in a commercial recreation setting may be found in a tragic accident in a large Eastern theme park where eight individuals died in a sudden fire in a "haunted house" facility. Apart from the safety standards applied in the design and construction of the facility, which became the subject of legal investigation and litigation, procedures for informing the families of the victims, bringing them to the site and meeting with them, were clumsily handled both from a public-relations and human-relations point of view.

While such concerns might *appear* to be administrative or managerial responsibilities rather than the function of those staff members involved in directing running programs, this is not the case. In the case of the "haunted house" fire, those individuals who were directly involved in operating the facility might have judged that procedures for emptying the building rapidly in the event of an emergency were inadequate, or that the very nature of the facility (with almost total blackness inside, tempting those going through it to light matches) involved a serious fire risk. If so, it would have been their responsibility to call this to the attention of higher-level personnel. In such settings, if a positive accident-prevention attitude is implanted and constantly reinforced among all personnel, such tragedies might in many cases be prevented.

Accident-Analysis and Risk Management

Based on such concerns, many leisure-service agencies have developed systematic accident-analysis and risk-management approaches. Today, such organizations must deal with a tremendous volume of visitors who come to outdoor recreation sites where their involvement is often unsupervised, and where natural hazards as well as the nature of activity (including scuba diving, cave exploration, mountain and rock climbing) have a high potential for injury or death. One useful approach is to develop a total risk-management approach that seeks to analyze and interpret accidents and to develop methods for minimizing them. This includes the following steps:

1. Systematic reporting and record keeping, which help reveal patterns of accidents and injuries as well as their severity and apparent causes—both in terms of specific parks (within a large state or national park system) and in terms of types of recreational activity.
2. Facilities inspection and hazard abatement, including inspection of sites with a possible risk hazard, and placing of speed-limit signs, rock-slide warnings, barriers, thin-ice warnings, or similar prohibitions to protect participants against natural hazards.

   Similarly, in recreation structures and facilities it is essential to correct such deficiencies as poor visibility, inadequate barriers or walls, blocked exits, or poorly marked emergency routes, accessible high-voltage transmission lines, or similar built-in hazards.
3. Participant-safety procedures that involve a regular, consistent approach to making sure that all participants understand the inherent risks in the outdoor recreation activity or sport they are engaged in. While waivers (signed promises not to hold the recreation agency responsible in case of accident) have limited value, conscientious efforts on the part of the organization to inform participants of the risks they face and of unsafe acts that must be avoided can be helpful in case of lawsuit. This can be done by posting rules, having briefing sessions, or similar measures.
4. Staff training and safety goal-setting are essential to make sure that the risk-management program works. Safety and accident-prevention must be made important items in personnel orientation and in-service training programs, and are regularly reinforced in meetings, evaluations, and other management procedures.

Ewert suggests that an intelligent risk-assessment process be carried out, which carefully measures both the predictable frequency of accidents and their potential severity in terms of possible injury or death.[9] If both frequency and severity are high, the odds are too great, and most leisure-service agencies will avoid such activities. With either a low frequency or severity rate, a given activity would appear to be a reasonable choice.

Usually, he points out, when a given type of outdoor activity is examined, three choices exist for the program planner: (1) to continue it in its present form; (2) to continue it with modifications; or (3) to discontinue it. If the decision is to continue it, a total risk-management plan should be developed, which includes such key elements as: (1) adequate preparations, in terms of a specified time schedule and clear objectives; (2) back-up resources, such as participant medical forms, emergency numbers, and facilities; (3) explaining hazards to participants, obtaining their consent, and having them sign risk forms; and (4) highly qualified leadership and carefully designed safety policies throughout the experience.

Despite the wave of public enthusiasm for high-risk outdoor recreation experiences, many public, voluntary and other leisure-service agencies have shied away from such programs because of their fear of lawsuits. However, a growing number of such organizations today are sponsoring adventure programming, and doing so with the kind of careful preparation and supervision that keeps injury and lawsuit to an unavoidable minimum. Recognizing that there are risks in all of life, with millions of injuries occurring each year in the home, this would appear to be a reasonable policy. At the same time, the field must continue to explore the use of new kinds of equipment, safety surfacing, and environmental designs that can provide excitement and creative exploration with a minimum of danger from built-in or behavioral hazards.

EXAMPLE OF PROGRAM IMPLEMENTATION

To conclude this chapter, a single major example of the process involved in carrying out a single major program event is provided. This consists of the plan for a large-scale swimming meet to be conducted by a Lancaster County, Pennsylvania, private swimming, racquet and tennis club. It is drawn from a report prepared by John F. Apple, Professor of Physical Education at Millersville, Pennsylvania, State College, who has had considerable experience in directing such a facility.

The plan is presented in full detail, with only minor modifications. It illustrates the underlying goals, preliminary arrangements, and other operational procedures of such an event, in carefully developed form—including budget planning, the selection of awards, handling of traffic, and maintenance arrangements—that were not discussed elsewhere in this chapter.

A Program Plan for the Administration of an Age Group Championship Swim Meet at Skyline Swimming, Racquet, and Fitness Center, Inc.[10]

Introduction

In Lancaster County, Pennsylvania, and in many counties around the country, every summer competitive age group swimming teams practice and have meets, while parent booster clubs raise money to support the above activities. A most effective way for a booster club to raise the funds necessary to provide coaching, equipment, awards, and the other essentials for an age-group swim program is the championship invitational swim meet. This paper deals with the organization, planning, and direction of such a program.

Skyline Swimming, Racquet and Fitness Center, Inc., is a private swim club and is a member of the Lancaster YMCA Summer Swim League along with twenty other teams representing private clubs, community pools, and recreation center pools in the area. Skyline is in Division I of the league along with six other teams. During the season, Skyline swims each of the teams in this division once. Following the completion of the dual meet season there are two championships hosted by the league. In addition to these league championships, several teams host their own invitational meets. Such meets serve primarily as fund-raisers for the teams in question. Skyline has recently discussed the possibilities of hosting such a fund-raising event. The guidelines outlined here could be employed by anyone proposing such a venture.

Purpose and objectives

The primary purpose of the Skyline Invitational Swim Championship is to raise funds to meet the annual swim team expenses and to provide the means needed to replace the bulkhead which was constructed in 1978 and which is now in very poor repair.

The objectives of such an event would include the following:

1. To provide a wholesome competitive event for area youngsters.
2. To encourage cooperation and "team unity" among the booster club parents.
3. To make it possible to replace the bulkhead.
4. To prevent an increase in swim team fees.
5. To eliminate the necessity for many little fund raising events such as hoagie sales, raffles, and bake sales.

Organizational meet committee

This is the group of people responsible for organizing, planning, and directing the meet. From this group will be chosen the meet director who is the person ultimately responsible for putting all the pieces together so that the meet runs smoothly. This group should consist of approximately six key persons. The most critical areas of responsibility are: the awards program, the officials, the printed program, the head table, concessions and admissions, and the facility set-up and maintenance. The meet director must select one or more people to head each of these areas. It must be recognized at the outset that an undertaking of this nature is quite extensive and requires a great deal of work and cooperation.

Time schedule

At least three months should be allowed from the time the decision is made to conduct a championship swim meet until the planning culminates in the actual event. The main reasons for this seemingly lengthy preparatory period are the plans for awards, the typed program, obtaining sponsors and patrons, printing the "T"-shirts, and obtaining special equipment such as bleachers, stop watches, and the refreshment set-up. A time checklist for the meet director might be as follows:

April 1st.	*April 8th.*	*April 15th.*	*April 22nd.*
Decide to host meet	Decide on Awards	Announcements	Notify league
Choose director	Design shirt	Order awards	Pool members
Choose date	Work committees	Order shirts	Design program
Establish committee		Interest Card	
Check with board			
May 1st.	*May 8th.*	*May15th.*	*May 22nd.*
Contract Officials	Concession Contacts	Follow up phone	Deposit reminder
Order watches	Equipment needed	Progress reports	Menu plan
Bleachers	Paper supplies		
Meet Equipment			
June 1st.	*June 8th.*	*June 15th.*	*June 22nd.*
Deposits due	Entries sent	Sponsors due	Arrange entries
Progress reports	Assignment areas	Patrons due	Type program
	Traffic flow plan	Entries due	Print program
	Practice schedule		Head table supplies
June 29th.	*June 30th.*	*July 10th.*	
Last minute check	Arrive early	Committee reports	
Set-up meet	Final check	Review meet	
Flag and anthem	Brief officials	Financial report	
Bleachers	Test all systems	Plans for bulkhead	
Restrain ropes	Meet with coaches	Bulkhead committee	
Maintenance	Call first event	What about next year	
Flood pool			
Check all supplies			
Committee heads meet			
Test all systems			

Personnel needed

The number of people needed to run a large championship meet will stagger the imagination. A rough number to start with would be fifty people including: judges, timers, clerks, starter, runners, physician, referee, recorders, announcer, admissions, meet director, refreshments, programs, parking attendants, lifeguard, and others. In championship meets it is not at all uncommon to require guest teams to provide two or more timers or judges for the meet. These arrangements should be made well ahead of time. For a six-lane pool the following may give a more accurate appraisal of needed personnel.

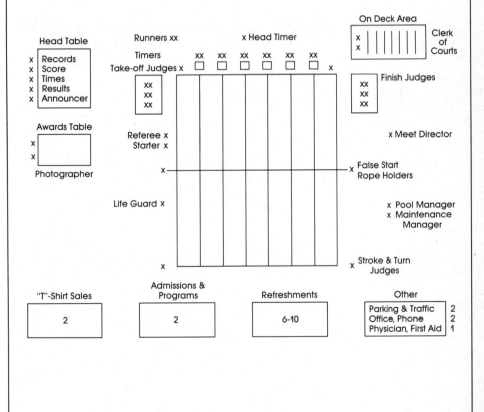

SKYLINE INVITATIONAL "MEDLEY" SWIM CHAMPIONSHIP

Meet information

Date: Saturday June 27, 1981

Starting Time: 10:00 A.M.

Entries Due: Friday June 19, 1981—Midnight Deadline!

Deposit: All teams interested in competing in the meet must submit a $25.00 deposit. The first eight teams to submit the deposit will be officially entered in the meet. Deposits are due on or before June first.

Minimum Entries: All competing teams must have a minimum of $50.00 in entries. Your deposit may be used toward the total fee.

Entry Fees: Entry fees must accompany all entries. Please deduct the $25.00 deposit from your total. Individual events are $1.00 each and relays are $4.00 per team.

Awards: There will be awards presented to the top six finishers—all events: Pewter cups, first; T-shirt, second; Meet patch, third; Ribbon, fourth; Wall certificate, fifth; and Card, sixth. Engraved Team Trophies—Awarded to top six teams for total score.

General Rules: Summer YMCA League rules will prevail. Each swimmer may enter three events. Each team may enter a maximum of three relays in each relay event.

Facility: The pool is seven lanes wide and twenty-five meters in length. There are lane lines, bottom lines, starting blocks, and wall targets.

Officials: All key officials will be provided by the host pool and the Lancaster officials club. Each invited team will be required to provide one timer and one judge for the meet.

Point Scoring: Individual Events—16,13,12,11,10,9,7,5,4,3,2,1
Relay Events—32,26,24,22,20,18,14,10,8,6,4,2

Souvenir Meet T-shirts: Will be available—cost $3.50/each.

Refreshments: Skyline Swim Team Parents will provide a full menu—Drinks, sandwiches, fruit, soups, desserts, etc.

Admission Fee: For nonswimmers/coaches admission will be—Children under 18 years, $.50; Adults, $1.00

Meet Programs: Will cost $.50 each.

Entry Forms: Each entry must be made individually on the entry cards supplied as well as indicated on the coaches' master entry form.

Budget and finances

It is not at all unusual for an age group championship swim meet to gross over $4,000. Of this amount anywhere from $1,500 to $2,500 may be profit. Major items of expense are the awards, the T-shirts, and key officials such as the referee, and the food. A good, unique, and attractive awards program will help ensure success by attracting more teams and participants, but such an effort doesn't come inexpensively. Fortunately, most of the personnel involved are swim team parents who are volunteering their time for their children's benefit. Usually the entry fees charged for the swimmers' entries in the events is sufficient to cover the cost of awards.

The admissions fees, refreshments, programs, T-shirts, sponsors' fees, and donations are all potential income makers. In the event of inclement weather, however, the booster club could be stuck with a lot of leftover shirts and food. A sample budget is included with a projected gross of $3,500 and a profit margin of $1,500. This would be enough to finance most of the bulkhead replacement. Invitations will be extended to twelve teams and the first eight to respond with a $25 deposit will be permitted to participate in the meet. The deposit, of course, may be used later toward entry fees. In addition to the deposit a minimum entry fee per team will be required and will amount to $50. This will yield a minimum starting figure of $400 income. The entry fees for events will be as follows and are in keeping with standard fees commonly charged: Individual events, $1.00; Relay events, $4.00.

Sponsors will be charged $10.00 to sponsor an event. With a total of thirty events this could bring in a potential of $300. In addition a page should be included for patrons and, for a donation of $1.00, such persons' names will be listed appropriately.

BUDGET

Expenses		*Expected Income*	
Awards	$ 725.00	Entry Fees	$ 800.00
Food	250.00	T-Shirt Sales (3.50)	750.00
T-Shirts (250 at 2.00)	500.00	Food	700.00
Officials (3)	75.00	Admissions	250.00
Bleachers	100.00	200 adults— 1.00	
Timing Equipment	250.00	100 children— .50	
Misc.	100.00	Programs .50 each	200.00
Total	$2000.00	Sponsors 10.00 each	300.00
Net Income	$1500.00	Patrons 1.00 each	50.00
		Total	$3500.00

Type of swim meet

The most common types of swim meets involve either individual events, relays, or both. The format that will be used in this meet will blend the above formats in a unique and distinctly different fashion. Medley events will be incorporated into both frameworks, those for individuals and those for relays. A medley event combines all four competitive strokes. To the writer's knowledge this particular construct has never been used solely as a meet format. It is hoped that the novelty of this new type of meet will be highly attractive to the various coaches and teams. This uniqueness will certainly tend to aid in the success of the venture. The age categories will be in keeping with existing league rules. There will be separate events for boys and girls. The events which will be used are as follows (event numbers are indicated):

	Individual Medley	Medley Relay	Individual Medley Relay
Age Group	100 meters	4x25 meters	4x100 meters
Eight & Under Girls	1	11	21
Eight & Under Boys	2	12	22
Ten & Under Girls	3	13	23
Ten· & Under Boys	4	14	24
Twelve & Under Girls	5	15	25
Twelve & Under Boys	6	16	26
Fourteen & Under Girls	7	17	27
Fourteen & Under Boys	8	18	28
Seventeen & Under Girls	9	19	29
Seventeen & Under Boys	10	20	30

Key: Individual Medley—An individual event where each swimmer must swim one length of each of the competitive strokes.
Medley Relay—A four-person relay where each swimmer swims one of the four competitive strokes.
Individual Medley Relay—A four-person relay where each swimmer swims 100 meters of the individual medley where all four competitive strokes are represented.

The awards program

The awards program is one of the key factors in the planning efforts. It is with a well-designed awards program that the host club will entice coaches and swimmers to compete in the invitational meet.

The following suggested awards set-up will be realistically presented with a full-cost analysis. As you recall from the listing of meet events there are a total of thirty events. Two thirds of these will be relays and one third will be individual events. The awards for relays will then naturally be four times as expensive as the individual events.

This awards program, as mentioned earlier, will be based on the assumption that eight teams will accept an invitation to attend. The size of the average team in the summer league is 100 so that the overall maximum potential in number of participants would be 800 swimmers. We will project that the participants may number 400, which would be typical at this type of meet.

The estimated costs for individual and team trophies, including pewter cups, pitchers, bowls, mugs, T-shirts, meet matches, ribbons and certificates, will be approximately $730. With the minimum team entry fee of $50 per team, and with eight teams participating, the meet committee will have a guaranteed $400 initially. The projected entries per team (with an average of fifty swimmers from each team and with each swimmer entering one individual event and one relay) will yield $100 per team, or $800 for all eight teams. These revenues will comfortably cover the cost of the awards.

Advertising

An event such as the one described here must be discussed about one year before it is actually considered seriously. This is done by asking other coaches and concerned people what they think about the idea and whether they would support the venture. If the person with the idea can sell it to four other teams and obtain their verbal commitment the venture is off and running. The next step is to formally organize the operation with a meet committee, etc. Advertising can be done through the league and directly to individual coaches and teams. With an invitational type meet set-up, specific invitations are only sent to those teams that the meet committee agrees to invite. Consequently, a great deal of advertising is unwarranted. Coverage of the actual meet by the press, radio, and T.V., is, of course, an important part of the overall preparation. Printing will include the meet announcement, the program, entry forms, and admission tickets. Public relations will include a good working relationship with parents, coaches, the news media, the patrons, and the meet sponsors. Copies of the results and sample programs should be made available to all concerned and thank-you letters as well as public recognition of important contributions the day of the meet must be taken care of properly. Often the entire meet may be dedicated to a local individual who is well known in the world of swimming.

Traffic flow

Traffic flow is an item often overlooked by planners, but it certainly deserves close attention. There are many facets to traffic flow that involve much more than merely parking cars. The meet planners must also consider crowd control, where the visiting teams will change, where the teams will locate themselves on the property, spectator areas, pool practice schedules for the teams, lanes designated for specific activities such as sprints, and areas roped off properly to prevent swimmers and spectators from interfering with the meet operation. When the meet is in progress the roped off areas are for actual competitors and officials only. All others must stay out of these areas for smooth meet operation.

Safety

Safety is an important item that doesn't just happen, it must be definitely planned! It begins with a fully equipped first aid station. Someone should be in the office at all times, and be able to respond to an emergency. The pool manager should be on duty the day of the meet and must be ready to act at a moment's notice. A lifeguard must be on duty and his or her only job must be lifeguarding and nothing else! The local police should be notified in order to assist with traffic flow into and out of the facility and to just be aware of the function. A medical doctor should be present at the meet. Steps should be taken to prevent running, dangerous play, vandalism, and theft the day of the meet. A second or third lifeguard assigned to roving the property will help in this regard. The insurance agent for the pool should be called and consulted about the meet in order to ascertain if everything is in compliance.

Head table

After the meet director, the meet committee, and all the subcommittees have done their jobs, it is up to the head table to see that the actual meet runs efficiently and effectively. In this regard it is often said that an announcer and a starter can make or break a meet. These two key personnel had better be very sharp. They can keep the meet running smoothly and quickly. There is nothing worse for all concerned than a meet that has frequent delays and drags. The results of each event must be brought quickly to the head table by the runners for recording. The clerk of course must have the next group of swimmers ready to move immediately to the blocks as soon as the group before them is sent into the water. The announcer must quickly read the swimmers' names and lanes. While the swimmers are racing the announcer must also give official results of prior races as he receives them along with team scores. He also calls swimmers to the on-deck area where they are arranged and lined up correctly for their events. These functions are all coordinated by the head table.

Maintenance and set-up

For an event of this magnitude, several hundred swimmers—along with parents, friends and family, and the maintenance staff—pool preparation and facility set-up is quite extensive. Advanced arrangements must be made well ahead of time for any equipment needed that is not part of the host pool's normal operation, such as electric timing equipment, bleachers, and the booster club's refreshment stand. One week before the meet, the booster club should run a "dry run" practice session to work out rough spots in the meet operation. Clinics should be planned to train the parents in meet operation, timing and officiating. The facility must be made ready the day before the meet. Systems checks should be done after all is made ready. The pool maintenance staff should have the entire facility in top shape. The pool water should be crystal clear with proper Cl_2 and pH. The bottom should be clean. The pool level should be higher than normal (flooded) to ensure a "fast" pool for the races. The rest rooms must be well stocked for the large numbers of people that will be present. Frequent checks of the rest rooms will be required. The booster club will assist in clean up following the meet. This is usually a big job requiring several hours.

Review and evaluation

During the meet accurate records must be kept. Results are not only announced as they are available, they are also posted so that spectators and coaches can copy them down. Following the meet, total meet results must be made available to the press. Frequently the press wants to take pictures of the winning team, coach, or outstanding swimmers who competed. New records should be carefully noted. A complete listing of the results will of course be sent to all participating teams. Results along with notes of appreciation should also be sent to all the event sponsors who helped to make the meet successful. A card or form for each coach's suggestions and comments regarding the meet should be available.

One week following the meet the meet committee should sit down and carefully analyze all aspects of the meet, especially if such events will be planned again. A full financial accounting should be given at this time by the club treasurer. Plans for repairing the bulkhead will begin at the conclusion of this meeting.

Closing comments

An event such as the one presented here is obviously an ambitious undertaking. It might easily discourage many swim clubs from even considering such a project. The rewards, however, can be just as great as the hard work and headaches. Everyone benefits from a well-run championship such as presented here. The booster club learns to function as a team forming many new and lasting friendships. The children can enjoy a wholesome event where they can have fun and demonstrate their talents and the results of their many hours of practice. The parents of the swimmers can enjoy watching their youngsters striving for and achieving goals and recognition in a friendly competitive setting. And if all goes well for the host team they might raise enough money to do bigger and better things for their children the following year.

This report of the program plan for a inter-club swimming meet illustrates many of the tasks that must be carried out to make any special event successful.

USE OF COMPUTERS IN PROGRAM IMPLEMENTATION

In earlier chapters, it was shown how computers could be useful in the process of recreation scheduling. Today, there is growing interest in the use of electronic data-processing throughout the entire leisure-service field.

Until comparatively recently, most computer use was devoted to payroll operations, to developing and monitoring maintenance plans, keeping inventories of equipment and supplies, and similar functions. For example, in Richardson, Texas, the public Parks and Recreation Department has used computers in handling such tasks as carrying out purchasing transactions; receiving, counting, depositing, and reporting program-derived fees; addressing, sorting, and mailing newsletters; preparing and processing program registration cards; maintaining personnel records; organizing and monitoring the community's parks maintenance operation; keeping program statistics; and assisting in planning athletic schedules and assigning fields for approximately 1000 teams, in several different sports.[11]

Computers are extremely valuable in carrying out such tasks, which involve working with large masses of data or with program elements that require organization, control, or recording. A major problem has been the lack of software programs that are directly applicable to recreation and park functions.

One agency that has pioneered in this area has been the Maryland National Capital Park and Planning Commission, whose Montgomery County Park Department has invested over $100,000 in the development of computer programs, resulting in an estimated annual savings to the Department of $480,000. Sharpless writes:

> Department functions using computer programs include: financial analysis and forecasting; policy development; long-range park planning; park police management; maintenance management; land records management; agriculture and property management; fleet management; nursery management; botanical garden management; general horticultural management; programs for use by the public; utility management; engineering and landscaping projects; and office management.[12]

Gradually, computer applications are being developed for recreation programming—which has not generally used electronic data processing approaches. Berryman and Lefebvre have developed a computer-based system for activity analysis and prescriptive therapeutic recreation programming for disabled children and youth, for example. The National Institutes of Health of the U.S. Public Health Service has developed a computerized recreation referral service for disabled individuals in the Southern and Mid-Eastern Regions of the United States.

Raiola and Sugarman describe the uses of computers in outdoor recreation programming at Unity College in Maine, where students have written programs for:

> an inventory program for the outdoor recreation equipment room, a computerized mailing list, and a section on state canoeing areas . . . rock climbing sites and day hiking areas. Using a menu-planning program, students can select the desired menu, input the number of people, and end up with the correct amount of each ingredient. Survival and decision-making simulation activities permit students to make mistakes without jeopardizing themselves or their groups.[13]

A number of recreation and park agencies have contracted directly with computer systems companies to develop packaged programs for them. Sharpless points out that several microcomputer programs in use by park and recreation agencies are available through a Seattle clearinghouse, Marketing Computing, Inc.:

> The inventory of programs developed or under development includes league standings, league scheduling, short- and long-term reservations, league registration, class registration, facilities reservation, maintenance scheduling, inventory management, workload-cost tracking, and cost management. The company's service includes tailoring programs to meet specific agency needs.[14]

Without question, computer technology will become increasingly important in the leisure service field, particularly in terms of such management processes as those described in this section, and for the purpose of maintaining a detailed, accurate, and readily accessible data base for management purposes.

At the same time, Jensen points out some forces that are working against increased computer applications in the fields of education and recreation. The mystique of electronic data-processing is compounded by the use of a strange vocabulary and the need to develop new kinds of technical skills. People, she writes, are concerned that machines will displace people in organizational processes, and resist change in work styles. In addition, there is growing concern about ethical issues:

> Data banks threaten individuals' right to privacy, and the use of robotics may eliminate or alter jobs. Computer crimes increase, and software piracy is rampant. The leisure ethic becomes more important. Concerns about an antitechnology revolution are raised as the gap widens between those who have access to technology and those who have not. The resolution of these issues must not be ignored.[15]

Clearly, the challenge will be to solve these ethical issues and to make the fullest possible use of this emerging technology throughout the process of delivering recreation and park programs and services. At all times it must be recognized that, while computers may be used to analyze problems and develop operational systems, they cannot provide a sense of values or make philosophical judgments; this is reserved to human beings.

THE NEED FOR SYSTEMATIC EVALUATION

In conclusion, this chapter has presented five important elements of recreation program implementation, including the assignment of personnel, the development of procedural manuals and guidelines, program publicity and promotion, continuing supervision of activities, and accident prevention and risk management. It also describes some of the growing uses of computers in recreation and park agencies, with special applications for programming.

The last step in the program planning and implementation process involves a comprehensive and systematic monitoring of the entire operation, and an evaluation of its effectiveness—both while it is going on, and at its conclusion. This important responsibility is described in Chapter 11, with examples of evaluation instruments and procedures in several types of recreation agencies and programs.

NOTES

[1]For a description of the staff-development process, see Richard Kraus, *Recreation Leadership Today* (Glenview, Ill.: Scott, Foresman, 1985), Chapter 13.

[2]*Program Planning Manual*, (Phoenix, AZ: Parks and Recreation Department, n.d.)

[3]"Overnight Camping," *Recreation* (May 1962): 237.

[4]*Official Brochure of the Pepsi Challenge/NBA Hotshot Contest, 1983*.

[5]Paul Wehman and Stuart J. Schleien, *Leisure Programs for Handicapped Persons* (Baltimore: University Park Press, 1981), p. 89.

[6]*Adventure Trips Manual* (Phoenix, Ariz. Department of Parks and Recreation, n.d.).

[7]Richard Kraus and Joseph Curtis, *Creative Management in Recreation and Parks* (St. Louis: C.V. Mosby, 1982), p. 97.

[8]Leroy Spivey, "Trends in Safety and Occupational Health: National Park Service Approach," *Trends* (NRPA/HCRS Park Practice Program) (Winter 1980): 3.

[9]Alan Ewert, "The Decision Package: A Tool for Risk Management," *Parks and Recreation* (April 1983): 40–41.

[10]John Apple, *Graduate Course Paper, Unpublished* (Philadelphia: Temple University, 1981).

[11]David L. Loughridge, "Richardson's Microcomputers Ease Growing Pains," *Leisure Today, Journal of Physical Education, Recreation and Dance* (April 1984): 58.

[12]Daniel Sharpless, "Navigating the Computer Maze Successfully," *Parks and Recreation* (May 1983): 40.

[13]Ed Raiola and Deborah Sugarman, "Bits/Bytes and Outdoor Wilderness Recreation," *Journal of Physical Education, Recreation and Dance* (April 1984): 59.

[14]Sharpless: 39.

[15]Marilyn A. Jensen, "Computer Applications: An Introduction," *Journal of Physical Education, Recreation and Dance* (April 1984): 33.

STUDENT PROJECTS_____

1. Based on the example of a private swim club meet presented in this chapter, develop a plan for carrying out a single large-scale event, such as an arts festival, health fair, citywide senior citizens day, or similar project.

   Develop specific plans for: (a) targeting audiences that will be involved in the event; (b) the actual activities that will be carried on; (c) the fiscal plan for the event, including a proposed budget of anticipated revenues and expenses; and (d) the plan for publicizing the event, with sample posters or news releases. *Note:* this program may be cosponsored with another organization; if so, describe the arrangement.
2. Select a recreation program setting which involves a fairly high degree of risk, such as a beachfront area, sportsman's center, or ski center.

   After carrying out research into the operation of such facilities, prepare an appropriate risk management plan, with specific safety guidelines and emergency procedures. *Note:* in each of these projects, show how computers might be used in gathering and analyzing relevant data, decision-making, and program evaluation.

SUGGESTED READINGS_____

Christopher Edginton, David Compton and Carole Hanson, *Recreation and Leisure Programming: A Guide for the Professional* (Philadelphia: Saunders College Publishing, 1980), Chapter 10.

Christopher Edginton and John Williams, *Productive Management of Leisure Service Organizations: A Behavioral Approach* (New York: John Wiley, 1978), Chapter 8.

Scout Gunn and Carol Peterson, *Therapeutic Recreation Program Design: Principles and Procedures* (Englewood Cliffs, N.J.: Prentice-Hall, 1978), Chapter 12.

Ruth V. Russell, *Planning Programs in Recreation* (St. Louis: C. V. Mosby, 1982), Chapter 7.

PART 3

Evaluating
the Recreation Program

Hobbies of every kind are found in recreation programs. Here, adults compete in a surf-casting contest in Mt. Vernon, New York. Youngster learns juggling skills from an expert at The Old Country, Busch Gardens, in Williamsburg, Virginia, and others are entertained by a master cartoonist at a family carnival sponsored by the Honeywell Corporation. Animals get a chance to shine at a Kids Dog Show, cosponsored by the National Recreation and Park Association and Ken-L Ration, in Dallas, Texas. Golfers, swimmers, and sunbathers enjoy outstanding recreation and park facilities in Vancouver, Canada.

CHAPTER 11

Evaluation in Recreation Programming

The Recreation Advisory Committee sat around the County government's board room. Finally, Aaron Marcus said to the Recreation Director, "Jim, we've had some complaints about the recreation program this year, and we feel that we need to have it evaluated by some outside person or group. How do you feel about that?"

Jim Morgan nodded. "I'd welcome it. I can justify everything I've done, but I'd be happy to get some outside opinions and ideas."

"Good," said Aaron. "How do you suggest we go about it?"

"Well, I have two ideas," said Morgan. "First, the president of the State Recreation and Park Society is Margaret Porter. She lives about thirty miles away, and I'm sure she'd be willing to head up a study team. She's a very experienced person. Or we could get in touch with the State University. Their recreation and park department has a field service unit, and they sometimes do program evaluations."

"Good suggestions," said Aaron Marcus. "We'll follow up on these ideas, and see what can be done. Frankly, I feel the program is fine. But we do need to get some experts to look at it."

During the past several years, increased emphasis has been given to the need for more systematic and thorough evaluation processes in many areas of public service—including recreation and park management.

DEFINITION OF EVALUATION

Briefly stated, evaluation means the following:

It is the process of determining the effectiveness of programs, leadership or other elements of professional service in achieving predetermined goals. The quality of a program may also be evaluated according to accepted standards within a field. Evaluations make use of a number of research techniques, of both a quantitative and a qualitative nature. Generally, evaluations examine specific agencies or situations.[1]

To the extent possible, evaluation should use scientific and valid data-gathering techniques and should be regarded as a form of applied, descriptive research.

Secondary Meaning. A secondary use of the term *evaluation* is found in therapeutic recreation, as it applies to the screening of patients or clients to determine their leisure interests, needs and capabilities. Through this process, which may also be called patient/client "assessment" or "appraisal," information is gathered that leads to the development of treatment plans, and overall therapeutic program planning.

Evaluation in Recreation and Parks

Within many areas of human service or daily life, evaluation is regularly applied. Teachers evaluate their students, and students evaluate their teachers, either formally or informally. Administrative policies and procedures are evaluated and employees are regularly appraised to assist in the personnel process. Special grants or government-funded projects normally include an evaluation component to determine their outcomes. In the area of medicine, new drugs or treatment procedures are thoroughly evaluated to measure their benefits and possible risks. Institutions like hospitals or colleges are periodically evaluated, as part of the accreditation process, by national or regional bodies.

In the field of recreation and parks, evaluation may be carried out as the final step in the program planning and implementation process, or as a regular part of the ongoing supervision of program activities and services. It has the following specific purposes:

1. It is used to measure the overall quality of an agency or program, based on the application of established standards and criteria to various aspects of its structure and operation;
2. It seeks to measure the effectiveness of an agency in achieving its overall goals, or in reaching specific short-term objectives and performance measures;

3. It gathers concrete information about specific aspects of the agency's operation, such as its administrative structure and policies, the performance of staff measures, the adequacy and quality of facilities and other physical resources, and similar elements.
4. It may also be used to examine the nature of participation in the agency's program, and the effects of participation in terms of behavioral change or other desired outcomes.

Given these purposes, evaluation's real contribution is to help the organization by providing direction and help in the program-planning process. Howe sums up the practical reasons for carrying out evaluations:

> Services must be improved, resources must be allocated or reallocated based on rational decision-making, the support of the grass-roots consumer must be expanded. . . . What all this means is that we must use evaluation to critically examine our effectiveness.[2]

Recent Emphasis on Need for Evaluation

There is widespread agreement today that evaluation is especially necessary to prove the worth of recreation services, in an era of financial stringency. By showing their positive outcomes, it is believed that a stronger case can be made for continuing the support of recreation and park programs.

Illustrating this position, Ellis and Witt point out that in the past, evaluation of recreation programs has tended to be "biased, self-serving, and ultimately misleading." Today, such "evidence" will not suffice. Instead, they argue, in an age of budget cutting and an increased concern for accountability:

> evaluation by design is a necessity. No longer will intuitive judgments suffice. The best proof possible is needed so that what is said to be done is really being done. There is a need for ammunition to fight to save park, recreation and leisure services from the tax cutter's axe. It is also essential to fulfill the responsibility to spend tax dollars in the most efficient and effective way possible.[3]

Similarly, Connolly makes the case that the limited resources available today for the support of human services make it essential that agencies demonstrate accountability as they compete for adequate funding for their programs. She writes:

> Accountability is a relative term that describes the capability of a service delivery system to justify or explain the activities and services it provides. Program accountability reflects the extent to which program expenditures, activities, and processes effectively and efficiently accomplish [their] purposes. Evaluation methods are employed to determine program accomplishments, thereby feeding into the accountability justifications.[4]

Numerous other authors have justified evaluation in similar terms. Woo and Farley, for example, write

> Ongoing evaluation of past policies and commitments is critical because public funding is shrinking and the era of cutback management has arrived. . . . Evaluation provides information that documents, supports and makes public programs accountable to their constituency."[5]

Unbiased Nature of Evaluation

It is important that evaluation *not* be perceived as a way of automatically justifying one's program. If it is carried out systematically and objectively, it may well yield negative findings—rather than positive and impressive outcomes. Like all forms of research, evaluation does not seek to "prove" a case. Instead, it asks a series of questions and gathers evidence as honestly and systematically as possible—not only to determine whether programs have been successful, but also to assist in future program planning efforts.

MAJOR MODELS OF EVALUATION

As indicated, much evaluation that has taken place in the past has represented informal judgments or subjective measurement of outcomes. Increasingly, however, evaluation is now making use of valid research techniques drawn from the social and behavioral sciences. Howe describes some of the techniques through which evaluation may be used to assist in agency planning and program development; they include:

> gathering and storage of demographic and attitudinal information; past evaluation and report reading; participation rate information; personnel time budgets; and accounts of income and expenditures for programs. [Such] information allows factually-based decision making to replace guess work.[6]

Among the most widely found approaches to evaluation are the following:

Application of Standards and Criteria. Usually, this approach makes use of a set of professionally developed guidelines describing effective agency structures and programs. An expert observer or panel of evaluators reviews the operation in detail based on these guidelines, which are usually formulated as standards and criteria.

Goals Attainment. In this action-oriented model of evaluation, an agency or program is judged based on whether it has been successful in achieving its stated goals and objectives. These normally would be stated in terms of events or programs sponsored, levels of attendance or participation, and other measurable outcomes, including effects on participants. The term *discrepancy model* is sometimes applied to this approach, referring to the gap between the stated objectives and the actual accomplishment of a program.

Transaction-Observation Evaluation.   Here participants in a program rate it, making use of evaluation forms, with emphasis on their personal experience and subjective judgment of the process and the dynamics involved in it. Often, emphasis may be placed on the degree of satisfaction derived from participation. Rossman points out that two distinct types of models may be used in evaluation: *process* and *preordinate* models.

> Process models delineate a set of steps and procedures to be used in conducting an evaluation without identifying the judgment criteria to be used in making judgments of worth. Preordinate models provide a process and specify the judgment criteria to be used in determining the worth of a leisure program.[7]

Two other kinds of approaches are found in program evaluation. As described earlier, the first is *formative* evaluation, which consists of an ongoing review or monitoring process while a program is going on, and which may yield direct feedback that results in changing a program's objectives and procedures, while it is still in action. The second is *summative* evaluation. As its name implies, it is carried out when a program has been concluded, and when it is too late to make changes in the ongoing operation; however, recommendations may be made for future action.

GUIDELINES FOR CONDUCTING EVALUATIONS

Recreation and leisure-service managers should regard evaluation as an important responsibility and should take steps to ensure that it is carried out effectively. This task will involve several steps:

Assigning Responsibility

To ensure that evaluation is carried out in a thorough and systematic way, it should be assigned as a continuing responsibility to a specific staff member, or possibly a work committee or task force in the agency. Having done this, it is essential that full support be given to evaluation as an important element in the agency's management process. In too many leisure-service settings, relatively little emphasis is given to evaluation, and even when it is carried out, it is done in a superficial or careless way.

Determining Evaluation Needs, Goals, and Priorities

This individual or group should take the lead in determining what the needs of the organization are for evaluation of the overall agency, specific programs, personnel, or other concerns. Based on this beginning analysis, a plan for conducting evaluation throughout the year will be developed, with a timetable and a precise statement of the resources that may be necessary to carry it out.

Many large national organizations urge that their local branches or units carry out periodic evaluations and, in fact, may require visitations and thorough examinations based on established standards if they are to maintain their status or accreditation.

Allocating Agency Resources to Evaluation

Some evaluation tasks may be carried out routinely without any special investment of time or money. Others may require special expertise, data analysis, or other resources that will need authorization and funding support. Typically, it may be appropriate to have regular staff members evaluate certain programs without any additional expense or commitments. On the other hand, to evaluate an entire agency or program, or to provide an objective, impartial, and highly skilled analysis, it may be desirable to bring in a visiting evaluator or team of observers.

Both approaches have strengths and weaknesses. Relying on "internal" evaluators is convenient and inexpensive, and it can be assumed that such individuals are quite familiar with the program and will not require a lengthy period of fact finding or detailed examination. On the other hand, they are likely to be biased or self-protective or—simply because of their limited exposure—not to have a full sense of what the program could and should be.

"External" evaluators may be drawn from many sources—faculty members of nearby colleges and universities, special consultants or authorities within the field, representatives of professional organizations, and leading practitioners in comparable leisure-service agencies. Their advantages are that they are likely to be extremely knowledgeable about professional practices and impartial in their approach to analyzing the program. However, they often require professional fees and travel or maintenance expenses, and may also need considerable time to become fully familiar with the agency.

In many cases, it is now recognized that a combination of both internal and external evaluators is an appropriate means of staffing evaluation efforts—although relatively minor self-studies can certainly be carried out by regular staff members. Major assessments should certainly make use of outsiders in key roles.

Developing Instruments and Procedures

Different kinds of instruments and other data-gathering procedures may be used, including checklists, observational forms, rating scales, and questionnaires. In some cases, instruments have been published by national organizations or may be found in the literature and will prove useful for a particular situation. However, it may often be necessary for a practitioner to develop his or her own evaluation form, to apply to the specific circumstances being examined. Useful guidelines for developing survey questionnaires were presented in Chapter 5 and may readily be adapted to developing evaluation instruments.

In general, it is advisable to use questions that have multiple responses, with a Likert-type rating scale approach (such as giving choices like Excellent, Good, Fair, or Poor. Pre-test the questionnaire to make sure that it is workable, in terms of clarity of questions, length of time needed to complete it, and similar responses. If at all possible, have responses pre-coded, so that they can readily be transferred to computer cards or other tally sheets for analysis. Finally, make sure that the population you are sampling is as representative as possible, so you can have confidence in your findings.

It is advisable also to develop a standardized procedure for distributing questionnaires, carrying out interviews, or conducting evaluation processes. In the evaluation of colleges and universities conducting summer youth sports programs under the sponsorship of the National Youth Sports Program, the following procedures are outlined in a manual of directions for visiting project evaluators:

> Each of the projects will be visited at least one week after the start of their project to allow the project adequate lead time to become fully operational prior to the visit. A minimum of one day will be spent at each site, and each evaluator or evaluation team will prepare an individual Evaluation Point Assignments and Values Form. The reports and recommendations of all evaluators will be combined into a final summary report which will be presented to the National Program Director of the National Youth Sports Program and the National NYSP Advisory Committee.

METHODOLOGY

1. The Project Administrator and Activity Director of the selected institution will be notified one week in advance of the site visit by the evaluator and will be requested to have the Visitation Report Form completed with all lists, schedules, etc. attached.
2. At the beginning of each visit, the evaluator will meet with the Project Administrator and/or Activity Director to discuss the nature and purpose of the evaluation, discuss the completed Visitation Report Form, and work out a detailed schedule for the visit.

3. The evaluator will attempt to observe the various program activities in operation and talk with staff and participants.
4. At the end of the project day, the evaluator will complete the Evaluation Point Assignments and Values Form. A meeting will be held with the Project Administrator and/or the Activity Director to discuss the evaluation and point assignment. Problem areas will be identified and specific suggestions for improvements will be recommended in writing to the Project Administrator and/or the Activity Director.
5. After the visit, the evaluator will submit the completed Visitation Report Form and Evaluation Point Assignments and Values Form with the Evaluation Narrative Report to the National Program Director within **ten days** after the site visit.[8]

Beyond such guidelines, it may be necessary to train interviewers or program observers—both as to the correct procedures for conducting surveys and interviewing subjects and to ensure that judgments or ratings are carried out accurately and are comparable among different evaluators.

Analysis and Reporting

It is important that all staff members have full input into the evaluation process, in terms of contributing their views or making suggestions for carrying it out. Following tabulation and analysis of data, the study conclusions should be summarized as objectively as possible, with a balanced presentation of positive and negative findings. The report should never take the form of a bloodletting attack on specific individuals.

If the full evaluation report is lengthy and detailed, it is important to prepare a brief, easily read summary report of its findings and recommendations. All staff members should receive copies of this and should be able to discuss the findings. When the study has been completed, it is essential that it be used, rather than filed and forgotten.

To illustrate several typical forms of evaluation as applied to leisure-service agencies, the following section of this chapter will present examples of: (1) agency evaluation; (2) program evaluation; and (3) participant-satisfaction evaluation.

EXAMPLES OF AGENCY EVALUATION

There are numerous examples of techniques used to evaluate entire agencies or leisure-service departments. Typically, these examine several major elements of the operation, making use of standards and criteria that have been developed by panels of experts and that provide a basis for observing and rating the agency within each area of operations.

NRPA Evaluation Manual

The National Recreation and Park Association (NRPA) has developed and published a manual titled *Evaluation and Self-Study of Recreation and Park Agencies: A Guide with Standards and Evaluative Criteria.*[9] It includes 35 standards, which are guidelines for high-level professional performance within six major areas: (1) philosophy and goals; (2) administration; (3) programming; (4) personnel; (5) areas, facilities, and equipment; and (6) evaluation. Each standard is accompanied by several specific criteria, consisting of detailed statements of practices that provide a basis for judging whether the standard is met. Figure 11–1 shows a section of this instrument, dealing with program evaluation.

To apply this manual, a study team should visit and systematically examine a municipal recreation and park agency, examining reports, interviewing personnel, and touring facilities and programs to determine whether the department is living up to the recommended standards. In scoring the results of the application, it is possible to obtain figures that provide a basis for rating the agency in comparison with others. However, the findings are also useful simply to provide a profile of the strengths and weaknesses of the department, and to suggest directions for needed administrative action or program development.

A number of somewhat similar instruments have been developed in other types of leisure-service settings. Doris Berryman and associates at New York University, for example, developed a manual of standards with evaluative criteria for recreation in residential institutions.[11] This manual has 55 different standards under headings related to philosophy and goals; administration; personnel; programming; areas, facilities, and equipment; and evaluation and research. It may be used as the basis for an outside team coming in to examine a therapeutic recreation program in a residential institution, or for a self-study in such a setting.

National Therapeutic Recreation Society Guidelines

A similar document has been published by the National Therapeutic Recreation Society. Titled *Guidelines for Administration of Therapeutic Recreation Service in Clinical and Residential Facilities,*[12] it presents a set of administrative recommendations or standards for effective practice. Unlike the NRPA

FIGURE 11–1 Programming Standards and Criteria of NRPA Evaluation Form[10]

	Is criterion met?					
	Yes	*Almost*	*To some degree*	*No*	*Does not apply*	*Comments*
Standard 10. Objectives There should be specific objectives established for each program element and service which are based upon and developed within the limits set by the philosophy and goals (see Category I) of the recreation and park department.						
Criteria The statement of objectives should: a. Be written.						
b. Cover program elements such as community centers and playgrounds; programs for senior citizens, the handicapped, and other special groups; special program fields; and services such as program consultation, provision of equipment and facilities, and literature.						
c. Be reviewed at the beginning of each year's or season's program and used as an evaluative tool at the end.						
d. Be prepared in consultation with appropriate groups, such as participant councils, planning committees, supervisory personnel, recreation leaders.						
e. Be specific and realistic in terms of what the program is supposed to do for the participant; not a statement of general values of an activity or program field.						

manual, it is not intended primarily for evaluative purposes, and does not include a rating or scoring system. Instead, it is designed simply to outline the appropriate philosophy and goals, administrative policies and structures, personnel practices, and other elements of effective therapeutic recreation programs. However, it may readily be converted to an instrument used for evaluation in such agencies. Figure 11–2 shows a section of this manual, illustrating the nature of the guidelines.

FIGURE 11-2 Program Section of NTRS Standards of Practice for Therapeutic Recreation Service[13]

Standard I. Scope of Service

Comprehensive therapeutic recreation program services are available to all clients in the agency/facility.

CRITERIA

A. Treatment services are available which are goal oriented and directed toward (re)habilitation, amelioration and/or modification of specific physical, emotional, mental, and/or social behaviors.
1. When interdisciplinary teams are utilized, the therapeutic recreation staff functions as part of that team.
2. The therapeutic recreation staff determine appropriate goals relative to therapeutic recreation and interventions to achieve the goals.
3. There is a written plan for implementing the therapeutic recreation goals.
4. There is periodic evaluation of the therapeutic recreation treatment program plan in accordance with standards of regulatory agencies.
5. The treatment goals and plan are modified according to the results of the evaluation and needs of the client.

B. Leisure education services are available.
1. Program Development and Implementation
   a. There is an established method for assessing leisure function.
   b. When appropriate, leisure counseling is available for clients and/or families.
   c. There is an established method for referral and follow-up when needed to assist clients make successful adjustment in the use of community leisure resources.
2. Program Content
   a. Opportunities are provided to explore and develop new activity skills that have carry-over value at home and in the community.
   b. Identification and instruction are provided in the use of appropriate leisure resources available in the client's community.
   c. Opportunities are provided for exploration of leisure concepts, attitudes, and values.

C. There are general recreation services which provide a wide range of activities designed to meet the needs, competencies, capabilities and interests of clients during leisure time.
1. Orientation
   a. Clients are assisted in orienting themselves to the physical surroundings and are helped to achieve maximum mobility and independence.
   b. Clients receive orientation to the available leisure programs, facilities, and resources with initial entrance into the program.
2. Program Development and Implementation
   a. Participant committees, when appropriate, are used in planning and implementing the general recreation program.
   b. There is an established method for assessing the needs, interests, competencies, and capabilities of all clients.
   c. Activities take into consideration the cultural, economic, social and educational backgrounds of clients.
   d. The therapeutic recreation program is carefully and consistently integrated with other programs to achieve maximum use of agency/facility resources.
   e. Provision is made for each client to participate at his/her optimal level of functioning and to progress at his/her own speed.
   f. Provision is made for clients to use their own initiative in selecting and participating in recreational activities.
   g. Provision is made for clients to assume leadership responsibilities.
   h. Activities are modified and special aids or adaptive equipment are utilized to assure success experiences and sequential development for each client.

i. Provision is made for bedside/
home-bound activities when and
where appropriate.

3. Program Content
   a. Opportunities are provided for
   clients to participate in activities
   which utilize physical behaviors
   (sensory-motor domain), mental
   behaviors (cognitive domain), and
   emotional behaviors (affective
   domain).
   b. In day and residential facilities,
   opportunities are provided for
   clients to participate in daily
   periods of activity.

c. Opportunities are provided for individual, small, and large group
participation.
d. The program provides both regularly scheduled activities and special events.
e. The program provides for the utili-
zation of a wide variety of public
and private community resources
and services.
f. The program provides for various
levels of integration of the client
population with the general
population.

EVALUATION PROCESS IN OTHER ORGANIZATIONS

Numerous other national organizations have developed evaluation
forms or promote systematic evaluation studies of their local chapters or units.
The Boys' Clubs of America, for example, strongly encourages local clubs
throughout the United States to carefully evaluate their administrative procedures
and their programs, and publishes several manuals to assist them in this task. It
stresses that evaluation must be taken seriously as an administrative responsibility, although it may take different forms

> Evaluation is a regular, integral part of Boys' Clubs operation, not just a
> procedure which is done because of pressure from an outside group or because
> of some crisis. [It is] the result of an honest desire on the part of the Board, the
> Executive and the Staff to determine how well the Club is doing and what can be
> done to improve itself. . . .[14]

Guidelines are presented in Boys' Club evaluation manuals, with recommended practices for each of the following program categories: (1) arts and
crafts; (2) citizenship education; (3) cultural programs; (4) game rooms, (5)
guidance program; (6) health program; (7) organized small groups; (8) physical
programs; and (9) special events. The study team, which may include board,
administration and staff members, as well as outside consultants, past and
present club members, and community representatives, normally examines the
agency's success in each of these program areas, and makes suggestions for
recommended changes to improve club operations.

In the late 1970s, the National Jewish Welfare Board carried out an
extensive evaluative study of its health, physical education, and recreation
programs in YM-YWHAs and Jewish Community Centers throughout the United
States and Canada.[15] It involved a survey of center presidents, executive directors, and HPER directors, as well as numerous interviews and meetings with

professional and lay personnel throughout the country. This unique study shows that evaluation is often more than simply appraising a given agency or program. It may involve an intensive self-study process of reviewing existing programs and practices, developing dialogues that examine old and develop new priorities, and creating entirely new approaches to agency management and services.

The American Camping Association carries out a rigorous program of evaluating organized camps, making use of an extensive set of standards that was developed a number of years ago, and has been brought up to date to reflect sound camping practices. The standards cover hundreds of specific requirements with respect to camp administration, staffing, transportation, housing, food, health practices, program, environmental practices, aquatics, facilities, and site development. They are used as the basis for intensive site visits by qualified teams, which then make recommendations with respect to accreditation of the camp.

> In the accreditation review process, camps are examined in four areas: site, administration, personnel, and program. A camp must receive a minimum score of 75 percent in each of these areas, and the overall score averaged from all areas must be at least 80 percent. In addition, there are 14 prerequisite standards which must be met, regardless of other scores.[16]

EVALUATION OF SPECIFIC PROGRAMS

Thus it may be seen that evaluation has become widely accepted by many social-service organizations on both a national and a local scale. In addition to evaluating the overall operation of local agencies, some evaluation efforts are directed to determining the effectiveness or quality of specific on-site programs. Several illustrations of such evaluation processes follow.

National Youth Sports Program. This is a project carried on with Congressional funding, under the aegis of the Community Services Administration and the National Collegiate Athletic Association. It consists primarily of sports and related activity programs provided for children and youth—drawn primarily from disadvantaged and minority-group populations in a number of cities throughout the United States. The actual programs are conducted by the athletic departments of colleges and universities in these cities. Each such program is visited each summer by an evaluator or evaluation team, who uses a checklist of statements or guidelines through which to measure whether it is living up to the operational standards established for the National Youth Sports Program.[17]

There are 106 such standards, relating to the following categories: (1) institution and institutional support, including provision and maintenance of facilities; (2) participants, including use of rosters, attendance records, collection of data on performance, and characteristics of participants; (3) project schedule, including having a minimum number of meeting days and hours, and early enrollment and staff orientations before the season; (4) activities, including the minimum of three sports, the provision of instructional swimming and lifesaving technique, the use of coeducational sports, and progressive instruction; (5) enrichment activities, including sessions on drug/alcohol abuse education, vocational and career outlook, and health and nutrition; and (6) other elements, such as the provision of meals or snacks, medical services, staff qualifications, project organization, and coordination and self-generated funding to assist the program.

Based on a camp's score, it may be rated as clearly "passing," "passing provided that certain deficiencies are corrected," or "failing" and not to be funded again.

EVALUATION OF PERFORMANCE OF CONTRACT AGENCIES

The preceding section shows how evaluation may be used to measure the performance of a contract agency that is carrying on a program with special funding from an outside source. In the leisure-service field, many such relationships exist and evaluation is frequently used to determine whether an agency should continue to be funded, based on its current performance.

United Way and Member Agencies.   As a specific example on the local level, United Way serves as an umbrella organization that coordinates and carries out a major fundraising campaign to support varied social services in many communities. In turn, it allocates funds to member agencies, roughly in proportion to their size and membership, and to the extent and importance of the services they provide.

To illustrate, the United Way of Greater Philadelphia provides substantial funding to the Young Women's Christian Association in Philadelphia. However, the money is not simply given as a flat sum or a proportion of the Y's budget. Instead, it is granted to support certain programs and services—and these in turn are clearly outlined in contracts between the United Way and the YWCA Board. Specific and quantitative performance objectives are stated, and it is up to the YWCA to demonstrate that it has met these objectives satisfactorily if it is to justify future support.

Program Budgeting as a Basis for Evaluation.   Similarly, many large municipal agencies may specify the objectives of different elements of their programs within a budget summary in order to facilitate review and clear understanding by their city councils, comptrollers, or other fiscal managers. For example, a public recreation and park department might prepare one-page budget statements for each major aspect of its overall program, such as playgrounds, community center operations, aquatic or beach programs, adult sports, programs for the aging, or special services for the handicapped. Such budget statements might include past, present, and proposed expenditure levels, sources of funding (including special grants), intended objectives of the program, and program performance measures stated in quantitative terms.

Figure 11–3 shows a one-page program budget for a municipal camping program in a midwestern city's Parks and Recreation Department for a recent year.[18] It describes the major objectives of the program and presents quantitative performance measures, in terms of the estimated daily attendance and participation in various programs. Obviously, this budget provides a useful means for determining whether or not the camping program has achieved its objectives.

OTHER APPROACHES TO PROGRAM EVALUATION

In addition to the methods just described, there are several other approaches to program evaluation that make use of appraisals by staff members, participants, or outside evaluators.

Evaluation by Staff Members

In many cases, staff members are expected to prepare and submit an evaluation report of a program that they have been responsible for planning and implementing. For example, the Portland, Oregon, Park Bureau has initiated a program known as *Recreation Integration,* which is designed to mainstream disabled persons into nonspecial programs offered by community schools, community centers, and other recreation sites which are designed to serve the public at large. It provides center and community school coordinators with general guidelines for cooperating in this mainstreaming effort, and concludes with a set of questions to be used in evaluating the program's success in each facility:[19]

What is success? Success can be measured in many ways:

1. Has your facility become more architecturally barrier-free? If so, how much?
2. Has your facility added disabled access signage—where appropriate—to its building/park or mailers?
3. Have you or your staff received any in-service training from Special Recreation Services for Disabled Citizens to increase your awareness of special needs or concerns regarding disabled persons?
4. Have you identified and formed a relationship with disabled individuals already using your facility?

FIGURE 11-3 Department of Parks and Recreation

Program: RECREATION PROGRAMS
Sub-Program: MUNICIPAL CAMPS

Expenditures by Character	Actual 1980–1981	Estimated 1981–1982	Estimated 1982–1983
Personal Services	$201,076	$224,200	$246,123
Contractual Services	28,675	45,900	58,675
Commodities	20,502	21,929	20,806
Capital Outlay	1,139	4,574	1,750
Total Expenditures	$251,392	$296,603	$327,354
Expenditures by Fund			
General	$219,814	$263,169	$291,703
Public Service Employment	31,578	33,434	35,651
Total Expenditures	$251,392	$296,603	$327,354
Regular Man Years	18.0	19.2	18.8
Special Grant Man Years	3.0	3.0	3.0
Total Man Years	21.0	22.2	21.8

Key Objectives
1. Conduct four ten-day sessions of resident camping and three ten-day sessions of day camping in accordance with the standards of the American Camping Association
2. Provide classes and informal learning experiences about the natural environment, ecology, archaeology and local history
3. Conduct a Learn-to-Ride program for children and adults

Performance Measures	Actual 1980–1981	Estimated 1981–1982	Estimated 1982–1983
1. Daily attendance			
Resident campers	59	80	80
Day campers	91	125	125
2. Program participation			
Outdoor School	2,200	1,000	1,000
Nature Wagon/Outdoor Discovery	8,532	9,000	9,000
Lakeview Nature Center	30,680	35,000	40,000
Red Creek Museum	17,145	25,000	25,000
Historic Village	10,494	14,866	28,000
Allen Park	820	1,250	2,500
Swadley Interpretive Center	10,814	15,000	20,000
3. Horseback riding/weekly average	79	80	80

Highlights
In 1981–1982 three seasonal positions were added to the Municipal Camps program to assist in the program development at Historic Village. In 1982–1983, program development will continue at this facility, as well as at Allen Park. Two seasonal cook positions at the resident camp have been eliminated from the 1982–1983 budget as food service will then be provided through a contractual arrangement. Participation fees from this program's activities are expected to generate $20,875 in 1982–1983.

5. Have you identified other disabled persons within your neighborhood who could become users of your facility?
6. Have you worked to find solutions for the barriers that make it
   difficult for disabled persons to use your facility? (e.g., architectural, attitudinal, transportation, economic).

Such questions not only provide the basis for an appraisal of the impact
of the program, but also suggest steps that need to be taken to make it effective.
This function of ongoing evaluation must be stressed—that it not only provides
a means of measuring the quality or effectiveness of programs, but provides
guidance for improving the program while it is being carried on.

Evaluation of Special Event by Staff/Participants

In many cases, specific events, such as sports tournaments, arts festivals, in-service training workshops, or similar one-time programs, are evaluated
by staff members and/or program participants. When this is done, it is usually a
good idea to use a comprehensive, detailed form that covers all important aspects
of the event, such as preliminary planning, site and equipment, attendance,
publicity, safety and crowd management, program effectiveness, financial arrangements, and other elements.

To illustrate, Figure 11–4 presents a rating form that may be used to
evaluate social recreation events, such as parties, carnivals, play days, or similar
programs. Such forms may readily be prepared to cover any type of continuing or
single events. In preparing them, members of the planning committee should
identify the key objectives or guidelines governing such activities, or should
prepare descriptive statements that give a picture of how the event should be
carried out successfully.

It is important that the forms be filled out promptly, when the program
has been concluded. In addition to having them filled out by staff members, they
may also be filled out by participants.

EVALUATION OF PROGRAM OUTCOMES

As indicated earlier, one approach to measuring the effectiveness of
recreation programs is to determine whether or not specific objectives have been
achieved. This may be done in several ways:

FIGURE 11–4 Evaluation Form for Special Event[20]

Social Recreation Event Rating Form

Instructions to raters: You are a leader or an active committee member who has just helped to conduct a party or other social recreation event. Please fill out the following form. Be as fair and accurate in your judgments as possible. The purpose of this rating form is not to praise or criticize any individual but simply to determine how successful the event was, what its strong and weak points were, and how it might be sponsored more effectively in the future. Please check the appropriate box for each standard.

	Ratings				
Standards	*Excellent*	*Good*	*Fair*	*Poor*	*Does not apply*
Planning and preparation					
1. Was there adequate planning and preparation for the event?	☐	☐	☐	☐	☐
2. Did the various committees coordinate their functions well?	☐	☐	☐	☐	☐
3. Was there sufficient and effective publicity before event?	☐	☐	☐	☐	☐
4. Were equipment and supplies obtained in advance as needed?	☐	☐	☐	☐	☐
Program					
5. Were early-comers welcomed and made to feel at home?	☐	☐	☐	☐	☐
6. Did program activities have good balance and variety?	☐	☐	☐	☐	☐
7. Were activities appropriate for the age level and other characteristics of group?	☐	☐	☐	☐	☐
8. Was the party carried on at a good tempo but with opportunity also for relaxed fun?	☐	☐	☐	☐	☐
9. Was there smooth transition from activity to activity?	☐	☐	☐	☐	☐
10. Was there a good level of active participation?	☐	☐	☐	☐	☐
11. Did the party end with an appropriate activity?	☐	☐	☐	☐	☐
12. Overall, was there a friendly spirit and good mixing of participants?	☐	☐	☐	☐	☐

Leadership

13. Were leaders enthusiastic and able to motivate participants effectively?   □   □   □   □   □

14. Were leaders well prepared and able to teach clearly and simply?   □   □   □   □   □

15. Were a number of different leaders involved in presenting activities?   □   □   □   □   □

Other details of program

16. Did decorations add to the party atmosphere and contribute to its theme?   □   □   □   □   □

17. Were refreshments well prepared and efficiently served?   □   □   □   □   □

18. Was the hall or room well lit, well ventilated, and attractive?   □   □   □   □   □

19. Was clean-up carried out efficiently, as a shared responsibility?   □   □   □   □   □

20. Was attendance at the level expected?   □   □   □   □   □

Other comments or suggestions: _____

_____

_____

_____

Measuring Accomplishment of Behavioral Objectives

Particularly in therapeutic recreation, objectives stated for individual clients or patients may be precisely monitored through the use of performance measures. For example, participants may be helped to learn certain basic neuromuscular skills, or to apply basic strategies in games, or to gain competence in other areas of daily living—such as the ability to travel on public transportation without assistance, or to carry out other self-maintenance skills.

Usually, such objectives are set forth in a logical sequence over a period of time, moving from the simplest or most basic tasks or skills to more advanced ones. By measuring the individual's success in accomplishing them, the effectiveness of the program can also be evaluated in convincing terms.

Impact of Program in Broader Terms

Many recreation programs are based on goals and objectives that are stated not in individual terms, but with respect to the programs' desired impact on an organization's effectiveness or its contribution to community life. For example, recreation in the armed forces is usually intended to contribute to the morale of military units or to the physical and mental fitness of uniformed personnel. Similarly, recreation in a corporate/employee setting has, among other goals, the purpose of helping to improve employee job performance. Varied forms of recreational involvement, with emphasis on sports and fitness activities, are believed to reduce absenteeism and the accident rate, and to contribute in other ways to company productivity.

Obviously, the determination of such outcomes cannot be done meaningfully through casual observation or by measuring the opinions of staff members or participants. Instead, they require carefully controlled and monitored programs that will yield comparative data that will stand up to rigorous scrutiny. A number of examples of such evaluative efforts and their findings in various areas of recreational programming are provided in Chapter 12.

Evaluating Participant Satisfactions

A final means of measuring both the overall quality of a program and its success in achieving stated objectives may involve evaluating participant satisfaction. Participants may be asked to rate or comment on the activities themselves, the quality of the leadership, the physical environment or setting, the publicity given to the program, or other elements. They may also be asked to indicate their level of satisfaction with these aspects of the program or with the entire experience, and to make suggestions for future activities.

Rossman has explored the effectiveness of an instrument designed to measure participants' satisfaction derived from program involvement in relation to such dimensions of leisure satisfaction as physical fitness, social enjoyment, or personal achievement. He concludes that this approach represents a useful method of generating data from clients that will be helpful in managing program operations:

> Three potential uses for these data have been identified. First, the strength and source of satisfactions with programs can be identified and documented, thereby establishing agency accountability for its services. Second, by comparing reported satisfactions with all programs, strong and weak programs can be identified. This will enable program managers to monitor operations and have programs needing additional attention pointed out to them. Third, the results of different organizational methods for delivery (of) program services can be explored by examining the differences in satisfactions they provide.[21]

A simple example of a form used to measure the degree of satisfaction of users of a service may be found in Figure 11–5, a sample travel survey distributed by Sky-Fly to airline passengers.

It should be noted that evaluation forms are not the only way in which participants' perceptions of programs can be measured. Obviously, staff members can observe programs in action to determine the reactions of participants. Verbal feedback can be gathered through personal conversations or meetings

FIGURE 11–5 Sample Airline Travel Survey[22]

Dear Sky-Fly Passenger:
Your cooperation in helping us evaluate our quality of service will be appreciated. Please complete this form and return it to your flight attendant.

Type of Food Service:

Breakfast ☐   Lunch ☐
Dinner ☐   Snack ☐

Type of Aircraft:
DC–9 ☐   727 ☐   747 ☐

Main Purpose of Your Trip:
Business ☐   Family ☐   Vacation ☐
Educational ☐   Military ☐   Other ☐

How Many Trips Have You Taken With Sky-Fly in the Last Year?
None ☐   1–4 ☐   5–9 ☐
10–14 ☐   15 or more ☐

Please Rate Your Flight by Putting an X in the Appropriate Boxes

Courtesy and Service	Excellent	Good	Fair	Poor
1. When making your reservation	☐	☐	☐	☐
2. At the airport ticket counter	☐	☐	☐	☐
3. At the boarding gate	☐	☐	☐	☐
4. From flight attendants	☐	☐	☐	☐

Other Factors				
5. On-time performance (this flight)	☐	☐	☐	☐
6. Cabin cleanliness	☐	☐	☐	☐
7. Flying conditions	☐	☐	☐	☐
8. In-flight announcements	☐	☐	☐	☐
9. Cocktail and beverage service	☐	☐	☐	☐
10. Quality of food served	☐	☐	☐	☐

How Would You Rate Sky-Fly's Overall Flight Today?
Excellent ☐   Good ☐   Fair ☐   Poor ☐

Please Indicate:

Flight number: _____   Date: _____
From: _____   To: _____

Additional Comments:
_____
_____
_____
_____

Thank You for Your Assistance—Sky-Fly, Inc.

with groups of participants. However, such sources are likely to yield scattered, highly personal views that may not represent a broad cross-section of all participants. Therefore, it is usually best to rely on a method that will gather information from a substantial and representative number of those involved.

In order to develop such an instrument, it is usually necessary to include very specific questions that deal with the unique circumstances of a facility or program. The scheduling, staffing, and other special circumstances may all be dealt with meaningfully in this way. Many recreation practitioners feel inadequate when it comes to preparing such instruments. It is important for them to realize that this task does *not* require an extremely high level of skill or sophistication. Following the guidelines for questionnaire construction provided earlier in this text and using common sense, a single staff member or small committee can readily put together an effective instrument.

To illustrate, Figure 11–6 shows a questionnaire which was used to survey the membership of the Hatboro, Pennsylvania, YMCA, regarding their satisfaction with the program. It was prepared by an undergraduate student at Temple University who was employed at the Y, and who had not had previous experience in program evaluation. Following its preparation as a course assignment, it was distributed at the Y building and filled out by hundreds of members, yielding considerable useful information to the agency staff.

ANALYSIS OF EVALUATION FINDINGS

Using the preceding instrument as an example, how should the resulting data be analyzed? What kinds of useful information or conclusions can be gathered from such a survey?

Obviously, the survey will help provide an overall picture of the nature of participation at the YMCA to supplement other sources of information— assuming, of course, that an adequate number of members fill it out. Beyond this, it will provide very clear judgments of the effectiveness of various components of the program, such as aquatics, child care, or senior citizen programs. Judgments will be offered regarding the performance of staff members, the maintenance of different facilities, or the value of such support services as baby-sitting.

Each set of responses should be tabulated, and the results interpreted. Based on the findings, the YMCA management may find it necessary to strengthen or improve certain elements of the program, or may conclude that other program changes are called for. If the staff wanted to dig more deeply into potential interests or possible new program activities, it might have asked respondents to rate these or suggest new activities.

FIGURE 11–6 Membership Survey Used at Hatboro, Pennsylvania, YMCA[23]

The following is a questionnaire that will be used to help the Hatboro Area YMCA serve you better. Please take a few minutes to fill out this form as honestly as you can. Any additional comments will be greatly appreciated and considered. After completing this form, please drop it off at the front desk of the YMCA. THANK YOU!

Age _____ Marital Status _____ No. of Children _____
Are you a YMCA member? Yes _____ No _____ If yes, specify_____
Sex _____
How often do you use the YMCA facilities?

5–7 days/wk.	1–4 days/wk.	1–3 days/month	on occasion	very seldom

How did you first find out about the Hatboro YMCA?
Mailed brochure _____ Newspaper Ad. _____ Friend _____ Other _____

PLEASE CHECK THE MOST APPROPRIATE ANSWER FROM 1–5
1 = Excellent   2 = Good   3 = Fair   4 = Poor   5 = Not Applicable

PROGRAM:
How well does the YMCA provide programs that meet the needs of you and your family in the following areas?

	1	2	3	4	5
1. Aquatic Programs					
2. Camps					
3. Child Care					
4. Children's Physical Fitness/Games					
5. Educational Programs					
6. Physical Fitness Programs (Adults)					
7. Senior Citizen Programs					
8. Social Programs					
9. How well does the Hatboro YMCA offer programs that involve the family, as a unit, in its programs?					
10. The scheduling of classes (hours & days) is					
11. Overall, the program quality at the YMCA is					

12. Are there any programs that you would like to be added or changed? (explain)

INSTRUCTORS/PERSONNEL:

Please answer by placing an (X) in the appropriate box

	YES	NO
13. Do you find the front desk staff to be friendly and helpful?		
14. Do you find the instructors to be knowledgeable?		
15. Are the instructors enthusiastic?		

16. Overall, I would rate the instruction at the
    Hatboro YMCA as

ADDITIONAL COMMENTS ON THE QUALITY OF INSTRUCTION:

_____

_____

FACILITIES:	1	2	3	4	5
Using the 1–5 scale, rate how well the following areas are maintained (clean, bright, sanitary, etc.)					
17. The main gymnasium					
18. The multipurpose room (upstairs gymnastics room)					
19. The universal weight room					
20. The upstairs club rooms					
21. The dressing areas of the locker room					
22. The showers					
23. The sauna					
24. The indoor pool					
25. The outdoor pool (during summer season)					

26. Overall, do the facilities seem to be well maintained? Yes _____ No _____
27. Do you feel that the facilities are adequate? Yes _____ No _____
    If no, state which areas could use improvement or explain what is lacking (suggestions for
    additional equipment that is needed, etc.)

_____

_____

GENERAL:
28. If baby sitting was available at a time when you took a class, would you use this service?
    Yes _____ No _____
    If YES, specify what time you would need these services. (list days and times)_____
29. If you are familiar with our baby sitting services, please give us your impressions of it
    (excellent—poor; reliable—unreliable; fun—unpleasant; safe—dangerous; etc.)_____

_____

	YES	NO
30. Do you find classes at the Hatboro Area YMCA to be enjoyable?		
31. Do you feel that the YMCA has enhanced your use of leisure time?		
32. Do you feel that the YMCA could do more to enhance your use of leisure time?		

    IF YES, PLEASE EXPLAIN

_____

_____

	YES	NO
33. Would you participate in a program at the YMCA again?		
34. Would you recommend the YMCA to your friends?		
35. Have your experiences at the YMCA been enjoyable?		

ANY ADDITIONAL COMMENTS:

_____

_____

_____

_____

_____

THANK YOU for spending the time to fill out this questionnaire. Your candid remarks are greatly appreciated.

** PLEASE DROP OFF AT THE FRONT DESK **

Use of Computers in Data Analysis.   Whenever possible, the data gathered in such evaluations should be of a quantitative nature, to permit statistical analysis and precise statements of findings. To facilitate this, increasing use is being made of computers to analyze survey findings. Computers make it easy to determine the statistical relationships among various factors in the study. For example, such elements as the age, sex, family status, residential area, or frequency of attendance of respondents can readily be correlated with different patterns of participation, attitudes toward programs, or other views. Through such computer-assisted analysis, it is possible to pinpoint specific populations and examine their needs and attitudes very directly, as part of the overall evaluation process.

EVALUATION AS A BASIS FOR ACTION

In concluding this chapter, it should be stressed that the purpose of evaluation is not simply to give a high mark to one staff member or program, or a low mark to another. And certainly it should not just be an academic exercise, resulting in a report that is permitted to gather dust.

When evaluation is approached as a continuing process carried on during the course of a program, it should include regular feedback to staff members that will help guide or redirect their efforts while the program is actually in process. As an example of such ongoing evaluation, the San José, California, Parks Division makes use of a regular monitoring process through its management operations.[24] In terms of maintenance procedures, it regularly uses both quantitative and qualitative methods of assessing the effectiveness of services being provided. At any point, if feedback indicates that the maintenance operation is not being carried out effectively in a given area, this may lead to new management policies or procedures.

When evaluation takes the form of a report at the end of a particular program unit or event, it should give a general rating to the activity and should specifically identify both strengths and weaknesses of the operation. Depending on the purpose of the evaluation, the appraisal might then lead to recommendations for continuing, expanding, or terminating the program activity or to recommendations for different procedures in the future.

In terms of evaluation of an entire agency, such as an accreditation site visit and report, the report is obviously put to immediate use, in that it will be used as the basis for recommending accreditation, certification, or other official actions. It may also be the basis for suggested policy steps or other actions that must be taken if the organization is to continue to receive funding support or professional recognition.

When evaluation has the potential for threatening staff members' job security, it obviously can be perceived as threatening. However, as indicated earlier, it should not be presented in this light. Instead, its major purpose should be constructive and supportive, and it should always be designed to result not merely in ratings of quality or objectives accomplished, but as the basis for sustaining and upgrading the quality of performance of a leisure-service agency.

NOTES

[1]Richard Kraus, *Therapeutic Recreation Service: Principles and Practices* (Philadelphia: Saunders College Publishing, 1983), p. 399.

[2]Christine Z. Howe, "Evaluation of Leisure Programs," *Journal of Physical Education and Recreation* (October 1980): 32.

[3]Gary Ellis and Peter Witt, "Evaluation by Design," *Parks and Recreation* (February 1982): 40.

[4]Peg Connolly, "Evaluation's Role in Agency Accountability," *Parks and Recreation* (February 1982): 34.

[5]Judith Woo and Michael Farley, "Portland's Program Planning and Evaluation Model," *Parks and Recreation* (April 1982): 50.

[6]Christine Z. Howe, "Models for Evaluating Public Recreation Programs: What the Literature Shows," *Journal of Physical Education and Recreation* (October 1980): 36.

[7]J. Robert Rossman, "Theoretical Deficiencies: A Brief Review of Selected Evaluation Models," *Journal of Physical Education and Recreation* (October 1980): 44.

[8]*Manual of Directions for Project Evaluation* (Washington, D.C.: National Youth Sports Program, 1983).

[9]Betty van der Smissen, Ed., *Evaluation and Self-Study of Public Recreation and Park Agencies: A Guide with Standards and Evaluative Criteria* (Arlington, Va.: National Recreation and Park Association, 1972).

[10]Betty van der Smissen (1972).

[11]Doris Berryman, *Recommended Standards with Evaluative Criteria for Recreation Services in Residential Institutions* (New York: New York University School of Education and U.S. Children's Bureau, 1971).

[12]Glen Van Andel, *Standards of Practice for Therapeutic Recreation Service* (Alexandria, Va.: National Therapeutic Recreation Society, October 1980).

[13]Van Andel, p. 1.

[14]*Program Evaluation in a Boys' Club* (New York, N.Y.: Boys' Clubs of America, 1967), p. 4.

[15]*Health, Physical Education and Recreation Study* (New York, N.Y.: Report of Study Committee, National Jewish Welfare Board, 1976).

[16]*Accreditation Manual* (Bradford Woods, Ind.: American Camping Association, 1984).

[17]*Manual of Directions for Project Evaluation* (1983).

[18]Adapted from *Program Budget Plan for Municipal Camps* (Kansas City, Mo.: Department of Parks and Recreation, 1978–1979).

[19]Adapted from *Program Manual, Recreation Integration,* Portland, Oregon, Park Bureau, 1983.

[20]See Richard Kraus, *Social Recreation: A Group Dynamics Approach* (St. Louis: C. V. Mosby, 1979), pp. 174–75.

[21]J. Robert Rossman, "Evaluate Programs by Measuring Participant Satisfactions," *Parks and Recreation* (June 1982), p. 35.

[22]Travel Survey Form adapted by author from forms in use by selected airline companies, 1984.

[23]Edward Cannon, *Undergraduate Course Paper* (Unpublished) (Philadelphia: Temple University Dept. of Recreation and Leisure Studies, 1983). Used by permission.

[24]Allan Mills, Richard Harris, and Kenneth Conway, *San Jose Brings Order to Hit-or-Miss Maintenance, Parks and Recreation* (January 1980), pp. 88–91, 99.

QUESTIONS

1. Evaluation is often perceived as a threatening process; supervisors and other professional personnel therefore tend to approach it in a superficial way rather than dig too deeply. Agency staff members often fear having their programs evaluated.

   Can you suggest a more positive and constructive way of viewing evaluation and gaining support for it? How should the process of program evaluation be approached, to make it more effective? How can its "threatening" aspect be reduced?

2. Assume that you are asked to design an evaluation process for a particular type of recreation program or service, such as a recreation program in a retirement community, or a voluntary youth-serving organization. Choose one of the following and prepare a preliminary outline of the evaluation process that might be carried out for the stated purpose. Whichever model you use, prepare a questionnaire or rating form to use in the evaluation process.

   a. A process based on the "standards and criteria" approach, relying on an outside evaluation team

   b. A process based on the "goals-attainment" model, relying on an inside evaluation team

   c. A process based on the "transaction-observation" model, relying on participants' ratings of the program

SUGGESTED READINGS────────────────────────────────

Christopher Edginton, David Compton, and Carole Hanson, *Recreation and Leisure Programming: A Guide for the Professional* (Philadelphia: Saunders College Publishing, 1980), Chapter 11.

Patricia Farrell and Herberta Lundegren, *Evaluation for Leisure Service Managers: A Dynamic Approach* (Philadelphia: Saunders College Publishing, 1985)

Scout Gunn and Carol Peterson, *Therapeutic Recreation Program Design: Principles and Procedures* (Englewood Cliffs, N.J.: Prentice-Hall, 1978), Chapter 13.

CHAPTER 12

Issues and Outcomes in Recreation Programming

Mr. and Mrs. Brevard were pleased and excited as they met with Phil Morris, director of the special camp program, two weeks after the session was over.

"We were really quite surprised," said Mr. Brevard. "Frankly, we have had a lot of difficulty with Donna. She is very bright, but she is often very disobedient and inattentive. Usually, she just won't stay with a task or accept responsibilities. But when she came home from camp two weeks ago, she seemed to have turned over a new leaf. Her mother and I feel that she seems much more willing to try. And she's much more pleasant to both of us."

Phil Morris replied, "Donna really wants to do well, but she's confused by the difficulties she has learning new things, and she often gets frustrated. This special camp program gave her some real responsibility and a lot of support, and she lived up to it. Also, we had some pretty strict rules, and we enforced them. It seems to have made a difference."

"Well," said Mrs. Brevard, "we're grateful. And I think we need to learn more about how to work with Donna."

The concluding chapter of this text has two purposes: (1) to sum up a number of major themes that were discussed in the preceding chapters, along with a number of the issues or concerns that are attached to them today; and (2) to present several examples of the documented outcomes of organized recreation programs, as disclosed through formal evaluation or research efforts.

These two purposes are closely linked, since a major premise of the text is that organized recreation service today must seek to assess and document its outcomes in a systematic, objective fashion. Since such findings are rarely summarized or reviewed in the literature, it would seem highly appropriate to do this at the conclusion of a textbook on recreation programming.

MAJOR THEMES OF THE TEXT

A key principle stressed throughout this book has been the need for organized recreation programs to be purposeful, and to have concrete, clearly enunciated objectives. These, however, *must* be formulated in terms of the changes that have occurred in the broader society and in the recreation movement itself.

Recreation programs can no longer be thought of as primarily geared for children and youth on playgrounds or in community centers, and consisting chiefly of sports, games, arts and crafts, and such traditional activities. While such programs continue to be an important part of modern recreation services, it is essential to provide a much broader range of activities and services that meet the needs of a highly diversified population in the typical American and Canadian community today.

Beyond this, it is important to recognize that recreation takes many forms today. It may be regarded as a fitness activity, a high-risk or hedonistic pursuit, a form of therapeutic service, a means of promoting important community values, a commodity that is bought and sold, or simply as fun.

Depending on the nature of the sponsoring organization, programming goals must be sharply tailored to meet the needs and interests of participants—and often general community or organizational purposes as well. In addition to serving participants, it is essential to realize that recreation may be specifically designed to meet these broader needs, such as improving job performance in a corporate setting or maintaining effective morale in the armed forces.

The text stresses the immense economic impact of recreational participation in modern society, and the need to recognize leisure programming as part of an economic system in which marketing plays a key role. Equally, however, it presents examples of the human-services approach to programming, as well as other important models of service. In terms of service delivery, the value of networking and participating in decision-making processes is emphasized, along with the use of a wide variety of program formats and specialized facilities to serve different populations.

Throughout, the text affirms that programming is a key element in all kinds of leisure-service agencies, and that it requires enthusiasm, expertise, and commitment—as well as faith in the human values that can be achieved through recreational involvement. In so complex a field, there are obviously a number of important issues or areas of concern or disagreement for which we need still to find appropriate solutions.

ISSUES IN RECREATION PROGRAM PLANNING

What are the issues and concerns of recreation program planning? A major one continues to be the need to define our purpose both as a field and within specific types of sponsoring agencies. Although the philosophy of organized recreation service has been widely expressed in the literature, in higher education, in recreation and parks, and at professional meetings, it continues to be in flux as society undergoes radical changes. The most obvious conflict lies between the marketing and the human-services models of leisure programming.

One illustration may be found in the recent trend toward wellness and fitness programming. This book has shown how adult fitness programs have become immensely popular, and how millions of adults have become involved in jogging and running, in sports and exercise activities sponsored by public departments, Y's, industry, the armed forces, and commercial recreation. It is obvious that this has become a multi-billion-dollar business, in which manufacturers, commercial sponsors, the mass media, sports and fitness associations, and other groups have joined together to create mass awareness of fitness needs and to provide equipment and programs.

Yet, at the same time, there is growing awareness that we are seriously neglecting the fitness needs of children and youth! Thanks to a sedentary way of life, fragmented or poorly suppported physical education programs, the lack of social reinforcement for vigorous recreational involvement, and the appeal of spectator-oriented or passive leisure activity, American youngsters are becoming increasingly flabby. When asked how the fitness of today's youngsters compares with that of previous generations, the Chairman of the U.S. Olympic Committee Sports Medicine Council replies:

> Youth fitness is at a very low ebb. A recent study shows that 57 percent of youngsters between ages 6 and 17 are unable to meet standards of fitness regarded as attainable by the average healthy child. . . . Young people in most other industrialized nations are in better shape. Such countries as West Germany, Sweden and Finland have programs for young people that are far more organized and comprehensive than our own.[1]

He goes on to comment that as fitness programs proliferate in the private sector, adults get strong social reinforcement for physical activity while children do not. In other words, because adults can be "marketed" in the sense that they can pay for fitness programs, they represent a prime target for exercise and popular sports programs. Children's programs must be subsidized, and therefore are given a lower priority in our society—which presents a clear challenge for recreation programmers on many levels.

Another important issue has to do with the responsibility of all types of recreation agencies for providing education for leisure. In the past we have tended to think of this as the responsibility of the schools. However, the reality is that few schools today regard this as a significant part of their mission; leisure education is only dealt with peripherally.

Today, we realize that education for leisure should be taking place on *all* levels, and should be an integral part of recreational programming. For example, leisure counseling is a key element in therapeutic recreation service for adults who are recovering from strokes or other physical trauma, or for teenage or young adult mentally retarded individuals who are about to enter the community. Mature employees who are facing retirement often profit from sessions on leisure values and opportunities, as part of pre-retirement seminars or workshops.

A vivid illustration of the need for leisure education is provided by a U.S. Navy Captain, John B. Bonds. In a discussion of recreation in the armed forces, he describes past attitudes which saw this as a minor concern:

> In the past, we [the Navy] seemed to assume that if we provided a place for inexpensive alcohol consumption, we fulfilled the requirement for recreation. Beyond that, if we provided a place for an informal softball game (preferably with free and unlimited beer), then we were taking care of our men.[2]

Today, Bonds writes, the serious problem of alcohol and drug abuse that is found in many armed forces units (as it is throughout the society) have compelled the Navy to face the issue of providing alternative recreation programs. Many military bases today have excellent recreation facilities and leadership. But, Bonds goes on to say, often there is great difficulty in persuading young recruits to take part in active, vigorous recreation. Often, he says, they feel most at home in passive pursuits and generally display a solitary, socially uncommunicative mode of behavior.

Bonds asks whether these young people have the recreational skills needed to take part in organized programs. He comments that members of his generations were taught these skills by parents or members of their extended families—or learned them from contemporaries in after-school activities in yards or vacant lots. Sports, hobbies, and social activities were a normal part of living for people in his generation. But, although some young Navy personnel still learn these skills as he did, Bonds adds that

> a large number of our volunteer sailors come from single-parent or latchkey households which do not teach recreational skills. They come from areas where there aren't any yards or vacant lots, and where the streets are too dangerous to use for a playground.
>
> Simply stated, these young people don't have many recreational skills. Since early childhood, their nearly singular recreation has been television and other pictorial imagery; TV replaced family and friends. Consequently, our youth feels most comfortable in a passive, receptive mode of recreation. They are uncomfortable in other modes, and perhaps in interpersonal encounters as well.[3]

Without question, this description of the need for leisure education applies to many more young people than young sailors alone. Given the growth of electronic entertainment in our society and the limited forms of recreational opportunity in many areas—as well as the frequent lack of family encouragement and stimulation—great numbers of teenagers and young adults would profit greatly from effective education for leisure.

In striving to equip people of all ages to use leisure more meaningfully, we must recognize that the modern concept of leisure has changed significantly. In past generations, leisure tended to be thought of primarily as freedom from work—a relaxed, contemplative state of being, slow-paced and free of constraints or obligations.

Glover describes Thoreau's life as an idealized example of the traditional concept of leisure. Throughout much of his life, he worked for no more than two or three months each year, and scorned the pursuits of wealth, prestige, material possessions, and social acceptance.

> His leisure pursuits were unhurried, simple and free. He never found it necessary to search the globe, as so many of us now do, for stimulation and excitement. There were a lifetime's worth of mysteries and miracles to relish within walking distance of his family's modest home.[4]

Most of what is aggressively promoted as leisure today, Glover writes, is the very antithesis of what leisure meant to Thoreau. It is hurried, complex, cluttered with paraphernalia, and dominated by machines. Most of all, it is expensive because that is how it best serves our consumer economy.

Much of what Glover says is true. Today, we tend to equate leisure with *doing* things—trips, hobbies, games, sports, amusements, and creative or cultural pastimes. We accept the need to have discipline and commitment in our leisure when we join a civic orchestra, train for a marathon, or enter a puppy in a dog-obedience class. Indeed, if leisure is to become truly a vehicle for self-actualization—that is, in Maslow's terms, a person's becoming all that he or she is capable of being, and of having "peak" experiences—this concept of leisure must prevail.

Probably few illustrations could be as vivid as the 1984 Olympics, which showed thousands of athletes who had trained for years (in many cases without the expectation of material reward) to be the best in their chosen fields of competition. In a sense, they epitomize the modern spirit of leisure expressed to the ultimate, in which it often becomes a highly demanding and engrossing experience, with deep emotional outcomes for the participant.

But one's philosophy of leisure must also be willing to accept other models, including the New Games approach, with its emphasis on cooperative, low-keyed rather than highly competitive forms of play. There is no single model of appropriate play or recreation, as earlier chapters point out. Given this great diversity, the only real criterion can be whether the experience enriches and enhances human personality and provides rewards that are, in the end, healthful. This brings us to the final question of this text: What *are* the demonstrated outcomes of organized recreation service?

OUTCOMES OF RECREATION

In the past, we have tended to rely heavily on casual observations of recreation programs or on subjective judgments to document their worth. Often, the assumed values of recreation were drawn from the personal testimonials of authorities. For example, in the early decades when the recreation movement was getting under way, law enforcement authorities, judges, school principals, and youth workers all enthusiastically supported its value in reducing or preventing juvenile delinquency. Others gave support to the claim that "the family that plays together stays together." Still others, including many mental health experts, agreed that recreation was a vital tool in maintaining emotional balance and sound mental health.

On the face of it, these claims appeared valid. Certainly, children and teenagers who were on playgrounds or sports fields or in recreation centers taking part in wholesome activity under adult guidance were less likely to take part in delinquent acts than gang members who roamed the streets looking for excitement.

But, in terms of the standards of modern, scientific research, most such claims were poorly based. Experimental research, which is the type of investigation most commonly relied upon to identify causal relationships (that one phenomena *causes* another) required such elements as pre- and post-testing of subjects, matched experimental and control groups, and other conditions that were extremely difficult to impose in real-life recreational situations.

As a result, it was often conceded: "We don't really have proof of what we claim. It can't be shown scientifically."

Thus, in many recent sociological discussions of juvenile delinquency, the role of play and recreation is dealt with in only the most cursory way. Few investigators of mental health tend today to look at the role of play, and often recreation services are placed far down on the "totem pole" of public support in modern communities because recreation services often cannot demonstrate their value as easily as other services can.

But the reality is that we have gradually been accumulating a significant body of literature about the worth of recreation. Many studies show that it is positively correlated with other desirable measures of social behavior or community change. It is highly important, in considering the process of recreation program planning, that we become familiar with such studies. They tend to be of several types: (1) studies examining the outcomes of different kinds of activities; (2) studies showing the effects of recreational programming with different types of special populations; and (3) studies showing the varied benefits of recreation for communities at large, or sponsoring organizations, from a cultural, social, or economic point of view.

The concluding section of this chapter summarizes the findings of several such studies. They are not described here in full detail; however, by consulting the sources that are given, fuller descriptions may be gathered.

General Values

Elsewhere, the author has cited some of the writings that support the value of play and recreation as developmental experiences for children, socializing experiences for teenagers and young adults, or important fitness and mental-health contributors for adults—to name only a few of the areas of benefit.

The leading authority on child development over the past several decades has been Jean Piaget, who recognized the value of play in the child's mental development.[5] Jerome Bruner, formerly director of Harvard University's Center for Cognitive Studies, found that children's play represented a valuable learning experience, and was closely linked to the development of creativity.[6] Leading psychologists like Erik Erikson and Bruno Bettelheim identified its value in the emotional growth and balance of children and youth.[7]

Numerous other studies have documented the value of recreation in achieving and maintaining cardiovascular fitness and contributing to overall health.[8] Without question, authorities agree that recreation provides an important form of release and relaxation that helps prevent stress and burnout among adults, and that leads to a sense of achievement and life satisfaction.[9] There is clear evidence that the ability to play is closely connected to successful accomplishment by adults in the business or professional world.[10]

In terms of its contribution to such special populations as the mentally retarded or the institutionalized aging population, a number of studies have shown the value of play and exercise programs, or creative and social programs for these groups.[11] To provide specific illustrations of such outcomes, the concluding section of this chapter will describe research findings in four areas: (1) outdoor recreation and camping for emotionally disturbed or physically disabled children and youth; (2) recreation and social programs intended to reduce or prevent social deviancy, such as juvenile delinquency; (3) the benefits of recreation in armed forces settings; and (4) the value of recreation and related services in corporate/employee programs.

Outdoor Recreation and Camping for Special Populations

Scholarly journals and the popular press have both given numerous accounts of outdoor recreation programs—including wilderness and adventure activities—designed to meet the needs of special populations. In a number of cases, the outcomes of such programs have been carefully assessed.

In the early 1970s, for example, Rawson described the success of special camping programs in working with disturbed children who were characterized by numerous behavior problems, including poor peer and adult relationships, marginal school behavior, and negative social attitudes. Based on three years of carefully monitored short-term therapeutic camping experiences sponsored by the United Presbyterian Church and Hanover College in Indiana, he concluded:

> The pre- and post-camp tests showed dramatic improvement in interpersonal relationship skills, self-control of socially inappropriate behavior, and positive response to authority figures. Attention span was drastically increased, as was academic motivation. Attitudes toward teachers and school were significantly improved along with feelings of self-confidence, especially in social and academic areas.[12]

Follow-up studies showed that campers obtained significantly better grades when they returned to school, were involved in fewer disciplinary actions, developed better friendships, and related more positively with their teachers. It should be noted that these results were not accomplished solely through a "normal" camp experience, but made use of special behavior modification techniques to bring about change. However, the recreational camp environment was an important part of the total therapeutic process.

In 1979, Gibson presented a comprehensive literature review of the outcomes of therapeutic camping programs for emotionally disturbed children and youth. These programs, which were carried on in wilderness settings, included such activities as backpacking, mountaineering, canoeing, cross-country skiing, and other outdoor recreation experiences. They were designed to strengthen the positive aspects of the participants' personalities, such as self-confidence and the ability to work with others, and to reduce such problem areas as anger, anxiety, or depression. They made use of a number of special behavior modification techniques, such as modeling, contingency contracting, positive and negative reinforcement methods, and a token economy approach.

Conceding that a number of the studies reviewed had methodological shortcomings, Gibson reported generally positive findings. In several carefully monitored studies, he found

> significant positive changes on the part of the experimental subjects in present and ideal self-concept, social maladjustment, value orientation, autism, alienation, aggression and repression [and] positive changes in [the] locus of control and behavior.[13]

Sessoms has described a number of other specialized camping programs conducted by the University of Kentucky and at Camp Allen in New Hampshire, as well as others sponsored by the National Easter Seals Society. In one three-year study of the effects of organized camping on physically disabled children, it was found that camping has significant positive effects on the self-concept and independent functioning of participants.[14] This program, carried out by a team from the University of North Carolina, offered a straightforward recreationally oriented camp experience, as contrasted to the specially designed therapeutic programs in the other camps described here.

Impact of Recreation Programs on Social Deviancy

One of the most important goals of youth-serving community recreation agencies has been to reduce or prevent varied forms of social deviancy—particularly juvenile delinquency. In general, there has been little documentation of their effectiveness.

However, a number of studies have given strong support to the hypothesis that recreation, in such forms as organized youth programs or competitive athletics, is an influential factor in reducing deviant behavior.

One such report in the mid-1950s showed that the delinquency rate for white boys in an area of Louisville, Kentucky, where a new Boys' Club had been built in the mid-1940s, declined steadily while increasing sharply in two comparable areas of the city where similar programs had not been developed. Recognizing the limitations of ex post facto studies of this type, in which statistics are analyzed after the fact without true experimental controls, Brown and Dodson concluded:

> the presence of an active, well-organized Boys' Club in an area where delinquency had been high . . . was associated with a decline in delinquency rate statistics, while these rates were increasing in other areas of the city. Although specific cause and effect relationships cannot be determined, the results of the study indicate that . . . the Boys' Club was a significant part of the community's arsenal in the battle against delinquency.[15]

In another ex post facto study, it was shown that only 7 percent of the boys who had participated for at least one full year in an interscholastic sport in several midwestern high schools were arrested for delinquent behavior during this period, compared with 17 percent of the nonathletes.[16] In the late 1950s and early 1960s, the establishment of a major new youth and adult center and an intensified program of recreation and other special services in East Harlem resulted in the disbanding of all eleven fighting gangs and a sharp decline in the juvenile delinquency rate in the area.[17]

The problem of youth gangs in both urban slums and many suburban areas is an increasing one today. It is recognized that the lack of adequate recreation continues to be an important factor in this serious social problem. *U.S. News and World Report* stated in the mid-1980s:

> Youth gangs are spreading in part because the conditions that spawn them in the old urban cores are becoming more prevalent in suburbs and small cities, experts say. They point to racial and ethnic separation, poverty, family breakups, high youth unemployment and lack of recreational activities.[18]

As an example of the programs that are being mounted to confront this problem, the Los Angeles Community Youth Gang Services Project makes extensive use of recreation as a "safety valve," as part of an overall prevention approach:

> With an annual budget of just over 2 million dollars, much of it contributed by business, the project employs a staff of 120, including many former gang members. Activities range from mediating disputes between gangs to sponsoring break-dancing competition, a junior Olympics, and other events that give teen-agers' energies a lawful outlet.[19]

Several recent studies have explored the value of specialized approaches to various aspects of the youth deviancy problem. In 1983, for example, Wright reported the findings of an Outward Bound treatment program for 47 primarily male juvenile delinquents. The research yielded significant positive findings among the participants. Wright summarized the outcomes:

adapted Outward Bound programs offer a viable treatment alternative for short-term change in the delinquent's sense of self-esteem, their willingness to accept more personal responsibility for behaviors, their belief in a sense of personal capability.[20]

Other important studies in this area have dealt with the use of positive youth motivation programs to control vandalism, and with the relationship between varied forms of recreation and alcohol consumption among adolescents.

A final interesting finding had to do with the outcomes of leisure education and programming in penal institutions. The need for such programs has become increasingly recognized; in its 1973 *Report on Corrections,* the National Advisory Commission on Criminal Justice Standards and Goals stated:

> The one specific area that has received little attention but has great potential as being a possible factor in the commission of crime is the ability of an individual to use leisure time productively and wisely.[21]

In this vein, Garibaldi and Moore sum up efforts to use recreation as a specific therapeutic technique in prisons. They describe an experimental program designed to modify socially deviant behavior and to reduce recidivism (relapse into criminal behavior):

> In a court in Indiana, it was determined that approximately 98% of the crimes committed by men being tried in that court were committed during leisure; further, it was revealed that 92% of the men placed on one-year probation were rearrested for subsequent criminal acts. In an attempt to reduce the recidivism rate . . . a condition of probation was added that required each man to learn new leisure skills. This new condition, along with the other conditions of probation, were strictly adhered to, and 24 months later the recidivism rate was 14% for those men placed on one-year probation.[22]

Values of Recreation in Armed Forces Recreation Programs

Apart from the positive outcomes of recreation programs with such special populations, it is also instructive to examine its values within different types of sponsoring agencies. For example, at Senate Appropriations Committee hearings on funding for military MWR programs, representatives of each of the four major branches of the armed forces testified regarding their value. The U.S. Army spokesperson concluded:

> Each installation must provide wholesome and diverse morale opportunities for the soldier and his family to a greater degree than the average civilian community because of the nature of the soldier's commitment to duty, and the threat of family separation caused by conflict or other duties. If [programs are cut] it will create personal problems for the soldier, degrade his performance and reduce his contributions to his unit's readiness.[23]

An extensive survey carried out by the armed forces showed that there is a strong level of support for such services and belief in their benefits. Over 230 Air Force commanders both in the United States and overseas who participated in face-to-face interviews, and over 6,100 active-duty personnel who responded to a mail questionnaire survey indicated that if the MWR program were withdrawn, it would have serious negative effects on job performance and mission accomplishment. Simonson summarizes the findings of the study:

> All commanders and 93.4 percent of the Air Force members believed there would be a negative impact on morale if MWR programs were not available. One hundred percent of the commanders saw MWR reductions having a negative effect on mission accomplishment, while 99.9 percent felt there would be an adverse effect on family life. The survey further showed 98.8 percent perceived a negative effect on the drug and alcohol program; 98.5 percent on job performance; 98.1 percent on discipline; 96.4 on retention.[24]

This study was carried out based on Herzberg's Motivation-Hygiene theory, in which MWR programs were classified as hygiene factors, similar to salary and working conditions, affecting persons only when removed or curtailed. Simonson explains that this meant that a person's playing intramural softball or attending the recreation did not mean that he or she would therefore do a better job for the Air Force. However, the study did demonstrate that if MWR programs were removed, it would negatively affect the job and mission accomplishment of military personnel.

Demonstrated Outcomes of Corporate/Employee Programs

Another field of specialized leisure service in which significant findings of outcomes have been gathered is corporate/employee recreation and services.

Byers has summarized a number of studies, both in the United States and abroad, which have shown a dramatic decline in employee absenteeism following the introduction of recreation programs and related services. For example, a careful analysis of the effects of such a program at the People's Jewelry Company, headquartered in Toledo, Ohio, showed a dramatic 23 percent decline in absenteeism, following the introduction of a new employee relations program, including recreation. Similarly, he cites a comprehensive study by Canada Life, which

> found that regular exercisers in its fitness program had a 22 percent decline in absenteeism, representing some $300,000 annual savings in a company of 1,400 employees. Also important, this group's turnover was 13.5 percent less than the control group.[25]

Byers also reviewed the findings of a study of 110,000 members covered by the Health Insurance Plan (HIP) of Greater New York, which showed that men classified as "least active" had twice the risk of a coronary, compared to those classified as "moderately active." Such statistics have led many major corporations to initiate extensive fitness programs, including aerobic exercises, team and individual sports, jogging, and similar activities.

Similarly, Myler summarizes other findings showing the positive effects of fitness programs, such as data indicating that absenteeism among exercising teachers in Dallas dropped to an average of 5.3 days from 8.5 days a year, resulting in savings of $452,000 for the school system. However, she concedes that many of the most important "paybacks" of such programs are such "unquantifiables" as:

> higher morale, improved company loyalty, a better public image and an edge
> in the labor market for "competitive, aggressive, into-life people"—the kind
> companies want to lead them.[26]

It should be noted that, although most of the emphasis in such reports is on the results of fitness programs, recreation and employee service activities involve far more than exercise alone. For example, Myler describes the Minneapolis-based Control Data Corporation's popular in-house "Staywell" package of smoking cessation, weight control, stress management, and programs on hypertension, fitness, and nutrition. In addition to the contribution of sports, social, hobby, and travel programs to this total effort, other services have directly measurable effects.

For example, the 6,000 employees of the John Hancock Life Insurance Company saved nearly $824,000 a year through the employee discount program, operated as part of the total employee services plan.[27] Thomas points out that a similar program sponsored by the Lockheed Employee Recreation Club in Burbank, California, saves its employees over half a million dollars a year through discounts in ticket sales and other products—including many forms of leisure-related admissions, products and services.[28]

Probably the most important outcomes, from the company's point of view, are not measurable, however. Carl Pirkle, manager of employee services at Healthdyne, Inc., in Marietta, Georgia, describes his initial presentation of a plan for employee services at Healthdyne:

> The bottom line in my proposal was profit. The company could—and
> would—profit from an employee program. . . . Employee services and recre-
> ation programs not only make for a healthier and happier workforce but one
> that, because of their psychological and physical states, is more productive and
> gives a greater effort to the company.
>
> [Our] employees like working at Healthdyne. The company shows that it is
> interested in them as individuals, as contributing members to the company and
> society. Employee services is a factor that keeps the personal touch in a
> company [that] ensures that an employee is not a number.[29]

LIMITATIONS OF RESEARCH

In reviewing these studies of the outcomes of recreation programs and the values of leisure involvement, it should be stressed that research cannot always tell the full story. Often, it is difficult to demonstrate scientifically that recreation has been a causal agent in bringing about certain outcomes. This is true in many other areas of human services and is generally the case in the behavioral sciences.

In part, this is because we have tended to assign preeminence to one type of research methodology—essentially empirical research that stresses quantitative measurement and statistical analysis. While such methods are appropriate for the "harder" and more traditional physical sciences, such as chemistry or physics, are they totally suitable for the investigation of such subtle forms of behavior as recreation and play, or to the role of leisure within complex human societies?

Hunnicutt, in describing play and leisure as "profoundly individualistic, subjective, and even 'irrational' areas of human experience," argues that there ought to be a place for more humanistic or philosophical approaches to studying them.[30] Calling the present approach an extension of "logical positivism," he urges the consideration of other, more meaningful ways of examining leisure, as well as the beliefs, opinions, intuitions, values, and tastes that surround it. Clearly, if we were able to use such techniques in measuring the outcomes of recreational experience, we would have a much richer understanding of its value.

The real truth is that many of the most significant and important outcomes of recreation can never be measured in a fully scientific, quantitative fashion, that looks for "proofs" in statistical terms.

If somehow we could probe into people's hearts and minds, we would know what it means to a ten-year-old from a city ghetto to camp for the first time in a wilderness setting or to canoe silently across a misty lake as the sun is setting.

We would be able to verbalize the mixed terror and joy that come from being in the front seat of a roller coaster as it creaks to its highest ascent and then begins to swoop almost vertically downward with a heart-stopping rattle.

We would know the triumph of the paraplegic patient who painfully learns to paint with a brush attached to his or her forehead, or to tap out a poem on an electric typewriter, letter by letter.

We would understand the elderly person who comes every day to a neighborhood senior center and says, "I would be so lonely if this weren't here."

We would cheer and cry with the millions—and through television, hundreds of millions—who watch the Olympics each four years and vicariously race, leap, swim, box, swing, ride, shoot, and compete in other contests, along with the Olympian athletes themselves.

We would be a child playing with his or her parents at a New Games Festival, or a mentally retarded youth who learns how to take a bus and go to a concert with his or her friends.

All these experiences are part of recreation. Whether or not their outcomes are measurable, they are the result of successful programs and skilled leadership. For people of all ages and many backgrounds, they enrich life and make it beautiful.

NOTES

[1]See Edward Colimore, "Young and Unfit: Physical Education is Declining," *Philadelphia Inquirer* (18 May 1984): 1; and Dr. Irving Dardik, quoted in "Why American Youth Has Turned Flabby," *U.S. News and World Report* (June 27, 1983): 70.

[2]Captain John B. Bonds, "All Work and No Play," *Proceedings* (October 1983): 144.

[3]Bonds: 145.

[4]James Glover, "In Defense of Simplicity," *Journal of Physical Education, Recreation and Dance* (February 1983): 62.

[5]See discussion of Piaget's views in Susanna Millar, *The Psychology of Play* (Baltimore: Penguin, 1968), p. 55.

[6]Jerome S. Bruner, "Child Development: Play Is Serious Business," *Psychology Today* (January 1975): 83.

[7]Erik Erikson, *Childhood and Society* (New York: Norton, 1950), 184; and Bruno Bettelheim, "What Children Learn from Play," *Parents' Magazine* (July 1964): 4, 9–10, 102.

[8]See Jane E. Brody, "Study of 17,000 Men Indicates Vigorous Sports Protect Heart," *New York Times* (29 November 1977): 1.

[9]Seppo Iso-Ahola and Ellen Weissinger, "Leisure and Well-Being: Is There a Connection?" *Parks and Recreation* (June 1984): 41. Numerous other studies have been done of the value of specific forms of recreation for different population groups. See, for example: Diane Wakat and Sarah Odom, "The Older Woman: Much Increased Psychosocial Benefit from Physical Activity," *Leisure Today, Journal of Physical Education, Recreation and Dance* (March 1982): 34–35.

[10]Judy Klemesrud, "Keys to Success: A Study of 95 Men," *New York Times* (28 September 1977); C–1.

[11]See Herberta M. Lundegren, Ed., *Physical Education and Recreation for the Mentally Retarded* (State College, Pa.: Penn State HPER Series 1975); and *Penn State Studies on Recreation and the Aging* (State College, Pa.: Penn State HPER Series, 1974).

[12]Harve E. Rawson, "Short-Term Residential Camping for Behaviorally Disordered Children Aged 6–12," *Therapeutic Recreation Journal* (4th quarter 1978): 17–23.

[13]Peter M. Gibson, "Therapeutic Aspects of Wilderness Programs: A Comprehensive Literature Review," *Therapeutic Recreation Journal* (2nd quarter 1979): 25.

[14]H. Douglas Sessoms, "Organized Camping and Its Effects on the Self-Concept of Physically Handicapped Children," *Therapeutic Recreation Journal* (1st quarter 1979): 39–43.

[15]Roscoe C. Brown, Jr., and Dan Dodson, "The Effectiveness of a Boys' Club in Reducing Delinquency," *Annals of Amertcan Academy of Political Science* (March, 1959): 47–52.

[16]Peter Donnelly, "Athletes and Juvenile Delinquents: A Comparative Analysis Based on a Review of the Literature," *Adolescence* (Summer 1981): 415–431; and Walter E. Schafer and J. Michael Armer, "Athletes Are Not Inferior Students," *Trans-Action* (November 1968): 10–12.

[17]See "Eleven Gangs Disband in East Harlem," *New York Times* (6 August 1960); 1.

[18]"Streets Gangs No Longer Just a Big-City Problem," *U.S. News and World Report* (16 July 1984): 108.

[19]"Street Gangs": 109.

[20]Alan N. Wright, "Therapeutic Potential of the Outward Bound Program: An Evaluation of a Treatment Program for Juvenile Delinquents," *Therapeutic Recreation Journal* (2nd quarter 1983): 40.

[21]Michele Garibaldi and Mary Moore, "The Treatment Team Approach," *Journal of Physical Education and Recreation* (April 1981): 28.

[22]Don A. Walsh, cited in Garibaldi and Moore.

[23]Paul Simonson, "Leisure-Time Activities: Fringe Benefit or Necessity?" *Employee Services Management* (December-January 1983–1984): 16–17.

[24]Simonson: 16–17.

[25]Melvin C. Byers, "Ideas Clinic," *Employee Services Management* (April 1983): 34.

[26]Kathleen Myler, "Exercise Can Firm Up a Sagging Bottom Line," *Chicago Tribune* (17 October 1983): 3–2.

[27]Kimberly A. Thomas, "Counting on Discount Services," *Employee Services Management* (April 1983): 14.

[28]Thomas: 15.

[29]Carl Pirkle, Interview in *Employee Services Management* (July 1983): 24, 27.

[30]See Benjamin Hunnicutt, "The Freudian and Neo-Freudian Views of Adult Play and Their Implications for Leisure Research and Therapeutic Service Delivery," *Therapeutic Recreation Journal* (2d quarter 1979): 3–4.

STUDENT PROJECTS

1. The text identifies three important issues in this chapter: (a) the unmet fitness needs of children and youth; (b) the need for improved leisure education programs for all age levels; and (c) the role that leisure should play in the lives of people today.

   Have the class divide into smaller groups, and ask each group to come up with a *different* issue of concern today. Examples might be the conflict between competitive and cooperative sports programming, or the strengths and weaknesses of the "marketing" approach to programming, compared to the "human services" approach. Have each group present the pro's and con's of the issue it has selected to the class, for fuller discussion and analysis.

2. The chapter presents brief summaries of research findings supporting the positive values of several forms of recreation service. Have the class divide into smaller groups, and have each group responsible for searching the literature to identify such findings or outcomes in areas not covered by the chapter. For example, one group might study and report on the economic values of recreation as a contribution to

community life. Another might do research on the role of recreation in improving intergroup relationships, or contributing to the mainstreaming of the disabled in community life. Following its research, each group would present its findings to the class.

SUGGESTED READINGS————————————————————————————

Reynold Carlson, Janet MacLean, Theodore Deppe and James Peterson, *Recreation and Leisure: The Changing Scene* (Belmont, Calif.: Wadsworth, 1979), Chapter 16.

John R. Kelly, *Leisure* (Englewood Cliffs, N.J.: Prentice-Hall, 1982), Chapter 15.

Richard Kraus, *Recreation and Leisure in Modern Society* (Glenview, Ill.: Scott, Foresman, 1984), Chapter 16.

Donald Weiskopf, *Recreation and Leisure: Improving the Quality of Life* (Boston: Allyn and Bacon, 1982), Chapters 21–22.

INDEX _____